Running a Restaurant

FOR

DUMMIES®

Running a Restaurant

FOR DUMMIES®

by Michael Garvey, Heather Dismore,
and Andrew Dismore

WILEY

Wiley Publishing, Inc.

Running a Restaurant For Dummies®

Published by
Wiley Publishing, Inc.
111 River St.
Hoboken, NJ 07030-5774
www.wiley.com

About the Authors

Michael Garvey was, at one time, an unassuming if not innocent soul from Brooklyn before he was grabbed by the clutches of the evil shadow known simply as the restaurant business. Starting as a resort waiter in the Poconos of Pennsylvania, he quickly became smitten by his new work and found himself a genuine masochist at heart. Garvey delved into other facets of the industry, from bartending in saloons to waiting in fine dining atmospheres. He also found time to volunteer in the kitchen of the Marist Brothers in Esopus, NY, manufacturing meals for handicapped and underprivileged children and adults. In 1994, he returned to New York City for some real brutality. He latched on to a small three-unit outfit by the name of Mumbles as a manager. After seeing action in their other locations, Michael landed a job as floor manager at The Oyster Bar in Grand Central Station owned by famed restaurateur Jerry Brody.

The Oyster Bar was a wonderland for the then medium-rare manager. Garvey took advantage of many opportunities including wine cellar stewarding which led to sommelier certification. He was part of the management team that rebuilt the institution in 1997 after a devastating fire. In 1998, he was offered the General Manager position and added President to his titles in 2000. Today, in addition to running the day-to-day operations in Grand Central, Michael has led efforts to franchise The Oyster Bar concept. While writing this book, he organized the first franchise in Tokyo, half a world and a culture away. At the time of printing, it is surpassing the franchisee's sales projections by over 100%. Garvey currently resides in Long Beach, NY, with his beautiful (and understanding) wife Vicki and their ridiculously cute daughter Torrance.

Heather Heath Dismore is a veteran of both the restaurant and publishing industries. She has published works including such titles as "Indian Cooking For Dummies," part of the compilation *Cooking Around the World All-In-One For Dummies, The Parents' Success Guide to Organizing, The Parents' Success Guide to Managing a Household,* and *Low-Carb Dieting For Dummies,* all published by John Wiley and Sons. This is her fifth published work.

A graduate of DePauw University, she succumbed to the restaurant business in Denver, Colorado while applying to law school. She rapidly rose to management at such regional and national chains as The Italian Fisherman, Don Pablo's Mexican Kitchen, and Romano's Macaroni Grill. She orchestrated the openings of 15 new restaurants and developed the training, procedural, and purchasing systems that were used as the gold standard in numerous concepts throughout her tenure. She currently lives in Missouri with her husband, co-author Andrew Dismore, and their daughters who are her first loves, inspiration, and never-ending source of new material.

Andrew Dismore, one of the catering industry's premier chefs, joined the foodservice marketing agency Noble & Associates in 2003 after amassing critical success and national recognition as Corporate Executive Chef/General Manager of Chicago's uber-posh Calihan Catering, Inc.

In a career spanning some 15 years, Dismore has amassed an expertise in the catering field few can rival. His experiences are a study in dramatic contrast. He has prepared seated dinners for over 10,000 guests, designed highly profitable operations that have fed over 200,000 diners in three weeks, overseen the execution of over 2,500 events annually, and directed the culinary operations for such mega-volume events as the Indianapolis 500, The Brickyard 400, The NCAA Final Four, The RCA Tennis Championships, and Formula One. He has participated in over 20 openings and has independently designed 12 new food service concepts. Yet he has catered intimate events for many of the world's social, political, and culinary elite.

Dedications

Michael Garvey: To Pat Tillman, a true American hero.

Heather Dismore: To my sweetest loves, Andy, Riley, and Lucy. You are my greatest joy and my greatest inspiration.

Andrew Dismore: To Heather, the love of my life, my beautiful girls, and the memory of my father who taught me the honor of a hard day's work.

Authors' Acknowledgments

Michael: The crews I've worked with over the years, big and small, for standing together in the trenches. Jerry Brody for acting on a feeling and giving me an opportunity. Marlene Brody for continuing to give me opportunities. The night manager who chopped open the door that pointed to the future. Craig Harrison for being a kind and understanding chef while still kicking ass. Jonathan Young for taking the training wheels off and making me laugh whenever I fell (even now). Tracy Boggier, Mike Baker, and the Wiley staff for pushing us with a patient stick. Dave Mazzorana, a fine technical reviewer. Wine salespeople for walking the tightrope of keeping me up to date without nagging. My Mother for giving me my first *For Dummies* book. Hiro Nagano, Ai Ito, Ishii Hideo, Master Toda, and all of the WDI staff for showing me while I showed you. Mark Abrahamson for letting a cellar rat run with it. Don and Debbie Richter for keeping me behind the bar and adjusting on-the fly. Austin Power for showing me how to have fun waiting tables. My co-authors for keeping me up at night and bringing back a lot of memories. My current staff for helping through another gut checking year. Vicki for leaving the light on so many nights.

Heather: A special thank you to Mike Baker, Project Editor Extraordinaire, who kept this project on track despite Murphy's Law, an influenza epidemic, and intercontinental communication challenges. And to everyone else at Wiley who made this book a success, including Diane Steele, Joyce Pepple, Kristin Cocks, Tracy Boggier, Tina Sims, Holly Gastineau-Grimes, Jennifer Ehrlich, Christy Beck, and many other behind-the-scenes folks in the editorial and production departments. Thanks for the opportunity to work with the best in the business. Thanks to Dave Mazzorana for a stellar technical review. Thanks for keeping us on our toes! Thanks to Mike Garvey, who managed to juggle writing this book, running a 500-seat restaurant, opening a new restaurant in another continent, and an NYC commute; just another day in the life. Finally, thanks to my incredible family for their patience and support during the never-ending writing schedule.

Andrew: Thanks to my family for your love, support, and much deserved kicks in the butt. I am truly grateful to all those that, without whom, I would never have made it out of the pantry: Chefs Dominic Menna, Scott Brittingham, Charlie Trotter, Dave Mazzorana, Todd Rogers, Frank Terry, Gabriel Viti, David Danielson, Mike Cansler and the entire staff at Calihan. A very special thanks to Chef Tony Hanslits, whose tireless dedication to pure cuisine continues to be an inspiration. I especially need to thank Kurt Layer. You are the greatest caterer in the business. You will never know how much you taught me or how often I recognize it. Special thanks to Bob Noble, Judy Sipe, and everyone at Noble & Associates. I have never worked with a more driven, dedicated, and visionary group of professionals. I am truly honored to be a small part of your team.

Publisher's Acknowledgments

We're proud of this book; please send us your comments through our Dummies online registration form located at www.dummies.com/register/.

Some of the people who helped bring this book to market include the following:

Acquisitions, Editorial, and Media Development

Project Editor: Mike Baker

Acquisitions Editor: Tracy Boggier

Senior Copy Editor: Tina Sims

Assistant Editor: Holly Gastineau-Grimes

Technical Reviewer: Dave Mazzorana

Editorial Manager: Jennifer Ehrlich

Editorial Assistants: Courtney Allen, Elizabeth Rea

Cover Photos: © Getty Images/Photodisc Green

Cartoons: Rich Tennant, www.the5thwave.com

Composition

Project Coordinator: Maridee Ennis

Layout and Graphics: Amanda Carter, Andrea Dahl, Denny Hager, Joyce Haughey, Michael Kruzil, Kristin McMullan, Rashell Smith, Lynsey Osborn

Proofreaders: Nancy Reinhardt, Brian H. Walls

Indexer: TECHBOOKS Production Services

Special Help: Georgette Beatty, Jennifer Bingham, Elizabeth Netedu Kuball

Publishing and Editorial for Consumer Dummies

Diane Graves Steele, Vice President and Publisher, Consumer Dummies

Joyce Pepple, Acquisitions Director, Consumer Dummies

Kristin A. Cocks, Product Development Director, Consumer Dummies

Michael Spring, Vice President and Publisher, Travel

Brice Gosnell, Associate Publisher, Travel

Kelly Regan, Editorial Director, Travel

Publishing for Technology Dummies

Andy Cummings, Vice President and Publisher, Dummies Technology/General User

Composition Services

Gerry Fahey, Vice President of Production Services

Debbie Stailey, Director of Composition Services

Contents at a Glance

Table of Contents

Introduction

The restaurant business is an exciting one, full of challenges and opportunities. We're glad you're interested in finding out more about it, and you've definitely come to the right place to get started. Years ago, going out to eat was truly an event — reserved for weekends or special occasions. Today, however, even a Tuesday, just another day, can be an occasion to eat out, especially when busy careers and overloaded family schedules leave little time to cook. Fortunately, consumers have more restaurant choices than ever before. And opportunities in the industry have never been greater. This book can help you minimize the challenges and overcome the obstacles before they overcome you.

We've managed, worked, eaten, mopped floors, tended bars, learned to repair equipment mid-shift on a Saturday night, hired, fired, trained, and done inventory in some of the best (and worst) restaurants in the world. We've worked in ultrafine dining, fast food, catering, and everything in between. We've worked dining rooms that sat 30 and catered events that fed 50,000 diners in a single day. Sure, each of these situations is somewhat different, but many aspects of running a restaurant transcend restaurant size, location, or dining style and fall under the category of universal restaurant truths. We do our best to bring all that information to you in this book.

Whether you're a seasoned restaurant veteran or just out of cooking school, we believe that if you're reading this book, you have the *desire* to run a restaurant. After reading it, you should know if you have a *passion* for it — orwhat we sometimes call The Sickness.

About This Book

Success in the restaurant business is the dream of many and the achievement of a few. Often, would-be restaurateurs have misconceptions about what running a restaurant is really like. Some folks are quick to see the glitz and glamour without also having the opportunity to see the anxiety and effort that accompany it. Others have seen the business from the inside and are sure that they can do it better than the people they've worked for, without feeling the true weight and complexity of the tasks and decisions that face The Boss everyday. On the other side of the coin, you find people who could do very well in the restaurant business but stay out because of the horror stories they've heard.

We want you to see the full picture — the good, the bad, and the absurd — so that you can make an informed decision about your place in this business.

We wrote this book because no Bureau of Restaurant Operators exists to test your knowledge and skills on the open road to determine whether you have what it takes to get into the business. After you've read the pages between these gorgeous yellow and black covers, you'll have a good idea whether this is the racket for you — and the knowledge to get started on the right foot.

You can find plenty of books that tell you how to open a restaurant, but you won't find many about how to *keep* it open. This book does both. Why? Because even after opening day arrives, you can never stop improving your service, evaluating your product, scoping out the competition, or researching opportunities in the marketplace. Change is the only constant in the restaurant business. To succeed, you must anticipate and act on new trends, new pressures, and whatever else the market throws your way. The spoils go to those who see opportunities before they happen.

Please don't mistake our realism for cynicism. We want you to be in the business. But we're going to make sure that you have the information you need to be a success. We show you many everyday realities that people don't always consider, but should. We hope that you take the information and use it to be wildly successful. You can do this, but you have to look at this business the right way. If you do, save us a table!

Conventions Used in This Book

To help you navigate through this book, we use the following conventions:

- ✔ *Italic* is used for emphasis and to highlight new words or terms that are defined.

- ✔ **Boldfaced** text is used to indicate keywords in bulleted lists or the action part of numbered steps.

- ✔ `Monofont` is used for Web addresses.

- ✔ Sidebars, which look like text enclosed in a shaded gray box, consist of information that's interesting to know but not necessarily critical to your understanding of the chapter or section topic.

Foolish Assumptions

Just as owners have to make assumptions about the customers who will be eating in their restaurants, authors have to make assumptions about their readers. If one or more of the following descriptions hits home, you've come to the right place.

- ✔ You're thinking about opening your own restaurant, and you want practical, how-to advice to accomplish your goals.
- ✔ You've worked in the business, and now you're thinking about getting in on the ownership or management end of things.
- ✔ You've never worked in a restaurant but you've met with success in other professional endeavors and possess skills that may be applicable to this business.
- ✔ You're fresh out of cooking school and thinking about putting those skills to work in your own place.
- ✔ You buy every book that sports a yellow and black cover.
- ✔ You currently own or operate a restaurant, and you're seeking advice, tips, and suggestions to keep things running smoothly and successfully.

How This Book Is Organized

This book is organized into five separate parts. Here's what's on the menu.

Part 1: Getting Started

In this part, we give you a crash course in the business, including tips for getting started, understanding your options, creating your concept and picking your name. We help you research the marketplace to determine whether your concept has a shot at success, and provide information on how customers approach the buying decision. We include a detailed timeline from idea to grand opening to get you up and running. We also help you decide whether you have what it takes to make it in the business.

Part II: Putting Your Plan in Motion

In this part, we focus on acting on your idea. We take you through the critical steps, like writing a business plan and getting financing. We work you through the ins and outs of finding the right location or making an existing location work for you. And we wrap it up by dotting some i's and crossing some t's, including help on getting the right permits and licenses, getting up to speed on local laws, and legally protecting yourself, the right way.

Part III: Preparing to Open the Doors

Here, we detail all the tasks you need to do to get up and running. We walk you through hiring and training your staff and developing your menu and beverage program. We show you how to set up your kitchen and dining room for the best flow of food and people. We also give you concrete tips for purchasing and managing your inventory, which can take you a long way toward profitability. And finally, we cover two often-neglected areas of the business: operating your office and promoting your business.

Part IV: Keeping Your Restaurant Running Smoothly

This part is for anyone running a restaurant today or tomorrow or considering doing it in the future. We show you how to maintain and build on your current operation, including tips for managing employees, keeping your diners coming back, and handling customer service situations. We explain how to keep your place spick-and-span and ensure food safety. We show you how to get great information about what your customers want. And finally, we wrap it up with a lesson in watching your numbers, with tips on what reports to run, how to analyze the numbers, and make changes to your business when necessary.

Part V: The Part of Tens

Here, we dispel the common myths about running a restaurant. We give you resources to help you take the next steps when you're ready. And finally, we give you some of our favorite only-in-the-restaurant-business stories.

Icons Used in This Book

Icons are the fancy little pictures in the margins of this book. Here's the guide to what they mean and what the icons look like:

The Tip icon marks ideas that can make your job a bit easier and help prevent problems from happening. The tips are often hands-on ways to improve your business today.

The Remember icon points out ideas that sum up and reinforce the concepts we discuss. In fact, if you're in a time crunch and can't read it all, you may want to go straight to this icon. It's your choice — read it as you see fit.

We use the Warning icon to alert you to potential pitfalls and to give you a heads-up on what mistakes to avoid. Pay particular attention when this guy rears his head.

Think of the Technical Stuff icon almost as bonus material. Usually, the info gives you some background about the subject that's not critical. We think it's interesting, so we include it, but you don't have to read it to get the ideas and concepts.

Where to Go from Here

We think that you'll find the information in this title valuable enough that you'll want to read it all. Doing so provides you with a strong, general foundation for starting and running a restaurant.

But one of the great things about a *For Dummies* book (among the hundreds that we can count) is that you don't have to read it word for word, front to back, cover to cover. If you're more interested in one particular topic than another, that's fine. Check out the corresponding part, chapter, or section and read up on that issue. You can find out about it without first having read the information that precedes it — get-in-and-get-out convenience. Interested in tips to create or improve your menu? Turn to Chapter 9. Are you currently looking for a location to plant your new shop? Check out Chapter 7. Is sanitation your thing? Chapter 18 has your name written all over it.

You can jump around, start wherever you want, and finish when you feel like it. So tie on your apron and get going.

Part I
Getting Started

The 5th Wave   By Rich Tennant

"It's an extension of the open—kitchen concept. We call it our open—owners office area where patrons can watch the owner fend off creditors, haggle with suppliers, and reprimand the staff."

In this part . . .

You're standing on square one. In the chapters that follow we introduce you to the business and help you determine if you have what it takes to make a go of it in the restaurant world. We give you the big picture, including a detailed timeline that takes you from today through the day you open the doors of your place for the first time. We also help you nail down your concept, come up with a name, and start researching everything from your potential customers to the competition.

Chapter 1

Grasping the Basics of the Restaurant Business

. . . .

In This Chapter

▶ Understanding the basics of the business

▶ Deciding whether you have the necessary skills

. . . .

*R*estaurants are fun. Whether you stop by to celebrate a special occasion, grab a quick bite for lunch, meet friends for a drink, or pick up dinner for the family on the way home from work, the experience is usually enjoyable. (At the very least, it's more enjoyable than not eating or being forced to cook!). Just about everyone associates restaurants with having a good time. If people didn't enjoy their experience, they wouldn't come back. So it's natural for people to think, "I enjoy going to restaurants, so I may as well get paid to do what I enjoy — hang out in bars and eat at great restaurants."

And you know what? Living the restaurant life is fun. We've been doing it for many a year, and we love it. But the problem comes when people see only the fun and never see the struggle. Viewed from the dining room or barstool (or from the kitchen, stockroom, or anywhere else other than the seat marked "Proprietor"), it's difficult to see the 95 percent of the picture that's pretty tough work. It's kind of like wishing every day was Christmas and actually getting your wish. In the restaurant business, you have so much fun that you can hardly stand it. You get tired of wrapping the presents, preparing the eggnog, and checking that the elves are on time for their shifts, and if you have to look at any more roasted chestnuts, you'll die. The restaurant business quickly becomes more work than fun, so don't be fooled.

In this chapter, we take you on a quick tour of the business. We introduce you to all the upfront work that you must do on paper before you can even think about picking up a pan or laying down a place setting. We move on to the physical preparations that will consume your every waking minute on the way to opening your doors. Then we remind you that the work has only begun after you first open your doors. Finally, we help you examine your motivations and expectations for pursuing your dream to determine if both are rooted in reality.

Getting a Feel for the Restaurant World

The restaurant world is more than glitz and glamour. It's truly a business, and if you don't look at it that way, you won't succeed. Ultimately, being a restaurateur is being a manufacturer. You're producing a product (food) from raw materials (your ingredients) and selling it to a customer (your diner). You're competing with lots of other "manufacturers" for that same diner. So you better do it better than the other guy, or you'll be out of business.

Laying the foundation

Sometimes the business of *the business* is tough for people to relate to. It's a hard concept for many people to get because your product isn't packaged in a box that sits on a shelf. Your product is packaged in many layers — including your exterior, your lobby, your staff's attire, the music playing, the aromas emanating from the kitchen, the friendliness and knowledge of your staff, your silverware, your china, and your glassware. All these things make up your packaging, affect the costs of doing business, and affect your diner's decision to come in and, ultimately, to come back.

As with any business, the planning stage is crucial, and you have to survive it before you can enjoy any of the fun. Right off the bat, you have to create a timeline for getting your business up and running (see Chapter 2), develop your restaurant's theme and concept (see Chapter 3), research the market (see Chapter 4), develop a detailed business plan and use it to find and secure financing (see Chapters 5 and 6), and find the best location for your new restaurant and get the right licenses and permits (see Chapters 7 and 8).

Buy your products at the right price and sell them at the right price. This simple tenet can make or break your business. Check out Chapter 14 for tips on getting the best price and look to Chapter 9 for pricing your food and beverage menus right from the start.

Setting up shop (with a little help)

Depending on how new you are to the restaurant biz, you may need accountants, attorneys, contractors, and host of other characters, all at the ready and working with you at various stages of the project.

Hire an accountant early in the process of setting up your business. She can help you get your numbers together for your business plan, which is a must-do if you're trying to get financing for your venture. Chapters 5 and 6 can give you the details. After you're up and running, you'll analyze your monthly financial reports and look for ways to improve the numbers. A good accountant, preferably one with restaurant experience, can help.

When starting any new business, you'll need to review contracts, file your permits, or maybe incorporate your business. Depending on how you set up your business, you may need to draft a partnership agreement or two. Before you sign franchise agreements or vendor contracts or fire your first employee, make sure that you're working with a good attorney, who can help you with all these tasks and more. Watch for details in Chapter 8.

Most people starting a new restaurant, or taking over an existing one, change a few things (or a few hundred things) at their new location. Maybe you need to set up a new kitchen from scratch or improve the air flow of the hood over the range. Maybe you want to upgrade the plumbing or install air filtration in your bar. Contractors can save you lots of time and trouble. Don't hesitate to ask them questions and check their references.

Check out Chapters 10 through 12 for the scoop on designing your exterior, dining room, kitchen, and bar — with or without the help of contractors, designers, and architects. Interior designers and architects come in very handy around renovation and revamp time. Sometimes they can come in and give your place a face-lift for much less than you might imagine.

Welcoming the world to your restaurant

All the hard work that's required to get to the point where you can open the doors will mean absolutely nothing if no one shows up. You have to start thinking about how to draw customers way before you open your doors (and every day after that). Develop your marketing plan based on what's special, unique, or different about your restaurant. Maybe it's the food, ambience, price, or value. Study your competition, watch what they're doing well (and not so well), and understand where you have the advantage.

Different groups respond to different messages. Figure out what works for the diners you're going after. Check out Chapter 16 for details on telling the world about your place and getting them to beat a path to your door. After you get the customers in the seats, you have to keep them there. We've heard that you can't use restraining devices in most states and municipalities, so you do have to let them go and hope they come back. We want you to do more than hope. Chapter 19 gives you concrete tips for building your clientele and ensuring that most of them come back — and bring their friends.

To be successful in this or in any business, you need to take care of your business today, tomorrow, and years from now. Stay up on trends in your sector and the restaurant business as a whole. Watch for information about shifting dining preferences and behavior in trade magazines, print publications, television news (and the not-so-news magazine shows), the Internet, or anywhere else you get information. And always keep an eye on your competition. Don't copy them, but know what they're up to. See Chapter 4 for information on how to conduct a market analysis. And check out Chapter 20 for ways to maintain what you create, using feedback from financial analysis and operational reports.

Discovering Whether You Have What It Takes

Culinary prowess, a charming personality, and an ability to smile for the cameras. That's about all you need, right? Wrong. Take a step back. It takes way more to run a restaurant successfully. And that's what we all want: anyone can run a restaurant, but not everyone can run one well. (In fact, we should've titled this book, *Running a Restaurant Really Well For Dummies,* but the publisher wouldn't go for it.)

Monitoring your motivations

This is a tough business, and if you want to succeed, you have to have the inner motivation — the drive — to sustain you through all the downs that accompany the ups. This isn't a venture for the faint of heart. If you want to own a restaurant to have a place to hang out with your friends and get free drinks, we say take the bar bill and avoid the hassles.

The first thing you need to do, before you invest any additional time or money in this venture (besides purchasing and reading this book, of course), is to examine and understand the factors that motivate you. Be honest with yourself.

There are lots of great reasons to want to run a restaurant. Here are a few of our favorites:

- You love an ever-changing work environment.
- You love taking on a challenge.
- You're passionate about the business.
- You have a passion for food.
- You hate having any free time (including the holidays).
- You're continuing the family tradition.

And the following list contains a few reasons that should send up a red flag in your mind:

- You think it will be fun.
- You want to be a celebrity chef.
- You want a place to hang out.
- If Emeril can do it, so can you.
- You're tired of having a "real" job.
- You've always wanted to run a restaurant after you retire.

If one or more of these reasons sounds familiar, don't be completely discouraged. Just make sure that motivations such as these aren't your only, or even your primary, reasons for wanting to get into the business. And do some further investigation before making the financial, personal, and professional commitment to the business.

Evaluating your expectations

Running a restaurant, either yours or someone else's, is a huge commitment. It requires long hours, constant vigilance, and the ability to control potentially chaotic situations — on a daily basis.

Think about *Cocktail,* the great (or not-so-great, depending on your point of view) '80s movie, in which a salty old bartender marries a rich lady and uses her money to open his own place. Just before he kills himself, he pours out his soul to his younger bartender friend, played by Tom Cruise, about what it's really like to own your own place. He confesses, "The only thing I know about saloons is how to pour whiskey and run my mouth off. I knew nothing about insurance, sales tax, or building code, or labor costs, or the power company, or purchasing, or linens. Everyone with a hand stuck it in my pocket."

Running a restaurant shouldn't be a leap of faith. You need to go into this with your eyes open (not with your *Eyes Wide Shut* — is this too many references to Tom Cruise movies in a single chapter?). Just as we suggest that you carefully consider your motivations (see the "Monitoring your motivations" section, earlier in the chapter), you also need to make sure that your expectations are firmly planted in reality.

Take out a pen and some paper. Divide the paper into two columns. In the first, list all of your expectations for the future business. From the profits you expect, to the lifestyle you hope those profits will support, to newspaper reviews or the customer views you hope to elicit, list it all. This is your chance to put your dreams on paper. Then, in the second column, write down what you expect out of yourself to make this thing happen — your contribution in terms of time and money, sacrifices you'll have to make, and anything else that you can think of.

Then it's time to determine whether the expectations on your lists reflect the reality of the situation. Reading this book is a great place to start — our goal is to present a balanced look at the joys and pains of running a restaurant. (If you want an instant reality check, skip over to Chapter 21, where we confront ten common myths.) But don't stop there. As we state in Chapter 2, you have to start researching every aspect of the business on Day 1, and you don't get to stop until you close your doors for the very last time. So you may as well start now. Minimize the mystery by getting out in the restaurant world — talk to owners, managers, waiters, and suppliers about their experiences and what you can expect. (Chapter 22 provides you with additional industry resources that you can consult.)

Tracking key traits

Based on our experience in the restaurant business, successful restaurateurs exhibit a few common traits. We list them below. Don't worry if you possess more of some traits than others. Just being aware of them is a great step toward making them all part of your world and succeeding in the business.

Business sense

This is probably the single most important trait. For all that the restaurant business is, it's still basically a business, subject to the same pressures as any other. Keep that thought in mind going into your arrangement. If you don't, you'll be hard-pressed to succeed. Skills that you've learned, developed, and honed in the real world can apply in this business, like buying skillfully, managing tactfully, and negotiating shrewdly. But many different facets of this business are tough to pick up.

Tolerance

The ability to keep your cool under pressure, thrive in chaos, and handle multiple points of view and personalities will serve you well in the business. Whether you're dealing with customers, employees, purveyors, changing trends, or a fickle clientele, you have to develop a thick skin. The inherent stress of the restaurant makes for short fuses. Your job is to dampen those tempers, smooth the rocky waters, and calm the storm.

Flexibility

The environment changes from minute to minute. You have to be able to adjust and think on your feet. You have to have a good balance of process- and product-motivated people. Process-motivated people microman-age what's going on in their organization. Product-minded people focus on the end result. Sometimes you'll wear both hats.

Creativity

Infuse creativity into every facet of your business from how you approach your customers and your food, to how you promote your business. That creativity affects how your business performs.

Positive energy

Whenever you're in the restaurant, you have to be "on" — all the time. Restaurants that have a positive vibe are the ones that make it. Positive energy is *the* differentiating factor, as intangible as it is, between the winners and the losers in this business. And your restaurant can't have it if you don't.

Ability to hold (or hold off) liquor

Coveted by many, achieved by few, the ability to handle one's liquor has been the downfall (physically, financially, and spiritually) of many a restaurateur. Per capita, no industry drinks more than the restaurant business. For some people, managing a restaurant is like getting the keys to the grown-up candy store, and the temptation is too much to resist. As a restaurateur, you often drink as part of your job. No matter what the circumstances, you still have to count the money at the end of the night, or you have to be ready to go first thing in the morning.

Leadership skills

Restaurateur /REST-o-ra-tor/: n. doctor, babysitter, marriage counselor, bail bondsman, parent, mediator, conscience, seer, sage. *See Patton, George; Ghandi; et al.*

Being a leader in this industry is being able to balance an entire range of different management approaches, knowing when to lead by example, and knowing when to give the troops their marching orders. Most importantly, a successful restaurant leader is able to find her own leadership style and deal with employees fairly, consistently, and with respect.

Schmoozability

Pucker up. People like to feel important. They want to be part of the inner circle of the restaurant, no matter how large that circle may be. It's cool to say, "I know the manager" or "The chef's a friend of mine." Nothing gets return business like calling a diner by name. That's why you put up with the pictures of grandkids, whines about their big project at work, or not-so-interesting travel tales. Always make the customer feel welcome, at home, and at ease. Turning a good mood into a bad one is incredibly easy. Turning a bad mood into a good mood is exponentially more difficult.

Passion

We call it The Sickness. To succeed, you have to have it. Running a restaurant is a business that eventually chooses you; you ultimately can't choose it. If you don't have passion for the business, you can't sustain, maintain, and overcome the obstacles that crop up.

You can't teach it or learn it; you have to feel it. If you don't have the passion, your task of becoming successful will be exponentially harder. You have to connect *everything* to your passion. You have to get the wait staff wired with it, because they're selling your vision to the customers. You have to get the prep guys pumped, because they're cranking on a tough schedule, without the natural excitement of a restaurant full of people. You have to get the dishwashers psyched about cleaning the dishes, because the dishes frame the experience for the customer. Diners should experience a buildup of expectation for their experience from the first time they come into contact with anyone from the restaurant (whether on the phone, in person, or online). Imagine doing all that without a passion for your restaurant, and you see why passion is mandatory.

Presence

Being there day in and day out has no substitute. Absentee landlords need not apply. Just stopping in to say hello or giving off an aura that you know what's up ultimately won't allow you to run the restaurant. If you're not there, those who are there in your stead will be the de facto rulers, and it won't be the same. If you're not physically present in the building most of the time, the schmoozing, the energy, the passion, and so on can't get to your staff and ultimately to your diners. You can't positively impact your restaurant if you're not there.

Chapter 2

Getting Everything Done before Your Grand Opening

••

In This Chapter

▶ Setting up your timeline

▶ Checking things off your master to-do list

••

*I*n this chapter, we help you plan for your restaurant's opening with a time-line of all the tasks you need to accomplish and track before you serve your first meal. Everything on the list is covered in detail in this book, so we include lots of references. From writing your business plan to opening the doors to the public, if it happens in the start-up cycle of a restaurant, it's on this list.

Every restaurant is different, so every opening timeline varies. Even if you're part of a chain, your timeline may be different from another unit's based on what side of the street you're on. This list is a guide. Check with all state and local governmental and regulatory offices to determine how long it takes to get the paperwork you need to open the kind of restaurant you want, keeping in mind that the processing time may be longer than quoted. And if we include things that don't apply to your restaurant, feel free to ignore them.

Figuring Out How Much Time You Need

Early in the planning stages, you may need to adjust your timeline and go with the flow, accepting the fact that timelines aren't always set in stone. For example, you may not need to have your business plan completed nine months before your opening if you're taking over an existing, established restaurant and don't want to make any changes. But, as you get closer to opening day, create and stick to a firm schedule to get everything completed on time.

If you're terrible at keeping a timeline, pad your schedule. This approach is similar to setting your own clocks 15 minutes ahead to be on time. But in this case, time is money. If you hire the chef a month earlier than scheduled, it's an additional expense you'll absorb before you're even open. You may have a very good reason, and it may be the right thing to do. Just be sure to factor the time and money adjustments into your schedule and expense projections.

In the checklist that follows, we group together similar tasks at each time interval. Use these categories to stay organized and eventually to delegate to the person who will handle the functions permanently. Here's the list of categories we use, shown in the order they appear in each time interval:

- **Administration:** Administration tasks include paperwork, phone calls, planning activities, and so on.

- **Construction:** Construction tasks consist of work related to designing and building your restaurant.

- **Human resources:** Anything concerning hiring, training, or managing your employees appears here.

- **Purchasing:** Purchasing tasks include buying equipment, supplies, and just about anything else your restaurant needs to get up and running.

- **Front of the house (FOH):** This term refers to any place a diner can be in your restaurant, including the dining room, restrooms, bar, and lounge. Tasks under this heading include organizing your bar, setting your dining room tables, creating and maintaining a floor plan, taking reservations, establishing your hours of operation, and all forms of customer service.

- **Back of the house (BOH):** This term refers to any place a diner can't be, including the kitchen, storage areas, the delivery entrance, the employee locker room, and the managers' office. BOH tasks include cooking, setting up a sanitation program, organizing your storeroom, and placing and receiving your first food orders.

- **Advertising and promotion:** This category includes any publicity, advertising, and public relations duties you should do.

- **Research:** Research is ongoing and forever. We list ideas to help you stay competitive and to reform and refresh your plans as you go along.

T-Minus One Year or More

Here's your chance to create the business you've always dreamed of. Use this time early in your schedule to thoroughly research your ideas, articulate your concept and vision, and put together a comprehensive plan for achieving it. Network with other restaurateurs and talk to everyone and anyone about the business, but keep the details of your plan (like your restaurant's name, menu specifics, and key points of difference) close to the vest. The first thing on your to-do list is one of the most important.

❏ Buy a copy of *Running a Restaurant For Dummies*. Use Chapter 1 to consider whether you have what it takes (and want to put forth the effort) to succeed in this business before you invest the time and money.

Administration

❏ Construct a detailed and professional business plan. See Chapter 5 for all the forms and lists you'll ever need.

❏ Develop and articulate your vision for the restaurant's physical layout, both the interior and exterior. The more detailed it is now, the better you can communicate it to designers, architects, and your general contractor as needed. Take a look at Chapters 10 through 12 for information on the physical layout of your restaurant.

❏ Develop your logos, trademarks, and brand identity. Chapter 3 helps you narrow down your theme and concept.

❏ Put together your team of advisers, including an accountant, attorney, real estate agent, designers, partners, and so on. See Chapter 8.

❏ Join trade organizations or local business organizations. Chapter 22 contains resources.

❏ Check with the local governing agencies to confirm timelines for your permits and licenses, especially your liquor license, if you need one. Requirements and schedules vary greatly from state to state, even county to county. See Chapter 8 for details on how (and where) to get started.

Research

❏ Formalize your process for conducting market, trend, and competitive research. See Chapter 4.

From this point forward, you have to continuously perform market, trend, and competitive research.

❏ Get a job. If you've never worked in a restaurant, now's the time to get started. Get a job doing whatever anyone will hire you to do, either in the kitchen or the dining room, and learn everything that you can. (We've done just about every job a restaurant can offer, including the less glamorous ones — taking out the trash, cleaning grease traps, cleaning bathrooms, shoveling snow, and the ever-popular dishwashing.) Any experience in the business is better than none. Use this time to look at how other people run their restaurants. Make lists of things you'd do differently and note things you'd like to implement in your place.

T-Minus Nine Months

At the nine months and counting mark, you should have your business plan in hand and be shopping for money. You can also begin researching specifics for your business, such as looking at prospective locations and researching your computer systems.

Administration

❑ Start meeting with potential investors. Explain your concept, business plan, and financial forecasts. Check out Chapter 6 for more information.

Research

❑ Shop for a location. See Chapter 7.

❑ Start researching point-of-sale (POS) systems. Much more than a simple cash register, a POS system can help you track and analyze just about any type of data you can think of. Check out Chapter 15.

T-Minus Seven Months

Around this time, your plan starts to become reality. Finalize your choice for a location and sign your lease. Get your money together and set up your bank accounts, credit card processor, and develop your other financial systems.

Administration

❑ Sign a deal with the landlord. But take a look at the chapters in Part II and Chapters 10 through 12 first to make sure that the location meets all your objectives and requirements for your concept and sales projections.

❑ Finalize your financing. Skip to Chapter 6 for the full story.

❑ Set up business bank accounts to pay deposits, rent office space, and deposit your investors' money. See Chapters 6 and 15 for help.

❑ Decide how you get cash from the restaurant to your account. You can use an armored car service or make a daily deposit at your bank.

❑ Establish a plan for regular financial reporting. Create the reports you'll use on a regular basis, such as an income statement and Cost of Goods Sold report. Check out Chapter 20 for what numbers to watch and why.

Research

❑ Research credit card processing systems. Kindly turn to Chapter 15.

❑ Check out payroll companies. Weigh your options for contracting with a company or doing it yourself. Chapter 15 can get you started.

T-Minus Six Months

Your biggest task at this point is to get — and stay — organized. Get your permits, licenses, and other legalities straightened out. Set up your temporary base of operations. And do your homework to figure out what equipment you need and whom you should buy it from.

Administration

❑ Set up water, electricity, gas, and other required utilities. Make sure that the billing is set up and the utilities are on *before* construction begins.

❑ Complete paperwork for permits and licenses. Figure out which permits your contractor will handle and which you must apply for on your own.

You may have to apply for your liquor license even sooner, especially if your concept depends on it. You'll need the restaurant's permanent address. If you change locations, you'll likely need to reapply for your license. And in some places, a finite number of licenses are available, so find out the specifics for your area. Check out Chapter 8 for details.

❑ Set up your temporary office space. Use a space in your restaurant that's away from the construction noise or work out of your home or even a trailer outside the restaurant while it's under construction. You need a space with electricity, lights, some form of climate control, desk space, a land-based phone line, and Internet access.

Get a fax machine for exchanging plans with architects and designers and other documents, such as specifications for equipment and resumes from management candidates. If you don't have a computer, get one. It's essential for doing research, ordering, creating your manuals, and developing your menu. Chapter 15 has info on equipping your office.

Construction

❑ Interview your contractor candidates. Check out Chapters 10 and 11 for information on working with a contractor and architect.

Make sure that you give your contractor your full specifications and your schedule. Make him or her commit to a detailed schedule in writing to confirm a completion date, with a financial penalty attached for not meeting the deadline.

❑ Meet with your kitchen and interior designers. Give them a tour of the rough space and discuss your ideas for final changes. Chapters 10 through 12 are your source for additional info.

We say "final changes" but realize that circumstances can arise that require changes later in the process. At this point the plans should be as close to final as they can be.

❑ Review your kitchen layout to make sure it fits your actual space. Take a peek at Chapter 11 for great ideas on ensuring an awesome kitchen flow and planning adequate storage.

❑ Review your dining room layout to make sure it fits your actual space. Chapter 10 gives you excellent hands-on advice for creating a dining room that flows well and captures the ambiance you're striving for.

❑ Review your exterior requirements to make sure they fit your actual space. Sneak a peek at Chapter 10 for the lowdown on the exterior.

Purchasing

❑ Start researching equipment suppliers and sourcing equipment. Consider new versus used equipment, and buying versus leasing options. You have to know your menu mix (see Chapter 9) to ensure your equipment provides enough capacity for your needs. It may seem early, but doing this step now is important, especially if any equipment needs to be special ordered or customized for your space. Do you need a chef? If you've done your homework and you know what you're doing, involving a chef may not be necessary. If you don't feel comfortable taking this step alone, consider bringing your chef or a consultant on earlier to help with this and other BOH functions. Take a look at Chapter 13.

T-Minus Five Months

Construction begins on your new site! Interview candidates for your key positions, such as your general manager (GM) and your chef, assuming that you're not either or both of them. Use any available time to work on manuals, job descriptions, and anything else you can get out of the way early.

Construction

❑ Begin construction. This schedule may be too soon or too late, depending on your operation. Take a look at Chapters 10 and 11 for more tips on working with contractors.

❑ Make sure that you and your contractor are still on the same page regarding the concept, design, and schedule and that anyone else involved with the process (such as designers) share your thoughts.

Human resources

❑ Interview general manager and chef candidates. Flip to Chapter 13.

❑ Develop job descriptions, pay rates, and benefits packages. Take a look at Chapter 17 for help.

Purchasing

❑ Order your kitchen equipment.

This stage is a great opportunity to get to know your business from the ground up. Don't pass it up by giving it all away to your chef. If you need help, definitely tap him as a resource, but stay actively involved. Know what you're buying and why. Look at Chapter 11 for details.

❑ Order your tables, chairs, and fixtures. Specify delivery for 30 days before opening. This schedule gives you time to allow for shipping and delivery delays. Review Chapter 10 for dining room layout and design.

❑ Purchase a POS system.

Research

❑ Research your beverage program. Take a look at Chapter 12.

❑ Investigate phone systems and phone service companies. All systems are not created equal. Check out Chapter 15 before making your selection.

T-Minus Four Months

Construction is well underway. Use this time to work on employee and operational manuals and create your beverage program. Check out the sidebar "Things to do in your free time" in this chapter to find things that you can complete now to save yourself time later.

Construction

❑ Check in with your contractor to make sure that construction is proceeding according to schedule.

❑ Finalize exterior construction.

Human resources

❑ Create employee and operational manuals. Spend some time in Chapters 13 and 17 for some direction on what to include in your manuals.

❑ Finalize job descriptions and pay rates. Chapter 13 can help.

FOH

❑ Finalize your beverage program. Create a beverage menu. Chapter 12 can help you with the details.

❑ Finalize your hours of operation. Do so before you hire your staff so they can coordinate their schedules with the restaurant's schedule.

Research

❑ Research pest control companies. Set up a regular schedule for treatment once you're up and running. Take a look at Chapter 18 for staying on top of your sanitation program.

T-Minus Three Months

Ideally kitchen construction is finished, and you can get a jump-start on cleaning it and placing equipment. If you haven't hired your general manager and chef by the end of the third month till opening, you'll definitely be behind. Delegate duties to your new managers, when possible. It's a great way to see how they work firsthand. Taste and test the menu to make the final selection. Firm up your beverage menu and start interviewing purveyors.

Administration

❑ Activate the phone lines in your restaurant. You may choose to do this later in the month, especially if you have office space somewhere else. Just make sure that your phone numbers are set and the lines are up and running when you're ready to begin pre-booking parties and accepting reservations. Choose an on-hold message. Chapter 15 gives you a great checklist for selecting all the features of your future phone system.

Construction

❑ Your kitchen construction should be in process.

❑ Review your final kitchen layout, including the eventual placement of all equipment. Look to Chapter 11 for tips.

❑ Dining room construction may be ongoing. Check out Chapter 10.

Don't install your FOH floor until the end of construction. Putting off the installation until as late as possible in your construction cycle minimizes construction-related dirt and damage. If people are wheeling heavy equipment through your dining room or banquet room, you may be able to save yourself some hard-core wear and tear. But you probably want to have the floor finished before you set up the tables and chairs. They're a huge pain to move while your flooring is being laid.

Human resources

❑ Hire your general manager and your chef (if they're not you).

❑ Start training your general manager and chef. Bring them up to speed on your plans and your progress. Set up your expectations for the rest of the start-up period and for the regular business period.

❑ Review resumes for supervisors and managers.

Purchasing

❑ Start sourcing food and beverage purveyors. Check out Chapter 14 for tips on negotiating the best deals and figuring out what you need.

❑ Order printed supplies.

FOH

❑ Review your beverage program. Sneak a peek at Chapter 12 for details.

❑ Develop your reservation system. Investigate online systems, phone systems, and computerized systems. Check out Chapter 10 for help.

❑ Deploy your reservation system.

BOH

❑ Review final kitchen layout, including eventual placement of all equipment. Chapter 11 is a great resource if you need help.

❑ Test recipes. Review Chapter 9 for help tweaking and cutting.

Advertising and promotion

❑ Begin preselling banquets, parties, and VIP functions. Make sure the phone numbers and reservation methods are in place.

If you're going to take early reservations, make sure that you're open when you say you will be.

❑ Revise the advertising and promotion plan you developed for your business plan. Work with a public relations firm as appropriate. Check out Chapters 16 and 19 for info on advertising and building a clientele.

Research

❑ Research your music options.

T-Minus Two Months

It's time to turn your attention to hiring your staff. At two months, create your plans for hiring, training, scheduling, and retaining your new team. Your menu should be set at this point. Hopefully, you have your liquor license in hand. You should also be working on any purchasing tools, like ordering procedures and forms, that you'll use after you're up and running.

Administration

❑ Make the final menu adjustments. See Chapter 9.

❑ Approve the opening menu items.

❑ Approve your menu design, layout, and fonts. Consult Chapter 9 to help you decide whether to print the menu on your own or outsource it.

❑ Follow up on any outstanding permits or licenses. Check out Chapter 8 for info on licenses, permits, and other legalities.

❑ Commission someone to create your Web site. Consider implementing an online reservation system, online ordering, and e-mail. Even if you can't support the cost for all features right away, make sure that your Web site is flexible and can handle changes when you're able to add them. Look at Chapter 16 for more info on inviting the world to your new place.

❑ Finalize your music program.

❑ Finalize your operational manuals. Chapter 13 gives you the scoop.

❑ Set up your trash services, including dumpsters and grease removal, recycling, and pest control services.

Construction

❑ All FOH areas should be completed at this time.

❑ Your kitchen construction should be complete.

Human resources

❑ Hire any other supervisors or managers.

❑ Create a blank interviewing roster for both the FOH and BOH. Look to Chapter 13 for details on the hiring process.

❑ Schedule times and dates for these hiring milestones:

- Initial interview

- Second interview

- Hiring

- Orientation

❑ Create a training schedule, including these specific training sessions:

- Steps of service (what you do when a guest sits down, when you offer bread, or how you present the dessert tray)

- Product training (menu, beverage, concept, and so on)

- POS

- Menu tastings

- Equipment training (dishwasher, food processor, slicer, coffee and espresso machine, and any other equipment you have)

Coordinate BOH and FOH job-specific training. Both teams should train on similar concepts at the same time. When you have your menu tasting, your kitchen should already be able to cook the food, and your wait staff should have an understanding of what your concept is. When it's time for your dry runs, everyone should be on the same page. If the kitchen is ready but you haven't hired your wait staff, you've wasted kitchen time.

❑ Finalize employee manuals. Chapter 13 is a great resource.

❑ Coordinate outside trainers as necessary.

Purchasing

❑ Create purchasing sheets with exact specifications of all products. Chapter 14 can give you a head start on purchasing.

❑ Review all printed materials, trademarks, and proprietary marks. Approve the specifications on all signage, business cards, menus, advertising, takeout bags and containers, letterhead, matches, beverage napkins, and stirrers. (Chapter 8 contains trademark advice.)

❑ Finalize all purchasing agreements with purveyors.

❑ Work with BOH to finalize smallwares order list and quantities.

❑ Create your purchasing manual.

❑ Create your purchase order for linen.

FOH

❑ Develop your floor plan (sections, table numbers, and section sizes). Chapter 10 can help you coordinate your furniture, your new dining layout, and your required sales projections to opt for the best setup.

BOH

❑ Work with purchasing to finalize your smallwares order list and quantities. See Chapter 11.

Advertising and promotion

❑ Finalize your campaign. Look at Chapter 16 for help.

❑ Finalize plans for your preopening party. Create a guest list and invitations for your preopening party.

❑ Provide tours to groups such as businesses in the area, corporate clients you're courting, and other VIPs. Tours can help you book and presell banquets and can also give a kick-start to sales of gift certificates.

T-Minus Six Weeks

Use this time to make sure that you have all the paperwork, training materials, and schedules ready when your prospective employees walk through the door. Set the expectation that you run a professional, organized, and well-run business and that you expect nothing less from them.

Construction

❑ Create a *construction punch,* or a list of unfinished items that must be completed before opening.

Human resources

❑ Print and collate your final employee manual.

❑ Make sure that you have all hiring paperwork in house, including applications, government-required forms (such as the I-9 and W-4s), uniform agreements, emergency contact cards, training materials, and so on. Check out Chapter 13 for the details.

FOH

❑ Finalize your opening floor plan (including sections, table numbers, and section sizes).

❑ Review FOH controls for maintaining optimum inventory levels while maximizing cash flow, and for minimizing your risk of theft. Take a look at Chapter 14 to get the full story.

T-Minus Thirty Days

The last month is a hectic one. You clean every square inch of your new restaurant. You set it up exactly the way you want it to look. Take pictures because you'll be setting the standard for how both the BOH and FOH should look before and after every single shift. You hire and train most of your opening staff during this crazy time, so make sure that you've set up your interviewing and hiring systems in the weeks beforehand to minimize the chaos and maximize the information transfer.

Construction

❑ Follow up on outstanding punch list concerns.

Human resources

❑ Start the hiring process for general employees. Place your ad and set up interviews at your location. Chapter 13 guides you through the process of hiring and training your employees.

❏ Hire new employees.

❏ Begin training new employees.

❏ Set up new employee files.

❏ Add new employees to the payroll systems, including to time clocks.

Purchasing

❏ Place food order for delivery two to three weeks before your opening. Coordinate the delivery so that you have time to train employees on food prep and menu tastings. See Chapter 14 for tips on buying right.

FOH

❏ Thoroughly clean all FOH spaces, including restrooms, dining rooms, the lobby, and the bar to get rid of any lingering construction dust and dirt.

❏ Set up all furniture and fixtures.

❏ Set up the managers' office. Check out Chapter 15.

❏ Finalize the table settings. See Chapter 10 for more info.

BOH

❏ Run a final test of all equipment (assembled as it comes in).

❏ Clean the kitchen, storerooms, and coolers to get rid of any lingering construction dust and dirt. Chapter 18 covers your sanitation system.

❏ Unpack, wash, and store all smallwares.

❏ Set up all storerooms. See Chapter 14 for tips on setting up your storerooms to keep the flow of inventory moving smoothly.

Advertising and promotion

❏ Get your signage in place.

❏ Send invitations for your preopening party.

❏ Continue to provide tours to groups, like businesses in the area, corporate clients you're courting, and other VIPs. Tours can help you book and presell banquets and kick-start gift-certificate sales.

T-Minus Ten Days

More of the same. You may be "just" the project manager at this point, overseeing the schedule to make sure that everyone is doing his or her job (rather than doing any of the jobs yourself). All employees should be hired by this point. Engage your staff's help in setting up your bar and assembling your menus. Continue to train and test your staff to make sure that they know your menu and processes in time for opening day.

Construction

❑ Follow up on outstanding punch list concerns.

Human resources

❑ Continue setting up new employee files.

❑ Continue adding new employees to the payroll systems.

❑ Continue training and testing employees on products, processes, and procedures. Test all FOH employees on menu knowledge, steps of service, table numbers, and so on, and test all BOH employees on station-specific menu items, station setup and tear down, and sanitation.

Purchasing

❑ Place your beverage order.

FOH

❑ Receive your beverage order.

❑ Set up your bar.

❑ Print and collate your final menu.

T-Minus One Week

The one-week-and-counting milestone marks the time when you want to have your restaurant completely assembled and in working order. Employees should be tasting the menu by this time and should be able to identify all dishes on sight. Each line cook should know the ins and outs of his station. All FOH employees should be role-playing and practicing mock service.

Construction

❑ Follow up on outstanding punch list concerns.

Human resources

❑ Continue training. Look at Chapter 13 for tips.

❑ Continue menu tastings. Chapter 17 gives great ideas for selling your employees on your restaurant. Start a tradition of tasting every dish and continue it as you change or add items to the menu.

❑ Work on mock service. *Mock service* lets servers wait on "guests" (other training employees), go through the steps of service, and practice fielding menu questions. Just like athletes actually practice how they want to play, you want your team to take this seriously and understand your systems and processes. You'll add real guests and real food very soon, so go through the drill to start working out the kinks.

❑ Continue setting up new employee files.

❑ Continue adding new employees to the payroll systems.

T-Minus Three Days

In the past four days, you've been focusing on developing your staff. Now it's time to see how they fare in an almost-like-real-life-scenario, the trial run.

Construction

❑ Follow up on outstanding punch list concerns.

Human resources

❑ Continue setting up new employee files.

❑ Continue adding new employees to the payroll systems.

❑ Conduct your first *trial run.* Some people call them *dry runs, soft openings,* or a host of other names. Before you open, invite employees' families, friends, investors, advisers, consultants, and others to eat in the restaurant. Treat them just like regular diners. They order off the menu, and the kitchen prepares the orders. Everything is the same as a real dinner shift, except the customers aren't paying. This is a chance to go through a practice shift and see how everything works together. You'll likely have a few things to iron out between your trial run and opening day, which is why you do it. Every restaurant should do at least one dry run, but do as many as you can afford to schedule-wise and money-wise. Trial runs aren't cheap, but they're well worth the money.

T-Minus One Day

Hopefully, you're having a fairly relaxed day. You may have your preopening party tonight, but your to-do list should be under control at this point.

Construction

❑ Follow up on outstanding punch list concerns.

Human resources

❑ Continue setting up new employee files.

❑ Continue adding new employees to the payroll systems.

Things to do in your free time

Okay, we know free time in this business is an oxymoron. Some tasks associated with opening a restaurant can really be done earlier or later in the process, depending on when you have time. It's simply a matter of choice. Consider getting some of these out of the way early. Your to-do list can quickly become unmanageable if you leave them all until the last couple of months.

✔ Develop your beverage program.

✔ Set up your training schedule. You probably can't know that on March 23 next year you'll be doing beverage training. But you can develop rough estimates and outlines for what new employees should do on Day 1, Day 2, Day 10, and so on.

✔ Establish your internal control mechanisms, such as procedures for cash handling, ordering, requisition, and receiving.

✔ Set up your credit card agreements.

✔ Figure out how you're going to get your money into your account. Are you going to schedule an armored car pickup or deposit it yourself everyday?

✔ Develop your preferred reporting systems. Develop your specific income statement format. Create your cost of goods sold report. See Chapter 20 for tips on which reports to use to evaluate your business.

✔ Research your music program.

✔ Develop your reservation system. Check out Chapter 10 for help.

✔ Interview pest control companies. They're one of those unmentionable necessities.

✔ Investigate phone companies and phone systems. Check out Chapter 15 for can't-miss tips.

✔ Research printers for letterhead, advertising or promotional materials, matches, napkins, and anything else you'd like to print with your logo.

✔ Develop your employee manual.

✔ Write job descriptions and establish pay rates for job classes.

✔ Pick your payroll company unless you're doing it yourself.

Chapter 3

Deciding What Kind of Restaurant to Run

*I*f you're thinking about getting into this business, and you're like most folks, you likely have an idea of what kind of restaurant you want to run, and you're looking for a way to get started. But before you run out and print your menus, think about your options. Better yet, take your time and research your options to set up the best plan for you and your restaurant.

In this chapter, we show you different ways you can get your business started, and give you some pros and cons for each. We walk you through the different styles of services you can offer. Finally, we help you finalize the theme and concept for your new restaurant. Your concept ultimately shapes all your research, planning, and design, so spend some time developing it.

Figuring Out Where to Start

For most restaurants, you have several possible starting points, including going with a franchise, taking over an existing restaurant, or starting from scratch. We give you the pros and cons of each in the following sections.

Buying into a franchise

In the restaurant business, buying a franchise is buying a license to sell a restaurant's food and use its brand, logos, and name. Wendy's, McDonald's Burger King, and KFC are examples of restaurants often sold as franchises. The company who sells its franchises is called a *franchisor.*

Not all chains are franchises, but all franchises are chains. A *chain* of restaurants simply means that there are more than one just like it. Many chains, such as Chili's, Starbucks, and Hard Rock Cafe, are chains all owned by a parent company, not by independent *franchisees,* people or companies who buy into a franchise. The terms *chain* and *franchise* aren't synonymous.

Buying into the franchise is the closest thing there is to a "sure thing" in the risky restaurant business. The pros of buying into a franchise are

- ✔ They typically have a proven track record and have worked out the bugs.

- ✔ Franchises have a consistent product, a set menu, huge brand recognition, and a built-in customer loyalty.

- ✔ Franchises help you with marketing, realistic sales projections, market research, and market analysis.

- ✔ You get a jump-start on all human resources (HR) and administrative issues, because franchises come equipped with all their own forms, policies, and scheduling philosophies.

As good as all that sounds, most of the cons of buying into a franchise are closely associated with the pros:

- ✔ You have to pay franchisors hefty setup fees and significant franchise fees monthly, usually a percentage of sales.

- ✔ You have to follow their rules, meet their numbers, and serve their menu. If you're the creative type, the franchise mold may be the wrong size or shape for you. Love it or hate it, when people see the golden arches, they know what to expect, and they don't want you messing with it.

- ✔ Because franchises are fairly lucrative, franchisors are very selective about whom they franchise to. Often you have to have a significant amount of money to invest and agree to open multiple units.

Obviously, this info is only a snapshot look at the world of franchising. If you decide that a franchise is the path you'd like to take, we suggest you check out *Franchising For Dummies* by Dave Thomas and Michael Seid (Wiley).

Taking over an existing restaurant

You may have an opportunity to take over an existing operation, either one you've been a part of or one that you're completely new to. Maybe your boss wants out, and you're going to buy into it. Maybe you're walking by and see a For Sale sign in the window of your favorite diner.

The primary positive and negative aspects of taking over an existing restaurant are relatively straightforward, but it all boils down to discerning the owner's motivation for selling.

- ✔ If the restaurant is relatively successful and the owner is retiring or moving, or has health concerns, taking over may be a head start. It presents you with instant client base that you can build upon.

- ✔ Often, though, restaurants are sold for reasons that paint a much bleaker picture of future success. The owner may be trying to pass along a loser.

Your job is to figure out which of these scenarios is more likely. Before signing on the dotted line, work your way through the following list:

- ✔ Open up the books and get the full financial picture. Chapters 5 and 20 cover what numbers to look at and information to gather.

- ✔ Find out the history of the space *and* the current concept. Just knowing it was a restaurant isn't enough. If it was a shop before that, why did it stop operating? How does the neighborhood work? Before you sign the lease, it's good to know that every three weeks the first floor fills up with water. Check out Chapter 7 for details on choosing the best location.

    A common reason that people sell a successful business is the landlord intends to raise the rent. If you're buying the business, you may also be *assuming* the lease or be required to agree to this increase. Talk with the landlord and the business owner about future plans for the space.

- ✔ Decide whether you're going to take over the business or just the location and equipment. If you're buying the business, you probably want to keep the name the same. If you do change the name, you'll probably be hurting yourself, at least in the short term.

If you determine that the current business is working well, you may want to keep quiet about the fact that new ownership is in place. Don't mess with success. Your regulars will know, but for customers who come in only occasionally, why bother notifying them about the change? The idea of new ownership or management can affect people's perception of the place as they fall into the "back in the good old days" mentality. Suddenly, their old favorites don't taste the same, or the wait times are too long.

You may incur lots of unforeseen costs when you take over an established restaurant, including repairs to older equipment and facilities. Work with a reputable contractor and inspector to thoroughly go through the restaurant from top to bottom before you finalize your deal. Check out Chapter 10 for tips on working with a contractor.

Partnering up with your current employer

If you're considering partnering up with your current boss, our advice is to look this gift horse in the mouth. When you buy into a restaurant, you buy into its profits *and* losses and its assets *and* liabilities.

If the restaurant is a profitable business that's well run, consider why someone is giving you a piece of it. Why is someone letting you buy into it? A number of legitimate and potentially profitable motivations exist:

- Reward for your hard work
- Part of an Employee Stock Ownership Plan (ESOP) that allows managers to buy into the business over time
- An owner who wants to retire

However, other, less-positive motivations may be behind the offer:

- The operation is leaking money like a sieve. If someone wants you to put money in right away, you should be leery. This is the one situation to immediately be very concerned about.
- The owner's attention is being diverted to another business, so he's giving you an incentive not to rob him blind while he's distracted.

Anytime you consider entering into a partnership, you want to see the books before you hand over any money. Make sure that you get involved with a financially sound business that offers the potential for success.

When getting involved in any partnership, get definite answers about how much and what kind of say you're going to have in day-to-day operations and long-term planning. Clearly define on paper who gets what, including compensation, profit sharing, the best parking space, and Christmas Eve off. If it's important to you, write it down and make sure that everyone signs it.

Starting from scratch

We can quickly sum up the pros and cons for this one: Starting from scratch is exciting and scary. You have a blank canvas: It's your baby from the ground up. You may be taking over an existing space that's been abandoned for years, or you may decide to convert a shop or a house into a restaurant. (Take a look at Chapter 7 before you sign on the dotted line for any space.) Either way, you'll have limitations for what your space can do, but you can get very creative with the obstacles in terms of layout and flow. It's like putting together a puzzle — rebuilding the pieces to fit your concept.

Taking this road can involve a lot of work. Very few spaces are ready and waiting for you exactly as you want them. And implementing your idea isn't as easy as saying, "I want to make this bar 40 feet long and 4 feet high mahogany with a marble top." You actually have to figure out how to build it and work out all the details. Work with a contractor to implement your vision because the devil is in the details. You'll face the fun of electricity, plumbing, heating, ventilation, air conditioning, placement of everything from ranges and coolers to the wait-staff stations . . . the list goes on. Check out Chapters 10 and 11 for info on laying out the front and back of the house. And get an inspector to come in and evaluate the space, just like when buying a home.

When you're starting from scratch, now's the time to plan ahead for the future. During the rebuilding after a fire, coauthor Mike left extra plumbing hookups under the floor in the middle of the lounge so he could add a sushi bar later if he wanted to. Always add more power outlets than you think you'll need, even in the office. Extra cable and wires for electricity are handy in case you have to move something around later.

Choosing the Best Type of Restaurant

Forty years ago, going out to dinner was an event. Now it's more routine, and the number and variety of restaurants that you can find illustrate the change in America's eating habits.

As a general rule, the atmosphere defines the type of restaurant more so than the food does, but they usually go hand in hand. For example, out-of-this-world carnitas, slathered in chili verde, with fresh lime and cilantro could be served from a cart on the side of the road, at a casual Mexican eatery, or in a world-class fine dining establishment like Rick Bayless's Topolobampo in Chicago. The atmosphere of each venue is very different, though, while some menu items may be similar.

There's no magic formula or dollar amount that you need to start a restaurant. The cost varies based on such things as the concept, size of your space, size of your menu, location of your space, number of employees you'll need to hire, and cost of insurance in your area. You need to do your homework to figure out how much money you need to spend and why. Chapters 5 and 6 can help you with the nitty-gritty details.

Dining in style

Fine dining, dining with the highest quality food, service, and surroundings, usually includes the highest prices as well. If you choose to run a fine dining restaurant, your restaurant needs to cater to the guest's every need.

Soaking up the atmosphere

When they walk in your door, your diners should know they're in a fine dining establishment. If you choose to open a fine dining restaurant, include these atmospheric factors in your plans:

- ✔ **Ambience:** The tables should have white linen tablecloths and top-notch dinnerware, glassware, and silverware. Choose lighting that's subtle, maybe even leaning toward the dark side. Select furniture and décor that reflect the mood you're trying to set. Decide whether you want to show the world a hip, trendy place or a more traditional restaurant.

- ✔ **Service:** The service is almost smothering. You escort guests to the bathroom rather than direct them to it. Your servers place napkins in your diners' laps after they're seated. You must train your staff in every service detail imaginable, such as removing crumbs from the table properly and serving plates from the correct side of a diner.

- ✔ **Amenities:** You offer amenities such as valet parking service and a coat check. You must have a reservation system. Many fine dining establishments get creative while trying to outdo each other. For example, a restaurant may offer guests a choice of 10 or 15 high-quality pens to sign their bill. Are you ready for the challenge?

Focusing on food

If you're thinking about opening a fine dining place, spend some time thinking about what kind of food you want to serve. People have very high expectations about what they eat when they're in a fine dining restaurant. Here are a few things to keep in mind while you're mulling it over:

- ✔ **Food quality:** In your fine dining restaurant, the quality of food should be exceptional. It's characterized by top-notch ingredients, precise preparation styles, and intricate presentations, with a wine list to match.

- ✔ **Menu selection:** Your menu doesn't need to be extensive, but the items should be intricate. Sometimes, fine restaurants don't even offer menus. Each guest is served the same food at a set price.

- ✔ **Wine and liquor:** Your liquor selection should be high-end with an extensive selection of cognacs and brandies. The wine list is perfectly paired with the menu items and includes selections of superior quality. Some of these wines might be quite expensive, but a well-balanced list includes options in all price categories.

Kicking back casual

The term *casual dining* is a catchall for anything that isn't fast food or fine dining. You can get a broad range of food and service quality in casual dining, but the dress code is consistently casual in every casual restaurant. In general, *casual* refers to the ambience or atmosphere of the place and the style of the service, rather than the quality of the cuisine. You can have remarkable food in a very casual setting. Think about a bistro concept: you can get fresh fabulous food while wearing your jeans and flip-flops.

Casual restaurants tend to be noisier than their fine dining counterparts with loud music, loud patrons, and maybe even loud service, if servers, bartenders, and food runners are calling out orders back and forth. The food is generally reasonably priced, somewhere between $4 and $18 per entrée. Guests tend to linger longer in casual restaurants than in fast food restaurants. They usually order from menus at the table rather than at a centralized menu at a cashier. Many chain restaurants are casual restaurants. Examples include Chili's, Applebee's, Bennigan's, Lone Star Steak House, Shoney's, and IHOP.

In casual dining, sometimes the food matches the level of service, and sometimes it doesn't. The Oyster Bar in New York's Grand Central Station has an extensive seafood menu, with high-quality products and innovative dishes, but the service is friendly and efficient, not smothering.

Many diners are opting for counter service these days and casual dining is filling that need. If a diner is dining alone, or in a hurry, the counter is a popular choice. Counter service is usually good for groups no larger than three or so. Typically you can get the full menu at the counter, usually in a hurry. If you choose to set up counter service, make sure you set up an ordering system that prioritizes counter orders, for this very reason.

Placing an order — to go!

You can view your takeout and delivery options as falling under one of two general categories:

- **Takeout/delivery-only operation:** This setup is most applicable if you're considering opening a pizza, Chinese (or other ethnic food), or sandwich shop. You may have one or two tables with chairs or just a couple of chairs where customers can wait for their orders.

- **Takeout or delivery as part of your larger operation:** Many restaurants successfully incorporate takeout and/or delivery options to varying degrees. Your options are numerous, including a dedicated carry-out counter (with a separate entrance even), ordering takeout from the bartender, or simply permitting eat-in guests to order food to go.

The menu for this option may be the same as your regular menu, or you may offer a modified menu. But takeout hours are often modified if it's part of a larger operation, usually with shorter hours for takeout and delivery. Takeout and delivery may stop one hour before close, while other takeout-only operations may be open 24 hours.

If you're not sure that your restaurant has a delivery market, consider looking into some kind of co-op delivery program. In some areas, a company contracts with restaurants to do delivery for them. Customers call the company and place orders with one of several different restaurants.

As with any restaurant, takeout and delivery business has high times and low times, and they usually coincide with mealtimes. Staff your delivery, kitchen, and ordering staff appropriately. See Chapter 17 for tips on scheduling.

Ordering

Make sure your customers can order in person at the restaurant or by phone, fax, or e-mail. Ordering online is also more and more common. Some diners order their meals, eat them in the restaurant, and then order more food to go (for a snack or for someone who couldn't join them for restaurant dining).

If you have some items on your menu that aren't available for takeout, make sure that they're clearly marked and your order taker knows which menu items aren't available for takeout. That employee also needs to be able to answer questions about menu options and ingredients.

If your takeout or delivery order system is integrated with your point-of-sale (POS) system, make sure to clearly differentiate the order as takeout in the system. Otherwise, takeout orders may get *plated,* or placed on plates for service, as dining room orders instead of being packaged in to-go containers. You can distinguish between the two types of orders by creating different POS items (French fries versus TG-French fries), using modifiers (French fries with cheese versus French fries with cheese to go), or by simply noting where the order came from (dining room — section 1 versus to-go window).

Delivery

You want to deliver a quality product to your diner's door. Establish your delivery radius by determining how long your food holds in the containers you use and how long it takes to get to your customers. You don't want to go farther than your food will hold. And consider that your delivery guy needs to get back to your shop to deliver the other orders. Make your delivery area as large as you can reasonably serve. Do it well or don't bother doing it.

If you offer delivery, you need transportation, probably either a bike or a car. You'll likely need some kind of ID (for secure buildings or gated communities) and/or uniform that indicates that the delivery person works for you. A recognizable uniform also help keeps you in the loop on what he's doing outside the restaurant. If he's rude to people, litters, or rides on the sidewalk, you'll hear about it.

Overestimate the amount of time it will take to get orders to your customer by at least 10 minutes. Things get dropped and lost, and you need some stub-your-toe room. Customers almost always react better when you call them to let them know a problem has occurred and give an estimate on how long it will take to fix it instead of just showing up late.

Selecting self-service or fast-food

Many fast-food, self-service, or quick service restaurants (QSR) are franchises, but you don't have to take that route for fast-food success. Pizza, Chinese food, and ice cream are all great choices for fast-food non-chain restaurants. Even an independent sandwich or burger joint can be successful.

You'll really need to hone your point of difference between you and your competition (see Chapter 4 for details). Generally, you'll need to focus on the difference in your quality because you likely can't compete, at least initially, with the big boys in terms of price.

Fast casual is the hottest emerging trend in restaurants at the moment. Fast casual takes the concept of a quick-service deli and blows it out into a range of cuisines combining counter service, comfortable but basic furnishings, takeout, and sometimes delivery. If you haven't tried one of these restaurants, look for names like Chipotle, Baja Fresh, and Noodles & Company. They're part of a whole new genre of restaurants that are delivering a level of freshness with less overhead.

Running a bar — with or without food

Even if you're opening a bar, you'll probably need at least limited food service. Check out the laws in your area because your liquor license may require you to serve some food during some of your business hours. Most bars offer some kind of food service even if the menu is very small and it's not available at all hours (the kitchen may close at 9 p.m., while the bar is open till 2 a.m.). The food may be something as simple as potato chips, popcorn, nuts, and pretzels. At a few places, when the kitchen closes, you can bring in food from other restaurants.

Lots of people eat at the bar, not out of necessity but out of preference. More and more operations are incorporating food service in their bars as part of their regular business. With no-smoking laws in place in many bars and restaurants, the trend toward eating in the newly smoke-free bars will continue. If you're not serving food in your bar, take advantage of this trend by experimenting with a limited menu. See Chapter 12 for details on setting up and running a bar.

Providing catering and banquet services

In general, both catering and banquets serve large parties, anywhere from 15 to 50,000 people at a single time. *Banquets* usually take place at a designated banquet hall or facility, and *catering* takes place at a customer's location. More and more restaurants are getting into the catering business, and you may want to consider it as a component to your operations (or consider basing your operations only on catering).

Catering lends itself to highly controllable costs and consequently high profitability. In catering, you generally have the luxury of knowing, in advance, how many guests will attend, exactly what they'll eat and drink while they're there, and how many employees you need to staff the event. Therefore, in theory, you should know all the costs in advance: what it costs you to produce 150 servings of lasagna in terms of food, labor hours to produce that lasagna, and labor hours to serve that lasagna and clean up.

In catering, all direct expenses associated with the production of an event are transferable to the client. In other words, everything you spend for food, beverage, labor, disposables, transportation, rentals, flowers, and décor are billable to the client. You only need to factor in your administrative time, overhead, and profit margin to arrive at a price. Simple, right? Wrong.

The art of profitable catering lies in understanding how to "work the numbers" (understanding how to prepare just the right amount of food, no more, no less).

Here's an example of how to work your catering numbers. If you have a party of 500 people outside in a tent, your prep list might look like Figure 3-1. Looking at Figure 3-1, you may say, "Hey! That doesn't add up! You've got 408 pieces of cake (34 cakes × 12 pieces per cake) for 500 people." See, we know that in one hour, the average guest consumes four passed hors d'oeuvres. We know that on a buffet, only 80 percent of guests have salad, and those who do have an average of 1 to 1.25 ounces of greens. If you have two types of salad dressing and specify 60 percent of the guest count for each, you'll be fine. (Here's the math: 80 percent of 500 guests = 400 guests having salad. Then take 60 percent of 400 to decide how many 1-ounce servings of each dressing you need, and you get you 240 ounces = 3.75 gallons of each.) We know that a hotel pan of food feeds 25 average people (less if they're NFL linemen or more if they're ballerinas). And we know to always have vegetarian meals available for 5 percent of guests (in this case 5 percent of 500 is 25), whether the customer orders them or not. These tricks of the trade can make the difference between having too much food and wasting profits, and having just enough to cover the count and maximizing your profitability.

Catering Event Order Sheet

Client: National Association of Sleep-Deprived Restaurateurs
Attendees: 500   **Date:** December 15
Location: Tent (Grant Park)   **Time:** 6 p.m.

DINNER MENU	PREP QUANTITY
6:00 – Passed Hors d'Oeuvres (30 minutes)	
Bruschetta ala Caprese	300 each
Seared Tuna on Wonton Crisp	300 each
Maryland Crab Cakes with Spicy Aioli	300 each
6:30 – Client's Award Presentation (15 minutes)	
6:45 – Buffet Dinner	
Tossed Mixed Green Salad	30 lbs.
Balsamic Vinaigrette	3.75 gal.
Buttermilk Ranch Dressing	3.75 gal.
Seared Sterling Salmon with Herbed Potato Crust	60 lbs.
Carved Beef Tenderloin with Horseradish Cream	40 each
French Green Beans with Tarragon-Shallot Butter	16 pans
Roasted Garlic Potato Galette	20 pans
Flourless Chocolate Torte (12 pieces per cake)	34 each
(vegetarian dinners not on menu)	25 each
Beverages	
Merlot	15 cases
Sauvignon Blanc	8 cases
Bottled Water	15 cases

Figure 3-1:
Sample of an order sheet for a catered event.

Learning what to charge and where the opportunities are for increased sales is the trick. Do you only sell food and beverage, or do you become an event planner and coordinate the flowers, décor, china and linen rental, and the like? You need more info and experience to do this effectively, but the profits are huge because you're simply the middleman for some of the services, coordinating them for a more-than-fair markup.

Many restaurants, such as Spago, have spawned hugely successful catering operations that have become as big as, if not bigger than, the restaurant because you can make big money feeding the masses. You get rid of the speculation of the restaurant, trying to decide how much food to prep, how many servers to schedule, and so on. Catering enables you to know there are going to be butts in the seats and about how many people will be present.

Your catering menu will be smaller than your regular dining room menu. Select items from your main menu that are easily produced in volume, don't require a lot of steps, and hold well. Your choices should embody your concept. People choose you to cater based in large part on your signature dishes. In most cases, you'll be fulfilling catering/banquet orders out of the same kitchen, so the items should fit the workflow you've established.

The scope of your catering operation varies with your own desire. One caterer we know started out as a single banquet hall in Indianapolis. It's now a $50,000,000-plus catering enterprise. Start small and work your way up. Maybe you do small in-home parties for key guests at the restaurant. Maybe you provide off-site lunches to doctors' offices in the city. Whatever you choose, remember that transporting food must be done professionally, cleanly, and with food safety as a priority.

Putting It All Together

Make sure that your theme is consistent with your décor, cuisine, and style of service. If you have a Latin American name and theme and customers are singing along with the mariachi band, it's a good indicator that you've met or exceeded their expectations.

Thinking about theme and concept

Just like in a movie or a story, a *theme* is a common thread, idea, or image that runs throughout your restaurant. You can base a theme on many different things. Your *concept* is the whole package, including your food, menu, price points, design, décor, ambience, and how that package marries the theme. Here's the short list of what you can base your theme or concept on, but your imagination is really your only limit.

- ✔ **A style of cuisine:** For example, you may decide to base your concept on Brazilian churrasco, a cuisine that delivers various kinds of roasted meats sliced from the spit tableside. You're not offering the entire scope of Brazilian food; you're focusing on a single cuisine.

- ✔ **An individual dish:** A pizza place isn't necessarily Italian; it may have Sicilian, Hawaiian, and Californian cuisine all on the same menu, but it focuses on pizza. Some places specialize in just desserts.

- ✔ **Ethnic influence:** Japanese, Italian, Chinese, and so on are all well-known examples.

- ✔ **Décor and ambience:** Maybe you want your guests to be surrounded by New Age music, soothing scents, sage green walls, and relaxing lighting. You then serve food that fits that environment.

- ✔ **A character from a book, movie, and the like:** Maybe you want to open the Sherlock Holmes Bookstore and Café.

- ✔ **Sporting events or hobbies:** Sports bars and Internet cafes are typical examples.

- ✔ **Games:** Some restaurants offer pizza for the parents and provide the kids with flashing lights, animatronic animals, and tokens for games. Others skip the kids' stuff and focus on video games, pool, and darts for adults.

- ✔ **Geography:** Maybe you're located in a train station. Continue the theme into your restaurant via your décor, menu titling, and uniforms. Or maybe you focus on cuisine related to your area of the country, like Cajun food in southern Louisiana or seafood on the coast of Maine.

If a restaurant's theme is very kitschy, it tends not to have fantastic food. Instead, it spends more time focused on the theme, décor, and look of the menu rather than the food. In these cases, a big part of their draw and of the product they're selling is the atmosphere. But for most diners, the food is always the most important thing. If the food is marginal, they won't be back, so spend some time on your menu no matter how kitschy you decide to go.

Make sure that your theme and menu match. If you open Mike's Indian Bazaar, it's up to you whether it's a bazaar or just bizarre. Just be sure to do your research (and don't serve beef on the menu; the cow is a sacred animal and is rarely eaten in India). If you open an Indian-themed restaurant, you're trying to create an atmosphere that lets diners imagine they're in India. The smells, sounds, sights, and tastes you create can do just that.

Choosing a name

Your restaurant's name should be catchy, easy to remember, unique, and somewhat descriptive. Picking your name is fun, but don't get so caught up in it that you forget to take care of the necessary legalities (like making sure someone's not already using your favorite pick). Check out Chapter 8 for details on searching for trademarks. You may have picked out a name already, but consider these ideas before you inlay it in 24-karat gold on your signage:

- ✔ **Name of someone significant to you:** Consider your name, a relative's name, or the name of someone that inspired you. You could choose a figure in history who's been dead long enough not to have trademarked his or her own name. Examples are Rocco's, Crazy Horse Saloon, and Mama Carolla's Old Italian Restaurant.

- ✔ **Geography:** You can borrow your restaurant name from a natural forma- tion, such as a river, lake, hill, crater, or mountain range. Or use your town's name, a street, neighborhood, bridge, park, sanctuary, or an area of town as an inspiration. Blake Street Tavern, James River Grill, Breckenridge Brewery, and Everest are a few geography-based names.

- ✔ **Historic or traditional names and spaces:** Urban sprawl has incorporated many once-independent neighborhoods into larger cities and towns. Maybe you want to incorporate that tradition into your concept. In some areas, restaurants have taken over locations that used to be occupied by other businesses, such as banks. Those old names may be perfect for your new restaurant, especially if elements of the old business are part of your decor. At The Broker in Denver, you walk through a vault door to get to some tables. The Chicago Firehouse is located in a turn-of-the-century, fully restored firehouse.

- ✔ **Ethnic and cultural names:** Maybe you want your name to describe the influences of your concept. Comanche Curry Café, a Native American-Indian fusion restaurant, is an example.

- ✔ **Pop culture:** Hard Rock Cafe, Jekyl and Hyde's, Planet Hollywood, Bubba Gump Shrimp, and the like make their bread and butter by tapping into people's love of pop culture.

- ✔ **Weather:** Extreme weather (even weather that implies risk or danger) can influence your name. Think about the Fog City Diner in San Francisco, Typhoon! in Seattle, and Rainforest Cafe in many locations.

- ✔ **Your concept and theme:** You might include the term "Sports Bar and Grill" in your name. Or choose to call your restaurant Polynesia because you have poi on your menu and serve drinks out of coconuts. Tommy Gun's Garage is a 1920s speakeasy in Chicago.

- ✔ **Your preparation methods:** You may want a name that reveals how your food is cooked. Wok 'N' Roll is a Chinese concept, and bd's Mongolian Barbeque serves — yes, you guessed it — Mongolian Barbeque. Il Fornaio means *oven* and serves lots of oven-baked Italian favorites.

- ✔ **Other business in the area:** Consider a name borrowed from a nearby business. Examples include The Bottom Line Bistro in a financial district, The Carnegie Deli near Carnegie Hall, The Green Room near the theater district, and The Bull and The Bear near Wall Street.

- ✔ **Humor and irony:** You may want to try a funny or ironic name, but be careful that the humor doesn't offend anyone. The Cellar's Market is a café. Hot Doug's serves some of the best sausage and dogs in Chicago. Maybe a bar called The Hardware Store would do well in suburban neighborhoods. The Library may work as the name for a bar on campus.

Certain names will alienate people. Avoid truly offensive terms at all cost. In your quest to appeal to your target market, you may ruffle some feathers — the extent to which you do so is a marketing decision you have to make.

Chapter 4

Researching the Marketplace

· ·

· ·

*C*ompetition is defined as the following:

- ✔ A test of skill or ability; a contest
- ✔ The act of competing, as for profit or a prize; rivalry
- ✔ Rivalry between two or more businesses striving for the same customer or market

Before you read one more page or take another step toward realizing your dream of crowded dining rooms, ringing cash registers, and vacation homes in Belize, reread the definition of competition again . . . again . . . and again. Think about what it means in the restaurant business.

You're reading this book because you're making a decision to enter a *competition* — the restaurant business. And this is not some friendly game of Old Maid. You have a lot at stake: your business, your financial future, and your family's sense of security. That's why you have to analyze the competitive environment to make sure that you have a shot at success.

In this chapter, we show you how to investigate your competition. We give you tips on evaluating their strengths and weaknesses. If you're developing your concept, we help you use this information to shape your decisions about how to develop your concept and how to position it in your market. After you're up and running, you can use many of these same tools to continuously analyze the market and stay ahead of your competition.

Getting Your Mind Right: Profits Matter

To the casual outsider, the restaurant business is attractive for reasons that are byproducts of success (the fun, the glamour, the status). But success, and all its trappings, isn't guaranteed — a fact lost on many would-be restaurateurs. At its core, success in the restaurant business requires you to look at the business differently than these misguided victims of their own lack of knowledge. You must understand and accept one basic concept that eludes many: A restaurant is a business, a manufacturing enterprise whose products are only as good as they are salable.

And the only way to measure success in any business is profits. Ultimately, nothing else matters. You can have the coolest space, the hippest crowd, and the trendiest cutting-edge food, but without net profitability, you might as well close the doors and save yourself a slow death.

You're a manufacturer, so accept that fact. We know that the title of manufacturer isn't as sexy as the titles *chef de cuisine* or *restaurateur,* but it's the most accurate label. (Or, if you still insist on a cool-sounding French term, you can use *fabricant.* That's French, too — for manufacturer.)

Creativity, vision, and equipment allow you to produce a product. That product is not just the type, quality, and presentation of your food or beverages. *Product* refers to the whole of your concept (restaurant), including the quality of the food, design of the space, appearance of the wait staff, and convenience of the location. All these factors affect the likelihood that a consumer will purchase your product over the competition's product. (Check out Chapter 3 for tips on choosing and developing your concept.)

You need to embrace the fact that your success is based on producing a salable product and turning a profit — just as it is with any business. If you create a product with no sale, you're only creating inventory. Profits come only when you make the sale, and everyone is competing for that sale. Your job is to continually win that sale over your competition.

The Buying Decision: The Big Why

Why does one car sell and another doesn't? Why do you buy one brand of beer and not another? Why do you go to the restaurants you go to? If you think about your own actions, you can begin to understand the criteria that others use in making the buying decision. This process (whether formal or informal) is called a *competitive analysis.* How your product positively influences the buying decisions of customers determines your market share, operational cash flow, and ultimately, your success. Perform a quick competitive analysis based on your own views. Here's how:

1. **Pick five grocery stores and five automobiles.**

2. **Compare and contrast your personal feelings on each one.** Evaluate them using criteria of your choosing. But definitely include price, value, design, practicality, and service. You can't have a good competitive analysis without them.

3. **Now take those same criteria and apply them to your concept in your market.** By doing so, you begin to see how the customer views your concept when making a buying decision.

As you go through this exercise, you gain an appreciation of all the factors that influence a buying decision. But you're only you, so take it a step further. You need to understand the potential consumers and what influences *their* buying decision as it relates to *your* market.

Figure 4-1 illustrates the *competitive response cycle* — the process of research and action that you *continually* follow to ensure that your restaurant *continually* meets the needs of the consumers you're going after. You study the marketplace (including customers and competitors) and changes in the marketplace (including emerging trends) and then implement responses to your findings (marketing programs, menu changes, and so on) to develop your business. Then you analyze how well your efforts are working, which leads you right back to square one. In the following sections we describe each part of the cycle in detail. The cycle never stops.

Information is the weapon in the restaurant wars. Base your decisions on sound intelligence.

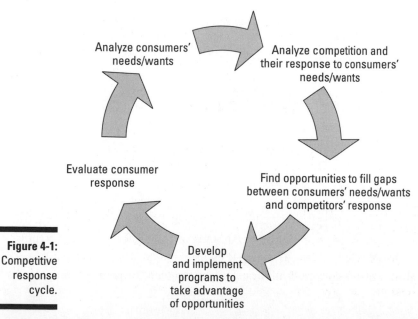

Figure 4-1: Competitive response cycle.

Identifying and Analyzing Potential Customers

Start by figuring out who you want your customers to be, and make sure they're likely to frequent your concept. Figure out what demographic group(s) you're likely to attract. The term *demographics* describes characteristics or traits shared by a group. A demographic group includes people within a specific age range or income level, or who share other distinguishing traits like gender or marital status. Ask yourself questions, such as:

- ✓ Are you looking for a male or a female clientele, or both? If it's both men and women, are you focusing on singles or couples?

- ✓ Is your concept geared toward families, or is it not kid-friendly?

- ✓ Are you targeting a particular ethnic or religious segment of your community?

- ✓ Do you want to attract people in suits, in hard hats, or in everything in between?

- ✓ Do you appeal to locals, or are you trying to draw out-of-towners, including business travelers and tourists?

You're not excluding anyone from dining with you; you're simply trying to identify the clientele who's likely to visit your restaurant. You must make sure that your menu offerings, music (and its volume), entertainment choices, décor, and so on appeal to your proposed clientele.

Over time, build a profile of your desired diners and tweak your concept, as appropriate, to appeal to this group. Figure out where they eat. Discover what motivates their buying decisions. Find out what else they do besides dine out.

Figuring out what you need to know

Deciding what information you need is half the battle (the other half is actually doing the research and analyzing the information, but hey, you can't expect us to do everything for you). Here are our tips for focusing your research on what your diners want from you:

- ✓ **Location:** Determine how much importance your potential customers place on location convenience and identify locations that fit. Maybe you're close to your customers' homes or workplaces, or maybe they drive past your place on their commute.

- ✓ **Hours of operation:** What hours are convenient to your potential customer?

- **Menu:** A big menu is a draw for some consumers; others prefer a short, simple format. Figure out what fits your desired clientele.

- **Food quality:** Given your concept, what do people expect?

- **Price/value:** The *price* is the amount of money that someone pays for a menu item. The *value* is how they perceive what they get (usually in terms of quality and quantity) compared to what they pay. Both need to be in line with the needs and wants of your consumer.

- **Service:** Determine the type, style, and efficiency of service that best fit your targeted customers' needs.

- **Applicable trends:** Determine how conscious your potential customers are of dining and lifestyle trends and how these trends are likely to impact their buying decisions. Do they largely ignore trends in favor of consistency, or are they largely trend followers? Keep in mind that a trend doesn't have to be glitzy and hip to qualify. Past trends like wraps, frozen yogurt, or low-carb dieting aren't real glitzy.

Depending on your concept and the trends in question, think about how to take temporary advantage of them. Don't retool your concept to serve nothing but trends, but you can use them as a component of your concept. By watching for and interpreting trends correctly, you can either create the next trend or have a plan ready when the market is ready for it. Maybe you notice that people are digging Asian flavors. Even if you're not running a Chinese place, you can add a grilled chicken salad with cilantro lime dressing and shiitake mushrooms to your menu.

Gathering this intelligence is a key component to getting your restaurant up and running, but you must continue to do so on an ongoing basis. Truly successful businesses foresee, adopt, and maximize opportunities as consumer behavior changes. They listen, and then give customers what they want.

Finding resources

In the following sections, we explain great ways to get the preliminary and relevant research information that you need. Just remember that you can read what other people have to say and listen to what experts think will happen, but none of it is a substitute for talking with *your* customers.

Demographic data

You can have the demographic part of your research done for you, but it may cost you some cash. Demographic research companies, like Claritas, establish their fee schedule based on how detailed you want your information to be. Believe it or not, this step isn't out of the realm of possibility for a single-unit startup restaurant. You can get good data, customized to your concept, for as little as a few hundred dollars. This route gives you specifics about your consumers in your prospective area including their income levels, age, ethnicity, and number of kids in the family, among other information.

Trade publications

One of the least expensive ways to find out about your consumers is to read trade magazines and newspapers. These publications contain info produced by trend watchers, industry analysts, and consumer groups. Publications like *Nation's Restaurant News, Chain Leader,* and *Restaurants & Institutions* are full of information on dining trends, culinary tips, and the business of running a restaurant (check out Chapter 22 for more information).

Other restaurants like yours

Go to every restaurant that's what you want yours to be. Walk in and look around. Pay attention to who's eating there. Look at the ages of the people who go there. Does the clientele change at different times of the day? What are they eating? Create a mini focus group by talking to everybody you can about the food, menu, and atmosphere. Ask them questions: "What do you like about the place? What do you wish you could have gotten there?"

Look outside of your geographic market as well. Look at a new hot chain that hasn't entered your market yet. What customers are they serving? Maybe you can be first to market with components of their concept and reap the success. But remember that being first to market with a copycat concept is no guarantee of success. If you open a fast food restaurant serving mainstay Mexican American cuisine until the wee hours of the morning, you need to be ready to compete should Taco Bell ever decide to roll into town.

Your community

Be your own consumer. Completely immerse yourself in your local dining scene. Know your local market. Put yourself in the shoes of your patrons in order to understand what motivates them, who they are, and what their perception of dining is. Know your community as a whole as well. Read your local newspapers and watch your local news. Get a feel for local events. The more you know about what's going on in your community, the better you'll be able to figure out how to connect with the folks who live there.

Consumer-oriented food media

Pay attention to the publications and broadcast media that target food fans:

   ✓ **Foodie magazines:** Publications like *Bon Appétit, Gourmet,* and *Food and Wine* report consumer info and help shape diners' expectations.

   ✓ **Newspaper dining and lifestyle sections:** Newspapers, whether they're local or national, contain useful info about foods people are interested in.

While you're reading these periodicals, pay attention to who's advertising there. What do you like about their ads? What can you incorporate in your own ads? What would you do differently?

✔ **Food TV:** The ability of Food TV to reach into the American household is probably the biggest single force that's made dining, cooking, and gastronomy cool today. It's motivated the way people eat in this country for the last five years. It made previously unheralded ingredients popular outside their indigenous markets. Foods such as andouille sausage, couscous, and mixed "gourmet" salad greens are now commonplace. Check out Food TV's lesser-known competitors as well.

Non-food TV and magazines

In all your free time, crank up the old boob tube and read magazines. Your customers are, and you should, too. See what they see and hear what they hear. Checking out general interest TV shows and magazines is also a good way to get ad ideas and help you decide whether you want to advertise there.

Focus groups

Focus groups are interviews with 10 to 15 people at the same time. The interviewer asks the group carefully drafted questions, and the group provides objective answers. It's a tactic borrowed from the biggest companies out there, and they're doing it for a reason. Focus groups create a forum where businesses can analyze their consumers and test new products or services. Focus group testing is crucial in making customer-centric decisions. People tend to respond to focus groups because they feel important and that their opinions matter. Typically, participants give you honest, critical opinions. Focus groups allow you to gather local customer-specific info that you can analyze along with broader, industry-specific information from other sources.

You can pay for this research. Impartial professional research teams develop well-designed, cognitively sound questions that ensure an objective, pertinent, and actionable set of results. You get the best information this way — at a hefty price. If you're a new business on a budget, do it yourself. It may not be as scientific, but you'll still get lots of great info.

Create an objective cross-section of your marketplace and potential customer, including Bubba, the banker, the stay-at-home mom, and the college kid. We recommend that you hold two to four sessions to get a large cross-section of data and to have the ability to make changes to your presentation to extract increasingly more pertinent data based on the results from previous sessions.

Identify what kind of insights you want to glean from your focus group. The more pointed you are in creating your questions, the more illuminating your group will be when answering them.

Sampling the local flavor

Focus groups are a great way to gather info from your potential customers. Here's an example of a focus group discussion guide to give you an idea of how to design your own. Say that you want to open a pizza place. So, you bring in a group to talk about the different pizza places in town. Here are some examples of questions you might ask if you want information about your menu:

- Name some examples of good pizza restaurants in our area. Tell me why they're good.

- Describe some disappointing pizza experiences that you've had.

- Do you use a pizza delivery service? Why or why not?

- Rate these ingredients from best to least liked: mushrooms, green peppers, onions, black olives, pineapple, jalapeños, mild sausage, fresh tomato, garlic, and pepperoni.

- Which blend of cheese do you prefer on pizza, A, B, C, D, E, or F? Maybe you make six different cheese pizzas with six different blends and ask participants which they like and why. You may get some great comments, "This might be really good on a spinach-and-artichoke pizza, but I don't know if I'd like it on my regular pizza."

- What do you order from pizza places besides pizza? What would you order if it were available?

- What kind of pizza crust do you prefer? Why do you like it?

Anonymity is the key to honesty and objectivity in focus groups. Don't meet at your restaurant. Don't announce who you are. Don't give them coupons or gift certificates to your place. If they're going to recognize you, get someone else to do the screening and interviews. You can watch the video later.

Compensate the attendees for their time. The concept of making a quick $50 or $75 is generally motivation enough to get someone to break from their busy schedule and offer their opinion. Oh, and feed them, too.

Keeping an Eye on the Enemy

Your competition is doing their own intelligence and implementing their own marketing strategies, just like you are. They're reaching out to the same group of potential customers. With your target customer in mind, you then have to figure out who your competitors are — both your *direct* and *indirect* competition. Here's the basic information that differentiates the two:

- ✔ Direct competitors share similar prices, a similar ambiance, a similar style of service, and similar food. If your customers see your restaurant as similar to another restaurant, you're probably direct competitors. If you're a burger restaurant, every other burger joint is your *direct competition.*

- ✔ But when people go out, they don't just go out for burgers. They also go out for Mexican food, pizza, and sautéed foie gras. These restaurants are your *indirect competition.* Indirect competitors don't share the same food, but they share similar prices, similar geographic areas, similar styles of service, and/or a similar ambiance.

Make a list of your potential competitors. Your research will confirm (or deny) that everyone on your preliminary list is indeed your competitor. The next few sections show you how. And remember that to be successful you must continue to do this type of research even after you open your doors. Old competitors die out and new ones are born on a regular basis. And some concepts that don't seem like competitors today may be tomorrow, depending on how you and they make changes to your businesses in the future.

Don't limit your attention to only direct competitors. Try to capture market share from indirect competitors as well. Chick-fil-A, a fried chicken concept, launched a campaign that featured cows holding up hand-painted (well, hoof-painted) signs that read "Eat Mor Chikin." Taco Bell uses the tag line "Think Outside the Bun," aimed directly at fast-food burger places. These companies have some of the most creative and calculating minds in the industry developing their marketing strategies for them, so learn from them.

You're competing not only against other restaurants; you're also competing against people eating at home. Think about the commercials for products like DiGiorno Pizza ("It's not delivery, it's DiGiorno") and frozen dinners. Swanson has developed two new lines of Hungry Man dinners, called Sports Grill and Steakhouse, aimed directly at restaurant diners.

Who do they think their customers are?

You can find out a lot about your competition and their perception of the consumer by studying where they choose to place their message. Every time somebody reads an airline magazine, a local community publication, a grocery store periodical, or watches TV, they're being motivated by your competition in varying degrees.

It's no secret that companies selling beer, pizza, cars, snack food, and burgers advertise during football games. Big companies spent millions of dollars to have someone tell them what may look obvious now: There's a gathering of their consumers at a certain time on a certain TV channel, so that's a good place to place propaganda — we mean ads. These same viewers are likely customers at your pizza restaurant. Maybe you can't afford Super Bowl advertising, but you can afford to advertise on the front page of the sports section of your local paper. Have your coupons delivered that Wednesday before the big game. They'll see the ads, be hungry, and have the coupons. Who knows what could happen? Chapter 16 has more on advertising.

Shop till you drop

If you really want to know your competitors, spy on them. Be their customer, literally. Dine at their restaurants and experience their products. Take notes and share them with the other managers in your restaurant. Use them as a starting point for brainstorming sessions for new services and products. In the restaurant and retail industries, these activities are called *mystery shopping,* or more accurately, *mystery snooping.*

Don't get too caught up in the "my duck à la orange can whip your duck à la orange" type of thinking. Be objective enough to say, "They're beating my pants off with their salads, sandwiches, and hip interior décor."

Initially, you can shop your competition on your own. But hopefully, you'll reach a point where you won't be able to mystery shop on your own. You'll be so prominent in your restaurant community that the competition will pick you out like a rookie restaurant critic. You may need to hire a professional mystery shopping service.

Mystery shopping services aren't always the way to go. We've had mixed luck with their results and accuracy. You can also get friends and employees to go in and spy for you. But give them the specific criteria you're looking for and remember that people you know may have a hard time telling you what you don't want (or what they think you don't want) to hear.

Examine your competitors that do it right. But looking at the failures is just as important. Spend some time thinking about why they failed. With few exceptions, they probably failed because they stopped being vigilant. They stopped being innovative. They ignored trends and failed to adapt to the ever-increasing savvy of the consumer.

Use Table 4-1 to define your direct competition (restaurants that consumers see as just like yours) and their strengths and weaknesses. We suggest using criteria, like those listed in Table 4-1, to begin to gather the facts about your competitors in the marketplace and to list your own. After you gather the info, you'll take the next step, evaluating the information and making judgments about it. (See Table 4-2 for an example.)

Table 4-1	Comparing Your Concept to the Competition		
Criteria	*Andy's Sports Bar and Grill*	*Bave and Duster's*	*Sports Zone*
Day parts	11 a.m.–12 a.m. (7 days/week)	11 a.m.–11 p.m. (7 days/week)	11 a.m.–1 a.m. (7 days/week)
Menu	Wood-fired pizzas, black angus burgers, wing flights	Burgers, wings, cheese sticks	Wings, pizzas, sandwiches
Price/value	Price based on "quality" brand costs of premium ingredients	Value-priced based on volume and lack of required labor for pre-prepared foods	Price based on national brand and image; portions and quality not in line with pricing
Efficiency	Personal service and physical layout expedite service; not the spot for a quick bite; more of a stay and linger destination	Quick service of foods due to convenience preparation	Slower service due to staffing levels
Location	Across from stadium; valet parking for VIP members	Suburban mall; outlot location	Downtown corner location; difficult parking
Targeted demographic	Affluent sports fans, regulars	Mid-market sports fans	Tourists, convention business
Type/style of service	Personal table service	Table, counter service	Table service
Novelty/other	Sport-specific rooms; distinctive	Peanuts on the floor	National brand image

Developing Your Battle Plan

How are you going to take your product, your information about your customers, and the scoop on what's going on with your competition and create a plan that brings people in *your* door, not to your competitor's door? Your plan should take the following into account:

- ✔ Your strengths and weaknesses
- ✔ Your competitor's strengths and weaknesses
- ✔ Your local marketplace

If you need information on refining your definitions of who your clientele and your competition are, check out the sections earlier in this chapter.

Creating a competitive analysis

Start to brainstorm what it is that you sell and what you're good at. Say that you sell innovative fresh Mexican food. Make a list of your strengths. Then figure out what strengths are yours alone. Decide whether your competition is better than you, equal to you, or deficient compared to you in this category. Unless you're the only person in town who does fresh Mexican cuisine, you don't own it. But if you're the only one who delivers, you own the delivery market for your type of cuisine. You're trying to find the things that your competition doesn't have an answer for. Your point of difference is what you see as your strength. From your customer's point of view it could be a strength or a weakness.

Use Table 4-2 to help you refine your points of difference. Your points of difference can become your greatest strengths. In Table 4-1, we focus on gathering the facts. In Table 4-2, you take the next step, evaluating the data and making judgments about the info. In the first column, we list everything that we want our restaurant to be known for. We want Señor Mike's Fresh Mex to be the market leader in each category. In this context, the market leader is the restaurant that's best known (usually measured in terms of sales dollars and reputation) in the category. In some cases, Señor Mike is the leader; in other cases he needs to improve to be the leader (–) while in others he may actually be better (+), but not yet known for being better.

Table 4-2   Refining Señor Mike's Fresh Mex Points of Difference

Your Desired Points of Difference	Market Leader	How Do You Compare?
Innovative Mexican	Poblano	–
American cuisine	Vera Cruz Fresh	+
Fresh (made from scratch)	Poblano and Señor Mike	Tied
Signature grilled flatbread tacos	Señor Mike	Leader

Your Desired Points of Difference	Market Leader	How Do You Compare?
"Create your own" counter service	Señor Mike	Leader
Service time less than 5 minutes	Señor Mike	Leader
Broad selection of Mexican and domestic beers	Poblano	–
	Vera Cruz Fresh	–
	Don Victor's	–
Authentic Latin market soft drinks	Don Victor's	+
Broad kids menu	Vera Cruz Fresh	–
Private-label salsas and sauces	Señor Mike	Leader
Location across from major mall and close to campus	Poblano	–
Low-carb menu	Señor Mike	Leader

The most effective point of difference that you can have is one your competition can't answer. If you have a location directly adjacent to a major destination (such as a stadium, cultural center, or mall), odds are your competition doesn't, and you can work this to your advantage.

Points of difference may be long lasting, or they may be fleeting, but while they exist, maximize them. Big corporations spend tremendous effort to develop the next point of difference that competitors can't immediately duplicate or copy. The chicken nugget, the drive-thru, and proprietary recipes or products are all historical examples of this type of temporary no-response point of difference. Eventually every fast food place developed its version of the chicken nugget, but for a time, a single restaurant enjoyed it as a point of difference. (For information on communicating those points of difference through advertising, see Chapter 16.)

However, most points of difference are subtler. These are the nuances that you "own." In Table 4-2, for example, Señor Mike "owns" several clear points of difference (like signature flatbread tacos and a service time less than five minutes) that he can leverage to his advantage. However, as in most competitions, his competitors also have their strengths (a broad selection of Mexican beer and a close proximity to campus). The process of analyzing competitive advantage requires that you objectively weigh your strengths against your competitors' strengths and develop plans to simultaneously improve your deficiencies while emphasizing your "ownable" strengths.

When weighing your strengths versus the strengths of your competition, you have to again put yourself in the shoes of your potential customers and determine which criteria matter most to them. You may own several minor advantages like a drive-thru, cute kids' toys, and free refills, but if your competition owns the categories of freshest, better-tasting foods; better service; and lower item-specific prices, you're in trouble, if that's what your consumers want.

Having a strength isn't enough; you have to have a point of difference that will be a deciding factor in motivating a potential customer to select you over the place down the block.

Acting on your information

You should now know who your most likely competitors and consumers are, so use that information to develop your plan. Here are the highpoints to help focus your evaluation:

- Play up your strengths as long as you can make them matter to your audience.

- Analyze your competitors and determine their deficiencies and exploit them.

- Continually strive to close the gaps on your own deficiencies because these are weaknesses that your competitors will counter-attack.

- Continually strive to create new points of difference. Your competitors aren't blind, so they'll develop new plans to counter your offensive. By creating new points of difference, you're always on the attack.

- Know your audience, how your points of difference matter to them, and how to reach them.

The strategy of evaluating and playing up points of difference helps smaller businesses exist in the face of competition from bigger ones. The simplest example of this is "You may be bigger, but I'm better." This works in all markets. Take fashion, for example. Levi's is bigger than Armani, but both companies are able to exist because they leverage their distinct points of difference to generally separate consumers.

The lines blur when businesses go after the same potential consumer. Now comes the time when the difference is in the details. All you have is small points of difference. So you must focus on the importance of these points of difference to your potential customer. For example, maybe your direct competitor microwaves all his entrées, while you prepare yours over a wood-fired grill. You take this point of difference and convert it into a message as to why your wood-fired cuisine is better, fresher, and less radioactive than your competition's.

Realizing the Research Doesn't End After You Open Your Doors

The minute you open your doors, you're in the battle. Every day is a battle. You can't just launch your plan and assume victory. The minute after you launch your attack, you need to analyze your competitors' reaction and retaliation. You're threatening their market share, and they'll fight for it. Only by observing the successes and failures of your strategy can you implement a successful campaign and claim the market share.

Suppose that you built your strategy on your wood-fired grill products, attacking your competition on the use of a microwave. You played up your quality and your investment in equipment to ensure the quality. You're targeting a consumer who values freshness, made-from-scratch cuisine, and trendy cooking methods and is conditioned to assume that microwaved products are inferior. Your plan went well for a while, until a competitor launched a two-fold strategy that included getting his own wood-fired grills and attacking your location by playing up his proximity to campus.

Now it's time to change your strategy. You must leverage another point of difference. If you're out of points of difference, you need to create one. By observing and evaluating the success and failure of your marketing strategy, and noticing your competition's response, you can continually develop new marketing strategies based on your point of difference (existing or new) and continue to capture or threaten the market share of your competition.

The restaurant business is noted for its ever-changing array of new competitors, new advances in products and technology, and increasingly savvy diners. You can stay competitive only by analyzing, reinventing, and reevaluating your strengths and weaknesses and those of your competition.

Take a look at Chapter 22 for resources on keeping up with trends and making sure that your restaurant is the best it can be.

Maintaining Your Competitive Edge

Some restaurateurs think that you can peacefully coexist with the competition because plenty of market is available. This point of view is wrong on two fronts:

  ✔ You're not accounting for new competition. The next guy might just be better, faster, cheaper, and sexier than you are. The new kid on the block steals market share, at least temporarily. And if he lives up to the hype, you're really in trouble.

✔ Peaceful coexistence doesn't actually exist. Think about Ford and Mercedes. On the surface, these brands cater to two different markets. But Mercedes didn't build a $30,000 car by accident. It's looking to leverage a market it didn't have before. Mercedes made a cheaper car that's still sexy. They've targeted customers who, above all things, want a Mercedes because they get prestige they couldn't afford before.

In today's marketplace, be wary of competitive threats from below and above. Casual theme restaurants can offer a gourmet experience without the gourmet price. Concepts like P.F. Chang's China Bistro, The Cheesecake Factory, Sullivan's Steakhouse, Fogo de Chão Churrascaria, and Grand Lux Café are grabbing market share from fine dining. Their common point of difference from their fine dining competitors is that they too are serving innovative, hip new cuisine, but in a less stuffy atmosphere and at much cheaper prices. Fine dining has responded with the message, "We still have better service and a proven track record of exclusivity, and we can make it accessible to you now." Many restaurants can create and offer a fine dining experience to new customers at a lower price point.

Casual dining is caught in the middle. It's attacked from below as people upgrade their menus. It's attacked from above as fine dining dumbs itself down, trying to grab back the market share it's lost in tough economic times. Even though casual dining is battling both fronts, it has managed to expand.

Don't rest on your past, or even current, successes. A shark that stops swimming dies and becomes food for the other sharks. Change is the only constant in this industry. The successful restaurateur is the student of information. Research means the difference between a sure win and a bloody fight for survival.

Part II
Putting Your Plan in Motion

The 5th Wave   By Rich Tennant

"It's hard to figure. The concept was a big hit in Nome."

In this part . . .

It's time to ramp up the activity and move from idea to action. We show you how to develop a restaurant-specific business plan, and we help you pound the payment to round up financing and scout out the best location for your concept. Finally, we cover permits, licenses, laws, insurance, and a host of other legal issues — including how and when to call on some professional help for these matters.

Chapter 5

Writing a Business Plan

· ·

In This Chapter

▶ Discovering why a business plan matters

▶ Reviewing the components

▶ Getting your financials into shape

· ·

*I*f you're going somewhere you've never been, you need a map to get there. Otherwise, you're going to get lost. If you have to stop and ask directions from strangers, doing so will cost you time and maybe even money. And who knows whether you're going to get the right information? If you're running a restaurant, you need a similar kind of map to help you reach your destination. The *business plan* is your map to starting your business — and achieving success. It answers the questions before your investors, financiers, partners, or employees ask them.

You need to do some things in a particular order when you're developing your business plan. Some steps are prerequisites for answering other questions. For example, if someone asks you about your advertising budget, you can't really answer until you know what your overhead is, what kind of food budget you're developing, what kind of sales you're forecasting, and so on. Feel free to skip around and read whatever interests you, but when you actually put pen to paper, remember that you need to follow some steps in order.

Don't Fly Blind: Understanding Why a Business Plan Matters

A business plan explains in a very detailed way what you envision your business to be. You clearly explain your concept and why it's viable and outline your budget. You're anticipating where you'll spend money (expenses), forecasting how much you expect to take in (sales), and estimating when the money will be coming in and going out (cash flow). Your business plan helps you in several ways:

- It starts you analyzing your restaurant in very detailed manner. This process can help you avoid some problems altogether.

- It helps you answer questions that many people involved in your restaurant will ask.

- It helps you identify and define the goal of your business, the customers you're hoping to serve, and your ideas for getting there.

- It provides a tool for potential investors to evaluate your business, your philosophy, your operating savvy, and your market.

- It provides a mechanism for figuring out how much money you realistically need to get started and to keep going until the business can sustain itself.

- It creates a tool for you to use and update regularly in your daily operations to get you on track and keep you there.

- It helps you decide whether your proposed business is doomed to failure from the beginning.

The more detailed your plan is, the better off you are in the long run. Do as much planning as possible and save yourself some time and money. But even with a business plan in hand, you're going to forget something. Pad your expense projections and be conservative in your sales forecast to account for this eventuality.

Business plans vary from organization to organization. It can be a relatively simple document, or it can be a book. Don't overwhelm yourself right out of the gate: Start with a simple one-page outline and flesh it out as you go. Not every business plan is an extremely detailed document, but we suggest you put in as much work as possible — to the point that creating the plan makes you think about even the smallest details, such as "How much does this teaspoon cost?" or "Should I go silver, stainless, or plastic?"

As a general rule, the more detailed your business plan gets, the more questions you find you don't have answers for. Including the details gives you great ideas for your to-do list and helps you realize the points you still need to ponder and research before you get your answers together.

Laying Out a Business Plan

Here are the basic pieces of most restaurant business plans.

- **Cover page and table of contents:** The cover page identifies your plan. Use it to differentiate your plan from those of other restaurants or companies that your potential investors may be looking at. The table of contents provides them with a map for perusing your plan. You may also want to include an *executive summary,* a brief couple of paragraphs explaining what the plan's about.

✔ **Management team:** This section provides information about you, your management team, and any other key employees. Detail the experience, expertise, and strengths of your team in this section. Place this section up front in your plan if your team is a strong selling point; otherwise, it's usually better placed later in the document.

✔ **Definition of your business concept:** Chapter 3 goes into detail about choosing your concept and theme. Take a look at the section "Articulating the concept and theme," later in this chapter, for details in communicating that theme in your business plan.

✔ **Your menu:** Include a copy of your menu. For details on developing, formatting, and figuring a cost for your menu, check out Chapter 9.

✔ **Market analysis and plan:** Here, you show the world how your business is different from other restaurants. You identify the market for your restaurant and discuss how you'll do it fresher, faster, cooler, or whatever and how that means "better" from your diner's point of view. Check out Chapter 4 for details on understanding your market and Chapter 16 for putting your marketing plan together.

✔ **Clientele demographics:** Discuss who your diners will be. Confirm that you have sufficient numbers to draw from in your market to make your business a success. Also detail why your concept and marketing plan will appeal to them. For more on winning and keeping your clientele, check out Chapters 16, 19, and 20.

✔ **Financials:** With this section, you're trying to communicate how much money you need, what you're going to spend it on, and how you're going to build upon it. Financial analysis is an important step, even if you're not looking to borrow money from anyone. You need to set up a realistic timeline for money going out and coming in.

Depending on your plan, you may break up your financials into a couple different categories, maybe assumptions (details about what you're basing your forecasts on) in one section and forecasts in another. You need to be the judge of what works for your business. But make sure that you include a few basic elements:

- Forecasted sales

- Forecasted cash flow

- Forecasted expenses

- A break-even analysis

- An income statement

- Balance sheet

In this section, and this chapter, we provide you with the basics on writing a business plan — including the financials — in general, and the restaurant-specific issues you need to account for. But whole books have been written on the subject. So if you want even more information, we suggest that you check out two — *Business Plans For Dummies* (by Paul Tiffany and Steven D. Peterson) and *Business Plans Kit For Dummies* (by Steven D. Peterson and Peter E. Jerat), both published by Wiley.

A quick example of all the variations: Some business plans also include *confidentiality agreements* that the reader signs and returns at the time he receives your plan. Others include technology plans, which detail computer systems, security systems, and other key electronics info.

Articulating the concept and theme

Most restaurants have a theme and a concept. They're really two sides of the same coin. The *theme* is the common thread, idea, or image that binds your restaurant together. The *concept* is the entire package, including your menu, price point, décor, and ambience. When someone tells you about a new restaurant in town, the person usually describes the establishment's theme and concept: the new *family-style seafood restaurant* or the new *Chinese buffet*. Definitely take a look at Chapter 3 for great tips on identifying and articulating your theme and concept.

This section of your business plan is where you get to relate your vision of the business to the reader. It's the qualitative, or descriptive, component, as opposed to the quantitative, financial portion that lays out the numbers. Here, you describe *what* you're going to do, not *how* you're going to do it.

Consider your audience when you're developing this section of your plan. Usually you write business plans for potential investors, a banker, and other financiers. But you may also use this section in other business documents down the road, such as your mission statement or employee manuals. The better you can communicate your vision of your restaurant to another person, the more likely you are to get the money you need to get started, and to keep your focus on your goals so that you can stay in business.

In the restaurant world, people sometimes use the word *concept* instead of the word *restaurant*. It's just sort of understood that you're talking about a restaurant, so you don't need to say it. For example, they may describe Papa John's as a delivery pizza concept or Applebee's as a casual dining concept. This convention is used most often when discussing chains of restaurants.

Creating your menu now

You need to develop your menu to match your concept, attract your desired clientele, and beat the competition. You can't do much in the way of predicting what you need to buy in terms of equipment, smallwares, table settings, and so on until you know your menu. You definitely can't predict how many clam chowders you're going to sell unless you know that clam chowder is on your menu.

You also need to figure out what your *menu mix* (how many of each dish you're likely to sell in a given time period, like a shift, a week, or a month) will be so that you can figure out how many people you need to do what jobs. If everything on your menu is fried, you may not need to budget for a grill cook. Figuring your menu mix also makes it much easier to figure out your forecasted *check average,* or the average amount an individual diner spends during a meal period, which you need in order to forecast your sales. Are you sensing a pattern here? For help on getting your menu together and forecasting your menu mix, check out Chapter 9.

You may also choose to include your projected menu mix in your business plan. We recommend that you do, because it shows potential investors that you've really done your homework. They can see that you're basing your numbers — like check averages and revenue projections — on calculated assumptions rather than random guesses. Include your menu mix for a month so that they can see what you're expecting to sell over a good chunk of time. Include your menu mix as supporting detail for your forecasted sales.

Describing your clientele

As you develop your plan, you must decide who your diners are. Who are you trying to appeal to? Who do you want eating in your restaurant every shift? You must know this information before you can even identify your audience or your competition, and in Chapter 4 we provide you with suggestions and resources to accomplish this task.

When you're ready to compose your business plan, put together a few concise paragraphs that describe your clientele. Include information about their income level, dining frequency, and where they currently dine. Make sure to include information highlighting why they're likely to frequent your restaurant.

You could contract with a demographic research company to put together reports for the geographic areas near your proposed restaurant, like within a 1-mile, 2-mile, or 5-mile radius. Include copies of these reports in your business plan. Check out Chapter 4 for details on working with a demographics research company.

Laying out your market analysis

Your business plan must include a thorough *market analysis.* A market analysis identifies and describes the market you wish to compete in and your competitors in the market. Include specific information about your competitors that's relevant to your business plan. You can include things like their proximity to your location, their hours of operation, and any special draws that you believe contribute to their success. If you're able to get any kind of sales information for your competitors, include that info as well.

Your competition doesn't have to be next door. It could be down the street, on the next block, or across town. Your *direct competitors* are those who are offering the same kind of food, the same style of service, and similar prices. Your *indirect competitors* are those who don't have the same concept or theme you do, but they're vying for the same customers you are. For example, say that you want to open a Mexican restaurant. Right next door is a fish and chips place. If you're both going for a lunch crowd, you're competing with each other. A diner is going to eat lunch only once a day, probably. Who is she going to choose? Check out Chapter 4 for all the details on researching the marketplace.

The Bottom Line: Focusing on Financials

Financial data helps you create a plan for making your business a reality, entices investors to take a chance on your venture, and can help you manage your business after you're up and running. In particular you'll continually project sales and expenses throughout the life of your restaurant. Stay at least six months ahead in your planning, but you can also devise long-term plans that cover one to five years. Plus, you'll use reports like the income statement, balance sheet, and cash flow analysis on a regular basis (with your real-life numbers, of course) to evaluate your business and it's success.

We introduce these financial tools in this section, and give you details about using them in the restaurant business. But to get a detailed picture on how to set them up and how to use them, check out the latest edition of *Accounting For Dummies* (by John A. Tracy; Wiley). If you choose to use a

software program, like QuickBooks, don't forget to pick up a copy of
QuickBooks All-In-One Desk Reference For Dummies (by Stephen L. Nelson;
Wiley) to go with it.

Ultimately, your business plan comes down to the numbers. Your business
plan must show that you can come up with the sales to fund the expenses
you plan to incur. If you can't, you should rework your concept. If you're looking for investors in your business, they'll pay particular attention to this section no matter who they are. Whether an investor is your uncle or a savvy
real estate developer, both of them will likely spend some time here to decide
whether your restaurant is a good place to invest their hard-earned cash.
(For tips on getting financing, take a gander at Chapter 6.)

To be thorough, you want to show three sets of numbers for each *forecast*
(prediction of what you'll spend or take in):

- ✔ A low-end, sort of worst-case scenario

- ✔ The best-case scenario that shows what'll happen if all the pieces of your
  puzzle fall exactly into place and the restaurant gods are smiling on you

- ✔ A mid-range set of numbers that show what happens if some things go
  your way and others don't

Take the calendar into account when you're forecasting your sales and
expenses. February is the shortest month, with the fewest operating days.
The months of January, March, May, July, August, October, and December
each have 31 days. But if you're not open on Mondays, for example, look at
the calendar for the years you're forecasting and make adjustments to your
projections. In the example used to create all the figures in this chapter,
March had the most operating days in the six-month period we were forecasting, and its sales *and* expenses are a little higher.

In the restaurant business, expect the worst and hope for the best to avoid at
least some disappointments by anticipating and avoiding disasters.

Forecasting sales

Start your foray into the world of financial forecasting with sales. If you don't
know how much you'll be taking in, you don't know how much you can
spend. Forecast your sales before you forecast your expenses.

You have to develop some assumptions for estimating what your sales will
be. Maybe you choose to estimate it based on your different *profit centers*
(separate areas in the restaurant that take in money, like the dining room,

bar, take out, and so on). Maybe you actually estimate how many guests you'll have at different time periods and estimate what each guest will spend. Or you can use some combination of both methods. Eventually, you'll have to do all of the above, but maybe you only use part of it in your actual plan.

In Figure 5-1, we start with a simple example. We figure how many guests we'll have during a meal period, also known as the number of *covers,* and multiply that by the *check average* (which we abbreviate as C/A in the figure), or the average amount that each guest spends in the restaurant. We're assuming that we have a 40-seat restaurant with a casual dining atmosphere.

Don't let the term *check average* fool you. The term may sound like it means the average for the entire check, no matter how many people are sitting at the table and paying on the same check. It's an industry standard to use this term to describe the per-person average spent in the restaurant.

Here's one way to forecast your sales:

1. **Figure out how many seats you have in your restaurant.**

   In the example used in Figure 5-1, the restaurant has 40 seats.

2. **Figure out how many guests will actually be in those seats for each meal period.**

   Depending on your business levels, every seat in the restaurant may be occupied multiple times. So take that fact into account when you decide how many covers you anticipate during each meal period.

3. **Try to estimate what each guest will spend during each meal period.**

   This number is affected by your menu prices, your clientele, and your concept. Diners usually spend more money at dinner because prices are higher (usually because portions are larger), they have more time to spend, and they're more likely to drink alcohol in the evening. So they may have a bottle of wine at dinner instead of a glass of iced tea. They may choose an appetizer, a salad, and an entrée at dinner, whereas they may order only an entrée at lunch.

These steps offer a super basic representation of how you start the forecasting process. Before you include your forecast in your business plan, you actually need to do some additional estimating to account for how your business levels will ebb and flow over the months. If you're a resort-based business that's open only four months each year, you want your business plan to reflect that schedule. If you're attached to a shopping mall and hope to get most of your sales between Thanksgiving and New Year's Day, your business plan should show that goal.

Cover Counts and Check Average

Food

Lunch	Mon	Tues	Wed	Thurs	Fri	Sat	Averages
Covers	40	40	40	50	60	70	50
C/A	$10	$10	$10	$12	$15	$18	$12.50
Dinner							
Covers	50	50	50	60	75	80	60
C/A	$20	$20	$20	$25	$35	$35	$25.83
Total:	$1,400	$1,400	$1,400	$2,100	$3,525	$4,060	$2,314

Beverage

Lunch	Mon	Tues	Wed	Thurs	Fri	Sat	Averages
Covers	40	40	40	50	60	70	50
C/A	$3	$3	$3	$5	$6	$6	$4.33
Dinner							
Covers	50	50	50	60	75	80	60
C/A	$6	$6	$6	$8	$9	$12	$7.83
Total:	$420	$420	$420	$730	$1,035	$1,380	$734
TOTALS:	$1,820	$1,820	$1,820	$2,830	$4,560	$5,440	$3,048

Average daily food sales:	$2,314
Average daily beverage sales:	$734
Average daily sales:	$3,048
Total weekly food sales:	$13,885
Total weekly beverage sales:	$4,405
Total weekly sales:	$18,290
Annual food sales:	$722,020
Annual beverage sales:	$229,060
Annual sales:	$951,080

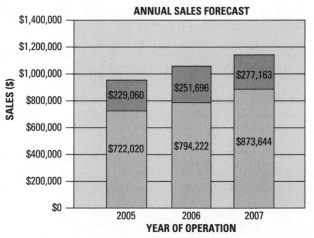

Figure 5-1: Developing a sales forecast.

ANNUAL SALES FORECAST

BEVERAGE SALES

FOOD SALES

Forecasting expenses

Even before you open the doors, your restaurant incurs expenses — time is money. Even if you're not paying rent, you've bought the fridge, stove, pens, papers, computers, and so on. You sink money into your business before you realize a single dollar in *income* — notice we did not say *profit.* That's way down the line.

You already shelled out money when you bought this book. Save the receipt to claim it on your taxes. Consider buying at least two copies: one in your office to loan out and one at home as a backup.

In some ways, forecasting your expenses is very different from running your business. When you're forecasting, you anticipate every possible thing you'll need to spend money on; when you're running your business, you should be looking at every opportunity to control the cost.

We know that we're repeating ourselves, but the more detailed you can be in preparing your forecasts, the better off you'll be in the long run. Figure 5-2 is a broad list for just about everything you could possibly need for your restaurant. Use it to start thinking about what expense categories you should forecast for your business. You may even find a few things that you hadn't thought about before.

Figure 5-2 is actually the restaurant chart of accounts for an income statement (see the "Estimating profits" section later in this chapter). The numbers in the column to the left correspond with the account codes used in your *general ledger,* the master set of books that tracks all the financial transactions in your restaurant. Use whatever number system works for you, as long as you're consistent throughout your system. The National Restaurant Association (NRA) recommends the number codes shown in Figure 5-2, so if you're starting from scratch, you may as well start here.

When you forecast expenses, include *everything* — from produce to salaries to advertising expenses. We provide a scaled-back version in Figure 5-3. If we were to show you a full year of an expense forecast with every category, it would take up way too much space in this book. Besides, you can really get a good picture of the process by using this snapshot. The next couple sections give you the details on what we summarize in Figure 5-3.

Include at least a full year forecast of expenses in your business plan. Make sure to include three possible scenarios: best case, worst case, and most likely to make your plan complete.

Income Statement Accounts

3000	**SALES**		4500	**MARKETING**
3010	Food		4510	Selling & Promotion
3020	Liquor		4520	Advertising
3030	Beer		4530	Public Relations
3040	Wine		4540	Research
			4545	Complimentary Food & Beverages
4000	**COST OF SALES**		4550	Discounted Food & Beverages
4001	Food:			
4002	Meat		4600	**UTILITIES**
4003	Seafood		4610	Electrical
4004	Poultry		4620	Gas
4005	Produce		4630	Water
4006	Bakery		4640	Trash Removal
4007	Dairy			
4008	Grocery & Dry Goods		4700	**GENERAL & ADMINISTRATIVE**
4009	Non-alcoholic Beverages		4705	Office Supplies
4020	Liquor		4710	Postage & Delivery
4030	Bar Consumables		4715	Telephone / Communications
4040	Beer		4720	Payroll Processing
4050	Wine		4725	Insurance - General
4060	Paper (QSR)		4730	Dues & Subscriptions
			4735	Travel Expenses
4100	**SALARIES & WAGES**		4740	Credit Card Discounts
4110	Management		4745	Bad Debts
4120	Dining Room		4750	Cash (Over) / Short
4130	Bar		4755	Bank Deposit Services
4140	Kitchen		4760	Bank Charges
4150	Dishroom		4765	Accounting Services
4160	Office		4770	Legal & Professional
			4775	Security / Alarm
4200	**EMPLOYEE BENEFITS**		4780	Training
4210	Payroll Taxes		4785	Miscellaneous
4220	Worker's Compensation Insurance			
4230	Group Insurance		4800	**REPAIRS & MAINTENANCE**
4240	Management Meals		4810	Maintenance Contracts
4250	Employee Meals		4820	R&M - Equipment
4260	Awards & Prizes		4830	R&M - Building
4270	Employee Parties & Sports Activities		4840	Grounds Maintenance
4280	Medical Expenses		4850	Parking Lot
4300	**DIRECT OPERATING EXPENSES**		5000	**OCCUPANCY COSTS**
4305	Auto & Truck Expense		5010	Rent
4310	Uniforms		5020	Equipment Rental
4315	Laundry & Dry Cleaning		5030	Real Estate Taxes
4320	Linen		5040	Personal Property Taxes
4325	Tableware		5050	Insurance-Property & Casualty
4330	Silverware		5060	Other Municipal Taxes
4335	Kitchen Utensils			
4340	Paper Supplies		6000	**DEPRECIATION & AMORTIZATION**
4345	Bar Supplies		6010	Buildings
4350	Restaurant Supplies		6020	Furniture, Fixtures & Equipment
4355	Cleaning Supplies		6030	Amortization of Leasehold Improvements
4360	Contract Cleaning			
4365	Menu & Wine List		7000	**OTHER (INCOME) EXPENSE**
4370	Pest Control		7010	Vending Commissions
4375	Flowers & Decorations		7020	Telephone Commissions
4380	Licenses & Permits		7030	Waste Sales
4385	Banquet & Event Expenses		7040	Interest Expense
4390	Other Operating Expenses		7050	Officers Salaries & Expenses
			7060	Corporate Office Expenses
4400	**MUSIC & ENTERTAINMENT**			
4410	Musicians & Entertainers		8000	**INCOME TAXES**
4420	Cable TV/Wire Services		8010	Federal Income Tax
4430	Royalties to ASCAP, BMI		8020	State Income Tax

Figure 5-2:
Chart of restaurant income and expense accounts.

Q1 AND Q2 FY'05

CONTROLLABLE EXPENSES	JAN $	FEB $	MAR $	APR $	MAY $	JUN $	TOTAL $	TOTAL %
Cost of sales								
Food cost	17,355	16,661	18,743	18,049	18,049	18,049	106,907	30.00%
Beverage cost	4,588	4,404	4,955	4,771	4,771	4,771	28,259	25.00%
Total COGS	**$21,943**	**$21,065**	**$23,698**	**$22,820**	**$22,820**	**$22,820**	**$135,166**	**55.00%**
Payroll								
Salaries	7,620	7,315	8,230	7,925	7,925	7,925	46,939	10.00%
Hourly wages	11,430	10,973	12,344	11,887	11,887	11,887	70,409	15.00%
Benefits	6,096	5,852	6,584	6,340	6,340	6,340	37,551	8.00%
Contract labor	0	0	0	0	0	0	0	0.00%
Total payroll	**$25,146**	**$24,140**	**$27,158**	**$26,152**	**$26,152**	**$26,152**	**$154,899**	**33.00%**
Other controllable expenses								
Direct operating expenses	1,905	1,829	2,057	1,981	1,981	1,981	11,735	2.50%
Music & entertaining	381	366	411	396	396	396	2,347	0.50%
Marketing	3,810	3,658	4,115	3,962	3,962	3,962	23,470	5.00%
Energy & utilities	1,524	1,463	1,646	1,585	1,585	1,585	9,388	2.00%
General & administrative	2,477	2,377	2,675	2,576	2,576	2,576	15,255	3.25%
Repairs & maintenance	762	732	823	792	792	792	4,694	1.00%
TOTAL CONTROLLABLE EXPENSES	**$10,859**	**$10,424**	**$11,727**	**$11,293**	**$11,293**	**$11,293**	**$66,888**	**14.25%**
NON-CONTROLLABLE EXPENSES								
Rent	5,334	5,121	5,761	5,547	5,547	5,547	32,857	7.00%
Real estate taxes	1,143	1,097	1,234	1,189	1,189	1,189	7,041	1.50%
Lease expenses	533	512	576	555	555	555	3,286	0.70%
FF&E reserve	1,524	1,463	1,646	1,585	1,585	1,585	9,388	2.00%
Insurance	1,524	1,463	1,646	1,585	1,585	1,585	9,388	2.00%
TOTAL OTHER EXPENSES	**$10,058**	**$9,656**	**$10,863**	**$10,461**	**$10,461**	**$10,461**	**$61,960**	**13.20%**
DEPRECIATION	991	951	1,070	1,030	1,030	1,030	6,102	1.30%
INTEREST	762	732	823	792	792	792	4,693	1.00%
TOTAL INTEREST AND DEPRECIATION	**$1,753**	**$1,683**	**$1,893**	**$1,822**	**$1,822**	**$1,822**	**$10,795**	**2.30%**

Figure 5-3: Sample six-month expense forecast.

Controllable expenses

Controllable expenses are expenses that you can change for the better by running your business well. At the same time, these expenses can quickly get out of hand. Here are the categories of controllable expenses:

✓ **Cost of sales:** This category includes your food and beverage costs. It represents your outlay for raw materials and reflects what you spend to buy the ingredients that go into your menu items. As the price of your ingredients fluctuates, your expense line will, too. If you're buying ice cream and dairy prices are high, your ice cream prices will be high.

If you sell anything else, like T-shirts or custom-labeled hot sauce, the expense you incur by purchasing them to sell to your customers goes in this expense line.

✓ **Payroll:** This summary category includes salaries and wages for both salaried and hourly employees. It also includes other costs associated with employees, such as benefits, taxes, and worker's comp insurance.

The more sales you generate, the more hours your employees work, the more you pay them, and the more you pay in taxes and some benefits. Take those facts into account when you're forecasting your expenses.

Salaries may not seem like a controllable expense, because you pay a manager the same amount each period, whether she's at the restaurant 10 hours or 110 hours. But ultimately, if your sales can't support the expense of another manager, you can't hire one. Coauthor Mike took on an additional responsibility of running the wine program at his restaurant to save money on hiring a *sommelier,* or wine expert. Although his budget might support the extra salary now, he's found that he really doesn't need a sommelier, thus saving himself thousands of dollars each year in this category.

✔ **Other controllable expenses:** This category includes the following:

- **Direct operating expenses:** Here's where you account for incidental expenses, like uniforms, linens, tableware, paper supply, cleaning supplies, and so on, that you must incur for your business. They're the result of your processes and are required to some extent, for every business.

- **Music and entertainment:** Include the costs for a live musician, satellite TV, or your sound system.

- **Marketing expenses:** You can control how much you spend, but most restaurants spend something on ad campaigns, PR, and research (trends, competitive analysis, and industry knowledge).

- **Energy and utilities:** These are controllable because everyone can turn off lights that aren't needed and fix leaky faucets.

- **General and administrative:** This category includes office supplies, postage, phones, dues, and subscriptions. Account for professional fees, such as attorney's fees, here. Credit card fees that you pay as a business owner and banking fees also go here.

- **Repairs and maintenance:** This category includes upkeep of your facility and your equipment.

Noncontrollable expenses

Some noncontrollable expenses are *fixed expenses* (or expenses whose amounts don't change). Some may be *variable expenses* (or expenses whose amounts change). The items in this list can get confusing, especially when you're just starting out. Get a copy of *Accounting For Dummies*, and keep it handy as you work through the first few months of your real restaurant reporting. Here are the details of the summaries we made in this section.

✔ **Occupancy costs:** This expense includes your rent (or mortgage), equipment rental, real estate taxes, insurance on the building and its contents, and personal property taxes. This number may be a constant flat rate, such as in the case of your rent payment, or it may fluctuate depending on your sales. Also think about any assessment for grounds maintenance or CAM (common area maintenance) when you're filling out this section. CAM includes the upkeep of things like the landscaping and snow removal. CAM also applies to tenants in malls or multi-tenant buildings for the upkeep of the lobby, public restrooms, and shoveling and sweeping the front sidewalk.

✔ **Depreciation:** Basically, this is the accounting process of booking the expense of a capitol purchase over a period of time known as its *useful life.* Depreciation is usually taken care of by accountants, so seek help from your accountant in figuring out your depreciation schedules.

✔ **Interest expenses:** Include any charges you will sustain for long-term debts or notes that you plan to take out. If you make payments to investors, it can show up here. These costs could be variable or constant, depending on what you set up with your investors. For example, some investors may want to be paid back in equal payments over five years, while some want a percentage back each year, with a *balloon payment,* a payment that includes the remainder of the principal in one lump sum, on the fifth year. See Chapter 6 for tips on finding financing and working out payment arrangements.

Figure 5-3 contains an FF&E Reserve line. FF&E stands for furniture, fixtures, and equipment. You can put money in an FF&E account in preparation for replacing these items. Your FF&E reserve account isn't a separate bank account; it's part of your operating bank account, but from an accounting perspective, this money is separate.

Breaking even

After you forecast all your expenses, run a *break-even analysis,* like the one in Figure 5-4. A break-even point is the point where your revenues equal your expenses. The break-even analysis helps you determine that point, or how much you need to sell to cover your expenses before you make even $1 in profit. This step is critical. If you can't possibly get the revenue to support your projected expenses, you must adjust your expenses.

In Figure 5-4, we add most of our projected monthly expenses from Figure 5-1 to create the Monthly Expenses line. We pull out the cost we pay for food and beverages (lumped together as Cost of Goods Sold or COGS) and show it on our graph as Monthly COGS. We add them together to get our Monthly Expenses + COGS so we can see what our minimum revenue must be to cover our costs.

TIP

We recommend splitting your expenses into these two categories, so that you can see how and where your cost control measures are helping you. So if you negotiate a better lease, it will show a dramatic improvement in your Monthly Expenses line, but will have less of an impact overall. If you negotiate a volume purchasing agreement for your food, you'll see a dramatic improvement in your Monthly COGS line, but less of a change in the overall numbers. Having this information cut into smaller pieces helps us manage our businesses more effectively. Ultimately, if you want to just provide the combined total of your monthly expenses and COGS to show your ultimate break-even point, you can do that. Use whatever method works for you. The important thing is to know how much revenue you need to cover your costs.

MONTHLY EXPENSES + COGS		$69,758	$66,968	$75,339	$72,548	$72,548	$72,548
REQUIRED REVENUE		$69,758	$66,968	$75,339	$72,548	$72,548	$72,548
MONTHLY EXPENSES		$47,816	$45,903	$51,641	$49,728	$49,728	$49,728
MONTHLY COGS		$21,943	$21,065	$23,698	$22,820	$22,820	$22,820

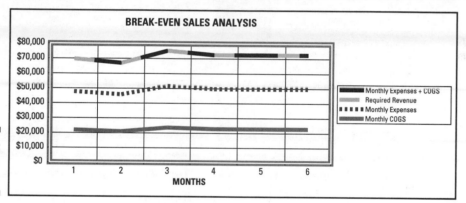

Figure 5-4:
Break-even
analysis.

Estimating profits

In a nutshell, you estimate your profit by taking your sales and subtracting your expenses. The remainder is your profit. In the real world, it's not quite that simple, but it follows the same principle. Figure 5-5 shows you a sample income statement. We use the same summary categories that we've worked with throughout the chapter, so if you need additional explanation on what detailed accounts are included in the summary categories, check out the preceding sections and look at Figures 5-1 and 5-3.

Basically, we take our forecasted sales, or revenue, and subtract all of our expenses (controllable, noncontrollable, and depreciation and interest) to come up with our final net profit/loss figures.

Q1 AND Q2 FY'05	JAN $	FEB $	MAR $	APR $	MAY $	JUN $	TOTAL $	TOTAL %
REVENUES								
Food sales	57,850	55,536	62,478	60,164	60,164	60,164	356,356	75.92%
Beverage sales	18,350	17,616	19,818	19,084	19,084	19,084	113,036	24.08%
Other income	0	0	0	0	0	0	0	0.00%
TOTAL REVENUE	**$76,200**	**$73,152**	**$82,296**	**$79,248**	**$79,248**	**$79,248**	**$469,392**	**100.00%**
EXPENSES								
Food cost	17,355	16,661	18,743	18,049	18,049	18,049	106,907	30.00%
Beverage cost	4,588	4,404	4,955	4,771	4,771	4,771	28,259	25.00%
Total COGS	**$21,943**	**$21,065**	**$23,698**	**$22,820**	**$22,820**	**$22,820**	**$135,166**	**55.00%**
Payroll								
Salaries	7,620	7,315	8,230	7,925	7,925	7,925	46,939	10.00%
Hourly wages	11,430	10,973	12,344	11,887	11,887	11,887	70,409	15.00%
Benefits	6,096	5,852	6,584	6,340	6,340	6,340	37,551	8.00%
Contract labor	0	0	0	0	0	0	0	0.00%
Total payroll	**$25,146**	**$24,140**	**$27,158**	**$26,152**	**$26,152**	**$26,152**	**$154,899**	**33.00%**
Operating expenses								
Direct operating expenses	1,905	1,829	2,057	1,981	1,981	1,981	11,735	2.50%
Music & entertaining	381	366	411	396	396	396	2,347	0.50%
Marketing	3,810	3,658	4,115	3,962	3,962	3,962	23,470	5.00%
Energy & utilites	1,524	1,463	1,646	1,585	1,585	1,585	9,388	2.00%
General & administrative	2,477	2,377	2,675	2,576	2,576	2,576	15,255	3.25%
Repairs & maintenance	762	732	823	792	792	792	4,694	1.00%
Total operating Expenses	**$10,859**	**$10,424**	**$11,727**	**$11,293**	**$11,293**	**$11,293**	**$66,888**	**14.25%**
GROSS OPERATING PROFIT	**$18,253**	**$17,523**	**$19,713**	**$18,983**	**$18,983**	**$18,983**	**$112,438**	**23.95%**
OTHER EXPENSES								
Rent	5,334	5,121	5,761	5,547	5,547	5,547	32,857	7.00%
Real estate taxes	1,143	1,097	1,234	1,189	1,189	1,189	7,041	1.50%
Lease expenses	533	512	576	555	555	555	3,286	0.70%
FF&E reserve	1,524	1,463	1,646	1,585	1,585	1,585	9,388	2.00%
Insurance	1,524	1,463	1,646	1,585	1,585	1,585	9,388	2.00%
TOTAL OTHER EXPENSES	**$10,058**	**$9,656**	**$10,863**	**$10,461**	**$10,461**	**$10,461**	**$61,960**	**13.20%**
ADJUSTED PROFIT	**$8,195**	**$7,867**	**$8,850**	**$8,522**	**$8,522**	**$8,522**	**$50,479**	**10.75%**
Interest	762	732	823	792	792	792	4,693	1.00%
Depreciation	991	951	1,070	1,030	1,030	1,030	6,102	1.30%
NET PROFIT/LOSS	**$6,442**	**$6,184**	**$6,957**	**$6,700**	**$6,700**	**$6,700**	**$39,684**	**8.45%**

Figure 5-5:
Income
statement.

This figure is a key indicator for many investors. Many consider the net profit/loss figure the bottom line. Of course, you must prove all your other assumptions are correct, but many people start with this number.

Projecting cash flow

Your *cash flow projection* maps out when your sales are coming in and when your payments are going out. It shows you how, over time, your business should be able to keep itself afloat. Take a look at Figure 5-6 for an example.

Q1 AND Q2 FY'05

	JAN $	FEB $	MAR $	APR $	MAY $	JUN $	TOTAL $
CASH RECEIPTS							
Food sales	57,850	55,536	62,478	60,164	60,164	60,164	356,356
Beverage sales	18,350	17,616	19,818	19,084	19,084	19,084	113,036
Sales receivables	0	0	0	0	0	0	
TOTAL CASH RECEIPTS	**$76,200**	**$73,152**	**$82,296**	**$79,248**	**$79,248**	**$79,248**	**$469,392**
CASH DISBURSEMENTS							
Cost of sales, food	17,355	16,661	18,743	18,049	18,049	18,049	106,907
Cost of sales, beverage	4,588	4,404	4,955	4,771	4,771	4,771	28,259
TOTAL COST OF SALES	**$21,943**	**$21,065**	**$23,698**	**$22,820**	**$22,820**	**$22,820**	**$135,166**
CONTROLLABLE EXPENSES							
Payroll							
Salaries	7,620	7,315	8,230	7,925	7,925	7,925	46,939
Hourly wages	11,430	10,973	12,344	11,887	11,887	11,887	70,409
Benefits	6,096	5,852	6,584	6,340	6,340	6,340	37,551
Contract labor	0	0	0	0	0	0	
TOTAL PAYROLL	**$25,146**	**$24,140**	**$27,158**	**$26,152**	**$26,152**	**$26,152**	**$154,899**
Operating expenses							
Direct operating expenses	1,905	1,829	2,057	1,981	1,981	1,981	11,735
Music & entertaining	381	366	411	396	396	396	2,347
Marketing	3,810	3,658	4,115	3,962	3,962	3,962	23,470
Energy & utilities	1,524	1,463	1,646	1,585	1,585	1,585	9,388
General & administrative	2,477	2,377	2,675	2,576	2,576	2,576	15,255
Repairs & maintenance	762	732	823	792	792	792	4,694
TOTAL OPERATING EXPENSES	**$10,859**	**$10,424**	**$11,727**	**$11,293**	**$11,293**	**$11,293**	**$66,888**
OTHER EXPENSES							
Rent	5,334	5,121	5,761	5,547	5,547	5,547	32,857
Real estate taxes	1,143	1,097	1,234	1,189	1,189	1,189	7,041
Lease expenses	533	512	576	555	555	555	3,286
FF&E reserve	1,524	1,463	1,646	1,585	1,585	1,585	9,388
Insurance	1,524	1,463	1,646	1,585	1,585	1,585	9,388
TOTAL OTHER EXPENSES	**$10,058**	**$9,656**	**$10,863**	**$10,461**	**$10,461**	**$10,461**	**$61,960**
Interest	762	732	823	792	792	792	4,694
Other deductions	0	0	0	0	0	0	
TOTAL CASH DISBURSEMENTS	**$68,767**	**$66,017**	**$74,269**	**$71,518**	**$71,518**	**$71,518**	**$423,607**
CASH FLOW FROM OPERATIONS							
Cash receipts	76,200	73,152	82,296	79,248	79,248	79,248	469,392
LESS: cash disbursements	68,767	66,017	74,269	71,518	71,518	71,518	423,607
NET FROM OPERATIONS	**$7,433**	**$7,135**	**$8,027**	**$7,730**	**$7,730**	**$7,730**	**$45,785**
CASH ON HAND							
OPENING BALANCE	0	6,433	10,568	14,595	17,325	19,055	
PLUS: New loan (debt)	0	0	0	0	0	0	
PLUS: New investment	0	0	0	0	0	0	
PLUS: Sale of fixed assets	0	0	0	0	0	0	
PLUS: Net from operations	7,433	7,135	8,027	7,730	7,730	7,730	
TOTAL CASH AVAILABLE	**$7,433**	**$13,568**	**$18,595**	**$22,325**	**$25,055**	**$26,785**	
LESS: Debt reduction	1,000	1,000	1,000	1,000	1,000	1,000	
LESS: New fixed assets	0	0	0	0	0	0	
LESS: Profit distributions	0	2,000	3,000	4,000	5,000	5,000	
TOTAL CASH PAID OUT	**$1,000**	**$3,000**	**$4,000**	**$5,000**	**$6,000**	**$6,000**	
ENDING CASH POSITION	**$6,433**	**$10,568**	**$14,595**	**$17,325**	**$19,055**	**$20,785**	**$20,785**

Figure 5-6:
Sample of
cash flow
projections
for six
months.

Buying in bulk hurts your short-term cash flow but helps you in the long run. But don't sit on the inventory too long, or you miss the opportunity to use the cash on another money-making opportunity. Check out Chapter 20 for details on managing your cash flow.

Keep the flexibility to cover some unforeseen expenses. Managing your cash flow is managing your sales and expense projections in a timeline. For example, why are you getting a lobster order on Monday when you know you're not going to sell them until Thursday, Friday, and Saturday? Your money is sitting in the tank for days waiting to be recouped.

Creating a balance sheet

A *balance sheet,* shown in Figure 5-7, is a summary or snapshot of your business on a given date, usually at the end of an accounting period. It summarizes the money you have (assets) compared to the money you owe (liabilities). One of the ways an operator can utilize the information on the balance sheet to help evaluate the efficiency of the restaurant is to measure the number of turns on inventory for the accounting period. The inventory dollar amount for the period is stated on the Balance Sheet in Assets. This figure is divided by revenues to arrive at a ratio that will tell you how efficiently you use your money. Every industry has an average number of turns they're trying to achieve. In the restaurant business, you want to get around four turns a month. Otherwise you are tying up more cash than you need.

Basically, balance sheets are designed to show that your assets (cash on hand, receivables, and inventory) balance out your liabilities (your upcoming payments and debts) and *owners' equity* (includes the amount you initially invested and anything you've earned and then reinvested in the business).

Assets

Current Assets:

Cash		$0
Accounts Receivable	$0	
Less: Reserve for Bad Debts	0	0
Merchandise Inventory		0
Prepaid Expenses		0
Notes Receivable		0
Total Current Assets		$0

Fixed Assets:

Vehicles	0	
Less: Accumulated Depreciation	0	0
Furniture and Fixtures	0	
Less: Accumulated Depreciation	0	0
Equipment	0	
Less: Accumulated Depreciation	0	0
Buildings	0	
Less: Accumulated Depreciation	0	0
Land		0
Total Fixed Assets		0

Other Assets:

Goodwill		0
Total Other Assets		0

Total Assets	$0

Liabilities and Capital

Current Liabilities:

Accounts Payable	$0	
Sales Taxes Payable	0	
Payroll Taxes Payable	0	
Accrued Wages Payable	0	
Unearned Revenues	0	
Short-Term Notes Payable	0	
Short-Term Bank Loan Payable	0	
Total Current Liabilities		$0

Long-Term Liabilities:

Long-Term Notes Payable	0	
Mortgage Payable	0	
Total Long-Term Liabilities		0

Total Liabilities	0

Capital:

Owner's Equity	0	
Net Profit	0	
Total Capital		0

Total Liabilities and Capital	$0

Figure 5-7:
Sample balance sheet.

Chapter 6

Show Me the Money! Finding Financing

. . . .

In This Chapter

▶ Determining how much money you need

▶ Figuring out how much you can contribute

▶ Turning to investors

▶ Asking a bank for a loan

▶ Working with your landlord and suppliers

. . . .

*F*inding the money to start a restaurant is one of the toughest hurdles for any budding restaurateur. You can have dreams of a popular restaurant, featuring great food and bustling with happy diners, but you need money to make it a reality. How much you need varies with how large your dreams are, the size of your own savings, and how many investors you can sway with your business plan (see Chapter 5 for the details on creating a business plan). In this chapter, we help you figure out how much money you need and how much money you already *have,* and we give you tips on getting more. Finally, we give you some tips on clever ways to free up some cash at start-up.

Knowing How Much Money You Need

Most people, including the experts, find it hard to start the process of figuring out how much money they need to run a restaurant. Every restaurant concept is unique. Your costs vary with your location, your construction costs, the china you pick out, and a thousand other factors. Use Figure 6-1 and the expense worksheets in Chapter 5 to help you figure out how much money you need.

Calculating start-up costs

Many of the things that you need for your business are one-time only purchases. Items such as tables for your dining room, racks for your glasses, and shelves for dry storage usually fall under this category. Unfortunately, you have to buy them before the cash starts rolling in, so you need to plan for these expenses when you're finding your financing. Figure 6-1 can help you get started. Make lists of all the items you need and then consolidate your list on this worksheet. So under the furniture category, include the cost of your tables, chairs, barstools, seating for the lobby, your host podium, benches for the bathrooms, artwork, vases on your tables, a fish tank (if you have one), your office desk, and so on.

Start-up Costs		
	Range of Costs	Final Projection
Deposits – utilities, landlord, and so on		
Construction, remodeling, and design costs (Chapters 10 and 11)		
Furniture and decor (Chapter 10)		
Signage (Chapter 10)		
Fixtures and equipment (Chapter 11)		
Licenses and permits (Chapter 8)		
Professional, legal, and consulting fees (Chapter 8)		
Initial advertising and PR (Chapter 16)		
Starting inventory of goods and supplies (Chapters 14 and 15)		
Salaries until doors open (Chapter 2)		
Operating reserve (this chapter)		
Other		
Total One-Time Start-up Costs		

Figure 6-1: One-time start-up costs worksheet.

We include chapter references in Figure 6-1 for where to find more information about each category of start-up expense. But remember, because all of these costs are directly related to your particular concept, location, schedule, day you hire the first manager and dishwasher, and so on, we can't give you specific advice on how much you will (or even should) spend. You have to research costs for your particular needs.

Opening with operating reserve

You probably won't be surprised to discover that you don't stop needing money the day you open your doors. When you're planning for the amount of money you need to get started, plan to include at least three months' worth of operating expenses. This cushion helps you stay open until your business level picks up. You'll have some sales early on, but you can't expect to hit your stride until a few months into the process. Take a look at the figures showing expense forecast and cash flow projections in Chapter 5 to help determine what your monthly operating expenses will be. Chapter 5 also gives advice on forecasting your expenses and sales.

Looking at How You Can Contribute

As scary as it may sound, you have to contribute a significant amount of your own money to your new venture. If you don't believe in your restaurant (and put your money where your mouth is), no one else will. Using your own money does have its benefits, such as keeping complete control of your business. You don't have to share control with investors (see the section "Working with Investors," later in this chapter). You can also skip the paperwork involved in getting a loan (see the section "Getting a Loan," later in this chapter).

Using your own money to finance your restaurant does have a downside: You have no guarantee of success, so you could lose all your savings, your credit rating (if you get behind on payments), and your home (if you've borrowed against it). You want to be able to feed yourself even if your restaurant doesn't succeed, so make sure that you don't compromise your future (or your family's future). Make sure that anyone who depends on you financially (such as your spouse, significant other, or children) understands the risks involved if you decide to sink your life savings into this kind of a venture.

People can contribute to their own restaurants in several common ways:

 ✔ **Use savings:** People use their general savings, retirement savings, and kids' college funds, and they cash in savings bonds. They also pilfer their Christmas club funds, securities accounts, and sell other investments to get money for their restaurants.

- ✔ **Get a home equity loan or line of credit:** Okay, technically speaking, this isn't their money; it's a bank's money. But should the restaurant go belly up, the loan taker is still *personally* responsible for paying back 100 percent of this loan.

- ✔ **Use credit cards:** Credit cards can be good for short-term financing options because the funds are ready when you need them. They can even help you order supplies, décor, and other items online. Plus if you shop for competitive perks, you can find low rates (usually only in the short term), get cash back on your purchases, earn reward miles, and get consolidated billing.

But rather than using credit cards to cover a liquor order or pay for COD deliveries, save them for true emergencies. One winter, an ice storm contributed to a broken water main that flooded the basements of several restaurants. The restaurants had to pay for the cost of pumping out the water, and they also suffered further financial losses resulting from flood damage to the heating units and the subsequent freezing from loss of heat. Settling claims with your insurance company for these types of losses often takes several weeks. You'll likely need to pay for the plumbers and other service technicians you might need and then get reimbursed later. Make sure that you have enough credit available on your cards to handle these emergencies.

Don't bite off more than you can chew on your credit cards. Pay the balance off as soon as possible to avoid paying high interest rates or worse.

Even if you don't borrow dime one from anyone else, we highly recommend that you write a business plan. A business plan is essential when searching for investors, but it's also a great tool for other reasons. Your business plan can save you a lot of your own money, help your restaurant make money faster, and hopefully, spare you a few headaches. See Chapter 5 for details.

Working with Investors

Most people can't completely fund their own restaurants, so they need to look for outside investors. Investors can include partners (both silent and not-so-silent), people looking for a new investment, your friends and family, or a combination of all of these people. We cover these scenarios in the following sections. (And check out Chapter 8 for the legal details on setting up your business as a partnership or corporation.)

Partnering up

A *partner* is usually an informed investor. Typically, a partner is more involved in the business than a typical investor, also called a *silent* or *limited partner*.

Tallying the types of partners

Some partners don't actually invest cash. Instead, they may invest their expertise. Normally, you select your partners because they bring something to the team that you're lacking. It could be money, bookkeeping abilities, or culinary prowess. Whatever the situation, each partner should bring something valuable to the party, or that person shouldn't get a seat at your table.

Bringing in a partner is always a strategic move. Here's a list of good reasons to bring in a partner or two:

- **They bring capital.** This is the most common reason to bring in a partner: You need the money.

- **They bring other financial services.** Sometimes, you can barter a percentage of your business for other services that you need accomplished. Get creative, but don't give too much away. For example, you probably don't want to give free meals for life to the accountant who prepares your tax return one time. Think about people who have these skills if you don't:

  - Accounting

  - Business acumen

  - Financial planning

  - Fundraising

- **They bring a particular restaurant expertise.** Maybe they've spent time in the business doing something that you have zero experience with. Teaming up can practically ensure your success. Look for these skills in a potential partner:

  - Culinary abilities

  - Efficiency expertise

  - Front man/host expertise

  - Local dining scene knowledge

  - Marketing skills

  - Operations skills

- **They bring reputation or name recognition.** Maybe your partner doesn't lend cash or involvement in the day-to-day operations of the business. But he brings a reputation and is available to consult as needed. For example, you may decide to bring in a big-name chef to consult on your menu and advise you on various aspects of your back-of-the-house operations (see Chapter 13 for more information on hiring a chef and other employees). Or perhaps you team up with a local wine expert who comes in to oversee changes in your wine program.

Making the relationship work

You may have heard the adage "Too many chefs spoil the soup." The more partners you have, the more different ideas you'll have about where the restaurant should be going and how it should get there.

Someone should have the final say in your restaurant. The best-case scenario is if one person makes the calls. If you need to have a committee meeting to take care of minor decisions, such as what brand of olives to serve in the martinis, you'll end up wasting a lot of time. Don't think, "We'll just come to a decision. We're united. No big deal." Think again, because it usually doesn't work that way. One person doesn't have to make every minor decision; in fact, different people can take charge of different areas in the restaurant. But you must have a clear hierarchy, and the ability to make a final decision should rest with a single person.

You should settle decision-making issues before you present your first business plan, seek the first dollar of financing, or even think about opening the doors. If all the partners can't come to an agreement about this point, you shouldn't go into business together. In fact, if you can't come to an agreement at this point, it's fairly unlikely that you ever will.

Seeking other outside investors

If you're considering going to outside investors, complete your business plan and figure in the one-time only start-up costs we outline in Figure 6-1. Before you have the first conversation with the first potential investor, you want to know how much you're going to need from your investors, and be able to tell them how soon they'll get a return on their investment and how much it will be. And of course, make sure that you have your business plan in tow (see Chapter 5 for the details).

People who invest in a restaurant may think they have a say in what goes on. Even those silent partners can become not-so-silent if they spend time in the restaurant. "Why did you get those curtains? They don't go with the spaghetti sauce." People may say that they don't want to get involved until things don't go as well, as quickly as you hope. Don't give them a valid reason to comment. Run your business right from the beginning.

Investors have friends; hopefully, they'll encourage them to come to the restaurant. If your investors are paying for their own meals, it's even better. Some investors expect to eat in the restaurant for free as one of the perks of "ownership." Consider offering discounted meals for investors if you think they're appropriate for your business. Make sure to write down the full terms of repaying your investors, including any perks like free or discounted meals, so that everyone knows what to expect.

Asking family and friends to chip in

You've probably heard all the warnings about being careful about borrowing money from friends. Borrowing from friends puts both the borrower and the lender in tough situations. You don't want to lose your life savings or your relationships with friends and family. Instead, rely on them for emotional support and encouragement.

If you do decide to borrow from friends and family, treat them with the same terms you'd treat your other investors, including a signed contract with deadlines for repaying the loan.

Compensating your investors

No one buys into the risky proposition of starting a restaurant without significant opportunity for a return on that investment. How you structure your compensation deals is important to the long-term success of your operation and the short-term success of your drive to raise money. You have to strike a balance between compensating investors fairly without burdening the business with high salaries, free meals, and unrealistic payment plans. The following sections explain a few typical compensation plans.

There's no right or wrong way to structure a compensation plan. Some investors don't want an open-ended deal. They're looking for a short-term investment. Others may want to stay involved in the business so they can say that they have a restaurant. No matter how you set it up, work with your attorney to draft the document that stipulates the terms of each agreement. Make sure that the attorney who draws up the agreement isn't also an investor in your business — it's a conflict of interest.

The sooner you pay back your investors, the faster you can reap the benefits of your hard work.

Earning your percentage

Suppose you have a partner who brings money to the operation; you, on the other hand, bring a little money but a lot of experience. In fact, you're the one who runs the restaurant day in and day out, and you draw a salary from the business. Assuming that the business goes well, the moneyman will get a return on his investment. Depending on how you structure the partnership agreement, you can gradually gain a larger equity stake in the business over time (meaning you earn a bigger share of the business), which, you hope, will then eventually pay you a larger return on your share of the investment. Or you could forgo the growing equity and get a return on your hard work through profit sharing. In this scenario, you won't build a larger share of the business unless you invest more cash, but you do get a chance to share in the profits of the business as soon as there are any.

Paying them back with interest

In this scenario, an investor provides you with an initial investment amount, with the assumption that you'll eventually return the stake plus interest. The timing for each — repayment of initial stake and interest payments — varies. You can find as many repayment scenarios as you can find investors. Each investor probably has certain things that appeal to him more than others. Suppose that you borrow $10,000 from an investor. In one scenario, you can pay him 10 percent annually ($1,000 each year) for each of four years *and* return the principal (the $10,000 you borrowed) on the fourth year, for a total of $14,000 over four years. Or you can pay him back another way, say over three years. Maybe you pay him $4,000 the first year, $4,000 the second year, and finally $5,000 the third year, for a total of $13,000 over three years.

Revving up performance-based percentages

If you pay someone back based on how the restaurant performs, this person is considered more of a limited partner. She's hoping for you to do well, so you pay her more money as a return, while she maintains a percentage of your business. Suppose that she invests $10,000 in your company, and that's 10 percent of the value of your business. For every $10,000 of profit you make, she gets $1,000. You could add a buyout clause to her compensation plan, so in addition to getting her principal back, she gets a lump sum cash bonus. You continue to pay her dividends until you buy her out.

Getting a Loan

Because the restaurant business is so risky, many banks won't loan money to one that's just starting out. If they do, they usually require the owner to personally guarantee the note, meaning that the owner is personally responsible for repaying the note, no matter how the restaurant does financially. In this section, we give you some tips on how to make yourself look like the best possible financial risk for a bank and then give you some tips on getting some help from Old Uncle Sam if you qualify.

Visiting your local bank

For most start-up restaurants, getting a bank loan is probably not an option. Even if you have a great reputation and working relationship with your bank, most banks look strictly at the numbers. You're better off looking for individual investors.

On the other hand, if you have a bakery and want to expand your business to include a café, you may have a shot at getting a loan from a bank. If you can show that you have collateral and a proven track record for success and are looking to expand an already-successful business, you may qualify for a loan. The bank may require a cosigner or ask you for collateral, such as your other business, your house, or anything that minimizes the bank's risk of losing its money.

Either way, the bank looks at some of your financial and business records to decide whether you get a loan. The bank will probably ask for the following info:

- ✔ **Proof of your ability to repay the loan:** Use your business plan to get this point across. For details on creating your own business plan, check out Chapter 5.

- ✔ **Your personal credit history:** The bank runs your personal credit report and assigns you a credit rating.

- ✔ **Equity:** It usually takes the form of your investment in the company. It's sort of like a down payment on a house.

- ✔ **Collateral:** This is any asset that you can use as security, like your house, your car, and certain kinds of investments, such as CDs, if you default on your loan.

- ✔ **Experience:** Here's where your industry-specific experience pays off. To leave the best impression, make sure that your business plan includes details of your experience in the business and managing in the business.

For more info, check out *Small Business For Dummies,* by Eric Tyson and Jim Schell, published by Wiley.

Finding government assistance

Most start-up restaurants are eligible for help from the Small Business Administration (SBA). In all likelihood, you'll work either directly with your bank or with an SBA *intermediary,* someone who helps you get your business plan together, helps you complete the required SBA paperwork, and gets you prequalified for an SBA loan.

After you're prequalified and your paperwork is complete, you then work with the bank to qualify for the loan. If you qualify, the SBA will guarantee the loan or part of the loan, reducing the bank's risk. So if you default on the loan, the SBA will pay the bank back.

This guarantee doesn't eliminate your responsibility to repay the loan. It only reduces the bank's risk, making it easier for it to lend you money.

As with any loan, the SBA evaluates your application, using the same standard criteria that we go over in the "Visiting your local bank" section, earlier in this chapter.

Some SBA services are free of charge, but others are provided by contractors who may charge you a fee, so make sure that you know what charges you may incur.

Considering Other Ways to Increase Your Liquidity

When most people think of getting financing together, they likely think of borrowing money, liquidating accounts, and maybe even looking under their couch cushions for loose change. But you can make the money you have go further if you know where to look and who to ask, in the form of deferred rent and extended credit terms. Check out the next few sections for details.

Securing landlord investments

One of the biggest expenses in your budget is your rent or mortgage. Negotiate the best deal you can to keep ongoing expenses as low as you can, and perhaps to even help with start-up costs. Look for a landlord who is pro-business. Hopefully, he's looking for you to renew your lease after the initial term ends. And maybe he even works to make it easier for you to make money. Ultimately, your success increases the value of his property.

Negotiating start-up savings

Many landlords give breaks on rent during the start-up phase of your operation. For example, if you need to *build out* the space, meaning demolish the existing space and construct a new space, and you're investing $50,000 to do it, maybe your landlord will give you three months of free rent. Check out Chapter 7 for details on finding and leasing your space.

Maybe you can take it to the next level. For example, you can propose that if you open up by a certain day, your landlord gives you another two months rent-free. A busy, successful restaurant benefits a landlord's other properties — if he has any. Perhaps the landlord also owns the space next door, down the block, or maybe just the rest of the building. Ultimately, a building's landlord doesn't want any of his space to be vacant. He makes money only when the space is leased. An operating business (especially a new restaurant) is much more attractive to a prospective tenant than an empty space or a store with a closed sign and painted windows. An operating business shows neighborhood vitality. If you're just coming in, he wants to get you in and up and running. The sooner you're making money, the sooner he is.

Negotiating your long-term lease

Consider making your landlord a partner. We don't mean that he should manage your bar or take over your ordering. But see whether you can work out a percentage-based rent. (For more information on partnerships, see the "Working with Investors" section, earlier in this chapter.) So if you're not doing well, you're not getting destroyed with a huge payment. But if your concept is going like gangbusters, you're bringing him along for the ride and stuffing his pockets. Another option is to try to negotiate a rent schedule that allows lower monthly payments in the early stages, with annual increases built into the term of the lease.

If you have a five-year lease and you're expected to make infrastructure changes to things like the heating and cooling units, electrical systems, plumbing and so on, make sure that you get some kind of a break in your rent. If you walk away, you can't take the plumbing with you, so you're really paying for an improvement to someone else's building.

Be the best tenant you can be. If you're not paying your rent on time, you can't expect your landlord to go out of his way to work with you. And if you're not paying your rent at all, you have bigger issues than dealing with your landlord.

Relying on suppliers' credit

Your vendors and suppliers, often called *purveyors* in the restaurant biz, can be a source of credit. They're not exactly giving you a loan, but they can defer the payment of your bills, which is sometimes even better. Basically, your purveyor approves you for extended payment terms, like net 30 or net 45 days (paying within 30 or 45 days). Then you can use your cash for other things in the short term. New restaurants may have a tough time qualifying for extended credit terms, but you may be able to qualify for smaller purchases. Check out Chapter 14 for more on dealing with suppliers.

Suppliers can offer you some equipment at no charge if you buy other products from them. So, for example, they may give you a dishwasher or espresso machine as long as you buy your soap and coffee from them. Such an agreement isn't exactly a loan, but if you need the equipment, it can help reduce your start-up costs.

Chapter 7

Choosing a Location

● ●

In This Chapter

▶ Checking out the real estate market

▶ Diving into location details

▶ Identifying cost considerations

● ●

*Y*ou've heard it countless times before: The cardinal rule in real estate is location, location, location. But finding the perfect location is much easier said than done. Part of the reason is that what works for some concepts definitely won't work for others.

The key in choosing a location is finding a spot that makes it easy for *your* targeted or desired clientele to reach *your* restaurant on a *regular* basis. It may be a freestanding restaurant in a busy shopping district. It may be by a kiosk in a mall. It may be a lunch truck in a parking lot. There is no right answer that fits every concept or area. Use the suggestions in this chapter to figure out the best spot for your restaurant.

Looking at the Local Real Estate Market

Everything starts with the local real estate market. Here are a few ways to find potential locations:

- ✔ **Work with a commercial real estate broker:** Finding one who knows the restaurant market is preferable.

- ✔ **Comb neighborhoods you think match your concept and desired traffic:** Look for locations that interest you even if it's not obvious that they're up for sale or lease. And check out the "Paying attention to traffic" section later in this chapter.

- ✔ **Check in with your local chamber of commerce:** It's a good source of information.

- ✔ **Get info from your local governing bodies:** Consult town councils, zoning boards, and any other agency or board that doles out licenses and is likely to know of new development and rezoning opportunities.

Most people look at the real estate market and potential locations in one of two ways.

- ✔ **A sure thing:** They start a restaurant in an already hip, trendy area of town, and hope to make some profit. Locations where people are often mingling provide a built-in customer base. But they come at a price — a hefty amount of money to get the space. (See the "Looking at other businesses in the area" section later in the chapter for related info.)

- ✔ **The ground floor:** Some folks choose to be prospectors and hit an area before it becomes a great restaurant neighborhood. Choosing to be one of the developers of the neighborhood means paying less in rent than in established neighborhoods. But it also means not having the built-in potential customer base of lots of traffic nearby (which can translate into increased marketing costs). Just keep in mind that with the greatest potential for profit comes the greatest possibility of failure. Your real estate agent should be able to help you find up-and-coming locations.

If you choose to establish your restaurant in an area before it becomes hot, you may not realize your business potential for a couple years. Make sure that you have enough cash to sustain the wait — few people have unending money supplies. Your overhead will be heavier while you wait for business levels to improve and sustain you.

The direction you take depends on your concept, business plan, and the specifics of each space.

Examining Location Specifics

No two locations are identical. What works for some restaurants definitely doesn't work for others.

Research the history of your proposed space, building, and neighborhood. Find out what was there before and what has succeeded and failed. Try to figure out why businesses in the area either made it or didn't survive. Here are a few ways to get started on your research:

- ✔ **Ask landlords for info.** Even if landlords can get you only the names of the previous tenants, you at least have a starting point for your research.

- ✔ **Visit the library.** The resources at your library can be helpful if the space you're interested in has been around for a long time.

- ✔ **Talk to past leasers.** If you can talk with the past leasers, you can get invaluable information on their problems and solutions for the space, saving yourself some trial and error down the road.

✔ **Talk to past owners.** Consider talking with your local building department for information on renovations that have been made, when they were made, and so on. All renovations, additions, and many minor construction projects require permits that must be granted by the building department. They keep a copy of all plans and permits on file.

✔ **Chat with the neighbors.** They're always a source of information, but take whatever info you get with a grain of salt. They may have accurate observations but off-base conclusions.

✔ **Contact your local restaurant association.** If the space you're considering used to be a restaurant, the association may have insights to share about why it is no longer used for that purpose.

You may not be in the market for a truly unique location, but here's a list of things to look for that benefit most restaurants:

✔ **Easy access:** Think about your restaurant from the guests' perspective. If they have to drive past your restaurant, turn left at the next light, and then backtrack to get to you, they may not bother. Having a traffic light with a protected left-turn arrow close to your location is a great plus. Often when people eat out, their first consideration is convenience. Make it as convenient as possible for them to get to you.

✔ **A high-profile location:** Corners are desirable because people can see you from two streets instead of one. You'll get more exposure, instead of being buried in the middle of the block. Say that your restaurant is close to the mall. If possible, you want to be out in front of, rather than behind, the mall because that's where the most exposure is. If you can get the front corner of a large parking lot (known as an *outlot*), right on the street, all the better.

✔ **Availability of parking:** Unless you're in an urban area that benefits primarily from foot traffic or public transportation, abundant, well-lit parking is a must. If you have to hire a valet, it will cost you some cash, so budget for it.

Paying attention to traffic

Traffic doesn't just mean cars. It means potential customers passing by your restaurant. Traffic includes walking people, biking people, people in cabs, people on public transportation, people driving by — any means people use to travel near your business.

Watch the traffic near your proposed location and make judgments about how well the people fit the profile of your proposed clientele (see Chapter 4 for more on targeting the right customers). If you have a concept nailed down and a great flow of traffic but the traffic is not your desired clientele, you'll have a tough time succeeding. For example, truckers want a good hearty meal that's a good value. If you're trying to sell them small, expensive portions, forget it. Here are some thoughts to ponder to get you started:

- ✔ Where are these people going? Are they going to or from work, shopping, visiting a nearby museum or theater, going to school? Are these the folks you're targeting? Are they likely to stop in?

Sometimes, putting a sign in a proposed location works better than placing a restaurant there. For example, being located along a busy commuting thoroughfare isn't a guarantee of success. People may see you but not want to give up their spot in traffic or return later to your restaurant if they'll have to fight the same traffic again.

- ✔ Do your proposed operating hours match the traffic flow? If you open at 5 p.m. in a business district, you may have already missed the traffic flow that existed from 9 a.m. to 5 p.m. But in a suburb, opening at 5 p.m. may be ideal — people start returning from work around that time.

Visit your proposed location many different times, at different times of day and on different days of the week, to get a feel for the traffic flow. Make notes about the volume and type of traffic you see. Look for patterns to help you evaluate the location.

Commercial sources, such as Claritas (`www.claritas.com`) or ScanUS (`www.scanus.com`), can help you identify demographics, average car traffic, and so on. Start with your local chamber of commerce, but then look for companies that specialize in segmenting the population into different demographic groups.

Knowing what locations to avoid

In a perfect world, people come to your restaurant for your restaurant's sake. If it's good, they come back; if it's not, they don't come back. But in the real world, outside factors affect your business more than you may guess. Your best bet is to pinpoint and avoid things that may keep customers away from your restaurant. For starters, avoid locations that feature

- ✔ **Businesses that your customers or others may find unsavory.** They may feel uncomfortable and may stop coming altogether.

- ✔ **Permanent construction zones.** You don't want heavy machinery and trucks going through during dining hours. Also, guests may have trouble getting to you through the construction mess. If the construction is short-term or pervasive throughout your area, you may not be able to avoid it.

Spend the necessary time talking to the people at your city, county, and state transportation departments. They can tell you what their long-term plans (one-, three-, and five-year time frames) are regarding road projects in the areas you're considering. Surviving and/or recovering from an extended road construction project can be difficult, or impossible. Many of your potential customers will choose other routes to their destinations and never even find out that you exist, and the ones who know about you won't want to deal with the hassle.

✔ **Remote or hard-to-find addresses.** Don't locate your restaurant in a remote or hard-to-get-to location. In a very few cases, remoteness can be a draw, such as in ultrafine dining, where you're going after exclusivity. In most cases, though, people want convenience to some degree. They consider the efficiency of their time when making dining and drinking choices. Another consideration is that people are less likely these days to venture far from home when drinking.

✔ **Other counter-productive features.** For example, if you're targeting a business clientele, don't locate your restaurant near a high school where kids go out for lunch. They may discourage other patrons from coming in. Depending on your concept, however, teens may be your ideal audience — they do have considerable disposable income these days.

Ultimately, let your own conscience be your guide when it comes to avoiding certain situations and neighbors. Remember who you want to attract to your business and how they see the world and your restaurant.

Looking at other businesses in the area

Your neighbors affect your business, and vice versa. Businesses such as theaters, entertainment, and shopping go hand in hand with restaurants. Attractions such as a scenic river walk in a downtown area, an ocean view, mountain peaks, and wildlife are great restaurant hooks.

Look for businesses that feed off restaurants. Think about the relationship between the remora and the shark. The shark attacks and claims its prize. The remora, swimming close to the shark, sustains its life off the successes of the shark. Restaurants and their neighbors are similar to the remora and the shark. Think about the number of chain restaurants located close to malls, tourist attractions, and so on. Many restaurants, chains and independents alike, locate themselves near a busy office building, office park, or business district, hoping to capture a booming breakfast, lunch, and even takeout dinner business. Putting a restaurant in such a location is a completely calculated move, designed to capitalize on already-present traffic.

Lighting the way

Make sure that your exterior is well lit. Cars are magnets for thieves looking for quick cash, stereos, CDs, cell phones, and other items often left in cars. Coauthor Heather recently had her purse stolen from a car while dining at a restaurant. She tucked the purse with its newly-broken strap under the front seat, but it still proved to be too tempting in the poorly lit, half-empty parking lot. Sifting through broken auto glass and chatting with the local police weren't the perfect topper to the fantastic meal. As the restaurant owner, you don't necessarily have a legal responsibility for what happens to your customers' cars, but over time, if your parking lot is the scene of many crimes, your business may decline. Do what you can to provide safe, secure parking facilities.

Also consider how your particular restaurant fits in with the current restaurant mix. If you want to bring in a Mexican café, but two other Mexican concepts are established within the open block, do you want to be the third? You may be successful if the other two are both highly commercialized versions of Mexican cuisine and yours is truly authentic *and* your clientele can appreciate the difference. But if you're offering more of the same, think about choosing a different location. There is a big exception, though. In larger metro areas, common cuisines can make up large city blocks that become areas known for different cuisines, such as Little Tokyo or Greektown.

Considering security

Security is a key concern for any business owner. Restaurants have a decent amount of cash on hand, despite the prevalent use of credit cards, and they can make a tough-to-resist target for thieves. Therefore, you must evaluate a potential location for security. Keep the following advice in mind:

- Avoid blind interior and exterior corners. Blind corners, like blind driveways, are corners that can't be seen from the normal flow of traffic.

- Stay away from buildings with poorly lit stairwells and hallways.

- In today's security-aware climate, consider potential terrorist targets in your location selection. If you're planning to be located near a courthouse, a power plant, or a federal building, consider the possibility that you may have to temporarily close your doors during erroneous bomb threats, evacuations, and the like.

- Avoid natural disaster areas (including flood plains) when possible. If you're in an area where natural disasters are prevalent, simply try to find the safest area possible in this regard.

In addition, make sure that your new location includes these safety features:

- ✔ Working locks and alarms on exterior doors or other secure areas
- ✔ Working security system with cameras
- ✔ Safe access to and from the garbage area
- ✔ Plenty of food storage in secured areas
- ✔ Well-lit exterior and parking lots
- ✔ A working safe

All of the things in these lists can be remedied with time and money.

Factoring In Cost Considerations

The primary cost of your location is your rent (or mortgage). For the most part, the restaurant owner isn't also the building owner. Purchasing the building is typically too expensive for a new restaurateur, so unless you're very established and successful, you'll likely have a landlord. Ultimately, a building's landlord doesn't want to keep the space vacant. He makes money only when the space is leased. Unless his is a highly sought-after locale, he should be motivated to help you get up and running. Check out Chapter 6 for more information about negotiating with your landlord.

Here's a quick list of questions that should affect your decision to lease a particular space:

- ✔ **Is your landlord pro-business?** Is he making it easy for you to make money? Your success increases the value of his property. You want to sign with someone who is looking for you to be there in the years beyond your initial lease.

- ✔ **Is your landlord willing to adjust your rent on a short-term basis?** Look for a landlord who's willing to give you some months of free rent — known as *rent abatement* — especially while you're setting up. It's not uncommon to ask for and get a 90-day abatement so that you can keep expenses down during your pre-opening period. Other tenants may depend on your being open because a closed space is an eyesore. If the rent is based on sales, the landlord wants to get you up and running as soon as possible. But keep in mind that it's also not uncommon for your landlord to give you nada, nothing, zip.

- ✔ **Is your landlord willing to foot some of the bill for construction costs?** This situation is less common, but you can still ask. Landlords are more likely to give you free rent rather than money out of their pocket. In some cases, you can get landlords to give you *x* amount of dollars per square foot toward the tenant improvements (known as TIs). One key factor in getting contributions is the state of the local commercial leasing market. If things are soft, and space is sitting vacant for extended periods you can be more aggressive in negotiating.

✔ **Is your landlord willing to help pay for required upgrades to the HVAC (heating, ventilation, and air conditioning system) and/or electrical systems as needed?** Sometimes when you get into a space, unforeseen complications occur that have more to do with the landlord's building than with your restaurant. Find out what the landlord's policy is on these kinds of upgrades before they happen.

If you're looking at a space that wasn't previously a restaurant, retrofitting it to accommodate the kitchen, dining room, and so on will be very expensive. Have an experienced restaurant contractor look at the space and help you understand all the ramifications of construction before you sign the lease. Ducts and plumbing don't just appear — they require hard work and money.

Depending on the age and configuration of the space you're considering, you may not be able to make the modifications necessary for a restaurant. Maybe the infrastructure of the building can't support the configuration, or perhaps the building's a historic landmark, and the modifications necessary aren't within the charter. You don't want to get locked into a lease and then discover that you can't install a range hood in your kitchen. You still owe five years' rent. Don't go bankrupt before you make a dollar.

If you decide to lease a space, consider talking with the other tenants about their experiences with the landlord. You'll get info that's not in the public record, shall we say, about the history of the space, and you can probably find out some details about why the previous tenant left. You're guaranteed to get a different perspective than the landlord gave you.

In addition, get the true story regarding the zoning situation of your space from the appropriate agency in your area. Make sure that you have the exact address of your proposed space because zoning ordinances can vary from block to block. Maybe ordinances don't allow for an outdoor café, but your business plan and concept demand one. On the other hand, the governing agency may try to promote outdoor eating in specific areas and provide financial incentives to develop restaurants that offer it.

Chapter 8

Paying Attention to the Legalities

•••

In This Chapter

▶ Figuring out who can help you with legal affairs

▶ Choosing the best legal setup for your restaurant

▶ Obtaining permits and licenses

▶ Putting together your insurance plan

•••

More than any other topic in this book, legal issues vary from state to state and concept to concept. You need to know about the specific laws in your area so that you stay out of legal trouble that could result in fines, loss of your licenses, or jail time. Laws dictate some details of your business that may surprise you. For example, laws tell you the number of alcoholic beverages that can be sitting in front of a single patron at one time, the hours your business can be open, whether you can serve diners on your patio, and how many people can be seated in your dining room at the same time.

To help sort through these complex issues, just about every restaurant needs the assistance of outside professionals, including a good attorney, a thorough accountant, and a reputable insurance agent. These business-savvy pros can help you navigate the legal necessities that are part of every small business and those that are unique to the wonderful world of the restaurant business.

In this chapter, we get you thinking about the legal realities of the business. We tell you exactly who you need to help you. Then we go over details concerning how to set up your business, what you need to know about local laws and licenses, and the types of insurance you need to be thinking about.

Identifying the Help You Need

Professionals you turn to for assistance should have experience in the business. If you get a "deal" from someone without restaurant experience, you may actually lose money in the not-so-long run. If your attorney doesn't know how to get a liquor license, you may get a license that won't work for your business. Then you're out the money you paid and you have no liquor license. And if your accountant doesn't depreciate your furniture correctly, you may not have the money to buy the new stuff when the old has got to go.

Find people with verifiable, positive references in the industry, and ask for a client list or a list of other restaurateurs they're working with. If they're not currently working with any, consider finding someone else. Call a few clients and get their impressions of the expert's service. Don't be shy; you can save yourself time and money by weeding out problems before they start.

Your local chapter of the National Restaurant Association (NRA) may be a good place to find some reputable professionals. Check out www.restaurant. org for the chapter nearest to you. Also, ask other restaurateurs and small business owners who they use and recommend.

Look for people who can understand your concept and goals. Because each restaurant is unique, make sure that they understand you and your vision. Bring them into your space or show them your plans. Be sure that they understand what you're trying to achieve so that they can help you get there.

The people you hire must be objective and able to have the hard conversations with you. Hire people who can tell you that you're spending too much money or the floor manager you really like has his hand in the liquor cabinet. You hire experts because they bring you knowledge that you don't have, and their input can ultimately benefit your business (even if what they're saying is hard to take). Don't let your ego get in the way of the success of your business. If two people in the room always agree, one of them is unnecessary.

Our advice is to contact experts with experience in the industry for specific advice in

- ✔ How to set up your business
- ✔ How to get the right insurance for your business
- ✔ How to get the necessary permits and licenses to do the business you want to do

Cross-examining attorneys

Lawyers can expedite your paperwork through the maze of bureaucracy and advise you as to what's necessary to do things the right way. Attorneys can be very helpful to the new restaurateur, especially when you're setting up your business. They can do the following:

✔ Recommend and file the appropriate paperwork to set your business up as a corporation, partnership, or sole proprietorship.

✔ Draw up partnership agreements and any other agreements.

✔ Review contracts, like your lease and your vendor agreements.

✔ Do the hard work of filing proper paperwork for permits and other licenses. In some states, you need an attorney to complete paperwork for your liquor license. Check with your local governing agency. For more help, see the section "Acquiring a liquor license," later in this chapter.

Depending on the size of your operation, you also may eventually need a few different attorneys, such as a labor lawyer, intellectual property lawyer, tax attorney, and divorce lawyer, er, we mean, general business attorney.

Your attorney may also have contacts, clients, or colleagues looking for a good investment. She may be willing to pass along your name to interested parties.

Auditing accountants

If you're brand new to running a restaurant, an accountant should be one of the first people you speak with. In the early stages, before you even open your doors, an accountant can walk you through the financial planning aspects of creating your business plan. He can explain complex financial stuff like depreciation, amortization, and capitalization. He can work with your attorney to show you tax advantages to setting up your business in one way or another. Using a qualified accountant to guide you can help you avoid paying for an attorney to get you out of trouble later. After you're up and running, he can help with preparing the monthly books and reports, preparing taxes, and conducting internal audits and reviews.

If your landlord bases your rent on the sales that you generate, you probably need to hire an accountant to review your books and make a statement to your landlord. See more about negotiating your lease in Chapters 6 and 7.

Ensuring your insurance agent

Insurance coverage is important in any business. You need liability insurance, property insurance, and workers' compensation. Your insurance agent should be able to walk you through the basics of balancing deductible amounts, giving you the appropriate amount of coverage with reasonable payments that protect your business without putting you in the poorhouse. See the section "Buying the Insurance You Need," later in this chapter, for more details.

Setting Up Shop on Legal Grounds

Your attorney and your accountant can help you decide how to set up your business. You have a number of options from going it alone to setting up a partnership to incorporating your business. Your decision determines how your company is taxed, how you earn an income from the business, what your obligations are if your business fails, and many other expensive decisions. In the following sections, we discuss some of the most common options.

Even if you're the only investor or are involved in a partnership, you still may want to incorporate. Without the legal protection of incorporating your business, your creditors can come after you if your business goes under. They can lay claim to your home, cars, savings, and anything else of value.

Going it alone: Sole proprietorships

A *sole proprietorship* is owned by one single person — in this case, you. Your attorney registers your business as a proprietorship by completing a simple form. You keep everything that you make, and you personally owe everything that you spend.

Teaming up: Partnerships

A *partnership* is similar to a sole proprietorship, but you're adding extra people to the mix. You share all the profits and all the risk. No two partnerships are the same, but the partners should spell out the details, in writing, with an attorney, before they begin. Each partner should consider hiring separate counsel to make sure that the agreement is on the up and up. (Check out Chapter 6 for info on finding financing through partners.)

Make sure that your agreement includes details about all of these concerns:

- ✔ **Responsibilities and hierarchy:** Figure out who's responsible for what tasks or areas of the restaurant, who makes which decisions, and who reports to whom.

- ✔ **Ownership stakes:** Whether a partner is contributing money, time, or both, she's making an investment in the company. In return for that investment, she owns part of the business. Spell out the details of your arrangement clearly, so that no one has any confusion.

- ✔ **Pay rates and profits:** Make sure that everyone knows how you plan to divide profits. Spell out who gets a salary and when it starts. Often, as you're building a business, the owners take a small salary (or sometimes no salary) until the business has the money to spare. Resolve all financial issues clearly and to the satisfaction of all parties involved.

✔ **Ultimate decision-making authority:** When humans work together for any length of time (usually no more than 15 minutes), disagreements pop up. Having more decision makers can mean that making decisions becomes more complicated, so clarify how your decisions will ultimately get made. Your first line of defense is to discuss, persuade, and then compromise. But the occasion will arise that requires one person's opinion to win the day. Write it down before you start.

✔ **Exit options:** You never want to think about this possibility before you start, but your partnership will probably end at some point. Make sure that you have an exit procedure outlined in your agreement. Usually, one partner can buy the other out, either in a lump sum payment or over time.

✔ **Death contingencies:** Definitely not a fun one to think about, but you need to consider it. Have a clear plan for handling this situation.

Almost teaming up: Limited partnerships

Limited partners are more like investors in the business than actual partners. They limit their liability legally because they aren't involved in the operation. Say that your friend, Joe Blow, wants to invest in your restaurant. He doesn't want to be involved in the day-to-day, but he thinks you're a savvy businessperson and wants a piece of the action. He gives you $25,000, and he owns a corresponding percentage of your business. You draw up an agreement that specifies what he gets as a *return on investment* (or ROI) and when he gets it. Maybe he gets a percentage of profits paid quarterly or annually. Fast-forward five years: Things have been going well for several years, but the worst-case scenario occurs, and your business folds. Joe Blow doesn't get his money back, but he also doesn't incur any debts as a result of your business folding. Creditors may take your house, but Joe's is safe and sound. That security for the investor is the beauty of limited partnerships.

As with any partnership agreement, have your attorney draw up a document with the specific language detailing the terms of your agreement with any limited partners.

Playing it safe: The corporate entity

Incorporating, or creating a corporate entity that owns your restaurant, offers you some protection if your restaurant goes under. Your attorney can set up your corporation for you, and you can be the only shareholder in your corporation and still own it completely. But incorporating also has some significant tax implications. *Double taxation* can be an issue: The government taxes the profits of the corporation and then passes them along to you. The government then taxes you on them again, as income. Depending on how you set up your corporation (different types of corporations exist), you may be able to lessen the tax burden. Definitely discuss your options with your attorney and accountant for the pros and cons of your specific situation.

Creating a corporate entity doesn't remove all your responsibility in the event that your business fails. As a new restaurant owner, many lenders require you to personally guarantee loans, which means that even if your business fails, you're still responsible for the debt. It's kind of like cosigning a loan for your corporation. Weigh the options. We know of many people who have lost both their businesses and their personal credit ratings when their businesses fell apart. And don't plan to use your corporation as a shield if you have less than honorable intentions. If you run out on your rent or creditors, you develop a negative reputation that will follow you throughout your career.

Knowing Your Local Laws

Laws govern just about everything about any business. The restaurant business is no different. Most laws related to this industry are governed and enforced by local and state agencies. Your local health department determines the many specific health codes you must follow to continue to serve diners in your area. Your local building department determines what steps you must take to make your facility safe to be occupied by people. And who knows who handles liquor licenses in your area? (Well, actually, we show you how to find out who handles them in your area, so don't worry.) Your local or state government probably has laws and ordinances governing the following:

- ✔ When you must close and when you can open
- ✔ How big you can make your signage and where you can post it
- ✔ The process for applying for required permits
- ✔ Where you can have your outdoor seating
- ✔ Details about building codes that you must follow
- ✔ How you can sell liquor

Most areas have very specific liquor laws. The government specifies when, where, in what container, in what quantity, and sometimes even at what price restaurants, bars, or clubs can serve alcohol. Here are some specifics that may apply to your business. Check with your governing agency for details:

✔ You may not be allowed to discount liquor in your area. Offers like Happy Hour drink specials or two-for-one deals are common in some areas and unheard of in others.

✔ Some states don't allow more than one drink in front of a patron at a time. Others limit only liquor and allow as many draft beers in front of a patron as you can fit on the table. You may not be able to serve liquor to a patron if she hasn't also ordered food. Some states require only that the drinker has access to a menu.

✔ Some states allow patrons to take their unfinished bottles of wine home. Others prohibit it.

✔ Liquor sales may be limited on Sunday. These laws, lumped together, are called *blue laws*. Some states don't allow the sale of alcohol on Sundays, others allow it in restaurants, and others have no restrictions.

Getting Permits and Licenses

A *license* is a legal document issued by a government agency giving you permission to do a very specific thing. For example, in the case of the restaurant business, you need a license to serve liquor. If you serve liquor without one, you can be shut down, fined, and even go to jail.

The words *permit* and *license* mean the same thing. Some agencies choose to use one word rather than another, but we don't really know why. Just call it whatever the agency calls it and don't worry about it.

In most cases, getting licensed is not a one-time thing; your licenses and permits usually need to be updated annually. Work with your attorney, bookkeeper, or other support personnel to create a system for alerting you when licenses and permits need to be renewed and processing any applications and fees required to get and stay current.

Make permits and licenses a priority. By doing so, you're not just trying to keep yourself out of trouble; you're truly making sure that everybody's going to be safe in your restaurant. Go above and beyond to assure that your customers and employees are safe and sound.

Acquiring a liquor license

Every restaurant that serves liquor must have a license to do so. Depending on the state, different agencies regulate and administer liquor licenses — the Department of Public Safety, the State Liquor Authority, and the Department of Alcoholic Beverage Control, to name a few. Start the process of getting your license in the early stages of starting your restaurant. Depending on the system in your area, getting this license could take a year or more.

Most licenses are valid for a year and require an initial license fee. If you maintain good standing with your local agency, you can probably get an automatic renewal for a smaller annual renewal fee. But if someone files complaints against you for overserving patrons alcoholic beverages, serving minors, or violating other terms of the license, your license may be revoked.

The cost of a liquor license varies greatly. If the government issues licenses directly, the price may be as low as $500. But if your area has no licenses available because it has met its quota and you need to buy one from an existing establishment or a third-party broker, the laws of supply and demand apply. In a really hot area, they may go for hundreds of thousands of dollars.

A *quota* is the fixed number of liquor licenses in a given area. Some states base quotas on the population living in an area. Utah, for example, allows one liquor license to be issued for every 5,000 people in the state. Other states set them based on population density or other criteria. So, for example, in some cities, you may find two to three licenses per city block.

The easiest way to get started: Get on the Internet and type something specific, such as **restaurant liquor license,** into your search engine. Also, `www.liquorlicense.com` gives a list of links to contact offices in all 50 states. Click on the State Government Offices button and then on your state to see which office handles the licenses in your area.

Your local agency offers liquor licenses in different *classes*. What kind of establishment you have determines what kind of license you need and how much you pay for it. The class of license you require depends on your concept. Here's a list of the broad, common classes of licenses. Similar licenses in your area may have different names, and licenses with similar names to these may have different provisions.

- ✔ **Beer and wine:** This license allows you to serve only beer and wine. Licensees can't sell liquor or distilled spirits. In some areas, smaller restaurants (40 to 100 seats) can get only this type of license.

- ✔ **Hotel and restaurant:** This license may be called a *resort-and-restaurant license* in your area. You may also be eligible for a *bed and breakfast license* (which you can find later in this list) at a reduced rate. Check with your local agency.

- ✔ **Restaurant:** This license usually requires that only a certain percentage of your sales come from alcohol. States have varying percentages, but most requirements fall somewhere around 40 percent. Some states require you to have a minimum number of seats to qualify for this license. A restaurant license usually allows you to serve beer, wine, and liquor. Some people call it an *all-liquor license* for that reason.

- **Eating place:** This license is usually reserved for carryout places, like delis, that may offer a small amount of carryout beer.

- **Retail:** A retail license applies to grocery stores, drug stores, liquor stores, or any other retail establishments where the average consumer can walk in and buy liquor.

- **Bed and breakfast:** In some states, this form of establishment is lumped in with the hotel and restaurant license. Some states have created two separate licenses to account for the size and sales of smaller establishments. This license may be cheaper in your area than the hotel and restaurant license. You're required to have a certain number of bedrooms, a separate kitchen, and so on to qualify for this license.

- **Tavern:** Some states require taverns to offer a food menu, but others don't. If you consider yourself a restaurant but half of your sales are alcohol, your state government may require you to apply for a tavern license. In some states, no such separate license exists.

- **Club:** Private clubs, such as country clubs and golf clubs, are eligible for a separate license allowing them to serve alcohol to their members. Some states allow only beer and wine in clubs, but others allow for all liquor.

- **Brewpub:** Many places brew their own beers, and in some states, you need a separate license to serve it to the public. Check your local agency.

Some states issue an *alternating premises* (AP) liquor license for places like wineries and breweries that allows these establishments to brew and ferment alcohol at certain times and serve patrons at other times.

- **Arts:** Some places, like theaters, may get a special license that allows them to serve alcohol in connection with certain kinds of cultural events.

- **Wholesale or distributor:** Some states require different licenses for importing liquor versus selling domestic liquor. If you're selling liquor to restaurants, retail establishments, hotels, and so on, you need this class of license. And on the other side of the equation, you need a restaurant (or retail, hotel, and so on) license to buy from a wholesaler.

Here are the general steps to follow when you're getting your liquor license:

1. **Figure out which government agency issues licenses in your area.**

   Conduct an Internet search or check with other restaurants.

2. **Research the classes of licenses in your area.**

   Request a list from your local agency. Many agencies post descriptions on their Web sites.

3. **Figure out which class of license works for your business.**

   Based on what you find out, look at your business, your projected food-to-beverage sales mix, and so on to determine which license you'll likely need. Do your homework and work with your attorney.

4. **Contact the local agency to find out the availability of licenses, costs, the application process, and a timeline for completing the process.**

   Your attorney may be able to handle this, but make sure it gets done.

5. **Update your business plan with the information on the cost and timeline.**

   Budget both the time and money to get your license before you open. This step is essential, whether you're using your own money or have partners, because you can't sell liquor without a license. Revise your plan anytime you run into a new schedule or budget factor.

6. **Apply for the new license or for the transfer of the soon-to-be purchased license.**

Consulting companies have sprung up because this licensing process can be so expensive and complicated. These companies can help you streamline your applications. They file your paperwork and the like — for a fee, of course.

Before you agree to work with any third party to secure a license, check with the state agency in your state that issues licenses and with your own attorney. You may be able to avoid additional fees and charges just by making a couple phone calls. Your local agency may have a list of recommended brokers that handle the buying or selling of existing licenses.

Heeding health codes

Every restaurant needs a permit from the health department to do business. And, as always, the permit requires you to complete an application and pay a nominal fee (usually under $500). In larger metro areas, the cost may be closer to a few thousand dollars per year. As with most legal issues in this business, the requirements vary from state to state, so check with your local health department for details. In some states, requirements and ordinances vary county by county or municipality by municipality.

In addition to the restaurant's permit, some states require employees to be licensed by the health department. The names for the licenses vary, but these licenses are sometimes known as *certificates of qualification, food handler's permits,* or *food protection certificates.* In addition to taking a test that ensures knowledge of proper food-handling techniques, employees may be required to submit to a health check for highly communicable diseases such as tuberculosis and hepatitis.

Check out Chapter 18 for an overview of food safety concerns and details on creating a successful sanitation program in your restaurant to keep your customers safe and pass your health inspections with flying colors.

Paying attention to building codes

Before you can begin construction or remodeling of your new space, you need to get the appropriate building permits. Check with your contractor and attorney to make sure that you have the appropriate paperwork in hand before starting construction.

After you finish construction, your local building department must issue your certificate of occupancy (CO) in order for you to open your doors. After you file your application for the certificate, an inspector from the building department visits your facility and inspects it. If you pass, he issues your CO; if you don't, you'll be reinspected later to see if you pass before the department issues your CO.

Be nice to your inspectors, but don't be too nice. It's absolutely no use, not a good idea, and, in fact, detrimental to your business to attempt to bribe or influence any inspectors. Be friendly and agreeable but always professional.

The certificate of occupancy shows the following:

- ✔ You've followed all building codes. You haven't knocked down load-bearing walls, for example.

- ✔ Your facility conforms to current safety requirements, which include things like having the right electrical systems and wiring and making sure that you don't have any asbestos or lead paint around.

- ✔ Any modifications that you've made to your space are sufficient and appropriate for your new use of the space. Typically, you must submit copies of your plans with your application for the inspector to review.

- ✔ Your building is safe to occupy.

Depending on the laws in your community, you may need another permit from the building department that stipulates your building allows smoking. Discuss the details of your business with your attorney so that she can advise you on what paperwork you need for your business.

Considering fire codes and capacity

Before you open, you must also get a permit from the fire department. The fire marshal inspects your facility during and after construction to ensure that you have appropriate emergency exits, determine maximum capacity, and check all fire suppression systems.

Expect annual fire inspections, but you may need more frequent inspections. Coauthor Heather inadvertently set off a fire suppression system during training for her first management position. The system had to be reset, and the fire department had to fully inspect the system to ensure it was again in full working order before the restaurant could reopen. Your fire inspector verifies that all your fire extinguishers are in working order, too. Make sure that you locate them in handy places with their current inspection tags attached.

Checking out other permits

Depending on your local laws, you may need to get these official permits:

- **Employer tax ID:** This permit identifies you when you're paying employee taxes and other required fees.
- **Business license:** Every business owner has to have these permits in some communities.
- **Elevator:** You need to get annual inspections done if you have an elevator in your establishment.

Depending on your business and concept, you may also have to get separate permits to operate specific parts of your business. Here are a few examples:

- Special license to sell specific food products, such as oysters
- Outdoor seating permit, which some areas require for outdoor dining
- Retail tobacco license, if you sell cigars

Taking up trademarks

As you build your business, you build your reputation. Customers come to understand your style of service, menu, and quality standards, and they have an expectation when they step in the door. If you're successful, they associate all the terrific things about your restaurant with its name and its atmosphere. The last thing you want someone to do is to sabotage your hard work by stealing your name and using it to open a restaurant.

Plan ahead and trademark your name, logo, tag lines, and so on. Get the proper paperwork to protect your intellectual property in your state and in the entire country.

An attorney can help you navigate through this confusing landscape. But to get started, incorporate you restaurant to make it a legal entity. Then check with the county or state governmental office that deals with trademarks to determine the protection you can obtain for your name, logo, and so on at the local level. Finally, check out the United States Patent and Trademark Office (USPTO) Web site at www.uspto.gov to find info on establishing trademarks and to search the database of registered trademarks to see if someone is already using your proposed name or logo.

Don't assume that because your future mark isn't listed that someone hasn't applied for it. The only way to be completely sure is to file your own application and get it approved.

After you're registered, you must protect your marks or risk abandoning them. Get your attorney to help you establish a strategy for maintaining your rights. You can also check out *Patents, Copyrights & Trademarks For Dummies,* by Henri Charmasson (published by Wiley).

Buying the Insurance You Need

The law requires you to obtain certain insurance, but other forms of insurance are optional. The amount of coverage you carry and the *deductible* (which is the amount you're required to pay before your insurance kicks in) you choose affects the amount of your *premiums* (the amount you pay for your insurance).

Talk with your insurance agent to find the best, most appropriate coverage for your business. Here's a list of common business insurance coverage:

✔ **Property:** Property insurance protects your property in the event of damage. Many policies cover only specific damages. You may want to consider other coverage, like earthquake, flood, wind, and hail insurance, if those natural disasters are likely in your area.

✔ **General liability:** Liability insurance protects you in case someone sues you for something. For example, someone may file a lawsuit if he falls on the sidewalk outside your restaurant or claims that he got sick after eating in your restaurant.

Check your lease for any required minimums for liability insurance. Your agent may have additional recommendations for how much liability insurance you should carry, based on the assets of your business.

✔ **Liquor liability:** When you get your liquor license, check with your local agency to see what amount of liquor liability insurance you need.

✔ **Automobile liability:** Automobile liability insurance covers any lawsuits that arise from an employee, including you, driving a company vehicle. Automobile liability may be covered in your general policy, but you may have to get a separate *rider,* or additional coverage, added to a larger policy.

✔ **Workers' compensation:** This insurance takes care of medical bills for employees injured on the job.

✔ **Unemployment insurance:** This insurance pays your out-of-work, ex-employees until they find another job.

The federal government requires you to have workers' compensation and unemployment insurance. Having the other forms of insurance on our list simply makes good business sense. Protect what you have with the right insurance. See your agent for the best coverage for you.

Consider protecting yourself with life insurance and long-term disability insurance, as well. If you're killed or injured in an accident, you or your heirs may need to pay someone to run your business. Having this kind of insurance can help mitigate the extra expenses.

And consider these additions (*riders*) to your policy. Some types of coverage are available only in certain states or are only available for established restaurants, so check in your area to see whether these policies apply to you:

✔ **Specific peril:** This policy addition covers flood, earthquake, or other weather-related perils.

✔ **Employment practices liability:** This addition protects you against wrongful termination cases, sexual harassment suits, and so on.

✔ **Loss of business income:** This insurance enables you to recoup income if you lose sales through one of the covered causes.

✔ **Food contamination and spoilage:** This policy covers your losses if something like a lightning storm knocks out the electricity that powers your coolers and results in large-scale food spoilage or contamination.

These additional policies may seem attractive, but the premiums required are often much more expensive than standard insurance. Think of it like insuring your jewelry: You can add the jewelry rider to your homeowner's policy, but the cost of the insurance can be close to the cost of replacing that jewelry. Consider what you're saving and gaining by adding the coverage. Your insurance agent can help you weigh the pros and cons of additional coverage.

Part III

Preparing to Open the Doors

The 5th Wave   By Rich Tennant

ORIGINAL WAITRESS UNIFORM FOR "HOOTERS" RESTAURANT

In this part . . .

We cover all the tasks you need to take care of to make your idea a reality. In this part, you can find information, tips, and tricks on planning your menu; setting up your beverage program; designing your exterior, dining room, bar, and kitchen; negotiating with suppliers; setting up your office (including all the electronics); and implementing a marketing campaign.

Chapter 9

Composing a Menu

● ●

● ●

The menu is the epicenter of your restaurant. *Everything* revolves around it: the ingredients you order every day, how you design your kitchen, which equipment you purchase, how you organize and train your staff, who your chef is, what selections are on your wine list, even the name of the restaurant. If the idea behind the menu wasn't the inspiration for your restaurant in the first place, then you must focus on it now. Creating your menu should be fun.

As important as the menu is, flexibility should be a consideration in almost every choice made for it. Ultimately, your diners make the final decisions about what's on your menu based on their consistent purchases of some items and avoidance of others. In this chapter, we go over what you need to know to plan your restaurant's menu, from deciding on core items, to determining its layout, to deciding how often to change it.

Making Some Initial Decisions

Your menu should match your restaurant's *concept* (or theme) and atmosphere, your guest's expectations, and your kitchen's capacity to pull it all off. Toss out any items that don't. After you have a general idea of what you want to put on the menu, you must decide what makes the final cut. In this section, we get you started with your menu planning by tailoring your menu to your restaurant, your clientele, and your kitchen.

The basic premise "quantity doesn't necessarily equal quality" applies. Some of the most acclaimed restaurants in the world have modest-sized menus. Other concepts are based upon the diversity of their menus. Success or failure doesn't depend upon the size of a menu in general. How well the size of your menu works within your overall operation determines your level of success.

The first thing you need to do is get together a core group of menu items that you think you want to serve. The number of menu items you begin with depends on the approximate number you envision ending up with. As a general rule, start with three times more items than you need. You can get a good core menu from this group, plus have some backup items ready when you need to revise.

Matching your menu to your concept

Do all your menu choices match the feel of the restaurant? Just because veal parmigiana is your favorite dish, having it on your Cuban restaurant menu doesn't make sense. Okay, maybe that example is too obvious, but you want guests to have a consistent experience the entire time they're in your restaurant. If your menu is inconsistent, now's the time to figure that out. Here are a few questions to get you thinking along a matching line:

- ✔ **Is your restaurant an ethnic restaurant?** If so, do all the dishes on the menu come from the culture or country that you're showcasing?

- ✔ **Is your restaurant themed?** For example, if you want to become known as the old-school Italian joint in your neighborhood, you may have decorated accordingly. Does your proposed menu match that theme, with spaghetti bolognese, lasagna, linguine with clams, and the like?

- ✔ **What's the atmosphere like?** Are you located just off the local walking trail? You may consider having a menu conducive to the activities going on around you. For instance, consider beefing up your takeout menu so people can grab snacks and bottled water and get back on the trail. But, if you have white tablecloths and candles, you may want to skip the bottled-water display and offer a wine list to diners as they're seated.

- ✔ **What cycle of service are you planning to follow?** If you plan on finishing all dinners with a traditional Tuscan salad, you probably want to make that plain on the menu and consider adjusting your salad section accordingly. If you're strictly a dessert joint, you may want to consider coffee drinks playing a starring role.

- ✔ **What are your hours of operation?** If you're open at 9 a.m., people will likely expect some breakfast items. But, they'll be surprised to see a ham-and-cheese omelet on the menu of your martini bar.

✔ **Are you a drinking place that serves food or a food place that serves drinks?** That particular question doesn't have a right or wrong answer, but it's one that you should answer. And when we say *drinks,* we don't mean only those that contain alcohol; drinks can be smoothies, coffee, and or anything else. If you're a bar, and your goal is to sell drinks, you'll likely have a limited menu, with some munchies and some salty things, which make people — you guessed it — thirsty. You get the idea.

Thinking about whom you want to feed

Think about your restaurant from the diner's point of view. What would they expect and demand? How can you delight and surprise them? How can you keep them coming back for more? Map your menu to your clientele and their needs. See Chapter 4 for info on figuring out your customers, and take a look at a few questions to get you started:

✔ **Are you looking to lure in the lunch crowd?** Because lunch diners often take a break from their workdays to visit restaurants, they have less time to linger. Be sensitive to their need for speed and efficiency. If you want to be a big lunch stop, offer items that can get them in and out in 30 to 40 minutes. They'll appreciate the consideration and may make you a regular stop on their lunch hour.

✔ **Do you want to focus on takeout?** Takeout customers want convenience: easy menus, easy ordering, easy pickup. Consider *combo-ing* — creating a single menu item that actually includes several menu items. For example your roast-beef-sandwich combo includes a small salad and a drink. That way, they can order a whole meal with a single item. If you're planning on doing a lot of takeout business, have food that is portable and *holds* (stays fresh after it's cooked).

✔ **Are you starting a family-style business?** Busy families turn to restaurants to give parents a cooking break. They want familiar, easy-to-eat items for their finicky pint-sized sidekicks. If you're targeting families, offer a few kid-friendly items or maybe a separate menu.

✔ **Do you want to be a destination?** People love to feel special, especially during a celebration in their honor. If you pride yourself on being a celebration or destination restaurant, make sure the customer-service touches complement your fantastic menu. Offer personalized menus for the guest of honor. Create a special dessert for celebrations. Give the party a behind-the-scenes tour of the restaurant. Do a follow-up call with them afterward. Find whatever works for your restaurant.

✔ **Is your food familiar to guests?** Consider how familiar the food is when determining the final menu. If you're going for eclectic (taking influences from many different sources or styles of cuisine) or haute (by which we mean *fancy* — *haute* is French for high cuisine), you probably want fewer items on the menu than you would if you were starting a diner or family restaurant. People will likely take longer with a menu full of items they're not familiar with.

Uncovering the links between your kitchen and menu

The size of your kitchen, its layout, the size of your coolers, and your dry-storage capacity all affect your menu. If you want to serve only from-scratch items, you need lots of refrigerated cooler space to store it. If you need to have 15 different kinds of ovens to produce the items on your menu, you have to determine whether you have the space (or budget) to accommodate them. Answer these questions early in your menu development process and save yourself hassle later on:

- ✓ **How big will your dining room be?** The size of your dining room dictates how much room there is for the kitchen and related storage space. Too much area dedicated to the dining room may severely limit what the kitchen can produce. You have to consider space for fixtures, equipment, storage, and maneuverability, but keep in mind that too much space in the kitchen could steal seating from the dining room and curtail revenue potential. In general, restaurants use between 15 and 25 percent of their total space for kitchen space. The perfect balance depends upon what you do with the space in each. Take a look at Chapters 10 and 11 for dining room and kitchen layout and design tips.

- ✓ **Does your menu have a diversity of preparation techniques?** Assuming that you have several different *stations* (areas to prepare food, like the grill and the fryer) in your kitchen, you want to have dishes with a diversity of prep techniques so that you maintain a balance of the number of dishes coming out of one station at a single time.

Finding a 57-burner range or managing that many sauté cooks in the kitchen at one time is difficult. Give the grill cook something to do. As they say, too many chefs spoil the sauté, er, we mean, soup. For more on the different stations in a restaurant kitchen, take a peek at Chapter 11. As with many things in this book, this is not an absolute rule. If your concept centers around a particular preparation technique, don't feel like you *must* diversify. A well-known restaurant concept fries chicken all day and all night. You can't argue with success!

- ✓ **Do your menu items have a consistent preparation time?** You want most items to be prepared in about the same amount of time. That way, all items are *fired,* or ordered to be cooked, at about the same time and come out at about the same time. Or if you have inconsistent preparation times, you can find ways to *par-cook* (partially cook) items so that some of the work is done early, and the dish is finished when it's fired.

✔ **Does your menu reflect a synergy of inventory?** Or more simply, do the items on your menu work well together and represent a modest, high-velocity inventory? For example, unless you're known for the variety of seafood you have available, you may want to just keep one variety of clams on the menu and use them for linguini and clam sauce as well as seafood stew. For more on managing inventory, check out Chapter 14.

Cutting Your Chef (If You Have One) in on the Action

Assuming that you're opening a restaurant that requires a chef, you may choose to hire her before designing the menu. Or you may opt to hire a chef later and determine the appropriate candidate based upon her expertise in light of the menu. If you're the chef, even better. Either way, the chef will run the show and must be completely synchronized with how you want the menu to be executed. Take every step to ensure this eventuality. (For information on deciding whether you need a chef, check out Chapter 13.)

Hiring your chef before you begin the menu-development process has several advantages and disadvantages. First, the good news:

✔ You can get a feel for her food style and creativity early in the process and ensure that your styles and philosophies mesh.

✔ If you're not a hands-on foodie, a chef's input isn't only valuable but also essential in the early stages of menu planning. Nothing is quite as disappointing to a diner as trying a new restaurant only to discover by taste that the menu creator has spent more time reading cooking magazines or watching cooking shows than she's spent in the kitchen.

Hiring your chef before you develop your menu has its downside:

✔ The sooner you hire her, the sooner you have to pay her. Depending on your budget, (and her salary), you can quickly rack up some cash before you even open the doors.

✔ The more people involved in planning the menu, the less control you have over the final product. If you're a control freak, developing a menu with a team of people may be a problem for you. ***Remember:*** Ultimately, your name is on the door, so win the war if not each and every battle.

Test runs of all recipes with the chef are essential. You can do this in a test kitchen, your home, or in the restaurant if you already have possession and the fixtures are in place. These very important sessions should occur as early in the process as possible. During testing, you'll likely decide to tweak some recipes or scrap ideas. An accidental discovery has also been known to occur.

Test runs are an excellent time to get a good sense of how you and the chef will work together. They're not real-time scenarios because you don't have the stress involved with guests waiting in the dining room. But you do get a good idea of your chef's food philosophy, creativity, cleanliness, management style, and efficient work processes (or lack thereof). And you get a sense of how a chef deals with feedback, both positive and negative. These important attributes don't show up on a resume, so pay attention.

Your chef will be instrumental in standardizing your recipes and creating production manuals for the kitchen staff to use each day to prepare dishes that are perennially on the menu. These manuals help train new staff and ensure that all staff members are making the dishes the same way, every time. The manuals establish the consistency that is essential to building and maintaining a clientele. These are particularly useful if you choose to change your menu less often (quarterly, for example). If you have a more dynamic menu, you'll need a much more experienced chef who can develop recipes and training materials, for both kitchen and front of the house (FOH) employees, like servers, quickly. For details on training employees, check out Chapter 13.

Don't give your chef carte blanche to buy a case of truffles to run a pasta special next month unless you know the specific reason. Know what she's ordering and why. In most cases, you want consistency over creativity, so make sure that you and your chef are on the same page when it comes to food costs and ordering procedures.

Figuring Out How Much to Charge

You can follow several different strategies when pricing a menu. No matter where you start, you'll end up with the old-fashioned, tried-and-true process of trial and error. Books, such as this one, can give you basic strategies, but ultimately, if your customers won't pay what you charge, then you have a problem. Conversely, if they'll pay more than what you charge, you're missing an opportunity.

Several components determine menu price points, including consumer demographics, competition, and accepted standards. In the following sections, we help you fix your price points and get a handle on food costs and how they affect your menu prices. We even show you how to keep your menu priced to compete even when some of your costs don't cooperate.

Determining your menu price points

Price points are ranges of prices for types of menu items. For example, on your lunch menu, your sandwich price points may be between $4.95 and $7.95, and your salad price points may fall between $7.95 and $10.95. Using price points to determine your menu pricing is particularly useful (and darn near necessary) if you're entering a highly competitive market. For example, if you're opening a steakhouse in an area with several successful steak-houses, you have to pay diligent attention to the prices charged by your competitors for what diners perceive to be like products. If you're charging more for your product, you must establish a point of difference (in quality, atmosphere, service, and so on) to justify the price.

A consumer will pay more for quality food, but exactly how much more is a question that only the consumer can answer.

Determining your price points isn't an exact science, but asking yourself a few key questions may help you get started:

- ✓ **What type of clientele are you trying to attract?** Suppose that you want to be a family restaurant that serves lunch and dinner six to seven days a week. Create an atmosphere through your pricing that encourages people to eat there on a weeknight and bring the family for sustenance. If you've done your research and determined that you can't sell an entrée that costs more than $12.95, stick with that plan even if it means you can't serve your personal favorite, filet mignon.

- ✓ **What are your competitors' price points?** Think about the $1 menu war waged by fast-food restaurants. Most have a $1 or 99¢ menu, but each restaurant varies the items on the list based on what it can sell at that price without losing money.

- ✓ **What price points are consistent with your atmosphere?** If you're opening a diner with counter service, you'll be hard-pressed to have many $20 items. When people pay $20 for an entrée, they usually expect to sit down at a table with a tablecloth. They may also expect to be able to order a drink from the bar or a glass of wine. If your restaurant offers neither, you probably want to lower your price points.

- ✓ **What ingredient solutions can you find to help you serve the food you want and hit your price points?** Can you use less-expensive cuts of meat to produce wonderful flavors through braising, and menu a fantastic pot roast for $12.95? Because pot roast has a much lower food cost than your favorite filet, you have a much higher profit margin. You make more money and have a great beef dish on the menu.

Looking at food cost percentage

Your *food cost percentage* is the cost of all the ingredients used to make a dish (your *food cost* for that dish) divided by the menu price. It's a benchmark used to help control costs and gauge profitability.

Restaurants take in money when diners choose items from the menu and pay for them. This stream is your *only* source of revenue. So your menu prices have to cover the cost of the food you're serving, the wages of your employees, your rent and utilities, and most importantly, your profit. So when you're running a restaurant, you set a target food cost percentage to cover all your costs of doing business.

Most restaurants target food cost percentage somewhere between 20 and 40 percent, but your choice will depend on a number of factors, including your actual overhead costs (like rent and utilities) and accepted pricing standards for your type of restaurant. To figure out your menu price of a particular item by using your food cost percentage, follow these steps (and see "Creating dishes and recipes and then costing them," later in the chapter, for more details):

1. **Find the food cost of the item.**

   You factor in all the raw ingredients costs associated with creating a dish, including any "freebies" like bread and salad (if these are complimentary in your establishment), to create your food cost.

2. **Divide the cost by your food cost percentage goal.**

   If you want to run a 30-percent food cost, a dish that costs you $3.75 in ingredients will cost the customer $12.50. ($3.75 ÷ 0.30 = $12.50).

So at various food cost percentages, your prices would look like this:

Percentage	Food Cost	Menu Price
20	$3.75	$18.75
25	$3.75	$15.00
30	$3.75	$12.50
35	$3.75	$10.75
40	$3.75	$9.50
45	$3.75	$8.50
50	$3.75	$7.50

If you get your calculator out to check our math, you may notice that some of these percentages aren't exact. For example, a 40 percent food cost is actually $9.38, but that price would be, well, just weird to see on a menu. Ideally, you want to round up and end in 25¢ increments (like $12.50, $10.75, and so on), or to an exact dollar figure (like $15.00) or just shy of full-dollar increments (like $12.95). There's no set rule, but you want your guests to be able to roughly add the prices in their heads.

At first glance, it may seem like you're making a bundle on each dish. In our 30-percent food cost example, you net $8.75 for each person ordering the dish. But before you book your next Caribbean vacation, don't forget all the overhead required to run the restaurant. You have wages to pay — including the greeter (hostess or host), the server (yes, the guests tip them, usually, but you still pay them some wages), the dishwasher, the prep cooks, the bussers, the line cooks, the chef, your bar manager, the delivery guy . . . the list is almost endless. And that doesn't even begin to cover the utilities, rent, linen service, plant service, décor, cleaning service, and so on. And what happens when the guest doesn't get the dish he ordered or a waiter drops a plate full of food? Guess who eats that food cost? You do. You get the point: Running a restaurant isn't a cheap endeavor.

Food cost is only one part of the equation. Ultimately, the lower the food cost you can run, the better off you are. That way, you'll have more left over for the other percentages, like labor, overhead, and the like.

Don't take the "lower the better" guideline as an absolute rule. Your food cost percentage is definitely affected by the kind of food you serve and your atmosphere, because they're key indicators of what prices your clientele will expect to pay. If they expect shaved truffles in their risotto, the darn things are expensive enough (at $150 per pound) that you'll likely not make a huge percentage off them, but you will make a decent dollar figure. Stay flexible! The other side of this issue is that in your drive to maintain low food costs, don't sacrifice your quality. Doing so will backfire on you eventually. As people see your quality deteriorate, they'll stop coming. Stay true to your concept and standards, but run an efficient business.

Creating dishes and recipes and then costing them

Go through each recipe and determine its food cost and food cost percentage. Determine if those numbers meet your goals for the restaurant. If they do, keep them. If they don't, toss them. If you still want to keep them, see whether you can adjust portion sizes and ingredients to bring the costs in line with your goals for the restaurant.

In this first scenario, you pick some recipes, test them (check out "Cutting Your Chef (If You Have One) in on the Action" earlier in this chapter), create standardized recipes, and then cost your menu. So if you're serving pasta with marinara sauce, follow these steps:

1. **Figure the cost of a serving of pasta.**

   If you're going to serve an 8-ounce portion of pasta for each serving, it costs you approximately $0.50.

2. **Add the cost of a single serving of marinara sauce.**

   If you make your sauce from scratch, it'll cost you approximately $0.85. So, you're up to $1.35 per serving.

3. **Add the cost of a sprinkle of Parmesan cheese.**

   If you use ½ ounce of Parmesan cheese on each serving, add $0.25. Now, you're looking at $1.60 per serving.

4. **If you garnish the plate with a little fresh chopped parsley, include it in the food cost.**

   A little sprinkle of parsley costs around $0.10, so your current total is $1.70 for this dish.

5. **Add in the costs of any complimentary items that each customer enjoys to the food cost for each entrée.**

   So if you serve chips and salsa or bread and butter to each visitor to your restaurant without charging for it, include that in your food cost. In this example, you may serve bread and butter to each guest, so add $0.50 to the food cost. Also, add an additional 5 to 10 percent of your current total ($2.20) to cover things like foil, plastic wrap, beverage napkins, stir sticks, and sugar packets, bringing your grand total for the food cost of this dish to $2.42.

This process is for costing a recipe. It tells you how much money you spend for the raw materials to put a dish on a plate and serve it to a guest. Determining the complete food cost percentage picture for your restaurant requires you to look further at your inventory to determine the extent of wasted food (which occurs when food spoils, is dropped, or is overportioned, meaning, for example, cutting a 10-ounce filet instead of the 8-ounce portion specified on the menu). You also need to consider factors such as miscooked food that must be cooked again or losses from theft. For details on gauging your restaurant's food cost percentage, check out Chapter 20.

Dealing with price fluctuations

There are no guarantees in the restaurant business. The price you pay for your products is no exception. Even if you negotiated the best possible pricing with your *purveyors* (suppliers), some products vary in price almost every time you order them. This variation can wreak havoc with your precisely laid-out food cost percentages and menu pricing. But never fear, because we have some strategies for dealing with these situations on your menu:

- ✔ **Use a "market price" designation in place of an actual price on the menu.** This strategy is acceptable for things such as seafood, imported items (like truffles), or seasonal or specialty produce (like broccoli rabe or ramps with very limited availability) that can have very large price swings (multiple dollars per pound). Normally, you communicate the daily market price to your staff, who pass it along to your diners.

- ✔ **Create a cost factor based on the worst-case scenario and price accordingly.** So if you know that tenderloin is $9 per pound during the holiday season but $7.50 per pound the rest of the year, cost your menu as if tenderloin costs $9 per pound year-round and price your item to fall within your margins. When tenderloin is cheaper, you make more, but you can still keep it available year-round. Items that experience massive price swings, like lobster, aren't good choices for this strategy. You could be cheating yourself out of revenue (and profits) because the highs are too high for your clientele but the lows are just right.

- ✔ **Print your menu daily.** This is a great choice if you have the capability to do it on site and you have many items with prices that fluctuate. Printing your menu daily is much easier than having a hostess or server rattle off the prices of 15 fish entrées to each table.

- ✔ **Deal with it.** Maybe the most common strategy for handling price changes is just dealing with it. This strategy is particularly effective when the price increase is only temporary (expected to last only a couple weeks) or it affects smaller components of your menu. For example, maybe a light freeze occurred in the citrus-growing states, and the immediate crop of lemons was damaged. As a result, for a week or two, your lemon costs double. You probably don't want to change your menu prices to account for the difference; the costs will return to normal soon.

Mixing your menu

Not all dishes will come out to a perfect food cost percentage; some will have a higher percentage, and others will be lower. Make sure that you sell the right amount of each, called a *menu mix,* to maintain your overall food cost percentage goals.

Check out Table 9-1 for an example of how this works. You may set a food cost percentage goal for the restaurant of 27 percent and achieve it with an overall food cost percentage of 26.8 percent. But notice that you don't set the price for each and every entrée at an exact 27 percent food cost. Instead, you *weight* your prices (price some a little higher and some a little lower) to achieve your overall goal. If you sell 20 steaks for $20 each at a 35 percent food cost, 40 orders of pasta with marinara for $16 at 25 percent food cost, and so on, you'll end up with a food cost well under your goal. To figure your overall food cost, take your total cost from all items sold and divide it by the total revenue from the items sold. For the details on creating a detailed menu mix analysis, see Chapter 20.

Table 9-1				Sample Menu Mix Analysis		
Item	Number Sold	Menu Price	Food Cost	Total Revenue (Number Sold×Price)	Total Cost (Number Sold×Food Cost)	Food Cost %
New York Strip	20	$20	$7	$400	$140	35%
Pasta	40	$16	$4	$640	$160	25%
Salmon	15	$18	$4	$270	$60	22%
Chicken	30	$16	$4	$480	$120	25%
Total				$1,790	$480	26.8%

Don't be afraid to include some dishes that are trendy, local, or just cool and that don't fit the food cost percentage mold. Experimenting is a good thing. But remember: Your overall menu should be priced so that the overall cost of the items you actually sell balances out to achieve desired food cost percentage. So the 25 percenters and the 40 percenters should balance out.

Deciding When to Change Your Menu

Even franchises change their menus, in large part because of an increasingly savvy dining public. With more people going out to dinner more often, the question isn't *if* you're going to change your menu but *when*.

Staying flexible when you first open

Give your menu a chance to work. After a change or new opening, allow at least a couple weeks or maybe a month to let people get familiar with your offerings, try out several different things, and establish favorites. Watch for trends at different times of the day and different meal periods. If your appetizers are selling better at lunch than at dinner, try to figure out why.

Don't get locked into a *tiered menu pricing system* (requires all appetizers to be $x, all entrees to be $y, and so on) with no room for change. If your appetizer list is really working well but no one is interested in ordering the crab-stuffed mushrooms, you may want to consider dropping the price by a buck or so. Be open to that possibility. Ultimately, diners determine what works and what doesn't based on their willingness to buy menu items.

Revisiting your menu later on

Ultimately, when you change your menu, you're trying to capture that new prospective diner and keep him coming to your restaurant while keeping your signature dishes that made you successful to begin with. Here are a few reasons you may want to change your menu:

- ✔ **Keep up with rising (or falling) trends and competition in dining:** Being at the forefront of the "wraps" trend was great, but if you're still tied to it, that's not so good. If the steakhouse down the street is packing them in and your steakhouse is empty, figure out why. Look at your competitor's menu and analyze what it's doing right and wrong. You can capitalize on its mistakes and improve on its successes.

- ✔ **Adjust for seasonality:** You may want to take advantage of the seasonal produce and other items. Or if you live in an area that sees dramatic climate changes, you may want to consider embracing the way dining habits change with the seasons. So in July you may include a gazpacho (a light, fresh, cold veggie soup) on your menu but replace it with beef stew in October. Seasonality dramatically affects top-end restaurants, but it's less important if you don't promise fresh items to your diners.

- ✔ **Generate new excitement within your concept:** You always want to "dance with the one that brung ya." But you can still try new items. If the name of your restaurant is Andy's Big Taco Shack, don't put lasagna on the menu just because you read an Italian cookbook this week. Instead, consider adding a taco bowl or a shredded beef option to your taco menu. You can also make these changes to showcase trendy, new, popular ingredients; celebrate holidays; or commemorate local activities.

Very seldom do you ever want to change the entire menu. In fact, we can't think of a single time when you'd change it all at once. Changing an entire menu isn't effective. Your regular patrons walked in your door for a reason. They probably developed favorites and may not come back if they can't get them. Plus, changing an entire menu isn't efficient; many hidden costs are associated with changing your menu including testing and tasting new recipes, reprinting the menu, retraining your staff (both kitchen and floor), retooling your processes, and reprogramming your ordering system.

Paying attention to specials

There are three big reasons to run specials:

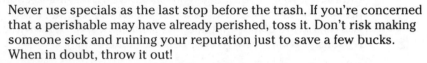

- ✔ **To showcase limited availability and truly special things:** Maybe you can order Copper River salmon (wild Alaskan salmon available only a few months each year) and want to offer it to your customers.

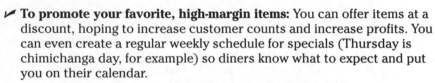

- ✔ **To create efficiency within your inventory by reducing waste from perishables going bad before they're sold:** Specials can repurpose these ingredients at a discounted price to sell them before they perish.

  Never use specials as the last stop before the trash. If you're concerned that a perishable may have already perished, toss it. Don't risk making someone sick and ruining your reputation just to save a few bucks. When in doubt, throw it out!

- ✔ **To promote your favorite, high-margin items:** You can offer items at a discount, hoping to increase customer counts and increase profits. You can even create a regular weekly schedule for specials (Thursday is chimichanga day, for example) so diners know what to expect and put you on their calendar.

One added benefit of changing the menu is your staff will be excited by the change. Consider giving your cooks or culinary team an opportunity to create items when you plan on offering specials or doing a menu revision. They get a chance to be creative, which usually increases morale. (For more on motivating employees, check out Chapter 17.)

Menu Layout 101

Designing the menu on paper can be fun and challenging. You must balance the artistic creativity of various menu selections with informational considerations in the design. The decisions you make here also depend on those you made elsewhere. Today, with simple software available, you can create new and attractive menu quite easily, every day, even every meal. But be careful. You don't want to change the menu *style* day to day. Your customers will note the change, which takes away from the familiarity you hope they develop.

If you don't want to invest in software specifically for menu development, consider using Microsoft Word or Microsoft Publisher. Both have a decent selection of templates, fonts, and graphics that add a professional touch to your printed menus, without costing much, and both are fairly easy to use. If you need help getting started, check out the latest version of *Word For Dummies,* by Dan Gookin, or *Office XP For Dummies,* by Wallace Wang (both published by Wiley).

After you know what to put on the menu, you must put pen to paper (or fingers to keyboard). Whenever possible, keep your menu printing options open. If you have the means and expertise on staff to print your menus yourself, do it. You'll likely save money, be able to fix errors and price fluctuations immediately, and make changes on *your* schedule, not the printer's.

If you're new to the business or you don't consider yourself a desktop publishing whiz, you may want to hire a firm to design your menu for you. If you had an outside firm design a company logo or signage, ask whether it provides menu services as well. At a minimum, it may be able to help you with layout and possibly set up a template so you can still maintain some independence to print your menu daily. Also check with other restaurant owners for suggestions for menu design firms. But even if you hire someone to design the menu, you need the information in the following sections to get that firm started and make some final decisions on the design.

Counting your main menu options

Most restaurants use a main menu and a supporting cast (like table tents, beer lists, wine lists, and takeout menus). As you develop your menu, consider which format best serves your diners' needs, matches the feel of your restaurant, and adequately showcases the items on your menu. An outdoor cafe, for example, might choose a one-pager, because the cafe offers a few simple items that diners are familiar with. A family-style diner might pick the multipage menu to show that it has something for everyone. And a Chinese takeout place may opt for the centralized menu to quickly move diners through the ordering process.

One-page menus

A one-page menu (or *one-pager*) can be one- or two-sided and has become commonplace in restaurants of every size, shape, and service level. These menus contain all the restaurant's offerings from appetizers and salads to entrées, desserts, and beverages. They can offer several advantages:

- **Flexibility:** One-pagers can be easily revised or updated without generating huge amounts of paper or going to a professional printer.

- **Simplicity:** They provide the guest with a simple and quick tool to guide her through the meal. Diners appreciate uncluttered menus that are straightforward and make their selection process smooth.

- **Quicker orders:** A menu that's easy and quick for the customer to read cuts down on her perusal time, which means you may be able to turn over the table more quickly. If you can seat more customers during a given dinner shift, you can make more money in the same amount of time for about the same overhead.

Quick turnovers are ideal (even essential) for just about any restaurant, with two notable exceptions: high-end-casual and fine-dining restaurants. If you don't encourage multiple courses or offer an extensive wine list, you make your money on the number of people you bring through the door each and every meal period. Turn 'em and burn 'em.

If you want to make sure a guest *doesn't* come back, make him feel rushed, like he's not welcome to linger as long as he wants. Making diners feel rushed or hurried is usually not a good idea. Your goal is to make it easy for them to get in and get out, without making them feel like you *want* them to get in and get out. A well-designed menu can help you strike this delicate balance. (For more on building a clientele, check out Chapter 19.)

Consider the complexity of your food when you choose your menu format. Although a one-page menu can prove advantageous for many restaurants, it does have a few downsides:

✔ **Space:** It reduces the space that you may use to explain a particular dish to your customer. We've had customers say, "I had no idea that the Cajun Grilled Catfish with Creole Rémoulade would be spicy."

✔ **Lack of variety:** A limited number of offerings may turn off some diners who choose restaurants because of the variety they offer. If you limit yourself to one page, you probably won't draw in those diners.

Multipage menus

A multipage menu consists of — you guessed it — more than one page. For example, it may include a page for appetizers, soups, and salads; another page for house specialties and entrees; and a third for desserts. This format offers the following advantages:

✔ **Details:** A longer format or multipage menu offers your guest a more detailed look inside your menu. You can list key ingredients and cooking methods if they aren't apparent in the name of the dish itself.

✔ **Busy work:** Multipagers can also provide a conversational icebreaker at a table or just enough literary substance for an on-time diner waiting for a tardy guest.

But every yin has its yang, and multipage menus have some drawbacks:

✔ **Intimidation factor:** Some patrons complain of the intimidation factor of a big menu. "There are just too many choices, I can't decide!"

✔ **Production issues:** Although you can print multipagers yourself, doing so is also multi-difficult. You must take special care to ensure all the old pages are replaced by all the new pages. Embarrassing customer moment #343: "Why is the dessert page between appetizers and entrées?" Also, the difficulty in producing and maintaining these menus will likely decrease your flexibility and increase costs in revising the menu.

Centralized menu

You may recognize the centralized menu from your favorite fast-food restaurant. Any establishment that has a single menu posted in a central location has a centralized menu. Usually, the order taker is also the cashier. Your diners order, pay for their meals, and then receive their meals.

This style of menu may be the way to go, thanks to the following advantages:

- ✔ **Ease of setup and maintenance:** You set the menu up once. When you change it, you change it once. No printing, no wiping down food spills.

- ✔ **Quick ordering:** People peruse the menu while they stand in line to order and then make quick selections when their turn comes up.

But the centralized menu doesn't work for everyone; here's why:

- ✔ **Limited space to explain menu items:** Because you're likely just starting out, your customers may need a little more guidance and explanation of menu items.

- ✔ **Doesn't match the atmosphere:** Unless you're running a quick-service restaurant of some kind, this style of menu may be off-putting to diners. As with just about everything we mention in this book, make sure that your menu decisions are consistent with the feel of your restaurant.

Although many very successful chains and franchises have adopted this style of menu, don't make the mistake of taking your imitation of it too far. They may be able to get away with centralized menus, sometimes showcasing just new items, but you probably won't. They rely on brand identity, the diners' familiarity with their menu offerings, and longevity of their product lines to lead diners to their menu selection.

Considering additional presentations

Most restaurants don't rely on a single kind of menu to address the needs of every diner. They often supplement the dining experience with other formats. Take a look at the following sections, and decide if your establishment could benefit from employing these hard workers of the restaurant world.

Table tents and special boards

Table tents and special boards serve the same purpose using slightly different formats. A table tent becomes part of the table decor and is typically multi-sided, offering everything from an advertisement of special events to drink specials to chef specials to, in rare cases, the entire menu. You may even consider it a one-pager in its crudest form.

Special boards are large chalk, marker, or electronic boards used to display specials. They sometimes morph into encompassing the entire menu. Place them in a prominent spot where customers can view them with ease. You may want the waiters to bring the board to the table and explain it there (or just leave it!). Special boards are handy because they're easy to change, but as a rule the simpler the better. Make the information large and clear enough that people can easily read it with just a few items, so it's not overwhelming.

Takeout/delivery menus

Takeout menus are particularly handy because guest can take them out, you can give them out, and so on. Many people collect them, so they have them on hand when making decisions on where to dine or order takeout. Takeout menus are great marketing items. Always have your address, phone number, and fax number on them. If diners can place orders at your Web site, include that address as well.

If you have items on your regular menu that aren't available for takeout, do not, we repeat, do *not* put them on your takeout menu. Most people assume that they can call in an order and come in to pick it up, or have it delivered, when they see the item on a takeout menu. If they choose a selection from your menu that can't be carried out, they get grumpy. You've now taken a prime opportunity to make a sale and blown it by frustrating your diner.

Selling the Sizzle

You can have the best food on the block, the most knowledgeable staff, and the best beer, but if diners don't order the high-margin items on your menu, you're missing a huge revenue opportunity. In this section, we show you how to lay out your menu and describe the items on it the most effective way.

Menu engineering

Menu engineering is the strategy of laying out your menu to encourage diners to order the food you want them to buy, usually your highest-margin items. The location of an item on the menu, highlighting, graphics, and formatting all have an effect on your customers and the choices they make.

Think about going to a grocery store. Grocery store shelves are like a menu. They put the things they want to sell you in the most accessible, most visible location, usually at the ends of aisles or at eye level on the shelves. Menus are very similar. The first place the diner looks on your menu is the middle of the upper half of the menu. Check out Figure 9-1 to see this in action.

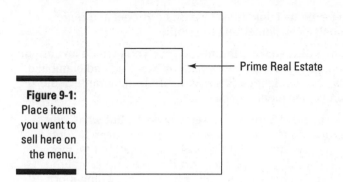

Figure 9-1:
Place items
you want to
sell here on
the menu.

Prime Real Estate

Understand the "power of three." If you have something you want people to buy, put two similar items on either side of it. Price one higher and one lower. They'll go for the middle-priced one all night long. For example, if you have three sizes of the same cut of steak, your menu may look like this:

Petite-Cut Rib-eye (8 ounces)	$9.95
House Rib-eye (10 ounces)	$10.95
Grande Rib-eye (12 ounces)	$12.95

You're practically guaranteed to sell more House Rib-eyes than either the Petite or Grande.

Money for ink: Lingo that sells

A few choice words can improve the perceived value of your menu items, which means you can charge more money and have more money in your pocket. When coming up with your own menu descriptions, think about these questions:

✔ **What's in the dish?** Great ingredients make for great descriptions. Are there any standouts or hard-to-find items? Does a dish contain seasonal items that you should highlight?

✔ **How is it prepared?** Many great menu items start with the preparation method. Words like *braised, seared, pan-fried, oven-roasted, wood-fired* and *poached* lend another level of prestige to a dish that increases a diner's perception of the value of it.

✔ **Why is it special, different, or unique?** Is your beef *aged to perfection?* Are your eggs *farm fresh?* Is your bread *baked in-house each morning?* Is your produce *locally grown* or *organic?*

- ✔ **Where do the ingredients come from?** *Kansas City* beef and *New Zealand* rack of lamb mean something to people.

- ✔ **Do all the foods in a dish share a theme?** Maybe you include an autumn root vegetable soup, an Asian chicken salad, or New England clambake on your menu. Use commonalities (seasonal, ethnic, geographic, and so on) to describe and name menu items.

- ✔ **Can you be more specific?** Sure you're serving *pasta,* but what kind of pasta? Say whether it's *fettuccine, linguine, capellini,* or *radiatore.* And that *sauce* you're serving tonight is probably great, but be more descriptive — *ragout, coulis, demi-glace,* or *reduction,* for example. Getting down to specifics has the dual advantage of providing more information and enhancing the diner's perception of the dish.

Be creative. Anything that makes $1.50 in food cost sound like $20 will work to your advantage. As an example, we once offered *andouille-crusted cedar plank Scottish salmon with horseradish whipped potatoes and vegetables jardinière.* It cost about $4.25 in food cost (including the board!) and sold on the menu for $24.95, making that a 17 percent food cost. If we'd called it *fish on a board with mashed potatoes,* we couldn't have charged the same price. By using descriptive language and cool cooking techniques, we sold more than 20 each night.

Never, ever mistake creative menu writing for misleading the diner or out-right lying. If you're cooking pizzas on a standard conveyer oven, don't menu them as *wood-fired pizzas.* Or if you deep-fry your shrimp, don't say they're sautéed. Diners will know the difference and feel cheated. Not only will you lose customers, but you could also be subject to legal action, including heavy fines for misrepresentation or fraud.

Chapter 10

Setting Up the Front of the House

. . . .

In This Chapter

▶ Considering the design of your restaurant

▶ Coordinating the exterior with the interior

▶ Laying out your dining room and waiting area

▶ Setting up supply and service stations

▶ Organizing your reservation system

. . . .

The *front of the house* (or FOH) is restaurant lingo for any place the diner can be. The FOH includes the dining room, bar, bathrooms, banquet rooms, lobby, exterior, and so on. These areas set the mood, set your guests' expectations, and set you apart from your competition. Spend some quality time developing the environment and atmosphere that you want your diners to experience. The front of the house is your face to the world. Show them your best.

In this chapter, we help you figure out what you want from your restaurant design and decide whether you need help. Then we take you through a tour of the inside and outside of your restaurant to help you decide what needs work. Finally, we go over two things you may not think of as part of the FOH but which are essential to creating a good impression on your clients: your wait stations and your reservations systems (if you choose to have one).

Because the bar is a key part of some restaurants and nonexistent in others, we separate the details about bars and put them all together in Chapter 12. If you're planning on incorporating a bar into your concept or opening a bar without a restaurant take a look at Chapter 12.

Digging into Design

Not everyone needs to worry about design. If your margins are low to begin with, and your concept doesn't require a particular ambience, don't spend a lot on your restaurant's design. For example, if you specialize in takeout, focus on speed and efficiency in your kitchen *and* in the front of the house.

Maybe your FOH just consists of a few chairs with or without tables, so people can sit while waiting on you to finish up their orders.

But the design and décor often impact the success of your restaurant. They provide a basis for diners to form initial expectations about your concept and the experience it'll provide. You have two missions: Provide a design and décor that accurately convey what you want your concept to be, and then live up to those goals. If you're going to charge $20 for an entrée, your customers expect a stylish design and expensive décor, and if you have expensive décor, you're customers won't be surprised to find $20 entrées on your menu.

Throwing money at the design doesn't make it good. Anything you do must fit with your concept. When thinking about design, make sure it's

- ✔ **Flexible:** Make sure that the design is flexible and can be updated. If you're adding a wall to separate a dining room, consider making it a movable (or *re*movable) wall to keep your options open.

- ✔ **Comprehensive:** Be sure that your designer covers all the bases, including furniture, floor tile, the ceiling, and ceramics. Small touches can make a huge impact.

- ✔ **Suitable:** Confirm that the design will fit in with dinnerware, glassware, silverware, and your menu. For example, if you're serving Chinese food, you don't want a Moroccan motif. Also, make sure that your chosen design works both inside and out.

- ✔ **Practical:** Make sure that the designer considers all the front of the house spaces and the flow between them before implementing the design.

Identifying pros that can help

If you're interested in creating a particular atmosphere or maintaining a theme throughout, a good interior designer, architect, and/or contractor can help you accomplish your goals. We say *can* because, depending on the state of the existing space, your budget, and your concept, you may want to perform many of the functions these pros provide on your own (or skip them entirely). But whether your restaurant is upscale, fine dining, casual, or quick service, these professionals can help you make choices to deliver a consistent experience throughout your establishment.

If you're taking over an existing successful restaurant, consider whether you want to change the look at all. If the design is working, consider how the décor benefits the atmosphere and decide whether your changes are improvements or may negatively impact your diners' expectations. Change is good, but too much of a good thing can be bad.

Anytime you deal with consultants or other contract workers, get the *detailed* terms of your agreement in writing. Always have a timeline for finishing work, with a financial penalty if not completed on time. Every day their schedules lag is a day that you're not open, not bringing in revenue, and not turning a profit. Be fair with them, but don't let them run the show. You're the customer, and your business is affected by how well they run theirs.

Be prepared to be the mediator if you're working with more than one of the folks in the following sections. They may all have different priorities, but you should have the final say.

Drawing out the designers

Look for a designer who can implement your vision — someone who can hear your thoughts and turn them into the restaurant of your dreams. Give the designer a budget and your vision and see what she can come up with. Or have several designers compete with each other by asking them to present sketches and bid on the job before you make a selection.

Make sure that the designer coordinates her work with any architects and contractors; the last thing you want is the beautiful fireplace to bellow smoke into the dining room because the new flue didn't make it to the contractor's to-do list.

Here are a few tips on finding a designer:

- ✔ Contact the American Society of Interior Designers (www.asid.org) for members in your area.

- ✔ Check out pictures of restaurants in trade magazines. Search for designs you like. Often the designer is listed, but you can contact the restaurant or the magazine for details if the designer isn't listed.

  Don't end your search with trade magazines. Consumer magazines, such as *Bon Appétit,* your local entertainment magazine, and so on, all do stories on restaurants, usually with pictures of their interiors and exteriors. Architectural trade magazines can also be good choices.

- ✔ Look in the phone book for designers in your area. Many take out large ads that give you information about the services they offer.

- ✔ The National Restaurant Association has a list of restaurant designers (and other suppliers) on its Web site, www.restaurant.org/business/.

Coming up with contractors

Basically, *contractors* supervise construction work at your site. A good general contractor can spot practical flaws in the design and suggest work-arounds. If your designer wants to remove a wall, your contractor should know whether it's load bearing and be able to suggest an alternative, such as adding support columns. If your contractor has restaurant experience, he'll be a huge asset to the process. Contractors should be familiar with all building and fire codes and maybe even health codes related to building issues, such as electrical requirements to maintain cooler temperatures required to hold foods at the proper temperatures while opening and closing walk-in doors all day.

Accessing architects

An architect is like the interior designer, but he deals in the structure of your space rather than the accessories. Many design firms have architects on staff and vice versa. Usually, you just select a single firm, and it provides both types of resources as you need them.

Architects are essential if you're putting a restaurant or other commercial space in what used to be a house or other nontraditional space. They can help you reinforce the floors to hold commercial equipment, widen stairs if necessary (for traffic flow and safety reasons), and make sure that your restrooms are up to code as well as aesthetically pleasing.

If you're located in a historic area, an architect familiar with your neighborhood can help assure that your design is consistent with integrity of the neighborhood. Preemptively plan your design with the neighborhood in mind. If you don't, you could get tied up in bureaucratic meetings and other red tape and end up where you should have started: with a harmonious design.

Getting the scoop on potential pros

These professionals are only as good as the projects they complete on time, on budget, and to the agreed-upon specifications. Check references, look at completed projects, and talk with satisfied clients. Here are a few ideas:

✔ If you go into a restaurant and love the ambience, ask the manager or owner whether he'd recommend the designer. If the design is great but you find out that the designer is habitually late or a bit flaky, you may want to keep looking. But always take this advice with a grain of salt. You don't want to be too cynical, but consider the manager's motivation for helping you if you're going to be a competitor.

✔ The Internet can help you make your first steps toward finding an architect, designer, or a contractor. Using Web sites may be more helpful as a way to rule out certain businesses rather than a way to actually choose a designer. Use Web sites to compile a list of a few firms you'd like to interview and collect bids from. Look at Web sites of restaurants similar to your concept. If they have pictures of the interior and exterior of the restaurant, use them to virtually visit their restaurant. If you like what you see, ask who the designer is.

Never base your decision entirely on what you see on the Internet. Anyone can design a site with flashy graphics and a fake client list. Check the references and confirm with clients who had projects similar to yours.

✔ Check your potential contract employees out with the Better Business Bureau. Doing so seems like a small thing, but it can make a huge difference. If you find out that they left the last three clients high and dry with no completed design, think twice before signing on the dotted line.

✔ If a contractor claims to be a member of a particular organization, check it out. Professional trade organizations often license their members.

Thinking Outside the Box — the Exterior

The exterior sets the tone for the interior and atmosphere. The exterior of your restaurant is your first impression to the public. Depending on what it looks like, potential diners may never make it through the front doors. Take your exterior seriously, or you risk failure before you start.

Here are a few points to ponder regarding your exterior:

✔ **Announce the concept with appropriate logos and signage:** Think about what works for your concept. Do you need signs that people can see (and read) from miles away? Are you located in an urban area with lots of foot traffic and in need of eye level signage?

One of our (Heather's and Andy's) favorite Mexican joints announces its presence to the world with a huge neon red pepper on the roof. (As a toddler, our daughter couldn't pronounce its name, and the whole family still calls it the Pepper restaurant in her honor.) A national chain of seafood restaurants publicizes each and every location with a glowing red lobster, even in Times Square in New York. Both restaurants want to draw in the masses with signs, specials, and a festive atmosphere.

On the other extreme, a world-class fine-dining restaurant in Chicago has minimal signage — only the chef's signature T on a plaque outside the door. If you don't know what you're looking for, you'll miss it completely. This signage matches the owner's goals, the restaurant's atmosphere, and the diners' expectations. It contributes to the exclusivity and understated elegance that the restaurant consistently achieves.

✔ **Fit in:** When designing the exterior of the restaurant, be sensitive to the neighborhood. If the neighborhood is full of restored Victorians and remodeled stone and brick row houses, don't panel your exterior with galvanized tin, wagon wheels and a life-sized sculpture of an Angus steer just because you're using a Texas barbecue concept.

✔ **Consider how guests will enter and exit your restaurant:** If you have tables near your entrances and exits, make sure that diners sitting there are comfortable. If you operate in a seasonally cold climate even part of the year, consider installing a second set of doors at the main entrance to keep the wind chill to a minimum. Set out floor mats to prevent slips and falls during rainy or snowy weather.

✔ **Decide how much of the outdoors you want indoors, and vice versa:** Outside noise from traffic and weather affects your atmosphere. Do you want to be able to open windows (or even move walls) on sunny spring days? If you have outdoor seating, is it an extension of the inside, or a completely different space? Maybe your outside dining is more casual, with all-weather furniture, awnings, and logoed umbrellas.

If you're planning outdoor seating, check to see whether you need a permit or any special or separate licenses. Permits are required in many areas. You may need a separate liquor license for an outdoor service bar. (Check out Chapter 8 for more info on permits and licenses.)

✔ **Keep it clean:** As smoking in public places decreases in popularity (and legality), more diners smoke outdoors, usually right outside a restaurant. If you keep ashtrays handy, make sure that you maintain them as needed. Pick up any trash in your parking area or landscaping. Find out whether ordinances in your area require a certain cleaning schedule. In some urban areas with lots of foot traffic, owners must wash the sidewalk in front of their stores at least once each day.

✔ **Decide how delivery and service people will enter the restaurant:** Do you have a separate service entrance or are deliveries coming through the front door? If it's separate, is it a secured entrance with a bell or maybe a video camera? Who has the key? Make sure that you control this entrance for security purposes.

If you share any common areas with your neighbors, make sure that they also maintain their responsibilities. Even if it's not your property, it's close to you and reflects on you and the neighborhood. Choose your neighbors wisely. For more on choosing the right spot for your restaurant, check out Chapter 7.

Laying Out the Interior

Your diners spend more time here than anywhere in your establishment. They relax in your bar. They wait for a table in your lobby. They read a menu and enjoy a meal in your dining room. They freshen up in your restrooms. Each area performs a different function, but they all must work together to deliver the same consistent experience.

Here are some questions to ask yourself when deciding how to lay it all out:

✔ How will your bar and restaurant affect each other? Will your bar be a service for your restaurant diners, or do you plan on doing independent bar business? The clientele can be very different for each, so consider creating a barrier, either a fixed barrier (like a wall) or a movable barrier (planters or a fish tank), if you want to keep them separate.

✔ Do you allow smoking in your restaurant? If you have a separate smoking section, think about where you want to place it. It probably shouldn't be right below a balcony that has nonsmoking seating, because the smoke will rise. Also, consider investing in some smoke eaters. *Smoke eaters* are commercial air filtering systems that "clean" smoke, allergens, and odors from the air. Installing these devices is a much better choice than relying on open doors or windows — you can avoid letting in nasty vermin with the fresh air, and you can maintain a more stable, comfortable air temperature.

Some counties, townships, and municipalities don't allow smoking in bars or restaurants in their jurisdiction. Know your local laws.

Allowing space for the flow

The flow of service in your establishment has a lot to do with the design and layout. The term *flow of service* means keeping service going at the pace and schedule that you've determined fits your concept. It's keeping guests flowing in and out of the restaurant at the right pace and continually producing food to flow out to the dining room quickly and harmoniously from the kitchen. Consider these points:

✔ Think about how your food flows into the dining room and how the dirty dishes flow out. Sometimes a side avenue for the dirty stuff lends itself to a better atmosphere for diners.

✔ Determine the paths diners will take to get to their seats, your bar, the restrooms, and so on. Make sure the paths are clear and easy to navigate. Minimize tight areas that would cause a guest to squeeze through or require them to move chairs or other furniture to move freely around the restaurant.

✔ If you offer food prepared or finished beside diners' tables (like mashing avocado with spices for the perfect guacamole or wrapping Chinese pancakes around moo shu pork), leave adequate floor space for it in your layout and logistical planning. If you need to move a cart around the dining room to prepare a Caesar salad at the table, you need plenty of aisle space to maneuver your cart, plus space to stand next to it and prepare the dish. And if you have low ceilings, you may want to rethink your idea about serving flaming dishes like bananas Foster. Safety first!

Keeping your kitchen in mind when you design

A new trend in restaurants is for kitchens to be partially or fully open to public view. As a result, kitchens now need to be a more important part of the interior design of the restaurant, meaning that more interior designers are more involved with restaurant kitchen design. But in most cases, their decisions are secondary to those of the kitchen designer, who's charged with creating an efficient, workable kitchen. A kitchen, no matter how open, isn't technically part of the front of the house, but the design matters here more than ever.

Building your floor plan

Check out Figures 10-1 and 10-2 for layout ideas. In both examples, the dining rooms, kitchen, and restrooms are equally sized. But the key differences can improve traffic flow and layout.

- Tough-to-seat tables are usually located near doors or heavily trafficked paths. We've marked these tables with an X in Figures 10-1 and 10-2. The placement of the front door and the host desk in one corner, rather than in the middle of the front wall, cuts down on the number of "bad" tables around the host desk. This layout helps cut down on traffic moving from the front door through the dining room to tables.

- Positioning the bar along a wall rather than in the middle of the restaurant cuts down on traffic around the bar. Check out the partition between the bar and the dining room in Figure 10-1 for extra traffic-flow control.

- Locate the service entrance in the kitchen rather than in the dining room. At some point you'll get an untimely delivery during the middle of the lunch rush. Running it through the dining room isn't an option. Plus, you can save some wear and tear to your dining room carpets if you accept all deliveries through a back entrance.

- Place bathrooms in a corner so you don't lose space on both sides of them. And avoid placing tables near them when possible. Seating people in these tables is tough because people line up outside, making the guests seated nearby uncomfortable. Also, whenever possible, make more space in the women's room than in the men's room. You won't be sorry.

Arrange your tables so that you can easily create and take apart larger tables. Booths are nice, but you can't really move them around. For flexibility's sake, use mostly tables rather than booths.

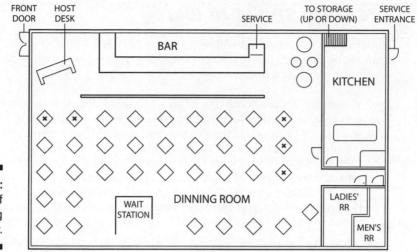

FRONT DOOR HOST DESK SERVICE TO STORAGE (UP OR DOWN) SERVICE ENTRANCE

BAR

KITCHEN

DINNING ROOM

WAIT STATION

LADIES' RR

MEN'S RR

Figure 10-1:
Example of good dining flow.

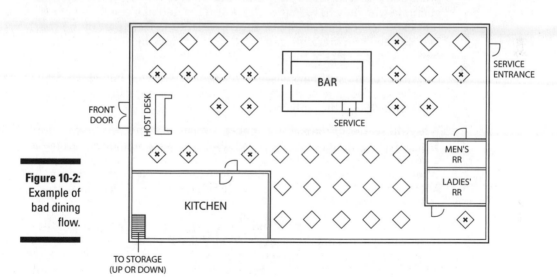

FRONT DOOR HOST DESK BAR SERVICE SERVICE ENTRANCE

MEN'S RR

LADIES' RR

KITCHEN

TO STORAGE (UP OR DOWN)

Figure 10-2:
Example of bad dining flow.

Creating space to wait

Hopefully, your restaurant will be so successful that you'll have more diners than tables at some time each day. Consider these ideas when you're deciding how much space to create for waiting:

✔ Where are people going to wait to be seated? Decide how much space you're going to allot to a waiting area, lobby, and bar. Decide what you want them to do while they're waiting. Should they admire your décor (or other interesting stuff to look at) or get a drink or appetizer? Should they have menus and wine lists to read? Will you offer cocktail service (service by a server at tables next to the bar), or will patrons get their own drinks from the bar? If video games fit your concept, do you offer them as a way to pass the time? How do you ensure that people are comfortable and that the thermostat is set at the right temperature?

✔ Where do people store their stuff? Are you located near or in a transportation hub (like an airport, train station, and so on) with a traveling clientele who may have luggage? Are you located in a geographic area that experiences cold, rainy, or snowy weather at least part of the year? People need to hang coats and weather gear close by. Are you going to devote space to a coat room?

✔ Do you want guests hanging around? Are you planning on being a take-out place, or do you want a restaurant where people want to come early, relax, and take in the ambience?

✔ Who will seat your diners? If you need a hostess stand, leave space for it and all the equipment involved, including menus, telephones, pagers, a computer, a reservation book, pencils, breath mints, toothpicks, and whatever else is essential for your operation. See the section "Setting Up A Reservation System," later in this chapter, for tips on getting all the necessities together.

If you don't have a hostess stand, diners usually take this as a sign that they will have to seat themselves. A centralized menu (see Chapter 9 for details) and a cashier may be other clues. Some restaurants allow the wait staff to seat patrons and then serve them as well. Many restaurants simply have a sign that says, "Please wait to be seated," which means that diners don't have to guess about what to do.

Nothing says *uncomfortable* from a customer's perspective like walking in the door to a restaurant and not knowing what to do. Make sure that the hostess stand is visible to all guests entering, even when the restaurant is very busy. By doing so, you keep your guests moving and the cash register ringing. Whatever your decision, make sure that it's obvious what the customers should do, either wait to be seated or seat themselves.

Keeping Service Support Close

Staff support is basically anything the staff needs to do their job and to provide the best possible guest service. Depending on your concept, you'll likely need at least one wait station and a few POS (or point of sale, meaning computers to order food and drinks) stations in your restaurant. The secret to good use of space in this area of the restaurant is efficiency. Keep everything you need to complete a task close at hand. Keep coffee cups and teaspoons near the coffee pot, glasses near the ice well, and so on.

For the following reasons, don't be tempted to combine your POS and your wait station:

✔ Your POS is electrical, and you want to avoid spilling ice water, tea, sticky sodas, and so on, on its components and backup supplies, such as printer ribbons and paper refills.

✔ You don't want servers waiting to ring up orders in the way of servers trying to get drinks to tables.

✔ You run the risk of waiters congregating, hanging around, talking, and holding up walls for you.

You want to keep service, and bodies, moving and flowing, not getting in each other's way. If you have to combine these stations, make sure that there's some sort of physical barrier, such as a partition, to divide the space and minimize the congestion.

Wait station

The wait station is the supply area for the FOH staff. They make and pour their nonalcoholic drinks here and may clean and restock the dining room tables from here. The wait station should contain anything that servers need to do their job. Here's the short list of things that you should include in your wait station:

✔ Coffee station, including the machine, pots, warmers, coffee, filters, teaspoons, and cups

✔ Reach-in cooler, stocked with milk, cream, half-and-half, and butter

✔ Soda station, including glassware, ice well with cover and scoop, and straws

✔ Iced tea station, including tea machine, lemons, ice, glassware, and spoons

✔ Hot tea supply, including tea bags, lemons, teaspoons, cups, and saucers

✔ Wine buckets

- Breadbaskets
- Extra linens, including napkins, tablecloths, and a few bar towels
- Sanitizer bucket, to clean and disinfect spills
- Clean china, silverware, and glassware (usually not barware)
- Carryout containers
- Ashtrays and matches, if your restaurant allows smoking
- Trash can
- Oil and vinegar cruets, a pepper mill, and any other condiments that *float* (meaning items that aren't on the tables but a guest might need on occasion)

Depending on the size and layout of your restaurant, you may need additional, or *satellite,* wait stations. A satellite wait station is usually smaller than the main station and contains less stuff. For example, your main wait station may have the coffee machine, while a satellite station may have only a warmer to keep already brewed coffee warm. It also probably won't have a reach-in cooler or plumbing. Satellites are designed to keep a few essentials at the ready but not take the place of the main station.

No restaurant rule says that you can have only one wait station, though. If you have the space, budget, and a logistical challenge, a second (or third) full wait station may help you solve it. If your staff has to use stairs to get from your kitchen to your diners, an extra station on the dining floor might really help. Or if you do an equal amount of indoor and outdoor dining, you might consider a second station close to your patio, or even a rolling portable station that you can bring inside when you close your patio.

POS station

Your POS (point of sale) system is the computerized system for ordering food and drinks. The system may consist of individual computers, or it may be dummy terminals connected together to a single computer in the office. At a minimum, each terminal allows a server to enter food orders, which are automatically sent and printed at the stations that prepare the items and to the expediter (the person in charge of the kitchen on a given night — check out Chapter 11 for details). Drink orders are automatically sent to the bar. Servers also prepare and finalize checks to present to diners in these stations.

If your budge allows it, we recommend having one POS terminal for every three servers on the floor per shift.

Your POS supply list is a little longer than you might think:

- **Backup ink cartridges:** Keep at least one ink cartridge in the POS station.

- **Check folders:** A check folder is the plastic or "pleather" holder that you present a guest's check in. You can usually get these from your credit card companies. Make sure that you have enough extras for servers to keep their working tickets in. The folders really help them stay organized.

- **Credit card imprinter:** Computerized credit card systems occasionally die, so it's good to keep these dinosaurs (and their corresponding paperwork) on hand for emergencies. Keep a list of the credit card companies handy as well, so you can call for a verification of charges. Servers can get an authorization code from the credit card companies and manually write it on the paperwork in case of a dispute later on.

- **Credit card machine:** Often this is just a swipe pad connected to the terminal. But if your system requires a separate machine, make sure to allot space for it.

- **Extra paper for the printer:** Store extra rolls of paper nearby for mid-shift changes.

- **Manual backup checks:** Computers are great — when they work. Don't get caught with your apron down; keep a supply of manual checks (with multiple carbons) on hand for emergencies. Match up the carbons at the end of the night to account for any tickets that may have gotten "lost" without being paid for.

- **Operation manuals for the POS and the printer:** Manuals are extremely helpful for new employees and veterans alike.

- **POS terminal:** This is the actual screen that servers use to process orders.

- **Printers:** A printer is attached to the system to print credit card receipts and copies of checks to present to diners.

If your staff handwrites orders and doesn't use a computerized system for ordering, you can disregard this supply list. Instead, you need only check holders, checks, and a central cashier. Make sure that you set up some kind of inventory and accounting of your check numbers so that guest checks don't "disappear." This loophole can be a slow leak of revenue that adds up quickly.

Computers are great tools for keeping track of these kinds of things, checks, money, and so on. If you're intimidated by the thought of it, check with other restaurant owners in your area to find a reputable hospitality software salesperson. She can demonstrate how a computerized system can benefit even small operations. (And check out Chapter 15 for more on the technical details of POS systems.)

Tabletop settings

Think of the tabletop settings as little self-service mini wait stations. They're made up of all the stuff your diners will need to comfortably make it through a meal. As with most things in this business, what shows up at your tables is based on your concept. There's no right or wrong answer. We've seen it all, ranging from a single linen napkin on the simple side of the spectrum to a pound o' individual butter containers, a roll of paper towels, and a galvanized bucket full of silverware on the other. You want to provide guests with the tools and condiments they need without encroaching too much on the eating area.

The tabletop is an extension of your concept. If you're a fine-dining establishment (with prices to match), your diners expect good linens, heavy silverware, and great glassware waiting when they arrive. If you're a family restaurant, they expect to find the familiar sweetening selection (the blue, the pink, and the white) and probably ketchup, salt, and pepper. Latin-themed and Japanese places often include their preferred pepper sauce and soy sauce selections, respectively, on the table.

Setting Up a Reservation System

Often, a diner's first direct communication with a member of your staff is via telephone. The diner may be calling about menu offerings or business hours, and will likely ask about reservations. Make the most of this opportunity by training anyone who answers the phone in basic phone etiquette and spend some time educating them on your reservation policy.

You can't stress enough that anyone answering the phone must be friendly, informative, and helpful. If people are treated with any kind of negative attitude, a harried voice, or lack of respect, they will not appreciate it. One restaurateur in New York has a centralized phone line for all of his restaurants, and two or three people do nothing else but answer the phones, answer questions, and take reservations. Spending this kind of time on customers pays off.

Decide whether you want to take reservations. More than just about anything else we cover in this book, this is a personal choice. There is no right or wrong answer to this question. Many places take only customers with reservations (sometimes months in advance), and others don't take any reservations at all — ever. If you take reservations and people stand you up, you lose revenue. At many exclusive restaurants, diners provide a deposit via a credit card to reserve the table. If the diners don't show up, their credit card is charged a standard amount.

If you decide to take reservations, you must do it well. You probably won't get a second chance with customers if you disappoint them. People expect their table to be waiting when they get there if they've made a reservation.

Here's a quick list of the basic supplies you'll need to get your system started:

- ✔ Clipboard and wait list
- ✔ Pens and pencils
- ✔ Phones
- ✔ Podium
- ✔ Reservation book

You can add convenience to your system with a few technological advances:

- ✔ **Computer:** Keep track of reservations and estimate wait times. People may argue with your hostess, but they won't argue with a computer. Many computerized reservation systems are available.

- ✔ **Online reservation system:** Some third-party systems, like www.opentable.com, process reservations for you and integrate their system with yours. You usually pay a fee for this service, so read the fine print.

- ✔ **Pagers:** These personal, hand-held devices alert customers when their tables are ready.

If you don't take reservations, have the overflow space to keep customers there while they're waiting. If not, people probably won't stick around, at least not until you've established yourself. Check out the section "Creating space to wait," earlier in this chapter, for tips on allocating this space.

Here are some tips for taking reservations:

- ✔ Reserve at least one table for special guests. You never know when one of your financiers, the bank managers, the restaurant critic you've been dying to impress, or Brad and Jen may stop in for a quick bite.

- ✔ Get a phone number when you take the reservation. Confirm the reservation with your diners the day before. Doing so is a great way to add a personal touch to their experience *and* protect against revenue loss from patrons who made other plans.

- ✔ Make sure that you have enough phone lines. If customers are calling your restaurant and the line is constantly busy, they will give up on it. A few may want to get in more, but most people will go down the street. If your manager is on the line talking to the ad guy, the chef's ordering on another, and your hostess is talking to a boyfriend, how many other lines do you have to take a phone call? Consider getting an intercom system on your phones to ease the flow of intra-restaurant communication. Also, limit personal phone calls to emergencies only.

✔ Consider getting voice mail or a message machine. Make the most of your message by giving directions, your hours, seasonal promotions, and the reservation number if it's different from the main number.

One twist on the reservation concept that's gaining popularity, particularly in casual restaurants, is call-ahead seating. It falls somewhere between a reservation and walking in the door and placing your name on a waiting list. When a person is ready to leave his house, he calls the restaurant to place his name on the waiting list. Basically, the guest shaves the driving time from his home to the restaurant off the wait time. Some restaurants hold the table for a certain amount of time as a courtesy, while others give it away immediately if the diners aren't in the restaurant when their name is called.

Reviewing Restrooms

Restrooms used to be a place to rest and refresh. Nowadays, people usually get in and get out. Decide whether you want employees to share the restroom used by your diners. Also decide whether you want your bathroom open to the public or reserved for customers and staff. Keeping the restrooms solely for guests can be difficult because you risk alienating potential customers.

If you have public telephones, locate them near the restrooms. Diners expect to see them here. Make sure that all your facilities are in line with ADA (Americans with Disabilities Act) code (`http://www.usdoj.gov/crt/ada/adahom1.htm`) and are fully handicapped accessible. Check the local code and ordinances when you get your permits.

Providing public facilities

Restrooms are an extension of the front of the house. You must spend just as much attention on maintaining these areas as you do on your dining room. Make appropriate supplies available, including (at a minimum) toilet paper, paper towels, soap, hot and cold running water, and plenty of trash containers. If you have the space, install diaper-changing areas in both the women's *and* men's room because dads share the responsibilities these days.

Conduct regular restroom checks to confirm that your facilities are clean, tidy, and in proper working order. If you want a constant presence in the restroom, consider hiring an attendant. Guests might appreciate the extra service and amenities. An attendant usually offers cologne, hairspray, and a nice selection of hand lotion. But customers may resent the feeling that they need to leave a tip. Decide what's best for your concept and clientele.

Whatever choice you make about maintaining your restrooms, make sure, at a minimum, that you have a schedule for checking it, a person assigned to do it (usually a porter, busboy, or hostess), and good follow-through.

Decide whether you have room for a lounge area. If you're drawing in families, a couch in your restroom is a nice feature for nursing moms or older kids waiting on moms and dads to finish up with younger siblings.

A full-length mirror is a nice addition to the restroom, especially if formal attire is standard at your place. Diners can confirm that all's well before returning to their table.

Earmarking areas for employees

Providing separate restrooms for your staff is a good idea. You can post staff notes and reminders on doors where everyone will see them at some time or another. You'll need to stock the basics in the employee restroom, including soap, hand sanitizer, paper towels, and toilet paper. Make sure hot and cold running water are available at all times.

At a minimum, you must post a sign stating something like this: "Employees must wash hands before returning to work." Depending on your staff, consider getting a bilingual sign. If your employees share a restroom with guests, the sign must go in that restroom. With a separate facility, you can add additional information, like the proper hand-washing technique diagram in Chapter 18. And you may want to include a friendly reminder that you won't tolerate any food or drink in the area.

If you take the next step and add a locker room to the employee facilities, keep the following things in mind:

- The locker room is not a place to hang out. Employees should change into or out of their uniform and move along.

- The locker room is a self-policing area. Make sure that the staff knows that the condition of the room is up to them. They have to clean it themselves.

- You can't post cameras or conduct locker searches. Employees legally have an expectation of privacy when using these facilities.

✔ Food and drink aren't allowed in the locker room. If you don't implement this policy from the get-go, the locker room will become packed full of dirty dishes and glassware. The next thing you know, it's packed full of pests (of the four-legged variety).

✔ Recommend that employees put dirty uniforms in the laundry hamper as soon as they take them off and then immediately place tomorrow's clean uniform in their locker. This system prevents employees from rushing when they report for work and keeps the dirty laundry from soiling the clean.

Chapter 11

Setting Up the Back of the House

• •

• •

Setting up the back of the house is even more important than setting up your dining room. The *back of the house,* or BOH, is any area of your restaurant that a guest can't normally see. If the dining room is the face of the restaurant, the kitchen is the heart. And how it works greatly affects the finished product that guests do see, including how long it takes their food to get to the table and what condition the food is in when it gets there. In this chapter, we reveal the first thing you need to consider when creating the back of the house — your menu and how it affects your kitchen. Then we cover the basics of layout, give you some tips on designing from scratch and dealing with an existing kitchen, and offer ideas on the kitchen equipment you need.

Planning a Kitchen with the Menu in Mind

Which came first, the menu or the kitchen? It's tough to say, because you can't have one that works without the other. And you can't be successful without both. Your menu and kitchen should be in perfect harmony or at least on the same page of the same book. Whether you're designing your kitchen from scratch or working with an existing kitchen, you need to figure out how your kitchen will run based on the menu you're serving in order to set it up right. (See Chapter 9 for more on composing your menu.)

Look at your menu item by item and determine what equipment you'll need to prepare it, store it, and serve it, from beginning to end. (The "Reviewing the basic kitchen stations" and "Taking control of your prep," sections later in the chapter can help.) Make a list like the example in Table 11-1 of menu items and the related equipment and stations you need to prepare those items.

Table 11-1	Equipment and Stations Needed in Kitchen	
Menu Item	*Station/Area*	*Purpose*
Oysters Rockefeller	Walk-in cooler	Store oysters until ready to shuck and serve; hold finished filling until needed
	Reach-in cooler	Store a few preshucked orders
	Prep area	Prepare filling, shuck oysters
	Oven or broiler	Finish stuffed oysters to order
	Expo	Check plate, garnish dish, consolidate order
Fried calamari	Freezer	Store calamari
	Prep area	Cut calamari to desired size, if necessary
	Fryer	Bread and finish calamari to order
	Expo	Check plate, garnish dish, consolidate order
Chicken Caesar salad	Walk-in cooler	Store lettuce, dressing, and cold plates
	Prep area	Cut or tear lettuce, prepare dressing
	Dry storage	Store canned anchovies
	Grill	Grill chicken breast
	Pantry	Finish salad to order
	Expo	Check plate, garnish dish, consolidate order

After you make your list, take a look at the forecasted menu mix analysis that you created in your business plan. Your *menu mix analysis,* sometimes shortened to *menu mix,* is a report, or in the case of a forecast, a prediction, of what menu items sell in what quantities. Among other things, it tells you how many orders of Oysters Rockefeller, Fried Calamari, and Chicken Caesar Salad you sell in a given shift. (Check out Chapter 20 for tips on creating a menu mix analysis if you don't have one.) Determine which stations will be getting a workout by looking at how many items in a shift will be coming out of each of them. Make sure that busy stations have enough reach-in space, counter space, and so on. Share reach-ins and counter space with less-often used stations. Look for other ways to improve efficiency based on your menu.

Laying Out Your Kitchen

As you design your brand-new kitchen or refurbish your existing one, a single word must be in the top of your mind: flow. How are things going to flow? Imagine your meal from delivery of product to delivery of the dishes to your guests. Picture the wine delivery person carrying a case of wine. Can he pass the dish area without falling, getting wet, and disturbing the dishwashers? Take a look at Figure 11-1 for an example of a kitchen layout with good flow.

Here are some ideas that can help you make sure that your kitchen design is going with the flow:

- Determine which stations are getting the heaviest (and the lightest) workload based on your menu.

- Make sure that you have enough *reach-in coolers* (think of these as the commercial versions of your dorm-room fridge) in the right spots (close to their specific stations) to keep your product at a safe temperature until use. In Figure 11-1, the pastry station (left side) has a three-door reach-in cooler; it's dedicated to products that might otherwise suffer from the constant in and out of the main coolers, and it's isolated from the heat of the hot line. *Fish files* (under-counter refrigeration drawers) are a space-saving way to bring refrigeration to the hot line while conserving space and avoiding the space association problems common with reach-ins.

- Keep your prep area close enough to the line to quickly restock it when needed. Notice in Figure 11-1 that the prep area is located between the main walk-in coolers (produce and meat/dairy) where food flows to the prep tables and then to the line.

- Ensure that your staff can efficiently get dirty plates, pots, and pans off the line and to the dish area. Waiters flow in the "in" door and stop at the dish area. The pot-and-pan shelf is located at the end of the right side of the line for the line cooks to place pans needing a wash.

- Keep the dish and prep workers out of each others' paths during busy shifts. The dish area is separate from the prep area in Figure 11-1.

- Keep the path to the ice machine clear so that bartenders and wait staff have easy access to refill ice wells during peak times. The ice machine in our example could be located along the front wall of the kitchen near the waiter station, with easy access for anyone who needs it.

- The wait staff and bussers should be able to get dirty dishes into the dish pit without falling and without hindering someone else's workflow. Our dish pit is the first stop on the way into the kitchen, with an extended table so waiters won't block the door or anyone else trying to come in.

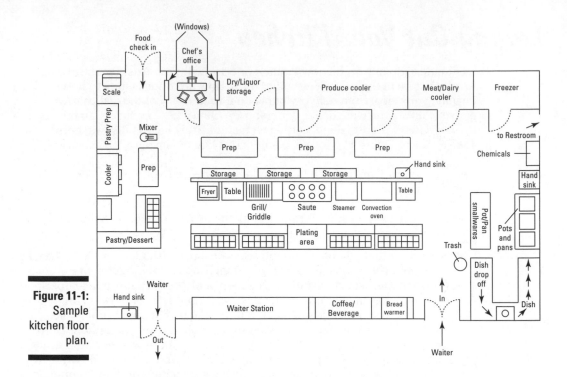

Figure 11-1:
Sample
kitchen floor
plan.

✔ Menu items should flow down the line and to the expo with ease and efficiency. The plating area in Figure 11-1 is located in the middle of the line, so plates come in from sides and through the plating area, for a check with the expo and then out the door.

Work smart, not hard. You and your employees will be on your feet many, many hours each day. Save as many steps as possible by designing an efficient layout. Get expert help if you need it; experts are available who deal specifically with flow and efficiency. Other ways to put experience on your side include:

✔ Turning to a broad-line equipment supplier who carries many types and brands of equipment for free design help. Edward Don is a national supplier of everything you need to get started, including planning guides; in your market, a local firm may also provide these services. You'll buy the equipment anyway, and many suppliers throw in free design help.

Nothing is actually "free." You'll pay for the design help through equipment prices that can be a little higher. See the section "Acquiring Your Kitchen Equipment," later in this chapter. Price the equipment from several sources and check into the cost of a kitchen design consultant to see which way you may come out ahead.

✔ Hiring an experienced general contractor who is familiar with outfitting restaurants and has excellent restaurant references. Not every contractor understands the needs and motivation of a restaurant. The ones who do are invaluable. They can help you get your range hoods working; make sure that you have enough power outlets for your blenders, mixers, food processors, and so on; and keep the plumbing flowing in your favor.

Each of your power outlets should be on a dedicated circuit with a minimum of 20 amps of power. Many restaurant-grade appliances use up most of that allotment, and if you try to plug in two on the same circuit, you'll trip the breaker.

✔ Reviewing your kitchen plans, especially the finishing details, with other restaurateurs. They likely have experience with a variety of setups and can help steer you in the right direction

Reviewing the basic kitchen stations

A *station* is an area of the kitchen designed to accommodate a particular cooking technique. So foods that are fried, like French fries, onion rings, and fried oysters, are prepared at the fryer station. Items that are grilled, like steaks, grilled veggies, and grilled chicken are prepared at the grill station.

A station is defined by the way the food is prepared, not by the kind of food prepared there. The station refers to the main equipment, such as a grill, and the setup and organization of the supplies and products that the cook needs to finish preparing menu items. In the case of a grill, the supplies and products could include the food to be grilled, brushes to clean the grill, side dishes to complete the grill menu item, knives, spatulas, tongs, plateware, and sauces to complete the presentations. Some foods have a variety of cooking techniques. Depending on your menu, a scallop could be grilled, broiled, smoked, steamed, or sautéed. So several stations could prepare scallops.

The *line* is the area of the kitchen where food is prepared, placed on a plate, garnished, and then sent out to the guest. The line is made up of all the stations in the kitchen. When a station receives an order to *fire* an item (cook a dish immediately), it means that a guest has ordered, the server has placed the order with the kitchen, and the kitchen should begin preparing the item.

Grill

The restaurant grill is just a bigger version of the grill you might have in your backyard. A grill is distinguished from equipment like a broiler or oven by the direction of the heat — the heat comes from under the food being cooked. (An oven's heat surrounds food, while a broiler's heat comes from above.)

You can find two basic versions: a *grated grill* (sometimes called a char-broiler) and a *flattop grill*. Depending on your menu, you may have one type of grill, both, or neither. If you're a steakhouse and want to serve steaks with nice little checkerboard grill marks, go for the grated grill. If you're a diner doing grilled ham and cheese and omelets, consider a flattop grill. If you have room for both, you can be more flexible with your menu offerings.

At the grill station, you need the following:

- ✔ Grill (surprise!)
- ✔ Cooler for your entrée items (like salmon, kebabs, chicken, and steaks for a grated grill, or eggs, pancake batter, and so on for a flattop)
- ✔ Seasonings (salt, pepper, signature spice blends, and so on)
- ✔ Grill brush
- ✔ Oil rag (to wipe the grill and keep it from sticking)
- ✔ Water bottle (to squirt down flames)

Sauté

This is the area you typically see in the open kitchen setup because it's usually busy and exciting. During busy times, several cooks work this station, preparing everything from pasta to poached fish, from sauces to sautéed spinach. If it's cooked in a sauté pan, it's cooked here. Next to sauté pans, tongs are the sauté cook's (sometimes shortened to "sauté") best friend. Sauté cooks usually use a multiburner range to prepare multiple dishes at a time.

If you have a sauté station in your restaurant, you typically want your most experienced cooks working this station, for a few reasons:

- ✔ Dishes cook quickly here, and you need people with speed and consistency to turn them out on time.
- ✔ The sauté station is often responsible for the most delicate, carefully prepared dishes on the line, so the items have to be finished with expertise in order to ensure a quality product.
- ✔ Sautéed items (like pasta dishes, saucy appetizers, and sometimes the veggie of the day) are usually popular and/or high-volume items, so you need people who can keep up with the pace for the entire shift.
- ✔ A sauté cook often tastes a dish to confirm consistent seasoning and must do so according to health regulations (this means taste-testing with a clean spoon, which must be sent to the dish area immediately after use — no double dipping!). An experienced sauté cook can take the proper steps to protect you and your customers from violations.

The European sauté station is vastly different from the American system described here. The American sauté system involves anything cooked on a gas burner. The Europeans break up this station into anywhere from three to fourteen different stations, each specializing in smaller pieces of the menu.

Fryer

The fryer is an extremely versatile station. You can use multiple fryers in a single station to finish dishes and supply other stations with a continuous stream of *parcooked* (partially cooked) product to stay ahead during busy times. Look for pressure fryers with lids or quick recovery fryers to speed up frying time if you're planning on doing lots of fried appetizers, or *apps,* and entrees. Always opt for a fryer with a working — and calibrated (accurate) — thermostat so that you can monitor the temperature and fry times on your menu items to get a consistent-quality product.

Several different types of fryers are available, including those designed to boil water. They're great for boiling seafood or pasta, or blanching vegetables. If you want to boil water in your fryer, purchase one designed for this purpose. You can damage the heating element in standard electric fryers by boiling water in them. Ask your equipment rep for the specifics on your particular model. If you're taking over an existing location with a fryer, have a reputable serviceperson look over all your equipment and confirm that you can use your fryer to boil water.

Other things that might be part of the fry stations include the fry baskets (for easy retrieval of items), plateware, breading, sauces, sauce cups, a skimmer for removing errant fries, a small reach-in cooler, a reach-in freezer, and anything else your fry cook needs to get the job done.

Broiler

Broilers are usually used for a short burst of high-intensity heat from above. You might use a broiler for melting Gruyère cheese on top of French onion soup, melting cheese on nachos, or providing that super crispy layer on an apple cobbler. A cheese melter is a lower-intensity broiler that really warms rather than cooks food. As always, your concept dictates what size broiler and what heat intensity you'll need.

Oven

An oven serves a few different roles in the kitchen. It can be a plate warmer or a sauté pan preheater and can actually cook food. The oven station can consist of any variety of ovens:

  ✔ **Combination oven:** If your budget allows, you can combine your oven and a steamer by using a combination oven. These freestanding cabinet-style ovens combine dry heat and moist heat, convection or conventional cooking, plus the ability to act as a stand-alone steamer.

- **Convection oven:** This type of oven uses a fan to circulate heat for quicker, more even cooking.

- **Conveyer oven:** The perfect choice for sandwiches and pizzas, the conveyor oven is usually an infrared heat source, heating food from both above and below. You control the cooking time by adjusting the belt speed and the temperature, and by where you place the food on the conveyor belt.

- **Rotary oven:** This large piece of equipment (the size of a small room) holds five to seven large trays that turn like a Ferris wheel. It may work for you if you're doing house-made bread, pastries, and desserts.

Your menu and your concept determine what type of oven you need in your restaurant. If you're a pizza joint, the majority of your menu items will likely come out of the oven. You need a different oven than the Chinese takeout place down the street does. Tailor your choice of oven to your menu needs.

Some restaurants don't have an oven station. Instead, they have an oven in the prep area and hold the already prepared food on the line, in the steam table (see the later section on steam tables). An Italian restaurant, for example, may use ovens in the prep area to bake lasagnas, roast large cuts of meat, or braise osso buco over a period of hours. Then it holds the items in batches (with the rest refrigerated) in the steam table on the line for service.

Pastry

The pastry station is typically reserved for dessert items. If your concept doesn't call for a pastry chef or even a pastry station, you can roll desserts into the pantry station. Alternatively, your wait staff can be in charge of *plating* their own desserts (putting them on a plate for service) in a station in the kitchen or in a wait station set up for this activity.

Steam table

The steam table is basically a huge chafing dish that holds items that have been previously cooked and keeps hot foods hot until they're ordered. The steam table is located on the line. Large and small metal pans fit into various configurations to make up the compartments of the steam table. For example, if you're a family restaurant or cafeteria, your line may consist of a steam table full of vegetables, roasted potatoes, braised meats, fried chicken, and so on, all completely cooked but held at the right temperature until a diner orders them. In this sort of concept, your prep area is where dishes are prepared, and then the entrée items are plated on the line.

Pantry

The pantry is the catchall center for cold food and, typically, a true assembly station. Salads, desserts, cold antipasto, unfried spring rolls, gazpacho, and tuna salad sandwiches could all make their appearance from the pantry. Anything to be cooked for the pantry (whether it's apple pie or hard-boiled eggs) must be done before it gets to the pantry. Even the few hot things that may appear in the pantry (warm bacon dressing for spinach salad or hot fudge for sundaes) are usually already prepped and then held nearby.

Expo

The *expo* is short for *expediter*. It's a station (and a person; if you're working expo, you're said to be the expo for that shift) that ensures that all the stations on the line are working in harmony. The expo ensures that all dishes going to the dining room are up to par with your restaurant standards, including presentation, portion sizes, temperature, within the specified time for an order to be prepared, and so on. The expo is the last quality-control check before a dish leaves the kitchen. This station often has some kind of communication tool (commonly a microphone or gopher) with the prep area, so that the expo can call for reinforcements, er, we mean replenishments, during busy shifts. Complete this station with a spindle (a metal stake to "stab" completed tickets), a highlighter, pen or pencils, a wet and a dry towel (for cleaning up plates), and any garnishes your expo might use.

The expo is the communication funnel. He protects the individual stations from things they don't need to know about, like waiters complaining about a missing entrée that should've been sent, side dish requests, and special orders. He sets the priorities for everyone working the line and serves as the kitchen's link to the dining room. If the expediter doesn't know everything that's going on in the restaurant, he isn't in control. Without good info flow, a kitchen can crash and burn at 7 p.m. and still feel the effects at 9 p.m.

Specialty equipment

Your concept may depend on a station or piece of equipment that we don't mention. If you're a casual Indian restaurant, you may need a tandoori oven. If you specialize in wood-fired pizza, you need a wood-burning stove or oven to create those menu delights. And believe it or not, the microwave isn't just for popcorn anymore. Restaurants, especially large casual chains, are increasingly taking advantage of this tool, paired with the power of food science, to ensure quick ticket times and consistent products.

Your menu will determine what equipment *you* need. Purchase, lease, and lay out your restaurant accordingly.

Taking control of your prep

You may have noticed that your average restaurant can get a pasta dish to your table faster than you can boil water at home. We assure you that no witches and wizards are hiding behind the curtain. The masters of the culinary world, whether on TV or at your local deli, rely on the time-honored tradition of *prep* (short for *preparation*) to make quick work of orders as they come into the kitchen.

In fact, most members of the kitchen staff have done some time as a prep cook in their restaurant career. It's a great place to watch and learn if you're interested in pursuing a career in the culinary arts. And in some of the more prestigious kitchens in the world, working prep is an initiation into the culture that is their restaurant. Whether you've painstakingly created 50 pounds of tournée potatoes (little fancy potato footballs), only to see the executive chef turn them into mashed potatoes before your eyes, or you've spent eight hours meticulously separating 300 quail breasts, prep can be a rite of passage.

More commonly, though, prep is just a means to an end — getting a product ready to go so that you can get finished dishes to the table as efficiently as possible. Most prep is done at off-peak times. If you do a busy lunch and dinner business, your prep staff will likely be working early, say, 6 a.m. to 2 p.m., to get the basics done before the lunch rush starts around 11:30. If you're a busy breakfast place, the prep staff may be in even earlier, maybe 2 a.m., and stay until 10 a.m. Consider a few pieces of equipment as you put together your prep area game plan. Read on for the specifics.

Coolers

In the restaurant world, a *cooler* isn't something that you carry your drinks to the park in. *Cooler* is the fancy restaurant lingo for refrigerator. No matter what size the cooler is, it's usually called a cooler. Most restaurants have at least one walk-in cooler (familiarly referred to as the *walk-in*) that's the size of a small, medium, or large room. Many stations have their own reach-in coolers (see the section "Laying Out Your Kitchen," earlier in this chapter) to store prepped food that's finished at the station.

Coolers hold anything perishable, from produce to butter to prepared sauces. All raw food, such as eggs or marinating meat, goes in a cooler. Anything wet, like egg drop soup or Alfredo sauce, goes in a cooler. Any food that isn't canned, dried, or frozen (from fresh fish to fungi) goes in a cooler. Even if you might not refrigerate it in your home (apples, for example), you'll likely refrigerate it here. Your restaurant's concept (and your purveyor's delivery schedule) dictates how many and what size coolers you need. If you're opening a place that deals mostly with canned or prepackaged foods, you may need only a small walk-in and a reach-in. If you depend on daily shipments of perishables, you may not need much refrigerated walk-in storage and can get buy with a single walk-in. If you're part of a franchise that delivers frozen products on a regular schedule, maybe you can get by with a freezer and a couple of reach-ins for the line and a smaller walk-in to thaw frozen products or store thawed products. Take a look at Table 11-1 to help you assess your need for coolers and other restaurant equipment.

Freezers

A freezer is simply a place to keep frozen foods. Freezers range in size from large rooms to smaller chest freezers, ideal for ice cream at a dessert station or backup ice in a service bar. Your concept and menu dictate what size freezer you need. If you pride yourself on serving fresh seafood, you may need only a small freezer area to store things such as French fries and ice cream. If you buy a lot of your food already prepared, a freezer may be an ideal way to save labor and still get a high-quality, consistent product.

When you're figuring out your freezer requirements, don't try to figure in your ice needs with it. Invest in a separate ice machine. You can get free-standing units that produce enough ice to keep up with a very busy restaurant, like the ones in hotel vending areas. Or you can get one that's part of your soda machine setup.

Prep tables

The rows of stainless steel tables known as *prep tables* are essential to a smooth prep shift. You need plenty of work surface and sinks for several members of your staff to prepare multiple items at once in a sanitary environment. For example, in one area, Maria may be washing lettuce for salads. At the same time, James may be slicing and weighing tuna steaks. You don't want these two to get in each other's way. If any of the fish bits get near the lettuce, you create a huge food safety issue (see Chapter 18).

Depending on your volume, you may need separate workspaces for two to eight people to work independently. Consider your prep schedule and par levels when determining how many prep tables you need. *Par levels* are the goal levels you set for each item on your prep list for a given day based on the amount you forecast using for that day. For each shift, you count your food on hand and then prep to your par level. For example, if the par level for clam chowder on Tuesdays is 3½ gallons and you have only ½ gallon on hand, you'll prep 3 gallons that day.

Make sure that the prep tables are at the right prep height, usually a minimum of 36 inches, to ensure comfortable standing while prepping. And leave plenty of space for garbage cans around your prep tables. Prep generates lots of trash, including cans, cartons, and vegetable remnants.

Dry storage

Dry storage is the commercial version of your home pantry — a walk-in storeroom that holds all your dry goods. Any food item that's canned (such as canned tomatoes, oil, and canned pudding), dried (beans or pasta), or shelf-stable (vinegar, margarita mix, or spices) can be stored here. You can also keep other consumables here, like beverage napkins, stir sticks, or candles.

Dry storage can be an organizer's dream or nightmare. Keep your dry storage organized to quickly know what you need to order and stay a step ahead at inventory time. Whenever possible, locate your storage area as close to your delivery door as possible. It saves schlepping time and energy and hopefully will be out of the way of the majority of your prep.

Consider creating a cage in your dry storage area if you keep expensive non-perishables on hand. A *cage* is simply a locked cabinet that can hold your saffron, truffles, caviar, or other expensive items securely. For more on managing inventory and purchasing, check out Chapter 14.

Tilt skillet

A *tilt skillet* is a huge freestanding skillet. It has a handy feature that lets you tilt the skillet (either by means of a manual crank or electric switch) to pour your finished sauce, soup, rice, or whatever into your storage container. You can use it for sautéing, searing, or braising large quantities of foods that don't fit into a conventional pan suitable for use on a range top. For example, you can sear 12 pork loins or 50 chicken breasts at one time, braise 20 osso buco at a time, or poach 100 eggs at a time. It's an indispensable tool for high-volume restaurants that prepare just about anything from scratch in bulk.

If possible, situate your tilt skillet near a grated floor drain to quickly dispose of used liquid, overflows, and spills. If you're opening a new restaurant or remodeling an existing one, build in drains where you need them now. Doing that job later is costly; you not only have to pay additional construction costs, but you actually have to shut down your business for at least a few days. Drains are also handy for easy cleaning of big pieces of equipment. Just clean them out and dump the rinse water onto the floor and down the drain.

Steam kettle

A steam jacketed kettle (the "jacketed" refers to the steam chamber that surrounds the kettle itself) can be as small as 5 gallons or as big as a hot tub. These specialized pieces of equipment use the even heating of superheated steam to evenly cook soups and sauces in volume. A crank system (similar to a tilt skillet explained in the preceding section) allows the contents to be carefully poured into smaller containers for storage. The even heating of a steam kettle is unmatched for preparing things like stocks, long simmered sauces like bordelaise, and chili for you and 500 of your closest friends. Locate your kettle near a grated floor drain for quick cleanup of spills.

Smoker

A smoker is a piece of equipment designed to do a specialized job. A cold smoker uses indirect heat to impart smoky aromas and flavors to the food, thanks to the fragrant wood that fires it. Cold smoking doesn't cook the food; it simply adds the flavor to create items such as smoked salmon or smoky cheeses, including some provolones and cheddars. A hot smoker uses direct heat — a smoke box with fragrant woods — to cook and smoke simultaneously. Barbecued items are often cooked in a hot smoker.

Most restaurants don't have a smoker. If you're a rib place or you specialize in wild game, you may consider investing in one. Because of the extensive time it takes to prepare smoked items, the smoker is not a line station. Items prepared in the smoker are held on the line until ordered by a guest.

If you want to offer the occasional smoked item on your menu, consider finding a vendor who deals in smoked or specialty goods. Smoked salmon is a good example. If you serve smoked salmon, you likely have a vendor that carries it. Save the labor and the equipment costs by purchasing the product.

Mats

Commercial restaurant floors are usually concrete or quarry tile. Standing on these hard surfaces for several hours a day causes stress on knees, leg muscles, and feet. General work processes can make floors wet and greasy. Invest in some well-designed kitchen mats to alleviate fatigue and eliminate slippery floors. Place mats in prep areas, on the line, behind the bar and host podium, and anywhere else people stand for long periods of time.

Working with an Existing Kitchen

Congratulations! You've found a site, and it already has a kitchen. A big piece of your business plan, including start-up costs and equipment is probably based on not needing to invest in a kitchen, because there's one in your space already. But many times, modifying an existing kitchen is more expensive than building a new one. After you figure in the costs of demolition and disposal, running gas lines, and updating the plumbing, ventilation, and fire suppression systems, you could really eat into your budget.

Plumbing is extremely important. Before leasing, have it all checked out, especially the sewage main to the city lines. Kitchens produce a lot of grease and food matter that can clog pipes. We recommend a thorough jet cleaning of all pipes before you open. Nothing kills appetites like backed-up toilets!

Ask yourself these questions before you sign on the dotted line:

- ✔ Is it the kitchen for you and your menu? Does it have the space to accommodate your food? Can you work with the layout to get the flow you need for your menu?

- ✔ Does the existing equipment work? Can you use it? Just because the equipment is there doesn't mean it's not held together by duct tape and coat hangers. Have it inspected by a certified restaurant service pro. If you find that the equipment isn't in top shape and can't be upgraded at the landlord's expense, exclude it from the deal and buy your own.

- ✔ Does the heating, ventilation, and air conditioning (HVAC) system work? A working HVAC system is a necessary asset; one that doesn't work is a liability.

- ✔ Do the wiring and the gas systems meet current building codes? Be wary that in some instances the previous owner may have received a code exemption through a grandfather clause, but now you may have to make major updates to fit in with current codes at your expense.

✔ What's the sale price of the kitchen? If the owner is charging a lot for used equipment, you may be better off starting over with your own.

If you choose to include the equipment in your deal, stipulate in writing that the equipment must be in good working order.

An existing kitchen that has a good flow relative to your concept can save you tens of thousands of dollars. But don't get caught up in the fact that a space already has a kitchen and then alter your concept to match. If you've done the work and created a concept you believe in (and have the numbers to back up your plan), fit the kitchen to your concept — not the other way around.

Going into an existing operation can be a little off-putting at first. You may be expecting something that's as clean as the pristine television kitchen. But look at the space with an eye for storage, immovable equipment like plumbing, the line, and so on. You can't move them, so make sure you can work with it. Don't worry if the kitchen is dirty. Floors can be cleaned, grease removed, and equipment repainted. Don't let the level of dirt and grime affect your decision. Look for floor drains to make floor cleaning easy.

Accepting the things you can't change

Suppose that you find the perfect space with one tiny problem: The kitchen is downstairs, and the dining room is upstairs. In the restaurant business if there's an obstacle, there's always an answer. With some creativity, time, and money, you can usually make it work. The most common obstacles that you'll find and need to address in existing restaurants are the following:

✔ **Stairs:** If you're going to make a two-level situation work, you need to install skid-resistant stair liners and paint the edges highly visible colors in accordance with local safety codes to help keep people from falling. Consider installing dumbwaiters (very small service elevators designed for transporting trays of food and beverages — not people — between floors). An elevator may be another solution.

✔ **Distance from dining room to the kitchen:** If the dining room is too far away from the kitchen, you may have trouble keeping food hot until it gets to the table. Perhaps you can set up satellite food stations, such as a soup station, close to the dining room to keep soup from cooling off on the way to the table.

If servers are regularly too far from the kitchen, they're not available quickly to answer questions from the kitchen or relay guest requests to the kitchen, delaying guest service times. Some places use headset microphones, hand-held-style ordering systems, or even vibrating pagers to assist in long-distance communication. The physical distance between the dining room and the kitchen can add miles to any shift, so consider adding a food runner to help lighten the load, if your budget permits.

✓ **Structural inconveniences:** Is a column located in a place where you want a cooler? You have to find a less convenient spot for your cooler. Is a load-bearing wall blocking your view of part of the dining room? If you can't easily see your diners, make an extra pass through in that part of the dining room to make sure that guests are being properly attended to. Usually, removing these kinds of structural elements isn't economically feasible, so you have to be creative and work around them.

With a little ingenuity, these structural inconveniences can become intriguing parts of your interior space. Coauthor Andy started his career in a Denver restaurant located in what had previously been a bank vault. Knowing that they couldn't remove the 3-foot-thick vault doors, the owners incorporated the design features into the concept and ambience.

Changing the things you can't accept

In some cases, you have to make modifications to your kitchen to make it workable for your concept. If your concept is based on rotisserie meats, for example, your kitchen must accommodate a rotisserie oven. If you're a wood-fired pizza place, you have to have a wood-fired oven and the appropriate vent work and floor supports to go with it. If your concept includes a drive-thru and one doesn't exist, you'll need to create one. If you can't add those things *necessary* for your concept, you have the wrong space.

The special features required for your concept don't need to already be present in your space, but you must be able to add them. Check with your contractor, kitchen design consultant, and landlord for advice (and for permission) on the cost and schedule for the modifications you must make to the space to stay true to your concept. If the modifications are too expensive for your budget, find a new space.

You may have to work with your existing plumbing because changing it is usually cost prohibitive, but you can usually add power where you need it. For example, bringing power in through a drop ceiling with hanging GFCIs (ground fault circuit interrupters) on a retractable pulley can solve the problem, if you're trying to run equipment at a location away from a standard wall outlet.

Look at an equipment solution to infrastructure problems. For example, if your water heater is in the basement and it's having a tough time keeping up through antiquated plumbing, you can buy a dish machine with a *condenser,* which reuses the hot water to save the cost of heating the water and save wear and tear on your hot water heater. Or you can add a water preheater to an existing dish machine. A *preheater* is a reserved source of hot water to make sure your machine is always running at the right temperature — important if you're using a heat-based (rather than chemical-based) sanitizing system.

Consider adding a reverse osmosis water system to your operation. It extends the life of your plumbing and increases the efficiency of your chemicals. Plus you can cook with and serve tasteless, purified water.

Power cleaning

If you start with existing equipment, get it the cleanest it will ever be again. Then establish a regimen to maintain that level of cleanliness, always. See Chapter 18 for more information on keeping things clean.

Getting started

Here are some suggestions on this part of the cleaning job:

- Remove anything that's removable, including smallwares (small equipment items like soup bowls, tongs, and spatulas), plates, mixers, pans, tables, and shelving units, that the previous owner may have left. Decide whether these items are worth keeping or should be replaced, and clean and sanitize each item before putting it into use. As you're cleaning the removables, check for any in need of repair.

- As you're removing items, watch for evidence of vermin (usually along the walls). The signs may include feces or shredded paper. Have an exterminator check inside the walls, particularly in dish and high-moisture areas — the most likely homes for creepy crawlies. Get a jump-start on pests immediately. Playing catch-up is a losing proposition.

- Pay particular attention to cleaning the underside of tables, often overlooked in the cleaning process.

- Check out anything with silicone seams — a possible bacteria breeding ground. Decide whether you can clean the silicone or should reapply it.

- Look at the corners and *coping* (waterproof molding that gradually curves to meet the wall from the floor) to see whether they're sealed to the wall and check for bugs, vermin droppings, and so on.

- Check all gaskets along coolers and ice machines. Gaskets are tough to clean but inexpensive to replace.

- Check for lime scale buildup in plumbing, particularly in the dish area. Lime scale, if left unchecked, can ruin expensive dish machines.

- After you take out all the removables, contract with a reputable cleaning company to power wash and sanitize the entire kitchen, walls, and floors.

A reputable company knows to avoid the equipment and electric outlets and gadgets. But walk the space with the cleaners to reinforce where you don't want water and make sure they understand your expectations.

Putting it back together

After you clean the floors and walls, you need to do the following:

- Reinstall, replace, and reset the tables, smallwares, and equipment according to the flow.

- Break the kitchen into stations appropriate for your concept.

- Reinstall equipment where it makes sense for your operation.

- Start to envision production. Walk through the experience of creating a dish from start to finish. Try to set things up so that cooks have to move as little as possible and can avoid a lot of bending and stooping. Most people are right-handed, so place reach-in coolers with that fact in mind. You won't be 100 percent right about your setup right off the bat, but the closer you can get the first time, the better off you are.

- Now is a great time to set the standard for cleanliness and organization. Take pictures of perfectly setup stations, well-organized storage areas, a clean dish area, and so on. Reference the pictures a week later and a month later as a gauge of how you're doing.

- Integrate a pest management system and set up contracted or internal cleaning procedures.

Acquiring Your Kitchen Equipment

New York has the Bowery. Chicago has Restaurant Row. Most major cities have this kind of restaurant supply street. Whether the products are new or used, you'll likely buy it here. If you're not located in a major city, going to one may be worth the trip, just for the money you can save and for the used equipment, but bring your bartering hat — and do your homework.

Know what equipment you need for your operation. Use Table 11-1 and Figure 11-1 to create a list of the equipment you need to produce the menu you've chosen. Know what it costs new and used. Shop around. Check out equipment Web sites, national companies, local companies, and restaurant equipment auctions. Talk to other people in the business about their good experiences and bad ones. Get names from them about good companies to work with. If they can introduce you to someone specific, you'll be a step ahead. Be savvy. Know when you're getting a good deal and when you're not.

Building a big kitchen is a huge expense. Consider hiring a consultant to advise you about purchasing equipment. Here's what a consultant can do:

✔ Review your concept plan and assist in choosing equipment for your concept. Together, you create a list of the equipment you need, including the quantities of each item, and whether it should be new or used.

✔ Develop a sourcing action plan for those pieces of equipment. The sourcing action plan includes using resources (online, network, and trade pubs) to figure out several sources for each piece of equipment, developing a process for evaluating the different options (manufactures, distributors, used equipment dealers, and so on) for each piece of equipment, and creating a schedule for acquiring the equipment.

✔ Solicit bids for new equipment. Your consultant should also help you evaluate the bids when they come in.

✔ Facilitate purchase of used equipment, including negotiating the purchase price, conducting inspections, clarifying warranties, and scheduling delivery.

In a restaurant situation, the simpler the equipment, the better. For example, skip the equipment that boasts internal sensors. They're virtually useless and just another part that can break.

Looking at leasing

Finding financing for equipment is tough until you're an established high-volume restaurant. But feel free to check with your bank if you need a piece of equipment you really want to purchase.

Leasing equipment has certain advantages. You pay for equipment only for the time you use it. When your lease is up, you get a brand-spanking-new piece of equipment with all the latest gadgets by signing a new lease. And when a piece of equipment breaks, it's not your responsibility to fix it.

Things shouldn't change between the time you talk to your salesperson and the billing department sends you a bill, but sometimes they do. Spell out all the financial details in the agreement so you're not surprised when the bill arrives. Get it in writing and check your invoices.

Here are a few items, in particular, that we suggest you lease:

✔ **Ice machines and coolers:** Both units have relatively short lives. Their motors and condensers work very hard and burn out. They're expensive upfront, and there's virtually no market for used ones. It's better to roll the price over in a lease format for a time, so that when your machine is about to die, your lease will be up, and you'll move on to a new unit.

- **Dish machines:** This equipment is the restaurant version of your home dishwasher. It's very expensive upfront and usually can be leased through your chemical supplier. Some chemical suppliers give you the machine if you buy your products from them.

- **Coffeemakers:** Coffee companies often give you the machine if you buy the coffee from them. You may pay a little more for the product, but this option gives you flexibility and more positive cash flow. Plus if there's a breakthrough technology, you can usually upgrade quickly.

- **Linens:** Lease, don't buy, all your linens, including entry floor mats, uniforms, towels, tablecloths, and napkins. Usually you pay a single bill to have them delivered, stocked, and laundered.

Depending on your volume of purchasing, food suppliers such as U.S. Foodservice, Gordon Food Service, and SYSCO give you a computer with their ordering software that you can use for other business applications. They want to make it as easy as possible for you to place orders with them.

Buying — used versus new

Wheeling and dealing with used equipment can be a lot of fun, but it's no different than buying a car. Be ready, willing, and able to tell the salesperson no and walk out of the store. It's no secret to him or to you (because you've read this book) that you can get the same thing two doors down. Expect to pay between 40 and 60 percent less for used equipment.

When buying restaurant equipment, negotiating is acceptable and expected. For example, say, "I'll buy this oven and grill if you throw in the stainless steel table." You may walk out with a mixer and food processor instead, but you probably need them anyway.

With used equipment, get some kind of a guarantee in writing. It may not be an extended warranty, but you need some assurance that it's gonna run for a while. When you buy used equipment, you trade off extended warranties and factory support in favor of a lower price. The only way that used equipment benefits you is by saving you money. If you don't save money buying used equipment, you might as well have bought new equipment in the first place.

Don't worry about missing knobs and handles. You can usually add them. Focus on the all-important questions: Does it work? Will it work tomorrow? Is there a guarantee that it will work a week from now?

Don't buy very specialized pieces of equipment used, such as a combination oven (a combination steamer and convection oven) or a conveyer oven. You benefit from a warranty and complete information on the ideal cleaning and maintenance regimen that comes with a new oven. But you can buy many pieces of equipment used, like those in the list below, and sleep soundly:

✔ **Gas ranges:** These appliances are excellent candidates for buying used. Unless you derive some sort of personal satisfaction from it, don't go for the copper-clad import from Lyon when plenty of sound products are available that don't command the price. The biggest consideration when buying a gas range is how many BTUs it puts out.

✔ **Ovens:** Gas ovens, like gas ranges, are okay to buy used. But be cautious of purchasing used electrical ovens because so many things can go wrong with them, including problems with the sensors and temperature controls.

✔ **Fryers:** Buy fryers used, but get a guarantee that the thermostat works. Calibrate the thermostat to make sure that the temperature is actually correct. If you don't know how to change the oil, when to change the oil, how to clean it, and so on, get the information from your salesperson. If you can get a manual with the equipment, even better.

✔ **Grills:** Grills are usually okay to buy used, especially the gas variety. But do a detailed visual inspection of wood and gas grills because, over time, the guts eventually burn out. The heat warps and distorts the grill's inner workings. Make sure the grill surface is flat. If the grates are removable, inspect them to make sure that the surface is level.

✔ **Smallwares:** You can buy almost all used smallwares (like tongs, salt and pepper shakers, and soup cups) with confidence.

Chapter 12

Setting Up a Bar and Beverage Program

● ●

In This Chapter

▶ Equipping your bar and keeping it clean

▶ Packing the house

▶ Serving beer, wine, and liquor

▶ Playing it safe

● ●

*W*hether you're looking to open your neighborhood's new favorite bar where regulars become permanent fixtures, the "in" club with the best music and drink specials, or an elegant wine bar attached to a chic new restaurant with an up and coming chef, this chapter is for you. In it, we cover everything you need to think about when opening your bar — from equipment and supplies to attracting customers.

But don't be so quick to skip past here if your establishment doesn't have an actual wooden bar with stools and all. If you're planning on serving alcohol, you'll want to stick around because we also help you set up a beverage program, including figuring out what you need based on your restaurant concept, tips on stocking, pricing, and selling beer, wine, and liquor, and important information on serving alcohol responsibly.

Setting Up Your Bar

Your bar must match your concept. If you have a bar and restaurant together, the themes should be connected. One successful chain of Australian steakhouses is basically bars that happen to have restaurants built around them. Most diners come in and have to wait for a table just long enough to sit at the bar and have a drink. Other successful restaurants have only a service bar, with no stools or counter, that's accessible only to the wait staff.

Before purchasing any bar equipment, think about your goals. Decide if you want your bar to be the primary source of income for your business or subordinate to the restaurant. This exercise helps you determine how much space to dedicate to your bar, your dining room, and all the other front-of-the-house areas. (Chapter 10 covers laying out the front of the house.)

Form and function go hand in hand when setting up a successful bar business. If you have a freestanding bar, spend time considering both factors in your design. The following sections focus on the specifics.

Selecting equipment

Decide where you want the basic structures of your bar to be. After you set these items up, they'll stay put for quite awhile. The basic bar equipment list looks a little something like this:

- **Bar:** Decide where to put the actual bar.

- **Bar stools:** Choose the number of stools you need based on the length of your bar. Each stool should have about 2 feet of dedicated bar space (So if your bar is 12 feet long, you'll need 6 stools).

- **Payment system:** Tie your bar payment system into your main system. The bar should have a separate cash drawer and computer terminal (if you're using a computerized system). If you plan to serve food at the bar, the bartenders need access to any food ordering system you use. If you plan to use a computerized system, your service bar will also need a printer to print out the restaurant's bar orders as they come in.

- **Pour options:** Weigh your options for metering, pouring, or strictly controlling the amount of liquor in each drink. Systems range from pour tops added to control the speed the liquor flows, to full computerized systems that dispense the measured amount of alcohol at the touch of a button and keep track of the number of drinks made from each bottle.

Bar customers like a free pour (pouring the alcohol without using any measuring device). Anything else seems chintzy. Decide how to balance your profit with their perception (see the "Lapping Up Some Liquor Learnin'" section later in the chapter).

- **Smoke eaters:** If you allow smoking in your bar, install these to help control the smoke. Check out Chapter 10 for details on smoke eaters.

- **Cooler:** Your cooler should be large enough to hold your inventory of white and blush wines, your beer kegs, your backup bottled beer supply, and any other supplies your bar uses regularly that must be kept cold.

- **Wells:** Each area where a bartender works needs a well. The well holds ice (with a dedicated ice scoop), well brands of the basic liquors (vodka, gin, whiskey, rum, and scotch), a garnish station, and a soda gun. Check out Figure 12-1 for how this looks.

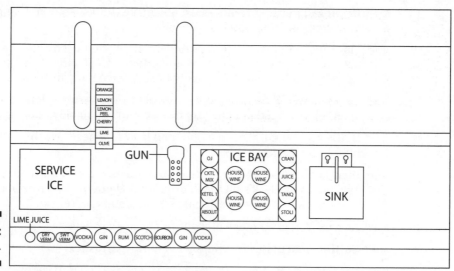

Figure 12-1:
A swell well.

✔ **Hand sinks with soap and sanitizer:** Hand sinks are small sinks reserved for washing hands only. Stock the sink with antibacterial soap, paper towels, and hand sanitizer.

✔ **Beer taps:** The kegs can be in the bar or in a separate cooler, with lines run to the bar, depending on your setup.

✔ **Reach-ins:** Reach-in coolers (usually shortened to *reach-ins*) are the restaurant equivalent of a dorm room fridge. Choose lowboys (reach-ins close to ground level) or highboys (reach-ins situated at about waist level), or both. Look for the best setup for your operation.

✔ **Soda system:** The bar usually shares your restaurant's soda system, with "guns" at each well.

✔ **Glass racks for hanging glassware:** Installing glass racks above the counters in the bar saves valuable counter space.

Here's a list of smaller, but important bar equipment. You probably need it all, but you can set it up in multiple ways and change it, as you need to:

✔ **Jiggers and shot glasses:** Use these to measure liquor for mixed drinks.

✔ **Cocktail shakers:** Use these items to shake cocktails such as martinis.

✔ **Cocktail strainers:** These gadgets strain ice from shaken drinks that are served *up* (without ice).

✔ **Garnish holder:** This item holds lime wedges and lemon twists.

✔ **Bar spoons:** These items are great for stirring drinks.

✔ **Muddlers:** These look like a small wooden baseball bat. They're used to crush mint leaves for mint juleps, or fruit and sugar for an old-fashioned.

✔ **Drink rail mats:** Bartenders usually make drinks while standing on these mats because they catch small spills.

✔ **Floor mats:** Industrial-grade rubber mats cushion achy knees and soothe achy feet. These mats are typically grids of small circles that connect at the edges and can be thoroughly hosed down daily or between shifts.

✔ **Corkscrews:** Depending on your level of wine service, determine whether you need industrial wine openers for quickly opening bottles.

✔ **Bottle openers:** If you do a booming beer business, get the ones with a built-in bottle cap holder.

✔ **Blender:** This small appliance is sometimes called a bartender's least favorite friend — it's all those drinks like daiquiris and frozen margaritas that typically take longer to make than a standard cocktail.

✔ **Knives:** You need these utensils to cut the garnishes.

✔ **Cutting board:** Here's where you cut the garnishes.

✔ **Specialty items for your concept:** Maybe you plan to keep a frozen beverage machine full of margaritas or sangria.

✔ **Glass-washing equipment:** Most bars have a system of three sinks designed for washing glasses. The first sink holds the motorized brushes used to clean the glasses. The second contains hot clean water to rinse the glasses. The third sink contains sanitizer to sanitize the glasses.

✔ **Containers with color-coded tops:** Keep a supply of bloody Mary mix, orange juice, and the like in your bar reach-in for easy access and to keep contents fresh.

✔ **Drink recipes:** Your collection may take the form of a binder, recipe-card box, or even a computerized database of drinks. It may be a comprehensive list of every cocktail known to mankind or just a quick reference to your house specialties.

✔ **Ice buckets:** Used for refilling the ice wells in the bar, these containers must be labeled *for ice only.* If anything else gets in these buckets, they must be cleaned and sanitized before using them for ice.

If your ice machine is a long way from your bar, get rolling ice buckets or bins for restocking the ice. The wheels save strain on the staff because they won't need to wrestle the bins through the dining room. Use bins that are small enough that people can pick them up to dump them in the wells without back strain.

Some restaurants place cappuccino/espresso machines behind the bar rather than in the wait station. So the waiters order the coffee drinks, and the bartenders make them. Be a little wary of this system: Bartenders typically ignore these drinks if other priorities compete and resent making these drinks for servers because they're not their specialty. There's enough potential friction between the bar staff and the wait staff without adding this stress.

Setting up a service bar

The service bar is the bar that *services* the restaurant dining room. When waiters order a glass of wine or a martini, they pick it up at the service bar. You can set up a service bar in many different ways, but your service bar must be separate from the main bar from the guest's perspective. They may see this open area as the perfect place to stand and order their own drinks, causing congestion for the wait staff. Make it easy for your staff to get in and get out without interrupting the customers. Here are a few of the most common options:

✓ **Separate well at the main bar:** This design is the easiest from a setup perspective, because the bartender can access the same beer taps, and less often used liquors, without moving too much. But it gets complicated from a customer's perspective if it's not obviously marked. The absence of bar stools isn't enough to distinguish it from the main bar. Add brass railings on either side of the service bar or a sign stating, "servers only." With this option, you also risk creating a gathering place for servers away from the dining room.

✓ **Separate window behind the main bar:** Bartenders still have easy access to the full bar, and customers can't get to it, but depending on the layout of your place (such as if your bar is situated against an exterior wall), this configuration may not be possible.

✓ **Freestanding unit not attached to the main bar:** This option is great if your main bar and dining room are on different floors or if the main bar is far away from the dining room. Easy access for waiters to the bar usually means more drink sales and more money. The downside is that you probably won't have everything here that you have in the full bar, so bartenders may have to go between the two to make certain drinks.

The service bar needs the same basic equipment and supplies as the main bar. You may not keep every brand of vodka there, but you need the common ones. You may not have a full cordial selection, but develop a system for quickly serving drinks that require them.

Surveying supplies

A *supply* is anything you stock and restock on a fairly regular basis. *Consumables,* such as napkins, straws, and garnishes, are supplies. So are *hard goods,* such as glassware, that are used, cleaned, and restocked. (Beer, wine, and liquor are supplies, and we cover each later in the chapter. And Chapter 14 gives you the lowdown on purchasing and management.) Your supply list will vary, but here's a general all-purpose list:

✓ **Glassware:** You need an assortment, from beer glasses to wine glasses to coffee drink glasses, depending on your concept.

✓ **Drink menus:** You may have an entire list of different martinis or just a list of spirits that you carry. Be creative, but informative.

✓ **Soaps, cleaners, and sanitizers**: Get the right cleaners for your equipment. Check with your manufacturer for details.

✔ **Garnishes:** Examples include maraschino cherries, lemon wheels, lemon twists, celery, lime wedges, lime twists, olives, and margarita salt.

✔ **Paper goods:** You need things such as straws, stir sticks, beverage napkins, coasters, and dinner napkins.

✔ **Towels, bar rags, and sponges:** Keep a supply of these items handy to wipe up sticky cordials, overflowing beer taps, and mixer mix-ups.

✔ **Sanitizing bucket:** Keep sanitizer mixed (at the proper concentration) and ready to sanitize surfaces quickly and keep from contaminating reach-ins, ice wells, glasses, and other items.

✔ **Menus:** Any food available in the bar should be on a menu there. If you have the same menu, keep a supply of dining room menus in the bar. If a limited menu is available in the bar, create a separate menu.

✔ **Requisition forms:** Employees use these forms to request more supplies.

✔ **Food-specific supplies:** If you serve food in your bar, you need other supplies, including silverware, plates, salt and pepper, and condiments.

Don't use glasses to scoop ice — ever, never, not under any circumstances. If your glass chips or breaks in the ice bin, you have to pour hot water in it to melt all the ice (*burn* it, in industry speak) in the ice well, remove the broken glass, and clean and sanitize it. Then you have to restock the ice before you can use the well again. In fact, anytime there's a chance that glass may have gotten into the well, you have to burn it, and sanitize it.

Having signature and logoed items, such as ashtrays and matches, at the bar is cool. But don't make expensive items — anything from glassware to ashtrays — too special because people will take them.

Keeping Your Bar Clean

Your bar should be just as clean as, if not cleaner than, any other area in the restaurant. Here, your patrons get an upfront, intimate look at the sinks, shelves, counters, and cabinets. If they see dripping, sticky bottles and a mildewed reach-in, how long do you think they'll keep coming back? Develop a cleaning and sanitation system immediately, before you open your bar. Your bar is subject to health inspections just like any part of your restaurant. We cover cleanliness and sanitation in detail in Chapter 18, but here are a few bar-specifics points to consider.

✔ Don't allow any eating behind the bar. Bits of food can get mixed in with supplies and equipment.

✔ Don't allow smoking and drinking behind the bar.

✔ Bartenders should wash their hands often. They shouldn't be mixing drinks and touching the ice scoop without washing their hands. In addition, after a bartender touches his own mouth or nose, he should wash his hands.

✔ Bartenders must use utensils — not their hands — to stir drinks.

✔ Bartenders should never, ever stick their hands in dirty glasses. It may seem efficient to pick up four glasses at a time by placing your fingers inside them, then clamping your fingers together, but each time you do it, it's like sticking your fingers in someone's mouth.

✔ Create a rotation system for garnishes and mixes, especially during slow times. Just because you have lime wedges left over from the weekend, it doesn't mean they're still useable for Wednesday night margarita specials. Rotation is often more of a problem in the bar than in the kitchen, because kitchen staff members are usually beat over the head with the info from Day 1. Bartenders aren't. Check your perishables and make sure you're practicing FIFO (first in, first out).

Drawing Crowds

Creative bar owners bring in the crowds in a variety of ways. Whether it's music, games, or drink specials, behind every busy bar is a reason why people come. Maintain flexibility in your design so that you can reconfigure your space easily as your bar business changes. In this section, we give you some pointers on what you may want to use to both draw and entertain the masses.

Promotions

Promotions are events you use to attract customers — and make more money. Your job is to find a balance between getting people in the door and actually profiting from this increased traffic. If a promotion doesn't make money, it's not successful, no matter how many people you get in the door. Planning and analysis are key: Use the same process for forecasting expenses and sales we show you in Chapter 5 to outline the best, worst, and most likely scenarios for each promotion. And then follow up to determine the actual outcome.

Promotions are only limited by your imagination (and all applicable laws, of course). Put yourself in your potential customer's shoes to figure out what will draw them in. Here are a few creative promotions we've heard of, which we include to spark your creativity. We don't recommend that you do or do not use them: Think about what works for the clientele you're going after, what fits with your local liquor laws, and what's profitable for your business.

✔ **Sponsor a softball team:** You get advertising space on the jerseys or in the league programs, and the players, and their friends and family become part of the greater bar family. This approach works with other sporting events (like golf outings) and leagues, too.

✔ **Take part in radio station promotions:** Partner with a local station to broadcast from your bar. Give away free stuff like shirts, merchandise, and event tickets to improve your chances of drawing a crowd.

✔ **Offer a free happy hour buffet:** Set up an appetizer buffet for a limited period of time, or simply offer complimentary snacks and appetizers at certain hours. You can also charge a small fee to cover some of the costs.

✔ **Create a bar event schedule:** For example, you can make Monday football night, Tuesday karaoke night, Wednesday mud wrestling night, and Thursday $2 draft beer night.

✔ **Feature a ladies night:** Women get two-for-one drinks or a free cover charge. Bring in the women, and the men will follow.

Successful bars advertise. Take a look at Chapter 16 for the full details.

Entertainment

Keep your sports ear to the ground and the other tuned to the local music scene. There are sports to watch, games to play, music to hear, and songs to sing. If you're looking for entertainment for your bar, start here.

If you're running a bar inside a restaurant, think carefully before adding entertainment. If the bar crowd gets rowdy, it can affect your restaurant patrons. Owners of stand-alone bars can be a bit more creative and/or edgy with entertainment options — people go to a bar for a reason, and it's not a G-rated show.

Flipping on the TV

Sports bars are common in most parts of the country. Many have satellite packages that let customers watch games from every type of league in every time zone. You need to pay a fee to display the programming for commercial use. Check with your satellite company about the regulations in your area.

Playing games

Besides being a way to draw customers, games such as pool, electronic darts, and video games are actually revenue generating. In fact, some restaurants rely on the income generated from games to support the business, offering food almost as an afterthought. Grown-up versions of the arcade-with-restaurant-attached — the Chuck E. Cheese's chain being on of the most popular among the smaller set — are becoming more common. Look for names like Dave and Buster's, Jillian's, and ESPN Zone, to name a few.

Gambling in bars is also becoming more common. Anything from video poker to keno on closed circuit TV is available. If you're into gambling, you can put together leagues for poker, football pools, and other avenues to drawing customers and increasing profits. But make sure that any gambling you offer is legal. Don't risk your operation by taking illegal bets.

Turning up the music

Adding music to your bar isn't always easy. You can get started with a jukebox. If you're looking to create a dance scene, consider hiring a DJ. DJs usually have their own collection of music they bring with them and play at your bar. You pay them a fee for their services. The fee can be a flat rate, a percentage of sales, or a percentage of the cover charge, if applicable.

Karaoke allows your patrons to get up on stage and sing along with recorded music. If you're interested in starting a karaoke night, consider renting a machine, or hiring a service to run your program to see how it goes. A full commercial-quality system can run anywhere from $500 to $5,000.

If you want to move beyond a jukebox, check out some other bars and restaurants in your area and get to know the local music scene. Live music is a great way to bring in customers. Many local bands have their own followings and bring their fans with them. Expect to pay between $500 and $5,000 to get a decent band in for a weekend night. Some charge a flat fee, and others charge a percentage of sales and the full cover charge. Usually, the bigger the band, in number of members and in popularity, the more you pay. Talk to other bar owners to find out acceptable rates.

Check out www.gigmasters.com — a Web site with a nationwide database of performers, from a cappella groups to zydeco bands. To get a list of available groups in your area, just type in your zip code and dates. You can even be specific about what kind of performers you're looking for.

Bartenders

Bartenders can bring in patrons. Attractive female bartenders bring in men. (Think *Coyote Ugly*.) Attractive male bartenders bring in women who bring in men. (Think *Cocktail*.) But looks are only one way your bartenders can bring in customers.

A knowledgeable bartender can also be a draw. They should be well versed in beer, wine, and spirits, with an emphasis on your specialty drinks. But don't stop with beverages. Educate your bartenders about your food as well. Even if they don't know the full menu, bartenders should know your specialties. If your bartender knows your signature hot sauces, the special cheeses, or the secrets of your simmered sauces, they can build a regular bar clientele and encourage them to bring in friends for meals in the dining room.

Many people invest in a bartender. They spend time getting to know them and, generally, appreciate bartenders who recognize and remember them as regulars. Maybe your bartender is the neighborhood counselor, or maybe he's in the know. Depending on the size of the town or the neighborhood, patrons may follow a bartender if he leaves one bar to work at another.

Providing Liquid Refreshment

The term *beverage program* generally applies to restaurants that serve alcoholic beverages. Nonalcoholic beverages are usually priced and inventoried with your food products. Typically, things like coffee, tea, and soft drinks are purchased from the same suppliers you get your food from, so they're subject to the same pricing plans (and hopefully discounts and rebates) as your food. If you serve smoothies, shakes, and juices, they're definitely food products, even though you drink them, because they're made from the same things your food products are made from.

Use the same creative drive in your beverage program that exists in developing your menu. (Check out Chapter 9 for help.) Before you can think about what you need from a beverage program, you must understand your concept and your clientele. Then make choices on what to include on your drink lists based on these factors. If your interior design and menu are taking some risks, your beverage program needs to stand out, too. If you're running a family restaurant offering traditional fare, plan a beverage list to match.

Decide how to focus your list. Are you going to offer boutique vodka, gins, and scotch, or does a basic well (the least expensive brands of basic liquors) do it? Watch your competition. Where's your point of difference from the guy down the street? Maybe being familiar (or edgy) is your point of difference. Do you want to touch on all the facets of the beverage program (wine, liquor, beer, and nonalcoholic beverages) or specialize in one area?

Don't try to support too much from the beginning. It's not a good idea to reduce the number of your beverage choices, especially alcoholic drinks, after your restaurant opens; it's much better to start smaller when you first open and add to your list later. If you serve 15 different domestic bottled beers when you first open but later reduce that list to 2 domestic beers to create inventory efficiency, you risk disappointing customers.

Becoming Beer Brainy

Many restaurants get away with a very limited beer menu. Unless you want to be known for your beer selection, you may be able to limit your beer choices to a domestic beer (such as Bud, Miller Genuine Draft, or Michelob), a domestic light beer (such as Bud Light, Coors Light, or Michelob Ultra), an import (Heineken or Becks), and an imported light beer (Amstel Light). Most beer drinkers probably can find something to satisfy them from that list. But your concept may require you to dig a little deeper. If you're a German restaurant, you probably have to have a German beer, or three, on your list.

Styles of beer

With the explosion of microbrews in this country in the last ten years, you're bound to see a few obscure styles. Here's a quick list of the most common kinds, with some distinguishing characteristics:

✔ **Lager:** Made with bottom fermented yeast, lagers usually have clean, crisp flavors and are generally lighter in color than other beers. A few examples of well-known lagers include original Sam Adams, Fosters, and Budweiser.

✔ **Ale:** Made with top fermented yeast, ales are usually flavorful and robust, and sometimes are fruity and sometimes bitter. They can have a range of colors, from very light (like India Pale Ale) to dark (Brown or Amber Ale). Newcastle Brown Ale, MacTarnahan's Scottish Ale, Fat Tire Amber Ale, and Boddington's Pub Ale are some of the big names in this diverse category.

✔ **Stout:** These beers are made with top fermented yeast and are usually extremely dark. They can be sweet or dry but usually are slightly bitter. They often have a creamy texture. Probably the most recognizable stout in the world is Guinness, but most breweries brew their own version of this popular style.

You can approach pricing bottles and cans of beer much like you do wine. See Table 12-1 for an example. But when you're working with pricing a mug of draft beer, put your calculator away. You'd need to figure the number of ounces per keg and the number of ounces per pour and hope that your keg system is working perfectly. If your gas isn't working properly, you could be wasting lots of beer. Keg systems require maintenance, incur lots of spillage and waste, and give you huge profits. The average draft beer costs somewhere between 4 cents and 10 cents an ounce in product.

Table 12-1	Bottle Beer Pricing Based at 3 Times Cost
Cost per 12-oz. Bottle	*Price per 12-oz. Bottle*
$0.60	$1.80
$0.70	$2.10
$0.80	$2.40
$1.00	$3.00
$1.10	$3.30

Because beer is so readily available and people know what you paid for it, price it according to market norms — and don't charge too much. You can't charge $6 for a Bud and sell very many (unless you run the concessions at a professional sports venue). People will rebel. But also keep in mind that lowering your prices can harm your credibility. From a customer's perspective, lowering your prices is considered a retreat or a sign of desperation. Bumping up your prices a bit is much easier.

Getting with It about Wine

As with most other facets of your restaurant, your wine list choices depend heavily on your concept because it affects customers' expectations for both your list and the food you serve. But whether you're a family-style restaurant or a fine dining establishment, you can use a wine list to your advantage.

Creating your list

Having a good rapport with wine reps helps your restaurant. When closeouts occur with certain labels and vintages, the reps can make sure that you know about them and help steer you toward the diamonds in the rough. Wine reps can help you get a great product before it becomes unavailable.

Customer expectations

Many customers know what they want in a wine; others are always open to experimenting and trying something new. A popular strategy for developing a wine list over time is to give your diners familiar choices to start with and then expand your offerings to include similar yet less familiar choices as you go along. You can introduce them to new wines and let them explore the unfamiliar ones by the glass.

Anything that makes your customers happy (and keeps them spending money) is a good choice for your wine list. If a customer comes in once or twice a week and wants a particular wine on the menu, give it to her.

Your customers may interpret your use of "grocery store" wines (wines that are extremely familiar and inexpensive) as being too low end. But, depending on your concept, your clientele may expect these wines. Make sure that you make this type of wine a deliberate choice, not just an easy out.

Menu offerings

The ability to match your wine list to your menu is key to running a good restaurant wine program. Coauthor Michael frequents a restaurant where a husband and wife run the restaurant. She does the wine list, which includes only 10 or 12 wines that go perfectly with the menu. She focuses on what's on the menu and pairs accordingly.

If you're just getting started or want to update your list but don't know where to begin, consider having your wine salespeople taste some recipes and help you pair your offerings with their wines. Wine reps love to give their input. Just know that they'll design the list around their own portfolio exclusively.

Length of list and quality level of selections

A wine list doesn't have to be long, eclectic, or familiar to be good. And a good wine doesn't have to be serious; it just has to be a wine that someone enjoys. Find a balance between the eclectic and familiar stand bys. Don't get too esoteric or you risk intimidating guests with your offerings.

If people don't recognize the types of wine you're serving, make sure that your staff knows them, can explain them in detail, and brings the diner a sample. Also, if pronunciation may be intimidating, give each wine a number on the menu so guests can order by number instead of avoiding the unfamiliar because they're afraid to look foolish.

The "grocery store wines," or wines that everyone knows, are definitely on the way out in restaurants because many diners can figure out what you paid for the bottle, so justifying the price you need to charge to make your margins is tough. But have no fear; plenty of other great wines are available at reasonable prices. Work with your wine rep to find wines that fit with your menu items and that you can buy at a low price and meet your margin.

Pricing your wine

Determining your selling price for wines by the bottle is relatively easy. You simply decide on the factor you want to multiply the cost by. For example, you could pick a factor of two to three times what you paid for it. This system is really just another way to look at food cost. Here you're multiplying, with food cost you're dividing. The more expensive the wine is, the lower the factor that you might multiply by. So, if you buy the wine from your supplier for $12, you might charge $36 (multiplied the cost of the wine by 3). But if you paid $50 for a bottle of wine, you'll likely charge closer to $100 than $150 per bottle. Your percentage is lower, but your profit is higher.

Fifty dollars in inventory does you no good on the shelf. Don't be tempted to overprice your wine — you could price yourself out of a sale. With wine, don't worry about keeping the percentage that you make off your program low. Move wine through your restaurant to keep money flowing rather than tying it up in inventory.

Pricing your wines by the glass is tougher, but you can do it. First decide on the size of your pour, usually either a 5- or 6-ounce pour. A standard wine bottle is 750 milliliters, so you get five 5-ounce glasses or four 6-ounce glasses from each. Then decide on the factor you want to multiply by, just like you do for your bottle program. Check out Table 12-2 for what this might look like at three and a half times cost.

Table 12-2	Wine-by-the-Glass Pricing at 3½ Times Cost			
Cost per Bottle	*5-oz. Cost*	*5-oz. Price*	*6-oz. Cost*	*6-oz. Price*
$6	$1.20	$4.20	$1.50	$5.25
$8	$1.60	$5.60	$2.00	$7.00
$10	$2.00	$7.00	$2.50	$8.75
$12	$2.40	$8.40	$3.00	$10.50
$14	$2.80	$9.80	$3.50	$12.25

This difference in the price you pay versus the price you charge may seem huge. But don't forget that you have to cover all your costs, including waste, if the rest of the bottle goes bad. Take a look at Chapter 9 for details on what expenses you need to cover with your food and beverage prices.

Storing your wine

Storage is a huge issue for wine. Wine's biggest enemies are air, temperature, humidity, and light. Most wine cellars are below ground, because the temperature underground is constant and cool. Caring for wine is relatively easy in your restaurant.

Take your cue from these wine cellars and guard your wine against these forces by picking a cool, dry, and dark location for your stock. And store the bottles on their sides or upside down while they're in their cases, which prevents the corks from drying out and letting air seep in. If your investment in your wine list is sizable, you may want to invest in your own climate-controlled wine cellar.

Beyond the bottle storage concerns, many bar owners worry about storing and preserving open bottles for their by-the-glass program. If you have an extensive by-the-glass program, consider investing in a wine preservation system. These systems evacuate the air in a bottle, replacing it usually with nitrogen, and then seal the bottle until you open it again. The price for a basic system starts at around $1,000 for a four-bottle system and goes up, depending on what gadgets you want and how many bottles you need to preserve. If you don't have that kind of budget, consider using a product designed for home use, like VacuVin brand products. These products remove the air from your bottle of wine and seal it until the next time you open it, preserving the quality of the wine for up to two weeks. They run about $30 for the vacuum tool and 2 stoppers.

If you can't afford a wine preservation system, a really competent bartender can be an ally, especially if she works almost every day. She can keep an eye on open bottles, steer bar patrons toward those selections, and help avoid waste. She should also know when to trash a bottle that's been open too long.

Lapping Up Some Liquor Learnin'

Vodka is the current reigning king of liquor. Forty years ago, brown spirits, like whiskey, scotch, and bourbon, ruled the bar roost. Lighter and clearer spirits (vodka, gin, and tequila) are definitely where the bar business is right now and probably will be for the next 10 to 20 years. So pick your brands and then focus on your pours and pricing.

Watch out for the urge to overstock. Allocate your valuable bar space to stuff that moves. You can probably skip Benedictine and sloe gin, no matter what your liquor rep says. And resist the sales pitch that promises free bottles of stuff you don't use. If the free liquor is only a dust collector, how does that help you?

You can't *marry,* or consolidate, bottles of liquor. Doing so is illegal. You may think that you're being efficient by adding your half bottle of well vodka from the south well, to the bottle of well vodka from the north well and then stocking a fresh bottle in the south well. But you can't. Basically, the government is trying to protect consumers from fraud — bartenders putting cheap vodka in a high-end bottle and charging more. So no consolidating.

Pour size and pricing

Your *pour size,* or how much liquor you pour into each cocktail, is important. It determines what the finished drink costs you, how much you can charge, and how much profit you make on each drink.

A typical serving of liquor in a mixed drink is 1 to 1½ ounces. If you pour 1 ounce per drink, you'll get 33 drinks from each 750-milliliter bottle. If you pour 1½ ounces, you'll get 22 drinks from each bottle. So if you pay $20 for a bottle of booze, those same shots will cost you 61 cents and 91 cents, respectively. Add in another 10 cents for each for ice and the mixers. So if you want to achieve a 20 percent cost on your liquor, you should sell a 1½-ounce drink made from a $20 bottle for $4.59. Check out Table 12-3 for the specifics. You probably want to round these up a bit because, honestly, who can keep track of a drink that costs $4.59? Round it up to $4.95. For more on why you round prices, check out Chapter 9.

You charge more than the drink costs you to make because you have to account for *buybacks* (buying the occasional drink for regular diners or for guests spending lots of money in your establishment), overpouring, spillage, breakage, employee drinks, the occasional unscrupulous bartender — and don't forget profit.

Table 12-3	Costing Cocktails			
Cost per Bottle	*1-oz. Pour Cost*	*1-oz. Pour Price*	*1.5-oz. Pour Cost*	*1.5-oz. Pour Price*
$18	$0.65	$3.23	$0.92	$4.59
$20	$0.71	$3.53	$1.01	$5.05
$24	$0.83	$4.14	$1.19	$5.95
$28	$0.95	$4.74	$1.37	$6.86
$30	$1.01	$5.05	$1.46	$7.32

Liquor lingo

Terms like *well, call* and *premium* refer to the cost, and presumably the quality, of the ingredients in a drink and, ultimately, what the customer pays for the drink. If a customer doesn't ask for, or *call,* a specific brand of liquor, you use what you're pouring from your *well,* which are the cheapest house brands. The pricing-tier system of vodka looks like this:

Tier	*Common Brands*
Well	Popov, Dark Eyes
Call	Smirnoff, Stolichnaya, Skyy, Finlandia
Premium	Grey Goose, Absolut, Chopin, Belvedere, Kettle One, Tanqueray Sterling
Super Premium	Liquid Ice, Turi, Ultimat

You determine the price you need to charge your customers to hit the margins you've set based on the pricing you get from your suppliers. Even if the percentages you make from each drink are equal, the dollar amounts you make from calls, premiums, and super premiums, are much higher, so encourage your staff to learn their liquor brands (liquor distributor sales reps can help train them) and to recommend the better liquor brands to your diners.

Serving Alcohol Responsibly

If you serve alcohol to the public, you need to be aware of the risks you're taking and take steps to minimize them. Use your local liquor licensing authority for specific guidelines on what you can and can't do. Take this agency's recommendations and stated penalties seriously. Check out Chapter 8 for information on finding out which agency handles licenses in your area. Here are a few tips that can help you and your staff keep your customers safe:

- ✓ Keep the phone numbers of several taxi services handy.

- ✓ Set up a program for designated drivers. Maybe you can offer them free nonalcoholic beverages all night long.

- ✓ Encourage bartenders to attend training on responsible alcohol service. In some areas, the law requires specific training for all supervisors and staff members who deal with alcohol. Even if it's not required in your community, these classes are great tools for training your team.

- ✓ Refer to Table 12-4 to help keep patrons in the safe zone as far as blood alcohol is concerned.

- ✓ Check with your insurance company for recommendations they may have on ways to lower your liability. They may recommend signage (for example, reminding patrons to give their keys to a friend) that you can visibly post to lower your liability and help keep your customers safe.

- ✓ Be vigilant about potential problems. For example, don't assume that you can give people darts and alcohol and expect nobody to ever get hurt.

- ✓ Decide whether you need to hire bouncers. If you have a rowdy crowd, bouncers can help deter dangerous behavior.

Be careful when hiring and screening bouncers. They can be the catalyst, instead of the deterrent, for violence. Conduct thorough background checks on them to discover any arrests, criminal convictions, or even complaints filed against them. You can be sued if your overly aggressive bouncer decides he needs to punch someone to keep him in line.

- ✓ Develop a system for consistent *carding,* or checking Ids, to confirm that your patrons are of legal drinking age, usually 21 in most places.

Table 12-4	Percentage of Blood Alcohol Concentration (BAC)				
Weight	*Number of Drinks in Two Hours*				
	2	*4*	*6*	*8*	*10*
120	0.06	0.12	0.19	0.25	0.31
140	0.05	0.11	0.16	0.21	0.27
160	0.05	0.09	0.14	0.19	0.23
180	0.04	0.08	0.13	0.17	0.21
200	0.04	0.08	0.11	0.15	0.19

The legal limit in most states is either .08 or .10. Make sure you know your local laws.

No matter what advice they receive, some owners insist on walking the line between what's legal and what they think they can get away with. Our advice: Toe the line. If you're open when you're not supposed to be, you could risk your business. If you consistently have underage drinkers in your bar, you'll eventually get caught. At best, you'll get points counted against your liquor license. At worst, say goodbye to your business.

Sometimes a bartender or manager just needs to be able to recognize potentially hazardous situations before they become problems. When you mix people and their emotions with alcohol, problems can escalate. Watch for the guy who's had too much to drink. Be wary of two guys going after the same girl. Preventing problems before they happen is more an art than a science.

Your bartender should be the authority figure. He has the responsibility to keep everything in the bar running smoothly and safely. No matter what gender (or size) your bartenders are, they should have control over the clientele. At one time or another, someone will challenge their authority.

Chapter 13

Hiring and Training Your Staff

• •

• •

A chain is only as strong as its weakest link. You've heard this idea related to business a million times. Choose a good team and train them the right way to maximize your chance for success. Whether you're starting a new restaurant from scratch or revitalizing an existing one, the information in this chapter can improve your staff development today.

Finding the Right People

Before you can figure out who you need to help you operate your restaurant, you need to fully develop your concept (see Chapter 3) and menu (which we cover in Chapter 9). Then put on your operations cap and think about what jobs you need to fill. If you're a fast-food restaurant, you don't need a host to help people find a table or take reservations, but you will need some cashiers to take orders and make change. If you're a fancy gourmet restaurant, you need at least two hosts, one to kiss each set of cheeks, but no cashiers. Use our suggestions in Table 13-1 (and the descriptions throughout this section) to determine the employees you need based upon your concept.

Different jobs in the restaurant world require different personalities. For example, a fry cook doesn't need an outgoing personality: You don't want him to be so chatty that he can't focus on what he's doing. And a hermit at the front desk will alienate customers. You need people to be friendly when they interact with guests, but focused on productivity where you need production. And you probably need a drill sergeant to make sure it all gets done.

Table 13-1	Employees Needed for Each Shift
Type of Restaurant	*Positions to Fill*
Casual/family style	Hosts or hostesses Servers Bussers Dishwashers Line cooks Prep cooks Cashiers Food runners Bartenders
Fast food with a centralized menu	Cashiers/order takers Line cooks Dishwashers
Fine dining	Hosts or hostesses Servers Bussers Dishwashers Line cooks (several with different specialties) Wine stewards (who pour and serve wine) Bartenders Sommelier
Bar and grill	Servers Bussers Dishwashers Line cooks (several with different specialties) Bartenders

In the following sections, we give you an overview of what to look for in potential employees. We break up the information by position, detailing the scope of the responsibilities for each one. We even include a sample organizational chart, Figure 13-1, to show you how everyone fits together.

Create your own formal job descriptions for each position, preferably before you hire the people to fill them. The process of creating job descriptions can help you immensely during the hiring process by clarifying who you need for your operation and defining their responsibilities. (Chapter 2 discusses when in your restaurant opening timeline you should develop job descriptions.)

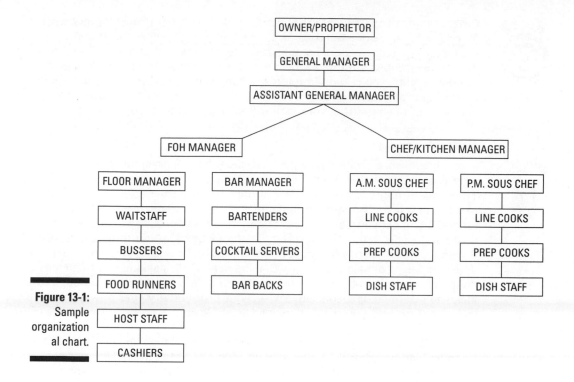

Figure 13-1:
Sample
organization
al chart.

Managing your quest for managers

Managers set the tone for the rest of the staff. So hire the best people for the job. They affect how smoothly your operation runs, how your staff controls the chaos and treats the customers, and how much money you'll ultimately make. In the following sections, we let you know about some key things to watch for when selecting the best people for your management team.

Hiring a recruiter to help you look for restaurant managers can be a smart move. Recruiters usually charge you, the employer, anywhere from 10 to 25 percent of the new employee's salary for their services, but they can really cut down the length of your search and improve the quality of your candidates. Also, take a look at Hcareers (www.hcareers.com) for a good Web site focused on hospitality-industry employment.

You should like the managers you hire, at least on some level. You're together for at least 12 hours a day, so you'd better get along.

Cross-training management team members is a good idea. Your bar manager, for example, may not need to know how to run the dining room, staff the kitchen, or expedite orders coming from the kitchen, but in most cases, the more cross-trained your managers are in each position, the better. You gain more flexibility, you respond rapidly to changes in business levels, and you're better equipped to deal with the inevitable vacations, sick days, late arrivals, and no-call/no-shows that your staff will take at the most inopportune times.

General manager

In any business, a *general manager* (GM) must have a grasp of all facets of the operation. You can hire a GM, but many owners choose to serve as the GM. They may or may not use the title, but they perform the duties, and save an extra salary. If you've never waited tables, checked coats, fried fries, or tended a bar, get yourself a quick education. If you don't, the employees in those areas will dictate the business. That may be okay, but think about this: If your chef says he has five guys but needs eight, how are you going to know if he's on target or asking for more than he needs? He's asking you to increase your labor costs by 60 percent for a single shift. You need to know enough to make an informed decision. Otherwise, your productivity goes down, your labor goes up, and your profits go out the window.

The GM is ultimately responsible for the staff's knowledge and commitment. He must lead by example. He must have a handle on the financial forecasts, budget objectives, and all the other numbers. Control of the restaurant is important as a means of maximizing profitably and maintaining cash flow.

The GM represents the restaurant not just while he's in the restaurant but out in the community as well. If he goes out and gets hammered down the street, sleeps with a competitor's wife, cusses out the mayor, and runs someone over on his way home from the bar, it's not good community relations.

Assistant general manager

The *assistant general manager,* or AGM, is the heir-apparent to the GM, or next in line. (See the preceding section for details on traits of a good GM.) The AGM should be aspiring to be a GM, trying to do the job before he gets the job. The GM delegates responsibilities to the AGM to prepare for an eventual promotion. The AGM either knows or is learning how to be the GM. As the owner, you may be attending to the GM's responsibilities without the title, and your GM may be acting as an AGM.

The titles matter less than the responsibilities. You need someone to be in charge and someone right behind him serving as a backup, the next in line, and learning all the ropes.

Chef

Most restaurants don't need a chef. Base your search for a chef on your concept. Anticipate your volume of business, the technical difficulty of your menu, and whether you want the chef to be part of your public relations push. Then narrow down your hunt. You can categorize chefs by their specialized cuisines or the types of operations that they have experience in.

A chef brings creativity, expertise, and leadership to your kitchen. Be aware that many people call themselves chefs when they really don't know which end of a knife to hold. The title has been diluted. A true chef will have a proven track record for the following:

- ✔ Managing, training, teaching, and developing a staff
- ✔ Developing a menu
- ✔ Running efficient, profitable, and clean kitchen operations
- ✔ Receiving accolades, awards, and positive critical reviews
- ✔ Demonstrating specific knowledge of service, wine, and spirits and how to apply them to your concept

If you don't need or want someone else to be that involved, consider hiring a kitchen manager (KM) instead of a chef. (See the KM description in the "Staffing the kitchen" section.) Then you can hire a consultant to make scheduled menu changes seasonally, something that a chef would handle.

Use quality chef recruiters to find a quality chef. Newspaper ads have limited success, but they may work if you're located in a large metropolitan area. Your choices may be more limited if you're in a smaller market. With a typical newspaper ad, your response isn't very targeted. You'll get resumes from every joker with an apron in your market. A recruiter can scour the country quickly for candidates that match your concept and budget, checking references and saving you time.

Be wary if your chef candidate says "No special orders." Diners who request special orders are by definition finicky, and they go where they can get what they want. A good chef is in his diner's psyche. He is current with food trends. He has the adaptability, creativity, and passion to see an opportunity where others may not bother with "difficult" diners.

Stereotypically, chefs are notorious for boozing, yelling, and the like. Your chef is a manager, just like any other restaurant manager. He should conduct himself in the same way you expect every other manager to behave. The restaurant is a tamer environment than it was 15 years ago, and that kind of behavior is no longer tolerated. Make sure that your chef got the memo!

Staffing the kitchen

We list these positions in order from most essential (dishwashers) to less essential (the sous chef or KM). Someone must be in charge of the kitchen, but it may be a single manager in charge of every restaurant employee, not a kitchen-specific manager, but no restaurant can survive for long without a dishwasher.

Dishwasher

The dishwashing job is very physical labor. Boots and an apron, preferably waterproof, are the standard uniform. Dishwashers are the serfs of the restaurant world. But most experienced chefs and managers agree that they're among the most important people in the building. The most amazing food in the world will do you no good if you don't have a clean plate to put it on or a clean fork to eat it with.

Many cooks and chefs start out in the dish area. If they have the desire, dishwashers can move from dish to prep to line to sous chef. Promotion from within your organization is an ideal way to sell an employee on working in the dish area. Motivating someone to "bust suds" and dig his elbows deep in discarded food is tough. Promotion can be the carrot dangling out in front of the employee. If you're able to hang on to your dish guy and move him up the ranks, you and he will both have a great story to tell.

When you're looking to hire dishwashers, start here:

- ✔ **Word of mouth:** If you have a good employee who recommends a friend or relative for a dishwashing position, definitely consider that person.

- ✔ **Newspaper ads:** For entry-level positions in your restaurant, newspaper ads generally get a good response from qualified candidates.

After you get some candidates in the door, make sure they have the following traits before hiring them:

- ✔ **Good work history (if they have a history):** Don't discount applicants just because this is their first job, but if they've been fired from their last five dishwashing jobs, you may not want to give them the sixth.

- ✔ **Punctuality:** If applicants are late for the job interview, it could be a sign of things to come. You definitely want a dishwasher you can count on to show up on time.

- ✔ **Organizational skills:** Keeping the dish area neat and organized is important in order to keep dirty dishes flowing in and clean ones flowing out. Make sure the person you hire is up to the task.

- ✔ **Necessary physical attributes:** Dishwashers must be able to stand for long periods of time. They have to be able to lift heavy loads, like stacks of plates or full garbage bags. They should also be fairly dexterous and not clumsy. They should be able to maneuver a rolling cart of glass racks through a busy kitchen without getting in someone else's way.

Prep cook

Prep is short for preparing, or making preparation. It's the root system of the kitchen. Your prep cooks are the unsung heroes of the kitchen, the ones who do the daily grunt work. Prep cooks touch every part of your menu and kitchen, whether they're cutting steaks off the side of beef; chopping lettuce; making soups, bulk sauces, frosting, or pizza dough; or wrapping and freezing compound butters. Prep cooks prepare your kitchen for the shift to come.

Many people believe that prep is the most important part of the cooking. If it's not done right, nothing can fix it. Take soups, for example. Soups aren't cooked to order. They're prepared early in the morning so flavors are melded by lunch or dinner. When a diner orders a piping hot bowl, the waiter serves up a ladleful and goes on her way. If the soup isn't prepared right in the prep stage, you can't do much to fix it after it's ordered.

In other cases, your prep cooks start the process, and your line cooks finish it. For example, your prep guys peel and devein shrimp for salad but don't assemble the final product.

Prep cooks should have a working knowledge of the storerooms and coolers so they know where to find product. They know where to find all the ingredients they need for whatever they're making. They also need to know how to operate many kinds of equipment — a buffalo chopper, food processor, tilt skillet, fryer, or even the grill. They could be roasting corn for a salsa and then frying noodles for a garnish — all within the same shift.

Look for the following traits and characteristics in a good prep cook:

- ✔ Punctuality and dependability
- ✔ Ability to take direction, criticism, and instruction well
- ✔ Organizational skills
- ✔ Ability to complete tedious, repetitive tasks over a long period of time
- ✔ Ability to read a recipe and apply basic math skills
- ✔ A real desire to be in the business (an applicant in it just for the money could be gone next week, searching for that extra 25 cents per hour)
- ✔ Ability to stand for long period of times and lift and move cases of food with relative ease

Experience in other restaurants is always a plus. If applicants don't have experience but seem like they could be good employees, consider them as candidates for the dishwasher position.

Line cook

A line cook is assigned to a station on your *line* (the section of the kitchen where food is finished, or cooked when ordered). The line is made up of kitchen stations dedicated to different preparation techniques, like the grill, sauté, fryer, and so on. See Chapter 11 for the full scoop on kitchen stations.

Most line cooks should have some kitchen experience before working on the line. Many people start in prep and work up to the line. Depending on your concept, you can start inexperienced line cooks on a cold station, like the pantry or pastry, and then cross-train them on other stations as their abilities and interests develop. Usually, these cold stations have a more limited menu than the hot stations and require fewer skills to run. Typically, the sauté cook needs the greatest amount of kitchen experience because this station has the most volume and requires the most expertise.

The key traits of a successful line cook are:

- **Punctuality:** As with any employee in the restaurant, line cooks need to show up on time.

- **Willingness to learn:** From what goes into the menu items to plate presentation, a line cook is always learning. Whether he's getting to know his station or learning to run the one next to him, successful cooks are those who are consistently learning.

- **Previous experience:** Line cooks need to have some experience before they start on the line. Figure out which particular station they're suited for by comparing their past experience with your needs and concept.

- **Positive attitude:** Because busy times in a restaurant are so busy and hectic, you need cooks who can keep their cool and go with the flow. You also need employees who can follow instructions and follow the directions of their supervisor, especially during shifts.

Cross-training is ideal on the line. During slow business levels, it's good to have cross-trained employees. If one guy can work one end of the line that consists of the oven and the fryer, plus he knows his way around the pantry, you have the flexibility to *cut* (send home early) some of your other staff. You save labor dollars but maintain your full menu and service levels.

If you have one, your *expo* is the end of the line. Basically, he gets all the line cooks working together on an order at the right time. See Chapter 11 for the full deal on the duties of the expo.

Sous chef

The *sous chef* (pronounced *sue,* French for *under*) is the kitchen's second in command. He's usually in charge when the chef isn't around. The sous chef is sort of the executive chef in training, but he may still train the underlings. A sous chef is in the process of learning ordering, inventory management, and food costing. Also, the sous chef is likely trying to pick up on the creativity of the chef, understanding his style of cooking and food philosophy. Some chefs use them as assistants. But other sous chefs are actually running the kitchen, and sometimes several sous chefs work in a single kitchen.

Kitchen manager

A kitchen manager, or KM, knows the nuts and bolts of running the kitchen machine. He may do the ordering and manage the staff, but he may not have advanced culinary training. KMs are great at maintaining consistency. A good KM knows the standards and can follow production manuals, but he doesn't have to be creative or focused on technique. He can teach the staff the basics. He should be very production-focused and efficient.

Filling the front of the house

The *front of the house* (FOH) is restaurant-speak for any area of the restaurant where a diner can be. (For more details, check out Chapter 10.) FOH employees have regular contact with your diners.

Host

You may call them *hosts* or *hostesses, greeters, seaters, reservations desks,* or a host (pun intended) of other names. Whatever name you use, the basic function is the same. These folks greet your diners, show them to their tables, and start their meal and experience on the right foot. They're also the last face that guests see on their way out of your restaurant. You want them to thank everyone and send diners off with a great final impression.

Look for composed, friendly, and organized people to fill these positions. They're essential to your success. This is one of the most difficult jobs in a busy restaurant. The nicest person in the world won't appear nice to prospective diners if she can't control the phones, deal with the customer who hated his soup, get the complaining waiter in Station 4 back on track, and deal with the smoke coming out of the kitchen, all while maintaining her composure. And if your host isn't taking down the correct time, number of people, and names for the reservation, it can be a disaster. Enough chaos will develop in the restaurant; you don't need a host staff contributing to it.

You don't need a beauty queen or Adonis to serve as your host, but she or he does need to capture the mood of the restaurant. Hip, trendy restaurants should have hip, trendy greeters. And communication skills are a must. Knowing when to communicate with the floor manager or the kitchen can keep the night running smoothly. Effective communication with the diners means going beyond friendly; it's understanding what you have to say to make this person happy.

Waiters often try to manipulate the host staff to seat them in a favorable way. Make your staff aware of the potential problem and give them tips to avoid it. If you're going to screw up the seating, do it on your own. Don't let a waiter do it for you.

Coat check

Coat check is often a function of the host staff. On busy nights, you may employ a designated coat-check person. This staff should be organized and methodical in how they take the coats, label the coats, and so on. The success of the coat check is determined by the equipment that you give them. If you have the right tools (like hanger tags, as well as labels for accessories such as hats, umbrellas, bags, and so on), you should have a smooth operation.

If you don't have a good coat check system, you *will* have problems that involve claims against your establishment for missing or damaged goods. You'll probably find yourself settling these claims in the spirit of goodwill, at a not insignificant cost. Copy whatever successful system your favorite upscale chain restaurant or steakhouse uses. These establishments have risk management people in their organization who have figured it out for you.

The coat-check room is a great place to put a camera. Theft does occur so having the eye in the sky as a backup is a help. It can also vindicate an accused employee who's innocent.

Cashier

Cashiers should be honest, organized, and friendly. If the cashier is the same person who deals with tipping out wait staff, she needs to be strong-willed and resistant to games that waiters may play.

Waiter

Waiters are salespeople. They're the most direct connection between your diner's wallet and you. They should be friendly and able to relate to people. Successful waiters are able to make judgment calls about what kind of customer they're waiting on and what their diners' expectations are. They should be able to read their diners and react accordingly. They should know when to chat people up or leave them alone. Is the couple that's been married for 40 years simply quiet but otherwise happy? Are they involved in an intense, private conversation? Or maybe the group is out to celebrate and want the waiter to entertain them.

Waiters should be able to smile no matter what happens. Coauthor Mike tells them, "Pretend this is a stage and you're entertaining these people. Don't let them see your problems. Don't let them even know you have any. They're supposed to have a good time, so let them."

Calling in the specialists

Some concepts require help from a few different specialists. Ice cream makers, *fromagieres* (cheese makers), and fishmongers all can be employees of your restaurant. In the following sections, we list a few of the more common specialists with brief descriptions. Most can be hired as full-time employees, but more likely they work as part-timers, or consultants, as needed.

✔ **Butcher:** Butchers are becoming less and less common in the restaurant due to factors like technology and improved food packaging. But if you want to be a world-class steakhouse, you may have one on staff. Butchers do much more than just cut a few steaks for the dinner shift on a single night. Butchers know how to break down an entire side of beef (or other meat) with very little waste. But if you don't plan to use the entire animal, you may be better off just buying what you want already cut and portioned.

✔ **Sommelier:** A *sommelier* is a wine expert. Many fine-dining restaurants have one or more sommeliers on staff to help pair food with wines that match the concept and explain the wine to customers and staff. He may or may not be in charge of the wine buying. If you're not going after a clientele that drinks quite a bit of wine and is looking for new, different, or high-end wine, you probably don't need a sommelier on staff. Instead, consider hiring one to help set up your wine list and update it seasonally or when your menu changes.

✔ **Pastry chef:** Pastry chefs can do much more than create amazing sweets. They can do pasta or pot de crème, crème brûlée, or crostini. Think of them as the all-around carb-chefs. If the recipe calls for flour and/or sugar, they can probably make it, and they can present these delectable delicacies in fun, exciting, new ways. They can develop a signature dessert for your restaurant or put new spins on beloved mainstays. Before you take on this hefty expense, decide whether you need a pastry chef. Instead of hiring a pastry chef, you could partner with a local bakery and pay more for the products but less in the labor.

Food runner

Depending on your service, you may include food runners on your schedule during busy shifts. Runners help get hot food out of the kitchen and to your diners quickly. They may be assigned to a particular section or could be available to help anyone who needs it at any point. Sometimes runners are waiters in training. They may be learning the ropes or are too young, based on local laws, to actually wait tables if beer, wine, and liquor are served. Or they could be waiters who take turns in a shift rotation to run food.

Runners should be knowledgeable about the food, the dining room layout, and your concept. Being a runner is a great way for an employee to get to know your restaurant and your food. A runner should be able to recognize dishes but may not be able to tell a guest every ingredient or preparation method.

Busser

A busser's job is to keep service flowing. Bussers clear and set tables to prepare them for the next set of guests. Some bussers may also be assigned to start service at a table. For example, they may pour water and bring bread and butter or other complimentary items to the table.

Bussers may have aspirations of being waiters. Like food runners, they may not be old enough to serve alcohol. Some bussers move from the back of the house to the front. Bussers should be quick and organized. They should know the proper table setup for your concept and their way around the dish area. They usually aren't required to have extensive food knowledge. But they should know your points of service and expectations for guest courtesy. They need some sophistication about when to clear and when not to clear dishes.

Bartender

A bartender should have an extensive knowledge of making cocktails, especially those that are associated with your concept. If you have a Mexican restaurant, the bartender needs to know how to make many kinds of margaritas, for example. She should also be likeable and friendly with guests. (We cover good bartending traits more detail in Chapter 12.)

Don't jump to hire a graduate just out of bartending school. Bartending is a skill that you learn from hands-on experience.

The *service bartender* makes the drinks for the waiters, helps other bartenders, and assists in prep work. The service bartender usually doesn't have much contact with guests. A bartender may use a bar back during busy shifts. The *bar back* can do anything except make drinks —stock glasses, ice, liquor, and other supplies and maybe wash glasses and empty the trash.

Cocktail server

Cocktail servers, stereotypically women, specialize in drink service. They usually wait on tables in the bar area of the restaurant. The cocktail server should know your menu if you serve food in your bar. She should definitely know the specifics of your liquor, beer, and wine lists. If you have any entertainment in the bar, she should have an idea of the schedule (like what time the band starts and who's playing tomorrow night). Depending on how busy your bar is, you may need a very experienced cocktail waitress who can handle multiple tables of patrons. If your bar isn't terribly busy, restaurant waitresses may be able to take on the task of cocktail shifts.

If possible, don't require a diner to pay his tab when moving from the bar to the dining room for dinner. Just add his bar tab to his dinner check. Making people pay two tabs usually makes diners angry, and using one check doesn't necessarily reduce the amount of a cocktail server's tips. People often leave a cocktail server a cash tip when transferring their bar tab into the restaurant.

Staffing office functions

The office is the nerve center of your restaurant where all the information in the restaurant gets tied together. Your POS (point of sale) system, payroll records, and telephone systems are usually housed here (see Chapter 15). Staffing the office can be as complicated as staffing any other part of the restaurant. Depending on the size of your operation, different people will wear different hats. In fact, until you can support the expense of hiring people, you may be wearing all the hats! Marketing, reservations, and accounting may all be handled by the same person. You, as the manager, need to know how your office runs, inside and out. If not, people will rob you blind. If you think the bartender can do it by giving away free drinks, just wait until the office does it.

Office staff should be honest because they provide the checks and balances for both the physical cash that moves through your restaurant — counting *banks* (usually cash drawers set up to give change at the bar and cashier station) and *drops* (cash deposits ready to go to the bank) and monitoring FOH cash handling — and the financial records. You may hire an outside accountant to come in to audit monthly, quarterly, or annually, or more often if you feel it's necessary.

Accounting

Your accountant may have no idea of what the business does, but she is responsible for checking numbers. The best bookkeepers can understand the numbers and give you advice on how they apply to your business's past performance and future needs. If you're new to the restaurant business, you need someone with this type of experience. Find an accountant who does the books for other restaurants. And purchase a copy of *The Uniform Code of Accounts for Restaurants* from the National Restaurant Association. If you have your accountant set up your books according to industry standards, comparing your operation to others will be easier. See Chapter 8 for more info on accountants.

Payroll

Many restaurants *source out* (hire an outside firm to do a job) some of their payroll processes. But you can't just turn payroll over to an outside company and assume that it will run without a hitch. Usually, someone in the restaurant confirms hours worked, pay rates, and so on and then sends the information to the payroll company, which just cuts the checks. The same internal person usually double-checks the checks against the data sent to the payroll company, verifies the payroll deposit has been made, and so on. This person is an initial investigator who identifies the discrepancies, asks the questions, finds the reasons, and conveys the potential problems to management. For details on planning for payroll, make sure to visit Chapter 15.

Marketing

Someone in your organization should be in charge of this important function, even if you get help from an outside source. In some cases, a general manager or owner serves as the liaison between an outside marketing consultant and the restaurant or may choose to perform the duties himself. If you hand off this job to someone else in your organization, pick someone who knows the operation and the concept behind the restaurant. If this employee doesn't know your business thoroughly when she starts, she has to get to know it quickly. If you hire someone without an interest in how the lamb is getting to the table with its special Armenian mint, what are the chances this person will have an interest in the long-term success of your business? Your marketing person should understand your passion and the nuances of your concept. Take a look at Chapter 16 for details on marketing and promoting your business.

Technical expert

You can hire outside people or outside firms to maintain your computerized POS system, but you need someone in your operation to watch over them. Even if you sign up for a 24-hour support team available to you with your newly purchased system, you need someone on your staff to be the liaison with them. You need someone who can handle the situation. This person may not have specialized training to handle the systems, but if he has an aptitude and an interest in helping out, you'll be a step ahead.

Interviewing the Candidates

When hiring, do your best to make a sound decision based on the facts and your gut instinct. But don't beat yourself up if it doesn't work out. In the restaurant business, lack of experience isn't always a good reason to not hire someone. The only way people really learn a job is to do it. If you think some-one has the right attitude, give him a try. If it works, let it keep working. If it doesn't work, cut your losses right away. Consider including a probation period, usually 60 to 90 days, for new hires. That way if someone really isn't working out, you can get rid of him quickly with very little trouble later.

Consult your state labor laws regarding probationary periods and unemploy-ment laws. If you've never managed a business (or even if you have), you'll be very wise to find an expert labor attorney. This legal expert can save you untold dollars and possibly even your business. The really good ones are expensive. But this is truly a case of getting what you pay for.

We recommend at least two interviews for most positions with at least two different people in your company. Use the first as a screening interview to get a feel for how the person fits into your organization. Many second or third interviews involve an audition or tryout, especially for kitchen positions.

Forms for new hires

After you pick your staff, they'll need to complete some basic government forms. Give them their employee manual, and have them sign for it. Also have them complete any helpful forms, like emergency contact information, at this time. Here's a quick list of the forms you'll want to keep on hand for new employees:

✔ **I-9:** The required I-9 form documents eligibility to work in the United States. It's a required document for every employee in your employ, whether a U.S. resident or an alien.

✔ **W-4:** The IRS-required W-4 forms allow employees to declare their number of withholding allowance to take from their pay.

✔ **Attendance calendar:** This allows you to quickly document any attendance discrepancies, calculate vacation days, and the like.

✔ **Emergency contact card:** This card is handy in case the unexpected happens in your restaurant. If you have to take an employee to the hospital, you'll be glad you have the name of a close friend or family member to call.

Keep a file on each employee, in which you retain all of these forms, along with the person's initial job application and/or resume. Doing so isn't just a good business practice; it's essential in case of a government audit.

Placing an ad and sifting through resumes

When you're looking to hire people to staff your new restaurant, start by placing an ad in the newspaper. Newspaper ads advertising new restaurant jobs get a *huge* response. The industry is full of job jumpers. If you're the newest restaurant on the block, servers assume you'll be busy, so you'll get swamped with applicants who jump from one opening to the next. Organizing your recruitment process to account for this volume of response is important to stay afloat in the sea of "people persons" and dependable, hardworking people who wonder if they can have Friday and Saturday off.

If you see obvious errors or red flags on a resume or application, don't bother to interview the applicant. If someone says she's an expert on Burgundian wine but she misspells *Burgundian,* it's probably a red flag. Or if she's worked three months at each of her last ten jobs, skip her.

Round 1: The meet and greet

Use this round for screening out people whom you *definitely won't hire.* Keep your questions short. Have the applicants fill out applications, get their background information and get a feel for how they answer questions. You won't have a lot of people whom you definitely extend an immediate offer to, at this point — save that for Round 2. Here's a quick list of good Round 1 questions:

✔ What's your employment background?

✔ Why do you want to work here?

✔ What are your strengths? Your weaknesses?

✔ Why did you leave your last position?

✔ What do you think is the most important aspect of the job you're applying for?

✔ Why are you equipped to succeed in this position?

✔ Are you looking for a career or a job?

Cull it down to the few applicants you'd like to find out more about. For FOH positions, put yourself in the guest's position. Do you want this person talking to you? Is she engaging? Is her voice nice to listen to? For BOH positions, does an applicant present herself as eager to learn? Is she modest, or very impressed with herself? Beware the hotshots in the kitchen; they're often resistant to training specific to your concept. Good candidates are attentive, willing to learn, and physically capable of doing the job.

Round 2: Comparison shopping

Make a list of the available positions, and add spaces for the number of people you need in each position. During Round 2, build a roster of candidates to fill the available slots. Use paper, a chalkboard, a dry-erase board, an emery board, whatever works for you. Think of it like the NFL draft. By the end of Round 2, you start to build a roster of your first, second, and third picks for each position.

The goal of the second round of preopening interviews is to ask the hard questions and get to the core of who the applicant is, in 15 minutes or less. Let the applicants know the good, the bad, and the ugly of the available position. Assess whether this discussion should continue to the next phase. Scare off the weak. Find out why they want to work at your restaurant — and it better be for reasons other than because you're hiring.

Get specific with the applicants' past background, job-related skills, techniques, and specific knowledge. Field their questions. Discuss pay rates, as appropriate. By the end of this round of interviews, you should start to feel comfortable making offers of employment.

When making your final hiring decisions, make sure that all applicants

✔ Have the applicable specific experience you're looking for.

✔ Meet the criteria you've established for the position they're applying for.

✔ Are available to work the number of hours you need them.

✔ Have a solid work history (or no work history for entry-level positions).

✔ Have a positive attitude, desire to learn, and enthusiasm for your restaurant.

✔ Mesh with your philosophy, company culture, and work style.

Never ask candidates about their religion, marital status, sexual orientation, age, gender, race, political affiliation, national origin, disability, or if they have children. Answers to these questions could be construed as a reason that someone didn't get a job and set you up for a lawsuit. Visit the U.S. Equal Employment Opportunity Commission Web site at www.eeoc.gov for details. Make sure that everyone in a position to hire on your behalf understands these rules. You're liable for their actions if they're on your payroll.

Training Your Staff

Assume that, when you hire your staff, they have no preconceived knowledge about your business. The more information you give them about the way your business runs, your expectations, your concept, your menu, and so on, the better they'll be as employees. Training is expensive. It uses up labor dollars to teach employees about your operation. It uses up supply dollars printing out manuals. It uses up manager time in putting all the materials together. But think about how much a poorly-trained employee can cost you in terms of wasted products and supplies, broken equipment, and lost customers.

Make sure you take a look at Chapter 2 for details on when to conduct specific training sessions during your opening schedule. There's great information in that chapter about how to hold mock service sessions and dry runs (serving food in a real-life setting to a few of your closest hundred friends) to make sure your staff is ready for opening day.

The employee manual: Identifying your company policies

An employee manual is your chance on paper to spell out for your employees what you expect of them in terms of performance, behavior, communication, appearance, and so on. You need to make sure everybody gets one, so every employee is on the same page. Get each employee to sign and date the manual, acknowledging that they've read it and have been given a copy for their personal records. If their signature is their statement that they've read, understood, and agreed to abide by the contents, give them a chance to read it thoroughly before signing. You'll eat it in court if you don't. Be sure to tell them that they should keep it and refer to it as necessary. Any changes that you make to the manual need to be handled the same way. The changes must be given to all employees and signed for. The following list contains some standard items that make an appearance in many employee manuals:

- Welcome letter
- Mission statement
- Company history
- Orientation period
- Communication policies
- Performance and job standards
- Code of ethics
- Confidentiality policies
- Emergency procedures
- Drug and alcohol policies
- Antiharassment policies
- Customer-service program
- Problem-solving procedures
- Safety issues
- Training meetings
- Performance evaluations
- Performance rewards
- Food-safety procedures
- Other policies

Use the manual to get your new staff excited about your restaurant. It's an opportunity to show your employees that they all contribute to the big picture and explain to them why they're important. Show them what safeguards are put in place to make sure the big-picture things happen.

The employee manual serves as documented proof of your policies. You can easily tell a server to remove his earring if you have it written in black and white that earrings aren't permitted. You have a consistent way to handle situations. If you have employees' signatures on file saying that they've received and read the manual, you have some protection if they sue you for terminating them based on something clearly spelled out in the manual.

No one employee manual suits every operation. Each is as different as the operation you run and the goals you set. If you're new to the business, don't let your GM write the manual because he has restaurant experience and you don't. This is one of those things you can't delegate: If he leaves in six months, you want the manual to reflect *you* and *your* philosophies. It's also an item that you need to have an expert labor attorney review before it gets issued to any employee. The money spent here will be minimal compared to the potential damages paid later. (And make sure that the GM reads and signs for his copy.)

Operations manuals: Understanding specific job functions

An operations manual helps you train employees to perform specific duties for each position, from pot scrubber to maitre d', from fry cook to general manager. Thoroughly explain each position, including duties, standards, and objectives. Tell them what they're here to do, how to do it, when to do it, your quality standards, and so on.

The more detailed you can be, the more successful your training will be. Outline in black and white what you want them to do. You may feel like you have to spend a lot of time putting your operations manuals together, but you'll more than make up for it by not having to take time to re-explain how to do things, when to do things, and so on. With the details written down for employees, their training time shrinks and they're up and running much more quickly.

Here are some examples of what should be included in the job-specific operations manuals:

- **Servers:** Your server operations manual includes standards of service, time cycling (when to order which food, when to clear plates, and the like), product knowledge, opening and closing procedures, side work expectations, kitchen interaction parameters, and cash handling procedures.

- **Bartenders:** The bartender operations manual includes standards of service, standardized pours, product knowledge, inventory procedures, cash handling procedures, guest interaction parameters, opening and closing procedures, and responsible alcohol service guidelines.

- **Line cooks:** The line cook operations manual contains station opening and closing procedures, standardized recipes for the station, prep amounts based on volume, station-specific proper food handling procedures, and the kitchen cleaning responsibilities chart. Each station may have its own manual with station specific info.

> ✔ **Managers:** This operations manual includes the master opening and closing procedures for the whole restaurant, instructions on using the POS software, overall daily cash handling and reporting procedures, instructions for dealing with employees, and instructions for dealing with guests. The manager operations manual should include everyone else's info and then some. Managers should know how to cook the whole menu, how to wait tables, how to light the pilots on the ovens, and how to change the paper in the POS printer.

Cross-training is important. Your fry cook should be able to work the grill; your pantry cook should be able to sauté. If you notice someone who's trying to learn more — a prep cook who wants to learn the line, for example — never discourage his efforts. Consider allowing him time during his regular workday to assist or learn the ropes. Not only will you be encouraging his interests, but you'll also have a possible substitute in case someone can't make it in one day or leaves.

Certification-based training, such as TIPS (Training for Intervention ProcedureS, a safe alcohol service, `www.gettips.com`), ServSafe (food-safety training, `www.nraef.org`), and HACCP (Hazard Analysis and Critical Control Point food safety training, `www.cfsan.fda.gov/~lrd/haccp.htm`), complement in-house training programs. Often, local health departments sponsor these training sessions at little or no charge. Encourage your staff to attend whenever possible. The info is valuable to every food-service professional.

Ongoing training

Don't think that, because someone's training period is over, he's trained. Training is an ongoing process. Keep products fresh in your employees' minds. Include training on current specials, new wines, or whatever else your staff needs every single shift. Hold weekly position-specific meetings and monthly all-employee meetings to go over important information with the staff. Regularly scheduled meetings keep lines of communication open and prevent misunderstandings. See Chapter 17 for more info on the subject.

Chapter 14

Purchasing and Managing Supplies

● ●

In This Chapter

▶ Getting control of purchasing

▶ Picking the right suppliers

▶ Working with prices, quality, and service

▶ Developing a solid inventory system

● ●

A wise man once said, "You make more money buying than selling." That adage is true in any business, particularly a competitive one like a restaurant. Purchasing takes vigilance and enthusiasm. You must be diligent in your research, knowledgeable about what works for your concept, current on the latest food trends and production techniques, and confident in your volume of goods purchased. Good purchasing decisions result in positive bottom lines.

In this chapter, we take you through purchasing from start to finish. We show you how to figure out what you need to buy and who you need to buy it from. From an inventory standpoint, you need to develop a system for confirming that you got what you ordered, it's stored in its appropriate location, and it stays there until you're ready to use it in your restaurant.

Getting Started in the Supply Room

Before you order that first supply, you have to understand your concept (see Chapter 3), your menu (see Chapter 9), the amount of time you have to devote to preparing your menu items, and the number of people available to produce them. If you have lots of time and people, you can start with less-refined products (like whole chicken instead of boneless skinless breasts).

But even after your menu is squared away, the purchasing work has only begun. You know that you'll need some specific things, such as a particular brand of pasta or a certain label of wine. But for the most part, you'll likely know only that you need tomato sauce; you may not know which particular brand of sauce or case size to get.

So how do you figure out what you need to order? Start by researching products you don't know: Go out to eat. Try new things. Read the industry magazines (see Chapter 22 for a list of resources). Any information you can get helps you make better decisions.

Purchasing entails buying anything you need for your restaurant: food, beverages, equipment, paper goods, tables, silverware, and everything else. After you purchase the basic equipment for your restaurant start-up, you spend the majority of your purchasing time buying food and beverages. If yours is like most restaurants, you spend not only lots of time but also lots of money buying these types of supplies. So we focus our examples in this chapter on food and beverage purchasing. But you can definitely apply these same principles and tips to purchasing just about anything else you need for your restaurant.

Making your lists

Make a list of all the food and beverage supplies you're going to need according to your menu. Organize the list by category, as we've done in our example in Table 14-1. You need to have this list in hand before you start locating and interviewing suppliers. (Although our example deals exclusively with food and beverage items, you can use this approach for every purchase, including bar equipment, paper goods, and linen.)

The categories in the table are organized the same way that most purveyors specialize. You might have a meat guy, a seafood guy, and a *broad line* supplier (a large supplier that carries a variety of goods across many product lines). The list in Table 14-1 is by no means comprehensive. Your list will be based on your menu.

Be specific with your final list. Don't just write "beef tenderloin." Instead, write "beef tenderloin, block ready, 5½ up, silver skin removed, prime," if that's your specification. If you just say "beef tenderloin," the supplier could give you a price on no roll (ungraded) or select (instead of prime) beef tenderloins that looks great from a price standpoint but that may not be the right quality match for your concept.

Deciding on your menu, your recipes, and desired end results before you draw up your list is a real plus when you're not sure about the exact product you want. You can then turn to your supplier for guidance. For, example, tell him that you need chicken fingers but want to taste all of his company's chicken fingers side by side. You can look at 2, 10, or 20 products side by side and discern why something works for your application and why it's the best choice for your operation.

Table 14-1	Sample Supplies List		
Item	*Category*	*Unit*	*Projected Weekly Volume*
Bread, French roll, 1.5 oz.	Baked goods	Case, 144 ct.	
Bread, roll, herb garlic, 1.5 oz.	Baked goods	Case, 144 ct.	
Bread, 3-ft. loaf, Italian	Baked goods	Each	
Pizza dough balls, 20 oz.	Baked goods	Case, 24 ct.	
Bread, sticks, 2 oz.	Baked goods	Case, 96 ct.	
Bread, wheat, French roll, 1.5 oz.	Baked goods	Case, 144 ct.	
Butter, unsweetened, 1 lb.	Dairy	Case, 36 ct.	
Butter, whipped, 5-lb. tub	Dairy	Case, 6 ct.	
Cheese, Asiago, shredded	Dairy	Case, 15 lb.	
Cheese, Bleu, crumbles	Dairy	Case, 20 lb.	
Cheese, Cheddar-Jack, shredded	Dairy	Case, 15 lb.	
Cheese, cream, 3-lb. tub	Dairy	Case, 3 ct.	
Cheese, cubed	Dairy	Case, 20 lb.	
Cheese, mozzarella, fresh	Dairy	Tub, 8 lb.	
Cheese, Parmesan, shredded	Dairy	Case, 15 lb.	
Cheese, provolone, longhorn	Dairy	Each	
Cream, heavy, 40%, 1 quart	Dairy	Case, 12 ct.	
Cream, sour	Dairy	5 gal. bucket	

Considering prep time as a factor

Convenience foods are popular, and there's no shortage of the restaurant versions of these foods. You can definitely save yourself time and money by using
them, but consider all the factors to make sure that they're economical for
your business. Think about going into a grocery store and buying a frozen
dinner. You may be able to heat it in 7 minutes, but you pay $2.50 to $3. But

you could've made the same meal for 95 cents in about 20 to 30 minutes. What you gain in convenience, you pay for in price. Determine whether you have an army of prep people skilled enough to create the items on your menu completely from scratch. Not all restaurants can do it, and it's very costly.

Don't have your prep team spend time on menial tasks that have little impact on your quality or bottom line. Throw your labor hours at the greatest product cost savings, and order the rest, when possible. For example, suppose that one person, who makes $8 per hour, takes four hours to cut all the potatoes for the 30 pounds of shoestring potatoes you need every day. By doing it yourself, you save $1 per pound on the cost of whole potatoes versus packaged frozen fries. It cost you $32 in labor (4 hours × $8 per hour) to make up $30 (30 pounds × $1) in food cost — at the end of the day, you're losing $2 on the whole deal. Not too efficient, eh? However, if that same person spent that same time prepping the 100 pounds of fajita chicken strips you need for the next two days for your signature fajitas and burritos, you could save $304.

Here's how. You buy 100 pounds of random-sized boneless, skinless chicken breasts for $184, 2 liters of olive oil for $18, 1 pound of the grill guy's addictive Fajita Fizzle for $12, and your cook's labor for $32. Your grand total is $246. Or you could buy 100 pounds of all-white-meat fully cooked, grill-marked fajita strips from Quick-E Poultry Co. at $5.50 a pound, for a total of $550.

Before you make a final decision to put prefab items on your menu, taste them and determine whether they fit your concept. Decide how close the quality of the commercial product is to the scratch version and whether the savings in labor is worth any sacrifice in quality. Ultimately, if your diners don't like it or it tastes like it came out of a box, they won't come back.

Here are a few examples of products that are available to make your prep labor dollars go further:

- **Sauce bases, such as demi-glace, pesto, and so on:** You purchase the base and add a few other ingredients to finish them as you need them.

- **Meats that are cut, portioned, and individually sealed:** These products are more expensive, but you have little waste and spoilage. Use them if you don't go through a lot of meat or don't have the skill to cut it yourself but want to keep some beefy options on your menu.

- **Baked goods, including breads, pastries, and other desserts:** Many good products are available prepackaged these days. Work with your purveyors to see what may work for your concept. Consider partnering with a local bakery to get locally known breads, pastries, and desserts.

Finding and Interviewing Potential Purveyors

Now that you know what you need, find out what's available from different *purveyors* (also called suppliers), both locally and via air or ground delivery. But keep in mind that there's a fine line between working with your sales rep in a partnership that benefits you both, known as *consultative selling,* and letting the sales rep run your show, known as *getting taken for a ride.* As often as possible, figure out what you need before the sales rep tells you what you need. They won't tell you about their competitors, so don't use them as your only research source.

Finding suppliers

The best way to find potential purveyors is to talk to other restaurant operators that you respect. Doing so saves you hours of looking in phone books, doing online research, and going to food shows. When you talk to other restaurateurs, you're talking to people who have made a conscious decision to go with one supplier over another. Find out why. Ask them who else they considered and who else is out there.

For example, seek out a restaurant that is doing the type of seafood you want to do or a restaurant that has fresh, flavorful products all the time and ask the owners which supplier they use. Usually, other restaurants are willing to pass along this information. Ask them why they purchase from Stanky Green Eyes Seafood rather than Rosy Red Gills.

This process works in all categories, from cleaning supplies to specialty foods. Make a list of supplies you need and next to each item write the name of the suppliers the competition is using for each category. Start with no fewer than three suppliers (also referred to as *houses* in the restaurant industry) in each category for the interviewing stage.

Interviewing suppliers

With your list of potential purveyors in hand, pick up the phone, call each supplier, and get a *sales rep* (salesperson) assigned to you. Set up times to interview each one. Have the meeting at your restaurant if possible. You may also choose to tour the supplier's facility to observe the sanitation level, the size of the operation, and how its warehousing systems work.

Engaging in your first conversation

When you talk to suppliers on the phone, tell them who you are and describe your situation. Let them know if you're new ownership, new management, or a brand-new restaurant. Maybe you have an existing restaurant and want to interview potential alternate purveyors.

Get the supplier's sales rep *and* her boss into your restaurant for the meeting. That way, your salesperson has a clear understanding of your objectives, and her boss gets the same info firsthand from you. Often, the real power in negotiating prices doesn't lie with the sales rep. Usually her boss or boss's boss gives the thumbs up or down on special requests. If they know that you're professional and organized, with concise needs and wants, the whole process goes much smoother, and you can cut out much of the game playing before getting to the real pricing.

Conducting your first meeting

Be concise in the meeting. Your goal is to educate the supplier about your concept, your specific needs (and limitations as you see them), your concerns, and what you expect from a supplier. Show them your kitchen, your equipment, your delivery dock — basically the whole operation — so you can make them aware of all the logistics.

When you have that initial meeting, bring copies of your supply list (the whole list), divided by categories (see Table 14-1 for a sample list). Purveyors may surprise you with a more broad-based inventory than you may expect. Coauthor Andrew worked with a dairy supplier who noticed that he was using a lot of imported olive oil and specialty goods. Two years earlier, the dairy supplier had quietly amassed an inventory of these items and was selling them at a significantly reduced cost compared to the local specialty house. This chance meeting became an exclusive purchasing arrangement for dairy and select specialty products at a big savings over the previous supplier.

Keep in mind that suppliers are salespeople — they're coming to sell you products. The more you buy, the more they make.

Go through the list item by item with each supplier, starting with the supplier's specialty. Explain what you're looking for in terms of flavor, performance, packaging, and cut, and provide an estimate of how much you'll need in a given week. The supplier may interject and say things like "We don't carry that, but we carry this kind instead" or "Ours is in a 15-pound case, not a 5-pound case." Your response should be a version of "I understand. My decision is simple. I'll give my business to the company that can service the needs on this list. I'm going to spend money, and this is what I'll spend it on. If you want my money, get what's on this list done for me. If you don't want my money, I'll find someone who does."

It's becoming increasingly common for restaurants to enter into *primary* (or *preferred*) *supplier agreements* with their vendors. In these contracts, a restaurant agrees to purchase selected items from one vendor in exchange for fixed prices, volume-based rebates, and the efficiency of having a minimal number of vendors. Make it clear that you're looking to establish primary supplier agreements and that you're going to buy a certain group of items from one company. If a supplier walks away understanding that they get all or none of a group of items, you'll be amazed to see what a supplier can make happen in terms of prices, discounts, delivery, and special orders.

Don't assume that a company can't bring something in for you packaged a certain way. Sometimes a supplier really can't, for lots of reasons. But maybe the only thing a supplier needs to do to get all your business is bring in a couple additional products, take a loss of a couple cents on the pound, or split a case of a product that comes only in a quantity that's more than you need. Then the supplier has to make a decision whether your volume of business is worth the additional inventory, reduced margins, and increased customer support. Not all restaurants qualify for these types of programs, but all restaurateurs need to understand that these volume-based incentives exist and that in most cases you get only the discounts, pricing structures, delivery schedules, and products that you *ask* for.

If suppliers aren't interested in getting your business, they aren't going to be interested in servicing your business. Make it clear to them that you want them to understand your restaurant and how you want it to work. You're setting up an ongoing relationship, not just buying groceries once a week. The best purveyors understand their clients' business and bring them ideas, new products, and opportunities in the marketplace that can benefit their business. They must understand your goals, business, costs, order and delivery requirements, and where you want to position yourself in the marketplace. If they can understand your business and maintain and increase your quality, while maintaining or decreasing your costs or your labor, then you're likely to buy that product from them.

Giving them a chance to respond

At the end of each meeting, send the supplier on his way with your list, an understanding of your objectives, and an understanding of your desire to have a purchasing program with a purveyor in this category. Remind him that the purveyor who can meet most of your needs will get the lion's share of your purchasing business. Give the supplier a definite timeline to get back to you. Make it clear that you're interviewing several purveyors in your category, and mention the competitors by name. Let the supplier know that you're willing to engage in a preferred provider agreement with his company, provided that he comes back with the best possible price guaranteed for one year based on your expected volume. This step shows the supplier that you know what you're doing and you're confident in your research.

Request your sales rep's office, mobile, and home phone numbers. Ask for her boss's office and mobile numbers, too, but make sure that the sales rep is aware that you've asked for the boss's contact info. Taking this step gives her the courtesy of not being blindsided if you call her boss, and keeps the pressure on because she knows that you may call.

Comparing Prices, Quality, and Service

After your purveyors get back to you with their prices on the stuff you're interested in, evaluate their bid. Their response should include more than just their pricing strategy. It should specify their terms of service, delivery schedule, credit terms, ordering process, any extras you've asked for, applicable rebate programs, and so on. If the agreement is to be *contractual* (agreed upon by a written contract with specific order volume or a specific time period), you need to get your attorney involved to review the contract.

Now's the time to iron out any logistical details as well. If you need your product before 8 a.m. every day, you need to tell the supplier that and make sure that the commitment is in writing. If you need net 90-day payment terms (90 days to pay the bill), you both should agree to that upfront. You're building relationships and goodwill with your purveyors, but not completely relying on the purveyor. You both should be comfortable with the relationship, but the supplier shouldn't get too comfortable.

How fast you pay can often dictate what your prices are.

Considering the size of suppliers

Working with a large supplier has a major upside. Because large suppliers buy in bulk, they get better pricing than smaller companies and can pass those discounts along to you. They usually carry more categories of stuff, and within those categories, they often have many choices. They probably carry thirty brands of tomato sauce, while a smaller company may have only five.

Larger suppliers often have additional bonuses and incentives for agreeing to sign with them for a particular volume. They may be able to schedule daily deliveries if you need it because they have a larger trucking fleet than the little guys. They may give you a computer, complete with their ordering software, which you can use for other office functions as well.

Larger suppliers can also provide you with other perks, such as electronics equipment or complimentary tickets to sporting events. Some companies frown on accepting these gifts, which can be considered kickbacks and could give employees and other suppliers the impression that improprieties are occurring. So carefully weigh the options before accepting any gifts, other than preferred pricing. And if your chef is getting freebies, make sure that you're still getting the best possible pricing.

The big downside when working with major suppliers is that you're one of many customers. They take your money but won't go out of business without it. They may be less likely to give you a generous pricing program unless you can give them a guaranteed volume. They can be a bit flakier with their deliveries, invoicing, and the like. As with any large company, considerable red tape is usually involved, and often what you and your rep discuss doesn't make it to the accounting department. A problem can take weeks to get straightened out. And major suppliers have been known to bully a customer here or there, especially when it comes to a verbal agreement. Get all agreements in writing.

Small purveyors offer excellent service. They have to, or they'll be out of business quickly. With a small purveyor, you *are* his business. Small suppliers will often go above and beyond to make sure that you're happy and satisfied with your service. You can often build business relationships that last decades.

Getting what you ask for the way you ask for it

After you set up your purchasing plan, you buy things a certain way for a good reason, maybe several good reasons. If the products you order aren't the products you receive, you have a problem. If you get bone-in chicken breasts priced at the boneless, skinless price, you're not only paying more for the product, but you'll throw good money after bad with labor dollars to debone the chicken. If you get a great price on liters of gin but receive fifths (which contain 25 percent less liquor) instead, you may not be getting a deal at all.

These kinds of problems happen regularly. The situation is compounded when the person who does the ordering doesn't do the receiving. Purchase order to the rescue! A *purchase order,* or PO, is a form that the purchaser fills out and leaves for the person who receives the order. Check out Figure 14-1 for a sample purchase order. The receiver compares the stock he receives, the PO, and the invoice and looks for things that don't match. That way, if you know that you got the wrong chicken, you can fix it before someone starts thawing and marinating it.

If you're signing for a product, you have to know what you're signing for. You can't just order things, think that you got a great price, and assume that everyone along the line will perform flawlessly and the whole process will run smoothly without a hitch. More often than not, mistakes are caused by honest human error, either on the ordering end or at the purveyor's location.

Date _____ Company Name _____ Order No. _____

Account No. _____ [Your account with the supplier] _____ Page ____ of _____

Salesperson _____

To: _____ [Supplier Company Name] _____

Fax Number: _____

Email: _____

Please send the following:

Deliver Via: _____ [Your transportation requirements] _____

Deliver By: _____ [Date and time you need it] _____

Special Instructions: _____

_____

_____

Quantity	Size of Unit	Item	Unit Price	Extended Price

Page Total _____

Order Total _____

Receiving Supervisor: Please complete the following information:

Rec'd by _____ Condition of order _____

Date rec'd _____ Other info _____

Figure 14-1:
Sample
purchase
order.

When trouble occurs, how do you resolve it? Your first call should be to your sales rep. For example, suppose that the supplier's delivery driver doesn't bring you everything you ordered on a certain day. Call your sales rep. If the rep wants to keep your business, the supplier will resolve the problem for you. The rep shouldn't give you a whole line of union drivers or a separate delivery company for you to contact to pick up the rest of your order. If suppliers promise to deliver in a certain way by a certain time, they should resolve any problems for you, delivering it themselves, if necessary.

Understanding how to negotiate pricing

Pricing figures prominently on both sides of the equation — buying and selling. Your goal is to get products that match your concept and meet or exceed your guests' expectations at the lowest price possible. Then you work to sell your menu items at a price that matches your guests' expectations, covers all your costs, and leaves you a nice tidy profit.

Twenty different kinds of breaded chicken tenders may be available from your local broad line supplier. The top-of-the-line product is all-white-meat, single-muscle chicken breast breaded with focaccia, Parmesan cheese, and herbs. The lesser-quality product is a chopped and formed mystery meat with extenders, gums to hold it together, and a nondescript flavorless breading. One is cheaper than the other, but which one matches your quality standards?

Minimize your physical inventory, but maximize the way you use what you get. If you bring in beef tenderloin for your entrée menu, think about where else you can use it. Can you bring the tenderloins in whole, so you get a better price, and then use the scraps for beef bourguignon, a stir fry, or salad? This type of purchasing helps you get more utility for the same product, increasing your volume and decreasing your cost.

The only thing that matters to a supplier is how much you buy from him, not your total purchases combined from all your suppliers. Utilize volume buying whenever possible. One company coauthor Andrew worked with thought that it was doing a good job by calling around to get the best price on a particular cheese. The company was buying 80 different cheeses from 8 different purveyors, diluting the power of its gourmet-cheese-buying dollars. Take your menu and winnow it down to a core group of cheeses that you need. Do you need eight varieties of blue cheese? Maybe the three varieties that one purveyor has will do, and while you're at it, cut down that list of cheddars to four, Parmesan to two, and so on, all from the same vendor. You're beefing up your volume with a particular buyer to get better pricing.

If you can't take control of the market with volume buying, take control of your menu to take control of the market. If one company sells shredded cheddar cheese, one sells block cheddar cheese, and another sells sliced cheddar cheese, why store three different varieties of the same cheese and hope that the respective menu items sell? Instead, bring in the core item, the block cheese, and then slice or shred it according to your needs, as part of the prep. You're buying more cheese from one person, driving costs down, and fulfilling the needs of your menu.

Building an Efficient Inventory System

Your *inventory* is the stock of supplies you have on hand at any given time. It's an investment, and you get no return on that investment until that product sells. You want as little money as possible tied up in inventory but still want to be able to efficiently run your business. You do need to have an adequate supply of product on hand, but keep backup stock on hand for a purpose, such as having enough key ingredients if an order is missed or you experience an unexpected upsurge in business. Not having a key menu ingredient can be bad for business. People understand that you may occasionally run out of a menu item when you're dealing with fresh products, like seafood. But if you're consistently out of beef for your tacos, they'll start to go elsewhere.

Inventory is also a warehouse of your cash flow. Excess inventory ties up money that you can't use for other necessities until the products sell. Not managing the balance between cash flow and inventory is the failing of many a restaurant. In a competitive business such as a restaurant, you want your money where it can work for you, not tied up in the skid of sugar packets that you got for half price and that are now taking up space in the storeroom.

Salespeople love to come up with incentives for you to buy in bulk, but examine the offer closely. For example, they may say, "If you buy 100 cases of water today, you'll save $2 a case." Take a look at that deal. If you buy 100 cases of bottled water at $20 per case, you've invested $2,000 in bottled water. Suppose that it takes you two months to sell this water, but you're on net 15-day terms with your vendor. In the meantime, at your margin of 50 percent (which means half the price to your customer goes to cover what you actually paid for the water) on bottled water, it will take you a month to break even on the investment and two months to realize your profit, all to save $200. For two weeks, you're in the red on that investment, meaning that you paid more than you made. If this is a pattern in your purchasing system, your money is tied up in inventory. Meanwhile, you have payroll to meet, a lease to pay, and repairs to the toilet that backed up during the Saturday night rush.

Managing the inventory

There's no *one* way to manage and track inventory. Many systems exist for tracking inventory. Some are high tech (such as scanner guns and bar codes that automatically update the system), and some are low tech (monthly hand counting your stock on hand). Some systems are fully integrated, tracking products from the time they're delivered, through the preparation process, to the time they make it to the customer. Other systems can automatically count down your inventory as you use products. If you're missing a single can, it shows up. The systems work well if you're planning on having an exceptionally stable menu. If you're planning any kind of a change, systems that are completely automated can be more work than they're worth.

Establishing your par levels: Keeping enough product on hand

Most restaurants resort to the tried-and-true process of manual counts for inventory purposes. In most cases, food is counted on a shift-by-shift basis. Use *daily par sheets,* (itemized lists of the amount of prepped inventory you need to have to enough product on hand until your next prep period), like the one in Figure 14-2, to count your food and set up your prep schedule. For example, in the kitchen you might set a par for the amount of Alfredo sauce to have on hand or the number of steaks ready to hit the grill. In the wait station, you set a par for the number of lemons to cut for iced tea. The bar keeps a par for everything from margarita mix to beverage napkins.

Daily Par Sheet

DATE <u>January 25, 2005</u>   DAY OF WEEK <u>Tuesday</u>

POSITION <u>Prep</u>

Menu Item/ Product	Amount on Hand	Par Levels		Amount to Prep	Shelf Life	Container	Comments
		Mon - Wed	Thu - Sat				
Shaved Beef for Philly Sand	5.5 lbs.	15 lbs.	25 lbs.	9.5 lbs.	3 days	6 inch plastic tray	Add 1 lb. Peppers and 1 lb. Onions.
French Onion Soup	2.5 gal.	4.0 gal.	8.0 gal.	10 gal.	4 days	5 gal plastic tub	Prep through the weekend.
Chicken-Wellington	6	16	30	10	2 days	Third pan	See chef for recipe change.

Figure 14-2: Sample daily par sheet.

Build a functional inventory by analyzing your recipe ingredients and historical or projected sales of an item. For example, if an ingredient is in your number-one selling item, you'll use a lot of that item, so you need to have a lot of them on hand. If you're McDonald's, you'll need more fries than apple pies. That information becomes the basis for your *ordering par sheet,* an itemized list of the amount of inventory you need to have to keep you up and running between orders.

This par plan doesn't work for some things that you purchase in *economic order quantities,* which refers to things that are packaged so that you have to buy more than you immediately need to get a reasonable price for them. For example, restaurants don't typically place an order for one 5-pound bag of sugar, which may last only a couple days and cost more per pound. Instead, restaurants buy a 50-pound bag of sugar, which is enough to last through the month and cheaper per pound than the 5-pound bag. Economic order quantities are usually nonperishable staples that you buy in bulk because the products aren't available in many different sizes.

Keeping par levels and doing *shift counts* (counting your products before or after every shift) help you stay on top of your inventory. Don't wait until the end of the month to find out that you're missing supplies.

Counting your inventory

As part of your monthly income statement (which you can read all about in Chapter 5), you count your inventory. Even if you have an accountant prepare your reports, you must provide the inventory count to the accountant. This count is a full and complete account of all supplies in your restaurant. Any items that are restocked or replaced on a regular basis are supplies, while things that are part of your restaurant for a long time, like tables and chairs, are called equipment. Don't include equipment in your inventory. You're reconciling your assets on hand (your inventory) against the liability of the invoices (the bills you've paid or must pay).

Use a spreadsheet program like Excel to help you calculate the value of your inventory. Do a physical count of the products you have on hand and then multiply that by the price you paid for them. This figure gives you the value for each item on your inventory. Add up the values you paid for everything you still have on hand (from lettuce to liquor), and you have your total value of inventory. This number will be listed as an asset on your monthly income statements. Check out Table 14-2 for an example. (We use just the dairy section of Table 14-1 to show you how it works.)

Table 14-2	Sample Monthly Inventory Worksheet			
Item	**Unit**	**Unit Price**	**On Hand**	**Value**
Butter, 1 lb., unsweetened	Case, 36 ct.	$75.00	0.75	$56.25
Butter, whipped, dairy, Tub, 5 lb	Case, 6 ct.	$38.52	0.05	$1.93
Cheese, Asiago, shredded	Case, 15 lb.	$53.70	0.1	$5.37
Cheese, Bleu, crumbles	Case, 20 lb.	$49.00	0.8	$39.20
Cheese, Cheddar-Jack, Shredded	Case, 15 lb.	$39.80	1.2	$47.76
Cheese, cream, 3-lb. tub	Case, 3 ct.	$17.00	0.66	$11.22
Cheese, cubed	Case, 20 lb.	$47.73	0.25	$11.93
Cheese, mozzarella, fresh	Tub, 8 lb.	$9.91	0.5	$4.96
Cheese, Parmesan, shredded	Case, 15 lb.	$16.69	0.66	$11.02
Cheese, provolone, longhorn	Each	$8.50	0.75	$6.38
Cream, heavy, 40%, 1-quart	Case, 12 ct.	$29.72	0.5	$14.86
Cream, sour	Bucket, 5 gallon	$24.00	0.25	$6.00
Total value of inventory				**$216.86**

Using requisition sheets

Requisition sheets are kind of like POs, but they can be less formal as your business dictates. Any form that you use to track requests for supplies can be a requisition sheet. Your bartender can use a copy of the wine list to request a new stock of wine. Your sous chef can use a par sheet to request more olive oil. Or maybe you actually create a separate form that people who need stuff fill out and give to the buyer for the restaurant. Whatever system you use, make sure that it's a written system, understood by everyone involved. It's tough to keep track of who needs what if you carry 50 wines by the glass or 15 different kinds of cheese. A written system provides an excellent way to communicate requests and start a paper trail for your supplies.

Requisition sheets also provide one more check to make sure that products are staying on the shelves until they're sold — and not walking out the door or being misplaced. If your chef needs a 5-pound bucket of liquid margarine but your purchaser just got one in the day before, a requisitions sheet can help start the search for the product.

Preventing theft

Maybe preventing theft is too lofty a goal. Controlling theft or managing theft may be a better way to put it. In the restaurant business, theft has always been a problem and will continue to be. Employees aren't the only ones guilty of theft; customers, delivery people, and neighbors may also be on the take. Robbery also falls into the theft category. Deterrence is as important as actually catching the thieves. Here are ideas that can help with both.

- ✔ **Put a lock on the door:** This suggestion sounds simple, but if you want to keep people out of something, lock it up. You can lock up coolers, storerooms, separate cages for very expensive items, offices, bar wells, liquor cabinets, and just about anything else. Locks don't keep out thieves, but they keep honest people honest. If you don't give people the opportunity to steal, most people won't. If people want to steal, they'll figure out a way, but locks are your first line of defense.

- ✔ **Give keys to as few people as possible:** The fewer people with keys, the easier to find out what's going wrong. And in this case, keys are a deterrent to the few people who do have keys — they know that it's usually not hard to figure out what happened.

- ✔ **Install security cameras, but move them often:** Cameras (even dummy cameras) can be a deterrent to theft. If people think that they're being watched, they tend to behave better. If you leave the camera in the same place too long, though, the camera becomes part of the environment. People forget it's there and don't continue to stay on their toes. Consider camouflaging cameras by hiding them in a plant or behind liquor bottles.

Don't install cameras, hidden or otherwise, in bathrooms or staff locker rooms. You could open yourself up to serious legal trouble.

✔ **Install a security system:** Use motion detectors and integrate it with local emergency respondents, such as the fire and police departments. Consult an expert in commercial, preferably restaurant, security before you buy a system.

✔ **Make cash handlers accountable:** Develop a system of checks and balances for waiters, bartenders, and cashiers to be accountable for accurate checkouts. Employees who accept cash must be accountable for their sales, cash, checks, charge receipts, coupons, and any other things you accept as legal tender. At the end of the shift, your POS (point-of-sale) system, the computer ordering system, should generate a report that tells you how much each waiter owes and how she owes it. Reconcile all the paperwork and collect all cash from each employee at every shift.

✔ **Change out banks in the middle of a shift:** And remove the working cash drawer and replace it with another one. Make it an expected part of the practice. Don't do it only if you're trying to find a problem, or it's a lose-lose proposition. You're giving a thief a clear warning or you alienate the honest person. If you do it on a regular but unscheduled basis (at least as far as your staff is concerned), you can deter thieves.

✔ **Stay visible and in the know:** Personal involvement is the best defense. Know the people you deal with and let them know that you're around. Having good, professional relationships with your employees will help you find things out through the gossip mill. If employees feel like part of the restaurant family, they'll have no trouble turning someone in. If you treat them badly, they'll feel like you get what you deserve.

Keeping breakage under control

How many times have you sat in a restaurant and heard the wonderful tinkling sound of breaking glass? Have you sat close to a busy kitchen door and heard the thudding and clanking of the dish area? Whether it's Shaky the Server or Dudley the Underenthused Dishwasher, all that noise costs someone money. You spend a lot of time finding china, glassware, flatware, and cooking utensils (and an equal amount of money), so it's important to preserve them as long as possible. Whether it's one glass or a handcrafted Limoges plate, the effect is the same: a pain in your wallet.

Accidents will happen. But the root of breakage is disorganization. If your servers are organized, your food is coming out of the kitchen on time, and your dish area is tidy, you're much less likely to sustain breakage than if everything is chaos. Breakage is an expense that you probably can't eliminate, but you can take steps to control it:

✔ Keep your dish tank organized and as clear as possible. Keep the dishes from piling up.

✔ You'd be amazed if you realize the amount of flatware that gets thrown away in restaurants. Busy servers scraping plates at the dish line inadvertently drop a fork, knife, or spoon in the trash. They may not even know they did it, so the chances that they'll go dumpster diving to retrieve it are small.

Magnetic trash can covers can catch an errant fork, before it ends up in the trash. The word *cover* might be a bit misleading because it only partially covers the trash cans. As servers scrape food from dishes into the trash (before stacking them neatly, of course), the magnetic force actually pulls the silverware out of scrapings before a utensil lands in the trash. The server then grabs the silverware and puts it in its proper place in the dish area.

✔ Try motivating the dishwashers to be careful with the flatware by giving them a monetary award for every piece of silverware they extract from the trash.

✔ Use the right racks for your glasses and stemware as they're washed and stored. Make sure that the dishwashers work properly and that you use the proper detergents and sanitizers. If not, you'll have to hand wash them, and there's no quicker way to break glasses than to handle them in bulk by hand.

✔ Organize your dish area so that plates, china, flatware, and so on are neatly stacked coming in and going out.

✔ Use rubber mats in the dish area and storerooms where glass items, from stemware to liquor bottles, are stored. A simple thing can go a long way in getting more bounce for your buck.

✔ Hire quality employees and then train and communicate with them. Educate them about your values. Reward them for following the rules.

Assess what hard goods you're buying on a regular basis. Some things are more prone to breakage. Make adjustments if necessary. If the breakage is too much, you can change your dishware and glassware. If you're serving soda in 10-ounce highball glasses but going through a ton of glasses, you can raise the soda price by 50 cents and serve them in a sturdier pint glass.

Reducing waste

Waste costs money, plain and simple. Waste occurs in many places: perishable food, utilities, labor, and so on. Spend some time analyzing your operation. Identify areas where waste occurs.

The easiest way to reduce waste is to be organized and be vigilant. When you're visible, your employees are less likely to leave the water running, steal something, or forget FIFO (first in, first out; see Chapter 18 for details). Train your trainers to have your eyes for waste. Financially motivating your employees about the importance of controlling expenses benefits you immediately and forever.

Here are a few key ways to reduce waste:

✔ **Keep your utility usage in check.** Close the cooler doors. Don't open windows when the air conditioning is cranked and it's 95 degrees out. Turn off unused burners on your ranges on a slow night. Turn off lights in storerooms and coolers when no one's working in them. Fix leaky faucets as soon as you can.

✔ **Keep tabs on use of office supplies.** Sticky notes, pens, paper, and menus add up. Don't let your employees stock their home phone centers and offices with your office supplies, which are the most stolen items in a restaurant. They're small and aren't usually tracked.

✔ **Ration your linens.** Cooks can use enough towels to scrub down the USS Enterprise in a given day. Once it's dirty, every towel has to go out to the cleaners at your expense. Many kitchens ration their towels. Each kitchen or bar employee gets, say, two towels to last them the whole day. Also, clean up floor spills with dirty linen, not clean linen. Doing so may seem gross at first, but it's much more efficient to clean up half a gallon of ice water with dirty linen and then sanitize the floor with a mop than to do the same exercise with fresh-from-the-package linen.

Short-sightedness can be a huge waste. If you buy cheap china, you'll have to replace it all much sooner, at a greater expense, than if you buy decent stuff to begin with. If you buy cheap pots and pans and kitchen utensils, they won't last two shifts in a busy restaurant. But don't waste money on buying items that are more expensive than what you need in your particular situation, either. Don't buy cookware just because it has some famous guy's name on it. Be realistic about what your needs are and buy with an eye for longevity. If you're a 500-seat dinner house focused on getting people quickly through your doors, leave the copper cookware for the TV guys. Buy what you need to get the job done. Buying too cheaply or too exotically is a waste of money.

Waste can be as simple as serving food portions that are too big. If your specification is 4 ounces of fresh vegetables on the plate, don't give diners 8 ounces. If you've done your homework and studied your food costs, put your knowledge into practice.

Eliminating spoilage

Most people have opened their fridge at one time or another and found a science project. It could be a pint of strawberries wearing a "sweater," rotting bagged salad, or pork chops bought on sale that smell a little funky. In the restaurant world, however, you'll find a flat of strawberries, a case of lettuce, and maybe the whole pig. The volume is greater in a restaurant, and the impact on your wallet is, too.

The good news is that spoilage can be prevented. Begin with an attitude that spoilage is unacceptable. Don't buy a case of shredded lettuce to serve the week after next, because it won't last that long. It doesn't matter if you got a good deal on it or your sales rep gave you two tickets to the big game. The fact is that you're not going to use that lettuce before it goes bad. So whatever you paid for it is wasted money.

Order the amount of any item that you'll use well within its shelf life. For example, you may need to order berries twice a week and fresh sushi tuna three to four times (or more) each week.

After you establish your pars and are organized about your ordering amounts, be vigilant and visible. The chef, the owner, or the intern should be in the coolers and storage areas looking at products several times a day. Fresh products are preferable over frozen ones, but fresh is more prone to spoilage.

Equip yourself with the means to properly store, handle, and extend the shelf life of foods. Invest in proper stackable food storage containers to store and hold food properly. See your equipment or broad-line food rep to purchase them. Make sure that items in your cooler are covered, labeled, and dated. (Look at Chapter 18 for details and tips on setting up a safe kitchen, rotating product, and establishing an effective sanitation system.) Vacuum sealing, individually frozen or ready-to-cook portioned food items, and advancements in shelf-stable technology are improving food safety and eliminating the risk of spoilage. (Chapter 18 has details on reducing the risk of foodborne illness.)

Spoilage can happen before the product even enters your cooler doors. If it's happening outside, you have to investigate. Did the delivery person handle it wrong, leaving your case of lettuce on the sidewalk for an hour while he delivered to another restaurant? Were your quarts of cream mishandled from the plant? After you find the cause, correct the problem. And make the person responsible for the mistake accountable for his or her actions.

Spoilage from the purveyor is more likely for restaurants that don't order in case quantities. Some purveyors (certainly not all) seize opportunities to pawn off less-than-fresh product on case-breakers. But don't ask for full cases if you don't need them. Order what quantities you need, but demand first-run (über-fresh) products when you do.

Believe it or not, beer and wine are perishable. If they're not stored at a consistent proper temperature, the perishing process speeds up. If you buy 20 cases of wine and your storage area temperature is fluctuating, you better be going through your stock quickly, or the wine quality will be affected.

Chapter 15

Running Your Office

*Y*our office is an important part of your restaurant. More often than not, however, restaurateurs give very little thought to its setup and location. But much of the important management of the business takes place in this space, so set it up right to maximize your productivity, maintain a close proximity to your diners and staff members, and protect your valuable data.

Deciding Where to Put Your Office

Your office size and location, along with the number of offices you have, are a direct result of the size of your operation. Most restaurants have a main office that's relegated to the least valuable storage space and serves as a shared office for all managers. (Sometimes a chef or kitchen manager gets a desk in the dry storage area, the kitchen area where you store dry goods and canned goods so they can be closer to the kitchen and closer to their staff.)

You'll likely be stuck with an existing office or have little choice of where to locate your office. But if you have the luxury of deciding where to put it, determine who will be using office space before you decide its final location. If your managers (rather than just an office staff) are using the office, it should be as centrally located as possible to give equal access to the various departments. You want to be as accessible to your staff as possible.

If your office is in the kitchen, consider having lots of windows looking into the kitchen so that you can still see what's going on there while you're in the office. You can add adjustable blinds for occasional privacy.

If you have the space, put all managers in the same office. If you have no other choice, all the better. Each manager can benefit, almost by osmosis, by knowing what's going on in other departments. The chef can hear how you buy advertising, which can impact how he buys produce. Listening to simple phone conversations conveys your purchasing philosophy, your employee treatment, and so on, which should be consistent throughout all the business.

Some people separate managers' office space due to personality conflicts or animosity. If your chef and general manager, or your general manager and controller, don't get along and don't want to work near each other, your problems are larger than the seating chart. Separating them is just putting a tiny bandage on a gaping wound.

Creating a Communications Hub

The office is the central place through which all internal (managers and staff) and external (customers and suppliers) restaurant communications flow. And, in the restaurant world, open lines of communication are key (despite the example of many screaming chefs and temperamental managers).

Counting on your computer

For most restaurateurs, computers have become essential for administrative and management tasks. Computers mean efficiency in all areas — ordering, tracking sales, financial analysis, menu planning, communications with customers, staffing, you name it.

You may find laptops more useful than standard desktop computers. They save space and are easily portable if you want to work in the bar or the storeroom, for example. But, the computers can get lost, stolen, or damaged if you move them around, so take proper steps to protect your equipment.

In addition to the actual equipment, also known as *hardware,* you'll need the following items to get your computer systems running smoothly:

✔ **Software:** You need a variety of programs, including software programs that protect your computers from outside attack (including firewalls and other security software), total your sales and sales tax received and owed, track your wait staff's sales and declared tips, and reconcile credit card receipts. You also definitely need the following software:

• A word processing program, such as Microsoft Word (for creating menus, business correspondence, and so on)

- A spreadsheet application, such as Microsoft Excel (for tracking inventory, ordering, and figuring daily food counts)

- An accounting program, such as QuickBooks (for tracking your accounts, writing checks, and managing receivables)

✔ **Printer(s):** You need to print out all the reports, spreadsheets, menus, letters, checks, and so on.

✔ **UPS:** No, not the brown company. The UPS we're talking about is an uninterruptible power supply, which helps keep your computer's data intact in case of a power outage. Most also have surge protectors built right in to protect your system in the event of a power surge.

Picking up the phone

Get with a reputable, authorized phone system dealer to help you pick the right system for you. But consider these issues to make sure that you get the features you need without paying for the ones you don't.

✔ **Number of lines:** Think about your volume, both personal and professional (especially during peak hours). If your purchaser and your Accounts Payable person are using two of the lines and you have three lines, you're left with one line for taking reservations. Maybe you just need a single line with call waiting. Or instead maybe you need several phone lines, each one dedicated to something different: reservations, carryout orders, general business, and so on.

Factor in extra phone lines for Internet, fax machine, and credit card modems. Think about losing five potential dinner reservations because you ran an American Express card during the lunch rush or faxed an order to your supplier (see the "Using e-mail and online services" section, later in the chapter).

✔ **Personal call policy:** Set a policy and make it consistent. Detail it in your employee manual so everyone knows the expectation. This issue affects both the number of lines you have and the location of phones.

✔ **Number and placement of phones:** Maybe you want one at the bar, one at the podium, two in the office, and one in the kitchen. Decide how convenient you want the phones. But remember that more convenience means more use — and abuse.

✔ **Long-distance access:** Requiring some type of code to dial long distance adds another level of protection against high long-distance bills.

✔ **Fax:** You definitely need a fax machine, with a dedicated line. Use your fax machine to accept takeout orders, receive contracts, and even send out your menu to diners who call and request it.

✔ **Voice mail:** Generally, you need voice mail boxes for anyone who has business-related contact with the outside world. These employees include your salespeople, public relations staff, accountant or controller, and anyone who places orders or supervises staff members.

✔ **Conference call capability:** If you need to place conference calls from your restaurant, consider investing in a system that has a speaker phone and allows you to tie in callers from multiple lines at a time.

✔ **Intercom:** An intercom system is a great addition to a busy restaurant. For example, a host can page the office or kitchen without leaving the podium and doesn't risk missing an incoming diner.

Adjust the speaker volumes for business levels. What's way too loud for a quiet afternoon may be inaudible for a busy Saturday night. And keep the microphones on the office phones on at all times. Nothing is more frustrating than responding to the intercom and not being heard on the other end.

✔ **On-hold recording:** Do you want hold music, a general message, or specific promotions? If you want the ability to change the message on a regular basis, make sure you know that before you buy your system.

✔ **Toll-free-numbers:** If you're a destination restaurant with people coming from far and wide, a toll-free number may be a good idea. If you expand your offerings to include a mail-order service, a toll-free number is a must. If neither describes your situation, skip the expense.

Don't get more phone lines than you can answer professionally and promptly. You don't want to make potential customers angry with long hold times and lost or dropped calls.

Call your local phone company to ask about business rates before you select a system. Sometimes it offers different rates for different kinds of systems, and the price difference may affect your buying decision. Ask them about different rates for Small Office/Home Office (SOHO) key systems (KSU) versus private branch exchange (PBX) phones. The differences between the two are technical and deal with how the phones work with the phone lines but don't really affect your daily use of the systems. Your decision can, however, affect what you pay.

Ask about used or refurbished systems. In most cases, restaurants don't need so many extensions and features that they demand the latest phone technology, so take advantage of a better price.

Using e-mail and online services

The restaurant business is slow to adopt technology, but the Internet and e-mail have finally made their way into restaurants. E-mail is now a necessity rather than a novelty. Here are three ways that the Internet and e-mail can benefit your business:

- ✔ **Patrons can contact you:** Providing an additional way for diners to contact you is a benefit. They can use e-mail (and Web sites) to make reservations, communicate satisfaction and dissatisfaction, and place orders for takeout and delivery. In some large metro areas, e-mail and online reservations are so ever-present that some diners make reservations only via e-mail. If you don't offer this service, they won't dine at your place. Period.

  If you decide to provide your diners with an e-mail contact, you must respond to their requests in a timely manner. Consider setting up an automated message that responds immediately with a generic thank-you message each time someone e-mails you — something as simple as "Thanks for using our Web site. Someone will respond to your question as soon as possible." But you still have to follow up quickly.

- ✔ **You can contact suppliers:** Having e-mail and Internet access for your managers to contact the outside world can increase efficiency and productivity, speeding up must-do day-to-day tasks such as purchasing and ordering. Many large food brokers accept orders via e-mail or their Web sites. If you develop your own spreadsheets, you can often e-mail them to your vendors to show them which items you need and in what sizes and quantities.

- ✔ **You can contact customers:** Develop a database of customer e-mail addresses when customers contact you. Then you can send electronic advertising, mailers, special offers, and other promotional material to diners who are likely to take advantage of it. You can even encourage your diners to register to receive promotions in exchange for a drawing for a free dinner. (Check out Chapter 19 for more info on mailing lists and other ways to build a loyal customer base.)

Tracking sales with a point-of-sale system

Much more than a cash register, a point-of-sale (POS) system can be your time clock, your ordering system, your credit card processing unit, your inventory manager, your calculator for food cost percentages, and so on. Many systems today allow you to manage the business in real time instead of requiring you to analyze them only after the fact. If you can, invest in an integrated system to ease the burden of watching your numbers.

Manual cash registers mean inefficiency and botched cash handling. A *point-of-sale* (POS) system is essential for just about any restaurant or bar. POS systems allow you to track sales of particular items, sales made by particular employees, special orders, and so on. You don't have to be able to perform a hostile takeover of the Federal Reserve with the thing, and it doesn't even have to be brand-new (if you're trying to save money, look for used systems).

At the low end of the operational scale, you simply need something to track the basics, things such as sales, tax, and labor hours. With a good POS system, you know not only how many people ordered the ahi tuna but also how many people ordered it rare with an extra side of wasabi.

A POS system comes with some basic standard reports. These reports can get you started and allow you to spot and analyze general trends in your business. Generally, they provide a big-picture view of your operation. But you'll likely need more targeted and segmented info so that you can watch specific areas of your business in specific ways. So if you want to track how much fish you're selling compared to beef, you need to add that report. Make sure that the system you buy has some customization features. Sometimes, you or someone on your team can customize the reports, but often you must work with the POS distributor's programming team to create the specific reports.

Here's a list of some of the data your POS should be able to provide for you:

- ✔ **Good basic info:** This category includes info such as check average (the average total check for each table), per person average (the average amount each guest spends), per person liquor sales (the average amount of beer, wine, or liquor each person orders), dessert average (the average amount of dessert ordered by each person), and average entrée price.

- ✔ **Sales trends by both major and minor categories:** Say that you have a major category like wine. You'll also have several minor categories, such as white wine by the glass, white wine by the bottle, red wine by the bottle, red wine by the glass, sparkling wine by the glass, sparkling by the bottle, and so on. Your system should be able to break up your sales info in many different ways, like all bottle sales, all glass sales, all red sales, and so on.

- ✔ **Sales by different cost centers:** A *cost center* is a different area of the restaurant that takes in money. Your system should be able to set up each drawer of the bar as a separate cost center, each server as a separate cost center, and so on. The system should also be able to combine them to take a look at the bar as a whole, or look at all the servers as a whole. Another feature of the system enables you to see what these groups or individuals sell during specific times and shifts.

As you refine your reporting and better understand your business, look for more specific trends. You may find that a customer who orders a bottle of wine also orders 20 percent more appetizers than a customer who doesn't order wine. Maybe when Joe the manager is on duty, you tend to be busier than when John's on. Then you can use the numbers to make adjustments. Janice has a higher check average than anybody. Don't you want her in the sections that serve the most people? If you discover that you're selling only three veal osso buco dinners each night, maybe you should stop offering it. All of this info is available if you track and analyze your sales numbers.

Look for brand names like Squirrel, Aloha, and Micros when you're looking at systems. Many systems, such as Aloha, can integrate your scheduling, inventory, labor costs, accounts receivable functions, and so on into a single system. (For more on integrating all the electronics in your office, see the "Interfacing your different systems" section, later in the chapter.)

When shopping, make sure that the paper that works with the POS printers is readily available and relatively inexpensive. If you're saving a ton on the system but spending a fortune in your monthly paper supply, what are you really saving?

Interfacing your different systems

The best time to think about interfacing, or connecting, your systems is before you buy them. The most likely candidates for connectivity are your inventory and sales systems, your scheduling system and time clock, and your online reservations and your phone reservations. Think about what you want from your various systems and how you may be able to save time by connecting them. Working with an authorized POS dealer is a great first step. Your sales rep should be able to help you interface anything you're willing to pay for. The easiest way to get your systems talking is to buy software that already works together. Such software isn't always the cheapest way to go, but you can expect that the systems have been tested together and are compatible.

Hardware (the Old-Fashioned Variety)

It may be the information age, but you still have to sit on something. Here are some un-techy things you need for your office:

- **Desk and chair:** Restaurants are notorious for bad furniture, especially in the office. How much you spend is determined by the importance you place on comfort.

- **Postage machine with scale:** This item may not be essential, but it's a huge help for mailing paychecks, checks, marketing materials, and so on. But it pays for itself only if you mail lots of items. Weigh the overall cost against the convenience of having the machine before signing for it.

- **Calculator:** You'll need a 10-key calculator with a roll of paper that keeps a hard-copy record of your calculations. This old-school device is still the standard for balancing drawers, checking out servers, and so on. It's a must-have item in any restaurant office.

- **Filing cabinets:** Make sure that they have locks to protect sensitive info, such as employee records.

- **Safe(s):** The fewer people with the combination the better. Your safe doesn't need to be huge. It should be able to hold however many cash drawers you use plus at least one extra, a supply of gift certificates, credit cards accidentally left by diners, and deposits until you can get to the bank. Some restaurants use a second safe, called a *drop safe* (a safe that functions sort of like a public mailbox; you can drop your deposit through the slot, but no one except the armored car driver can open it), for holding the deposits. These safes are a good deterrent to guard against employee theft or an inside job robbery (because insiders know you can't get to the money), but they can be very frustrating to an armed robber who may not believe you can't access the money.

Here's a list of some basic office supplies you need to start and will replace as time goes by:

- **Paper:** You need legal pads, message pads, the paper you print your menu on (if you do it yourself), letterhead, paper rolls for POS printers and the 10-key calculator, and so on.

- **Envelopes:** Your supply should include legal envelopes with or without the company logo, larger envelopes for mailing banquet pricing proposals and press kits, and envelopes to match your checks.

- **File folders:** Usually letter-size folders will do the trick.

- **Forms:** Keep a supply of employment applications, I-9 forms, W-4 and all applicable tax forms, time cards, deposit slips, and so on.

- **Miscellaneous office stuff:** Don't forget things such as paper clips, scissors, sticky notes, tape, pens, pencils, trash cans, clipboards, stapler, staples, staple remover, and the like.

- **Mailboxes:** Each manager needs a plastic tray, cubby, or some kind of bin. You'll use these to disseminate written info, such as schedules, new policies, and department-specific paperwork.

Preparing for Payroll

You should have two bank accounts:

- **Operating account:** You pay all your bills from this account.

- **Payroll account:** Use the money in this account only to pay payroll checks. Shuttle money *from* the operating account *to* the payroll account, never the other way around. After you put money into the payroll account, it's gone. Even if it stays there and an employee doesn't cash his check, that's his business. Resist the urge to "borrow" from this account even if things seem tight.

As soon as you hire someone, you need to have the new employee fill out the necessary paperwork, like the I-9 and W-4 forms (see Chapter 13 for the list), so that you can properly process their paychecks. You have to pay them if they work for you, but you can't pay them without the right paperwork. This is the *ultimate* case of dotting your i's and crossing your t's. If your records are audited and you don't have the proper paperwork, you could face devastating fines, or worse.

Farming it out or doing it in-house

Depending on the size of your operation, you may opt to do all the payroll duties yourself from start to finish (or assign it to someone in your operation) or outsource some of the work to a payroll company. If you keep everything in-house, typical duties of the assigned payroll guru for each pay period include the following:

✔ **Calculating and verifying hours:** If you use an integrated computerized system to track hours worked, you should be able to print a report to verify the hours worked by each employee. If not, collect those time cards and start adding.

✔ **Confirming employee pay rates:** Computers are only as flawless as the people who program them. Data entry errors are common, so a human needs to do a double-check on this important piece of info if your time clock is computerized.

✔ **Crunching the numbers:** You have to calculate gross pay and take out taxes and FICA for each employee.

✔ **Tallying the total deposit for the payroll account:** Figure out the full amount of net pay (the amount owed after all the withholding is withheld) that you owe to your employees.

✔ **Transferring the payroll deposit from the operations account to the payroll account:** In most cases, both your accounts will be held at the same bank, so you can make a phone call or an online transaction to move money from one account to another and post it by the end of the day.

✔ **Cutting checks for each employee:** Print a separate check for each employee. Make sure that each check includes details about the number of hours the employee worked, his gross pay, and any deductions.

✔ **Distributing checks to employees on payday:** Establish a scheduled time, usually between the lunch and dinner rush, to distribute checks.

Payroll companies generally calculate the amount of withholding tax, Social Security contributions, and so on and cut the checks.

But even if you hire a payroll company, you still need someone in house to double- (or triple-) check the records and perform the functions listed earlier that the vendor doesn't cover. So decide whether that service is worth the amount of money you'll pay for it. Check with a payroll company such as ADP, Paychex, or PayMaxx for quotes and details of the services they can provide.

Deciding on a payroll period

There's no right or wrong payroll period, but once a week or every other week is pretty standard for restaurant pay periods. Every choice has its advantages and disadvantages. Pick the period that works best for you.

- **Weekly:** You keep a fairly consistent expense each week, but your payroll management time (verifying hours, cutting checks, and so on) increases.

- **Every other week:** You have no payroll expense one week and then a big expense the next week. Paying less often cuts your payroll management time virtually in half compared to paying weekly.

After you pick a pay period, pick a day to hand out or mail the checks. If your pay period ends on a Saturday, maybe you hand out checks the following Wednesday or Thursday. If you're using an outside company to cut the checks, make sure that they commit to delivering the checks by your payday. Also, always deposit money into your payroll account before you hand out the first check.

Not paying your employees on time is a telltale sign that the restaurant is in its death throes. If the employees aren't getting paid on time, everyone will know about it. Set a pay period and stick to it.

Choosing salaries or hourly wages

A *salary* is a regular wage that does not change no matter how many hours the employee works. *Hourly wages* are paid to employees at a set rate for each hour worked. Here's a list to help you decide which system works best for your employees:

- **Salary:** Team members with managerial, supervisory, or accounting-type functions usually are salaried. They include the following positions:

    - **Back-of-the-house employees:** General managers, assistant general managers, accountants, bookkeepers, controllers, kitchen managers, chefs, and sous chefs (see job descriptions in Chapter 13) are in this category.

- **Front-of-the-house employees:** This category includes front-of-the-house managers, floor managers, bar managers, the maitre d', and possibly cashiers whose cash handling and money management responsibilities are extensive.

✔ **Hourly rate:** Some staff members clock in and out at the beginning and end of each shift. Tipped employees make less of a wage than other hourly employees, usually half of minimum, and make most of their money in tips.

- **Back-of-the-house employees:** Line cooks, prep cooks, and dish staff are in this category.

- **Front-of-the-house employees:** This group includes wait staff, bussers, food runners, host staff (except the maitre d'), most cashiers, bartenders, cocktail servers, and bar backs.

Choosing a method of payment

You have several different payment methods available to you. The most common form of payment is an actual physical check, but many restaurants opt for the other forms as well.

Physical checks

Checks are the most mainstream form of payment for restaurants. The check should itemize the hours worked, taxes withheld, Social Security taxes paid, deductions for insurance payments or 401(k) contributions, and any other deductions relevant to your benefits plan.

Direct deposit

Direct deposit is a service you may want to consider extending to your employees. Instead of a physical, depositable check, the employee gets a receipt that shows his hours worked, deductions, and the amount automatically deposited in his account. Salaried employees are the best candidates because their pay amounts are the same, and their Social Security, FICA, health insurance, and other deductions are the same each pay period.

Cash

Cash is kind of an old-fashioned method of payment, but it's completely legal. Most restaurants are cash businesses. Nowadays, banks charge businesses for converting checks into cash and vice versa. If you're doing it the right way, why pay the penalty, also known as the fee, and go through a bank? It's almost an incentive to use the cash because you have it. If you legally can work in the country, you still might not have a bank account, and cashing a check may be tough for an employee, especially one new to the area or the country.

Even if you pay employees in cash, you still must withhold the proper amount of IRS-required tax and so on from their pay. Keep good records regarding all of this information because you're required to pay your portion to the government and report all the employees' wages for tax reasons.

Opting for bonuses and incentive plans

Incentive programs vary from company to company and business to business. Most people recognize incentive plans as a plan to reward employees for doing a specific job at a certain level. Common incentive plans include profit sharing, or a flat amount if managers keep their liquor costs under a certain percentage. Other incentives, like Christmas bonuses, are more like expected gifts, having very little if anything to do with how the business is performing.

The formula or criteria you develop for paying incentives must be fair, consistent, and understood by anyone eligible to receive them. Incentive programs should be keyed for very specific things, or you may not get the outcome you desire.

If you're thinking long term, you're actually going to pay the incentives that you're promising, so make sure that you can afford whatever you say you will pay. The quickest way to guarantee high turnover of your managers is to tell them that you'll give them a certain thing and then fail to do so. No one's going to stick around if you don't keep your promises.

Saving, Storing, and Protecting Your Records

Record keeping is an important part of any business. Various government agencies require most businesses to save certain information for a certain period of time. Check out Table 15-1 for our recommendations.

Table 15-1	Recommendations for Keeping Records
Records	*How Long?*
Balance sheets	Permanently
Bank statements	7 years
Cash receipts	Permanently

Records	How Long?
Cash sales slips	3 years
Credit card receipts	10 years
Contracts: employee, government, and labor union	Permanently
Contracts: vendor (after expiration)	9 years
Equipment leases (after expiration)	6 years
Equipment repair records	Life of equipment
Financial statements	Permanently
Franchise documents	Permanently
Garnishments	6 years
General ledger	Permanently
Inventory records	3 years
Inspection reports	5 to 10 years
Invoices	7 years
Job applications, nonemployee	1 year
Leases	Permanently
Payroll records (after termination)	10 years
Mortgages	Permanently
Income statements	10 years
Permits and licenses (fire, elevator, liquor, and so on)	Current on file
Tax records	7 years

Depending on the office and storage space your restaurant offers, the length of time you'll be storing particular documents, and the amount of access you'll need to the document, you can store your records on- or off-site. Wherever you store them, though, remember that temperature and moisture can be the enemy of both paper records and computer disks. Make sure that your long-term storage area protects them from excessive heat and the possibility of flooding or fire.

You also have to ensure that the information stays out of the hands of prying eyes:

- ✔ **Secure the office:** You probably keep many records stored in your office, either on the computer or as hard copies in a file cabinet or safe. Job one, then, is to secure this area. Make sure that your door has a heavy-duty lock.

  If you have a security system with cameras, you can train one camera on the office itself. You may even consider putting the recording device in a safe in the office so it can't be erased or damaged.

- ✔ **Lock all filing cabinets:** Ultimately, if someone wants to get into your file cabinet, he will. Locks don't keep criminals and thieves out of your stuff, but they do keep honest people honest. Lock up your employee records, bank account numbers, and credit card numbers.

- ✔ **Use passwords:** Make access to computers password dependent, and give access to only a limited number of employees. Also, make sure that all managers promptly log off when their computer session is finished.

- ✔ **Install firewalls:** A *firewall* is a software application that protects the restaurant *and* its clientele from hackers attempting to gain access to your computer records to either destroy them or use the information for illegal gain. Talk to the sales rep who sells you your computer systems about the best plan for protecting your system.

- ✔ **Secure credit-card transactions:** Hackers can attack your credit card system as well. Use a reputable credit card company and make sure it has protection, insurance, and *encrypted,* or secure, systems. Talk about what services the company can offer, and pick what's best suited for you.

Chapter 16

Getting the Word Out

· ·

In This Chapter

▶ Creating your message

▶ Making the most of PR

▶ Understanding advertising

▶ Bringing in repeat customers

· ·

*Y*ou may have the most incredible menu, the hippest atmosphere, the most hospitable wait staff, the hottest chef, or the best wine list in town. If no one knows about it, however, your restaurant will fail. Getting the word out about your new place isn't as easy as telling your friends and family and waiting for the word to spread around town.

Using public relations (PR) and advertising to your advantage is essential to your restaurant's success. Pick the message that you want your potential diners to hear and make sure that it gets to them loud and clear. Of course, you have to live up to your own hype, or they'll never come back. But the first hurdle is getting them in the door. This chapter gives you the details for creating your own marketing machine to bring them in.

Customers return to your business because they like it. You may get them in the first time because you sent out coupons or offered a buy-one-get-one-at-half-price night, but they probably won't come back unless they enjoyed their first experience. We get them in the door in this chapter. Check out Chapter 19 for tips on how to keep them coming back.

Defining Your Message

Purposefully crafting your *message* (what you want people to remember about your restaurant), is the key to marketing success or failure. It's understanding *what* you want to say, *who* you want to say it to, *how* you reach this group or groups and *why*, operationally, you're choosing this particular strategy. Create a *marketing plan* to get your message to the group you want to reach.

Success is rarely an accident. It's a function of motivating the buying decision of the potential customer. Efficient operational practices, consistently delicious foods, and an attractive, accessible location don't guarantee success. With all the dining choices available, consumers expect those things at a minimum. You, therefore, have to clearly communicate your message to your audience. Build your message to speak to these components:

✔ Preferred clientele

✔ Concept

✔ Competition within that segment

✔ Desired business outcomes

Simply put in restaurant lingo: It's all about butts in seats. Unless you attract a consistent flow of paying guests to your tables, you'll have a For Sale sign in your windows before you can say, "Table for . . . none."

Focusing on the consumer

One size doesn't fit all for restaurant marketing. Just as neighborhoods and cities feature cultural and economic differences, your marketing plan should address the varied needs and wants of your consumer, whose dollar you're competing for. Each scenario requires an individualized marketing plan.

The simplest advertising plan is the shotgun effect. You throw it all out there, anywhere, and see what happens. Some consumers don't care, and others will hear it, see it, or read it and then reject it. Still others won't pay any attention. So the most successful ad plans target specific consumers.

Big restaurant companies spend millions to understand the demographic (who they are) and psychographic (what they think about) profiles of their consumer. To run your advertising and promotions program well, you need to understand your targeted clientele as well. In Chapter 4, we provide you with concrete suggestions and resources for researching and defining your potential customer. After you have a handle on who your potential customers are, they become your *target audience* for marketing purposes. You need to craft your message with them in mind.

You can have multiple messages based on the differences of your consumers. You can break them up categorically to focus on gender, geography, income levels, age, interests, or any other demographics of your consumers.

Communicating your concept

Your concept is the combination of your type of restaurant, your menu and prices, the ambience your offer, and the style of service you provide. We help you establish your initial concept in Chapter 3. And your concept will likely become more concrete as you analyze your local market (as we explain in Chapter 4). But, to get folks in your door, you have to tell them who you are, what you're offering, and why they should care. Your message should express these points.

Keeping up with the competition

You're competing for just one thing — the discretionary food service dollar of the consumer. Those food service dollars are owned by a spectrum of consumers more or less likely to use your concept, with varying frequency. Your job is to identify your competition and then determine their strengths and their weaknesses and determine your points of difference. (We guide you through both processes in Chapter 4.) Simply put, a *point of difference* is how you're different from your competition. At that point, you're ready to tailor your marketing plan to counter your competitors' strengths or attack their weaknesses in an attempt to attract a segment of the market.

Emphasizing points of difference

Your message can focus on a clear-cut point of difference versus your competition. This tactic is extremely common, but you have to decide how aggressively you want to point out your competition's weaknesses, rather than simply emphasizing your own strengths. "We don't microwave our burgers" clearly conveys the fact that the others do, so diners should choose you over them. Or your message could be a more subtle statement of a great feature of your concept that leads the consumers to compare your features with another place: For example, "We cook our pizza in a wood-fired oven." You're not saying that the other guy doesn't, but you're leading the customer to think about how the pizza they ate yesterday was cooked and how it could've been better if it had been wood-fired.

When you're defining your own point of difference, think about the burger wars. McDonald's, Burger King, Wendy's, and Hardee's all have similar menu items on the surface: burgers and fries, basically. But for years, they've focused their marketing on a point of difference, such as the following:

- **Price:** Enter the 99-cent menu.
- **Value:** The combo meal concept is an example.
- **Quantity:** Think super-size.

✔ **Quality:** Flame-broiling versus frying may be the difference.

✔ **New menu offerings:** Examples include premium salads, popcorn chicken, and low-carb dishes.

These companies spend millions each year trying to leverage their individual points of difference — whether it's their combination of offerings, size of portions, extended hours, kids' toys, co-branding with the hottest new movie, or dollar-burger days — and make it resonate with consumers. They're answering the needs and wants of their targeted consumers and shaping the future of the market by centering their marketing campaigns on emerging trends and development of new products that their competitors will have to respond to in order to protect market share.

After you're established, don't fall into the trap of just marketing to your strengths. You don't need to target that segment that will visit your restaurant whether you advertise or not. In a competitive marketplace, you must highlight the "WOW" (the new and exciting parts of your business) to attract a constant flow of new diners looking for variety.

Facing off — head to head

You can always choose to go head to head with your competition. "My secret family recipe fried chicken will kick your fried chicken's butt, Colonel!" Your competitor launches a French toast breakfast sandwich, so you counter with a sausage, egg, and cheese grilled waffle panini. Just don't make the mistake of always being the copycat. Create your own point of difference instead of taking a me-too approach all the time.

Maybe you have pizza on your menu, but you can't make it like Mike's Pizzeria pizza, which has been the favorite in your area for 36 years. Instead of trying to imitate its deep-dish, Chicago-style pizza, try focusing on your thinner crust, European-style pizza. You're still doing pizza, but you're offering consumers a different choice in the same type of food. You're not going head to head in a war you may not win.

Conceding strengths

Another approach is to concede a competitor's strength and focus on something it doesn't do at all, such as breakfast or steaks. For example:

✔ Arby's served basically only hot roast beef sandwiches for years. Then, instead of going after the traditional burger market, it got some really good bread and developed its cold sandwich program, called the Fresh Market program.

✔ Domino's also tried something new. Instead of relegating itself to being just another pizza joint, Domino's branched out with its delivery options. It added chicken wings and dessert items for more variety.

Introducing the new and improved Us

For years Hardee's continued down the path of touting its burgers, but the product just wasn't going over well with consumers. "Stick to biscuits" was a common slam hurled at the fast food restaurant. Then it started spending big bucks to launch an ad campaign highlighting its own reinvestment in the quality of its products. The ad campaign was well received even though it was essentially an apology: "The last place you'd go for a burger will now become the first." You must be honest about the marketplace identity of your restaurant if you're going to continue to improve it. Understand your goals. Be honest when you fall short and, most importantly, live up to your message.

In your case, suppose that two identical restaurants are located on the same block, but one offers a 15-minutes-or-it's-free lunch menu. Instead of adding your own 14-minute menu, maybe you offer a lunch buffet.

Getting tactical

You can also craft your message to achieve strategic results. For example, if you were fortunate enough to lock in a great price on 500 kilos of free-range, all-white-meat chicken nuggets hand formed into the lifelike image of Michael Jordan, you might design a marketing strategy to drive sales of these signature items and take advantage of your razor-sharp business acumen.

You see examples of this type of strategic marketing everyday. Simply consider the strategy behind "value meals," "super-sized" menu upgrade options, and "add a side of popcorn pigeon for $1.99." These suggestions appear as attractive discounts offered by a generous operator grateful for your patronage. In reality, they're carefully crafted strategic marketing decisions designed to increase customer traffic, maximize profitability, and drive customer purchases toward high-margin menu items. In short, it works like this: "I'll discount the soda that costs me 10 cents per serving if you purchase the 'Half-Pound Holstein Melt' that I make nearly $2 on."

Look at your marketing plan as your best opportunity to control the buying decision of your customer. A well-designed, purpose-driven marketing message can both increase your operation's top line by attracting new customers to your restaurant and increasing the frequency-of-use by your existing customer base; the same plan can also increase the all-important bottom line by inducing patrons (consciously or unconsciously) to select those items on your menu that are the most profitable.

Using Public Relations

Public relations, or PR, means developing a positive public perception of your restaurant with the local community and the media. Here are some examples of PR:

- ✔ Stories about you appear in the media, featuring you feeding volunteers at the toy donation drop-off site.

- ✔ A radio station mentions you have the best fries in town.

- ✔ A local restaurant critic reviews your place.

- ✔ A magazine includes your Mississippi Mud Pie recipe in its decadent desserts feature.

- ✔ An airline mentions your restaurant in an in-flight movie on what to do in Memphis, Tennessee.

- ✔ Travel and restaurant guides rate you.

Usually, PR is something you don't pay for. The tools to get the PR may cost you, but usually PR doesn't have a direct cost like advertising does. You didn't pay to have the article put in that magazine about your mud pie, but the guy who wrote the article came in for lunch twice and dinner another time and you paid for it. The chef spent time describing the recipe, and you spent time with him and impressed his friends. Maybe you even paid a PR company to contact him about writing the story, but you didn't pay for the story.

Planning for the good and the bad

Good PR is a fantastic asset. If you have a good PR machine working, you spend less time and money on other promotions, including advertising. If everybody already wants to come in, then you don't need to advertise in the local dining magazine every week or hold special events.

But PR can also hurt you. If you have a British burger joint and Mad Cow is running rampant in the press, that's bad PR; it will hurt. Sometimes media stories are political, over-hyped, health concerns, but no matter how true or false, they alter public perception, which affects your business. If you get a bad review from a critic, it can hurt. If people haven't been to your restaurant before, this may be this first thing they hear about you. If you don't make a good first impression, you may never get a chance to make another one.

Positioning positively: The press kit

Your *press kit* is the package of promotional materials that you should have at the ready to send to people who want details about your restaurant. It should contain all pertinent info about the restaurant including the phone and fax numbers and Web site and e-mail addresses. Include information about designated contact people, like the chef, general manager, PR person, owner, banquet planner, and so on. Any positive press clippings about your place should make an appearance. Add a summary of your restaurant's history or goals and specifics about your cuisine. Detail your mission statement. Include business cards, a copy of your menu, and something that tells someone what the restaurant's about, such as a postcard if you're in a scenic area or a matchbook if you're a cigar bar. In general, the more unique, the better. Anytime you can do something that separates you from everybody else, it's great. Put it all in a sturdy folder, preferably one with your logo.

Preparing for the worst: Contingency planning

Drawing attention to yourself is good. But after you're up and running, you become a target. You need to have a game plan for handling negativity, whether it comes from the competition, a disgruntled critic, or a disappointed customer. Role play or run through different negative scenarios with your staff and your managers. Ask specific questions related to your concept. Here are a few to get you started:

- ✔ What do we say if people get sick from an oyster? A green onion?
- ✔ What do we do if we have an underage drinker in the bar?
- ✔ How do we handle an aggressive newspaper reporter asking about our employee strife?
- ✔ How do we respond to a less than glowing review? Or do we?

Make it a regular practice to anticipate bad scenarios. The exercise helps you prevent the situation by taking the precautions against it. It heightens awareness of potential issues, improves food safety, and ensures product quality enhancement. And it helps you to be better prepared for dealing with the customer or press questions.

Going it alone

As with most things, you can manage your PR yourself, hire someone to do it, or hire someone to do part of it. Depending on your budget, you may start doing it yourself and then work up to hiring others after you're running a 150-restaurant conglomerate.

The do-it-yourself (or with your team) approach can work very well. You know your product and your concept, and you can make quick decisions about specials, promotions, and incentives. You save money because your time is paid for already and time because the communication is more direct. The downside: Tons of work and another serving of stress to your already full plate. Plus, you don't get the different perspective of your operation that an outsider can bring — a fresh pair of eyes and some new ideas.

Getting noticed in the community

PR is the public perception of both your restaurant and the most visible people in your restaurant, most likely you. Our best advice is to simply do things the right way. The goal here isn't to avoid attracting negative attention. Your goal should be to make a positive contribution to your community — a positive *visible* contribution to your community. The rewards are twofold: You make a difference, and you generate goodwill for your business.

Have the restaurant participate in charity events, including silent auctions or special dinners. Encourage your chef to teach cooking classes on occasion at the local community college or gourmet shop. You can build community relationships and relationships with other restaurant peers.

Make the most of these opportunities to let people try your food. Be in the booths at the major events in your area, like charity events, neighborhood or community events, or street fairs — whatever is appropriate to your business.

You, personally, have to make the effort as well. Volunteer for a board or join the Chamber of Commerce or the food service advisory board for a country club. Find something that gets you noticed within your clientele group. Or even better, join the group that your clientele wants to be. Coauthor Mike is on the board of Grand Central Neighborhood Association, a social services organization that feeds, shelters, and gets work for the homeless in the Midtown area near his restaurant. Coauthor Andrew served on the board of Second Helpings, an Indianapolis-based food rescue organization that repurposes food that restaurants and caterers donate for homeless shelters and missions, as well as provides culinary training for the homeless.

Generating positive PR from the inside

The ideal situation is to have a staff that works as a mini-PR machine. Bartenders build up the waiters. Waiters talk up the chef. The chef meets people at the tables or has an after-dinner drink in the bar. Good service equals good PR.

These examples aren't only ways to generate good internal PR; they also generate word-of-mouth PR — the good word about your restaurant that spreads outside the restaurant. There is no word of mouth until you start it.

Word-of-mouth PR includes diners telling their friends about their experience at your place and talking about your ads, PR, location, and so on. Basically anytime anyone is talking about your establishment, it's word-of-mouth PR.

People gravitate to busy restaurants. If your restaurant is too big, your options include moving to a smaller location (expensive) or building a visible partition to make it look busier. Otherwise, just wait for the axe to fall. Here are some ideas for building the buzz and creating the initial prestige:

- ✔ Get a plug from a writer, DJ, or sports figure.

- ✔ Make the most of a celebrity sighting in your place. Anonymously leak the information to the local entertainment reporter. You can also casually mention it to regulars, who in turn (hopefully) pass it on to others.

- ✔ Seed the parking lot with expensive cars and the occasional limo if you want a higher end clientele. Rent them if you have to.

- ✔ Make it hard to get reservations. But don't make it too hard.

- ✔ If you're serving a particular ethnic cuisine (like Mexican, Chinese, or Indian), get diners who are originally from those cultures to frequent your place. Nothing says "authentic" better.

- ✔ Create buzz about a signature dish by giving free samples to everyone. If you want to be known for the best onion rings, make sure that each person who comes in the door gets a sample. They'll tell their friends how great they are and hopefully order a whole batch next time.

Courting your neighbors is a good (and necessary) first step because you them on your side. But be careful: Don't exclusively target your neighborhood unless it can fully support you. You may suffer from "secret syndrome" — neighbors don't want to share it with the outside world. Long-term success comes from a balance of neighborhood support and extra-neighborhood support. If you make your restaurant a destination, as word spreads, it'll become bigger than the neighborhood.

You can generate a ton of talk and a huge buzz, but to move from being the "in" place of the moment to a perennial favorite, you have to deliver on your promises and exceed your guests' expectations (see Chapter 19).

Getting some help

A PR firm should have connections already. In addition to talking with several people at the firm, speak to the person who's actually handling the account before signing with the firm. If you don't feel comfortable with the account rep, pick another person or even a new firm. You're looking for someone who's personable and charismatic. If you don't enjoy talking with someone, how will your potential diners feel?

Pay someone by event

Say that you're having an event in your restaurant and inviting all the major chefs in town. Or you're having a blueberry-pie-eating contest and promoting it in the media. A PR rep or firm can help you spread the word. Maybe you're trying to promote a holiday dinner or a recipe, and you just want someone to get this one thing done. Use it as an opportunity to audition a PR company. Start small with a single event and then add a few things to the firm's plate.

Some PR companies specialize in restaurants in large cities. In smaller areas, you may find a more general PR company who may do PR for the local hospital, charities, a new gym on the west side, and a few restaurants as well.

Hire a person or a firm for full-time work

Even if you source out your PR work, you must remain actively involved in the process. You get as much out as you put in. A PR professional is the multiplier of your effort. If you put in zero effort, you still get zero out of it. Confirm that everything is meeting your expectations and approval. Review all press releases. Stay on top of things.

A good PR agency probably has a well-oiled PR machine already working and a system already in place and is fitting you in as a client. Such a business won't be reinventing the wheel or using you as a guinea pig. You should be able to get fairly quick results, compared to doing it all on your own.

Creating an Advertising Plan

An *advertising plan,* the plan you use to inform the world about your restaurant, is as unique as your restaurant. Advertising differs from PR in that you always pay for advertising. No one plan works for everyone. And the same formula probably won't work for your restaurant from year to year, or season to season. What works in January doesn't necessarily work in July. Maybe in 2000 your $50 burger was a great idea, but a few years later, the economy was completely different, and people were looking for value.

Developing an advertising plan is an investment in both time and money. Make sure that you're managing advertising like any other expense of time or money. It should be efficient and offer the greatest return on your investment. But unlike other expenses in your business, it's a *speculative* investment, meaning you're rolling the dice and saying, "I'll make this investment in hopes that I'll see a return in the food service dollar."

After you know your target audience to a T (see the "Focusing on the consumer" section, earlier in the chapter), figure out where to reach them. Many of the same sources you initially look at to research these folks are the same places you use to reach them — local newspapers, foodie magazines, TV, radio, and other sources we provide you with in Chapter 4.

Make concerted decisions about what outlets you choose to convey your message. You should know which section of the newspaper to put your ad in. If you're opening a sports bar with beer pitcher specials and the obligatory "I ate the whole thing" T-shirt you win for eating the 40-ounce steak, don't waste your ad dollars in *Ladies Home Journal.* Find out enough about your potential consumer to know that if you're in the Upper Peninsula of Michigan, you may well reach more people in the hunting and fishing publication than on the local sports scores and stats page. (And if your ad includes a picture, show somebody just like your desired clientele.)

Put together a plan to reach your clientele in as many ways as you can. Think about the reach of really big companies. Ask yourself what age you were when you knew every component of a Big Mac (two all-beef patties, special sauce, lettuce, cheese, pickles, onions, on a sesame seed bun). These folks have reached you since you were born. They continue to speak to you, consciously or unconsciously throughout your life, and it's no accident.

Here are some successful strategies we've used to get people in the door:

- **Use incentives:** Send coupons to your targeted clientele. This approach traditionally works for casual concepts, diners, and family restaurants. You can offer 2-for-1 entrées, a free appetizer, a kids-eat-free meal with paying adult, or anything else relevant to your concept and clientele.

- **Run TV commercials:** This approach can be expensive. You pay for the creation of the commercial (including actors, writers, a director, and production personnel) and the airtime to run the commercial.

- **Place print ads:** Use local newspapers and magazines and dining or entertainment papers. If your potential diners are reading the periodical, let them see your restaurant. Alumni newsletters are an idea — former classmates may be interested in checking you out.

- **Sponsor a local athletic team or event:** Don't just consider softball and bowling teams. Peewees to blue hairs, fishing tournaments to soccer leagues should be considered.

- **Find exposure on buses, trains, or cabs:** If your potential patrons use these modes of transportation, you may find an interested audience.

- **Go global on the Internet:** There are innumerable ways to promote your establishment using ads here. Connecting to other Web sites (cross-pollination), pop-ups, banners, and the like are relatively new and more and more effective.

If you're a new restaurant, your primary advertising objective should be to make people aware of your existence and your offerings. Therefore, your ad has to be informative and educational. Answer all the questions you ask when somebody mentions a restaurant to you that you've never heard of or dined at. Your consumers can then become word-of-mouth advertisers and help spread your message. You want consumers who see your ad to be able to answer specific questions about your restaurants like what you serve, when you're open, and where you're located. They can't talk about you if they don't have anything concrete to say.

Your message should speak to your to your target audience and tell them who you are, where you fit into the local dining scene, and how they should respond to your ad. Figure 16-1 contains our example of a well-rounded ad that addresses each point. Say we're opening Andy's Sports Bar and Grill. From a menu standpoint, we're serving burgers, sandwiches, and wings. We plan to focus our beverage sales on beer. The theme is sports friendly. We're trying to bring in a clientele comprised mostly of males between the ages of 18 to 45, middle to upper-middle income, with free nights to pass in our place and disposable income to spend. Who are we competing with in terms of our menu? Our concept? Where else do our customers go to eat? They probably also go to Hooter's, Dave and Buster's, and ESPN Zone. But that same segment, or group, of men eats at fast food and pizza establishments, with a skew toward delivery. We plan to target those who need to get in and out. This thought process gets us to the point where we can establish our point of difference. Our ads should target the audience we've identified.

Suburban Greencastle's first and only destination sports bar, featuring Hand-Pattied Black Angus Burgers, Wood-Fired Pizzas, Garlic Cheese Fries, and our signature Wing Flights where the flavor builds from ho-hum to HOLY S@#!. Our spacious bar offers an ever-changing selection of over 100 domestic, import, micro-brewed, and locally-produced beers on tap in addition to the most expansive collection of artisan bourbons, fine whiskeys, and small-batch tequilas in the Midwest.

With over 80 television monitors, including four 72" high-definition plasma screens, you'll never miss a moment of the action. You can count on your favorite sporting event to be on at Andy's. We carry all the big games from the NFL, NBA, MLB, NHL, and college. Or join us in the recently expanded Pit Lane for real-time racing action from NASCAR, IRL, CART, and Formula One. And don't forget to step into The Ring, our private cigar lounge for all your boxing action.

Andy's Sports Bar and Grill, right across from Blackstock Stadium at the corner of 1st and Park. Open seven nights a week with convenient, complimentary, valet parking for members of our Hall of Fame VIP Club.

Come for the food, stay for the game. It's on at Andy's.

Figure 16-1: Sample ad copy.

Part IV
Keeping Your Restaurant Running Smoothly

The 5th Wave   By Rich Tennant

©RICHTENNANT

"I showed Patrick where the pots and pans are.
Now he wants to know where to go to sharpen
and hone his compensation package."

In this part . . .

Whether you're currently running a restaurant or you're still in the planning stages, this part is for you as we focus on maintaining and building on your current operation. We offer suggestions that can help you improve your current style of management, attract and retain long-term customers, take another look at cleanliness and safety, and crunch the numbers to improve your financial standing.

Chapter 17

Managing Your Employees

• •

• •

*B*usiness would be great if it weren't for people. We say this with tongue firmly in cheek, but some days, it definitely feels that way. When you have three servers clamoring for the same Saturday night off, your dishwasher didn't show up, and you discover that an expensive bottle of wine is missing, you just might agree. In this chapter, we help you work through some of the common obstacles that come up while managing employees, and we give you tips on how to avoid most of them.

Selling Employees on Your Restaurant

Whether you're opening your doors for the first time or ten thousandth time, your success is intrinsically linked to the performance of your staff. And the way to get a top-notch performance out of your employees shift in and shift out is make sure that they feel like they're part of something special. You have to continuously sell your vision, your restaurant, your food, and their vital role in the process to every staff member.

Simply hearing about your enthusiasm for your business and concept only takes you so far with employees. You must talk the talk, but you also have to walk the walk. Make sure they see you consistently exhibiting your standard of guest service, insisting on meeting and exceeding diners' expectations, and maintaining high food-quality standards. Don't just *tell* them how they should perform; *show* them every single day, every single shift.

Educating your employees

Continuous employee education keeps your staff informed about and interested in your business. Correct training from Day 1 is essential (see Chapter 13 for details). But *educating* your employees entails more than initial training programs. Use weekly, monthly, and daily staff meetings to educate, inform, and motivate your employees. Share as much information about your business as you can. Investing the time to train and educate them properly shows that you view your employees as an important asset to your business. A good place to start the education process is with the food and the beverage program:

✔ **Periodic menu tastings:** If you're just opening your restaurant, have a complete menu tasting. You train two teams at once: The kitchen trains on preparation and presentation, and the wait staff gets lessons on the taste and appearance of the food. Let the wait staff develop a subjective opinion about the menu by describing, in their own words, how they feel about the offerings. You run the risk that they'll impart personal preferences on the diners' experience, but if they're good salespeople, they can find a pleasant, honest way to describe any dish.

If the restaurant is in operation, conduct mini-menu tastings on a regular basis. Once a day, or at least a couple times a week, bring out items that are on your regular menu, not just the daily specials. These tastings affect food cost but give your wait staff more knowledge and confidence in what they're serving, and that leads to better service (and sales).

✔ **On-going beverage training:** Any day's a good day for employees to learn more about your beverage program. Your beverage sales reps should be willing to come in and talk with your staff about any category of liquor, beer, or wine (on their own dime). The more your staff knows about a product, the more likely they are to sell it.

Reps can let the staff taste different vodkas side by side or introduce your employees to the nuances of scotches or ports. And schedule time with your wine reps. Ask them to pair their wines with your food and let your staff taste them together. Wine reps can provide your staff with good basic information about wine, like the terminology used to discuss it, as well as details about the specific wines in their portfolio.

Motivating your staff

Keep the momentum going by praising your employees often, encouraging them to praise each other, and displaying a positive attitude. Keeping morale up is key. The following are ways we've found to be effective in boosting and maintaining morale:

✔ **Encourage communication:** Keep an open door policy. Make yourself available to listen to the staff when they have something to say. And encourage them to communicate with each other. Their feedback may not always be positive, but if they get some say in resolving a problem, they're likely to stick with the solution.

✔ **Offer constructive criticism:** Clear, concise feedback to employees on their performance is essential, and often, the message is that they need to improve. But don't beat them up with the criticism. Get your point across in a way that also encourages the employee to perform at a higher level.

✔ **Praise them:** Pat them on the back for a job well done. If they only receive negative feedback, you're the one doing something wrong.

✔ **Know your staff:** Demonstrate a real interest in (and knowledge of) what's going on in employees' outside life (like tests, school, and other jobs). Talk to them and ask specific questions, such as "How's that Juliet part going?" or "Did you get that gig at the Sly Fox?" Such questions show employees that they matter to you and that you're paying attention. Small things, like acknowledging birthdays, also go a long way to build morale. (Add the birthdays to your calendar as a recurring annual event.)

Asking your staff personal questions also can be a minefield. Don't get too personal or ask questions that could darken their mood. Understand their individuality. What one person may appreciate another may consider an intrusion or an insult.

✔ **Encourage camaraderie among your staff:** Look at how the informal hierarchy treats different people, both veterans and newbies. When new people are treated well, they're much more enthusiastic about their training and tend to stay longer.

The pecking order should have zero impact on how you treat your staff and the amount of respect you pay them. A kitchen can't run without a dishwasher, and don't forget it.

✔ **Don't lose your cool:** Employees (and customers) can smell fear. If they see you act rattled or distressed during busy times — or feel that you're not in total control — your behavior may be infectious. The people around you may start feeling uncomfortable and become upset. Don't let it show if you feel out of control. Staying composed is half the battle.

✔ **Implement specific staff incentive programs:** Small-scale incentive programs are a tried-and-true path to boosting morale. Don't focus staff incentive contests on general stats, such as overall sales for a shift. Instead, get your staff focused on specific products or categories of products to build enthusiasm. Do a training session on your wine-by-the-glass program and coordinate that with sales contests and incentives during the following shifts. Get creative with the prizes: Give them a bottle of your house wine, a preferred parking space, or an extra day off. Motivating your staff doesn't have to cost you lots of cash.

✔ **Encourage apprenticeships, either formal or informal:** You want experienced staffers to take the new ones under their wing. When possible, give perks, such as preferred schedules or free lunches, to trainers and mentors.

✔ **Watch for animosity between front-of-the-house (FOH) staff and back-of-the-house (BOH) staff:** If you've spent more than a minute working in a restaurant, you know that this problem is all too common. The best way to combat it: Keep the lines of communication open. Have meetings that include both FOH and BOH staff to ensure that everyone hears the same info delivered the same way. Don't favor one department over the other. Keep in mind that the chef is more likely to side with the cook rather than a waiter, and a manager is more likely to see the waiter's point of view rather than the cook's. In order to succeed, both departments need to work together.

✔ **Turn the mirror on yourself:** What you do is reflected in what your staff does. You can't expect the cook to be nice to the waiter if you're not nice to the cook. You can't expect friendly service from your busser if you're not smiling at him. And don't forget managers are staff, too. How you treat them affects how they treat the rest of the staff.

Sure signs of good and bad morale

Morale, both good and bad, trickles through your organization straight down to your diners. It shows in how the employees treat each other and how they work together as a team. Keep on the lookout for both kinds of morale. Here are examples of both to help you keep your eyes peeled:

The good:

✔ The staff goes out together after work.

✔ The sauté cook helps out the fry cook when he's overwhelmed with fried calamari orders.

✔ A waiter sees a group looking around, and even though it's not his table, he helps out to take the order.

✔ Waiters restock service bar glassware.

✔ A pantry cook helps busy bussers sort dirty dishes at the dish counter.

✔ Waiters deliver food for the bar customers.

✔ Waiters make a new pot of coffee when they take the last cup instead of expecting someone else to do it.

The bad:

✔ An employee has a restraining order out against a coworker.

✔ A waiter berates a busser in front of a customer for *any reason*.

✔ A waiter gives the bartender attitude because she needs to wait for drinks even though the bartender is trying to break away from a conversation diplomatically.

✔ A hostess doesn't seat a particular waiter's section because he didn't clear a table fast enough.

✔ A waiter doesn't clear a table because it's not his job.

✔ A cook makes a waiter wait for food just to teach him a lesson.

✔ Waiters berate the kitchen staff and vice versa.

Making Staff Schedules

Creating a schedule is a necessary step for any business that relies on shift workers with changing hours. A posted, written schedule communicates who will be working and when they should be in the restaurant. Making schedules for the wait staff in the restaurant is one of the toughest jobs in the working world. You're dealing with part-timers, many of whom have other jobs, attend school, are aspiring actors, and so on. Many employees may have scheduling needs that change from week to week. Back-of-the-house employees tend to be a bit more consistent in their schedule expectations.

Adding it all up

The best way to create your schedules is to start with a job slot list. A *job slot list* is a chart that helps you determine the number of people you need, doing a particular job, at a particular time. Your job slot list will change for different shifts, or meal periods like breakfast, lunch, and dinner, and change based on the days of the week, weeks of the month, and months of the year, just as your business levels change.

Check out the job slot lists in Figures 17-1 and 17-2. These job lists are for the back and front of the house for the fictional restaurant Heather's Bistro on Batavia. First, a bit of background: Heather serves casual French-American fusion cuisine to a bustling lunch crowd that comes for her croque monsieur, cassoulet, and tarte flambé. *Cover counts* (the number of diners in her establishment) for dinner are steady during the week and peak on the weekends, when the pre-theatre rush brings diners looking for steak au poivre, pommes frites, and escargots Pernod.

	Monday	Tuesday	Wednesday	Thursday	Friday	Saturday	Sunday
	Average Covers Lunch/Dinner	*Average Covers Lunch/Dinner*	*Average Covers Lunch/Dinner*	*Average Covers Lunch/Dinner*	*Average Covers Lunch/Dinner*	*Average Covers Lunch/Dinner*	*Average Covers Lunch/Dinner*
	60/100	*60/100*	*60/100*	*75/120*	*80/165*	*100/165*	*100/60*
Job Classification	*Employees Required to Fill Position*						
Dish	0.5/1.0	0.5/1.0	0.5/1.0	1.0/1.0	1.0/2.0	2.0/2.0	1.0/1.0
Sauté	1.0/1.0	1.0/1.0	1.0/1.0	1.0/1.0	1.0/2.0	1.0/2.0	1.0/1.0
Fry	0.5/1.0	0.5/1.0	0.5/1.0	0.5/1.0	1.0/1.0	1.0/1.0	0.5/1.0
Broiler/Grill	0.5/1.0	0.5/1.0	0.5/1.0	0.5/1.0	1.0/1.0	1.0/1.0	0.5/1.0
Pantry	1.0/1.0	1.0/1.0	1.0/1.0	1.0/1.0	1.0/1.0	1.0/1.0	1.0/1.0
Prep	1.5/0.0	1.5/0.0	1.5/0.0	1.0/1.0	1.0/1.0	1.0/1.0	1.0/0.0
Totals	**5.0/5.0**	**5.0/5.0**	**5.0/5.0**	**5.0/6.0**	**6.0/8.0**	**7.0/8.0**	**5.0/5.0**

Figure 17-1: Job slot list — back of the house.

Heather's Bistro, via Figure 17-1, provides examples of common staffing techniques used to conserve labor and maximize productivity that you may want to use:

✔ **An overall buildup of labor commensurate with anticipated business levels:** Traditionally in the average restaurant market, here's what you find:

- Thursday is busier than other weekdays.

- Friday and Saturday are busy all day.

- Sunday is busy early; business then tapers off in the early evening.

✔ **Job sharing during slower shifts:** Some stations are shared on some lunch shifts. One employee works the fryer and the broiler for early week lunch shifts. The dishwasher and prep share some duties on Monday.

✔ **Concentration of morning prep labor early in the week:** This scheduling gives the staff time to prep items like salad dressings, desserts, and soups for the whole week. And notice that more prep people are scheduled for lunch than dinner. Most prep takes place during your slower periods so that you can gear up for your busy times. See Chapter 11 for details on prep and the stations in the kitchen.

The job slot list in Figure 17-2 is also based on business levels that increase toward the weekend, through a busy lunch on Sunday but earlier dinner. In the front of the house, you may make other adjustments as well. For example, you may need only five waiters to handle your Friday night dinners if they're experienced and reliable. If you have newer, less experienced people, you may need seven waiters.

As with the back of the house, always look to save FOH labor dollars during traditionally slow shifts. In Figure 17-2, notice that an a.m. bartender is scheduled on Monday to put away the big weekly liquor order, and then none are scheduled again until Friday. Managers can handle any guest orders for alcoholic beverages during these shifts.

Schedules aren't set in stone. You can make adjustments later based on experience (yours and theirs) and business levels. During each shift, you cut one or more employees (end their shift early) if your sales don't meet your projections during a certain time of the day.

Consider implementing an on-call system if you have very dynamic business levels, especially until you establish some patterns. An *on-call employee* calls into the restaurant an hour or so before a scheduled shift to see whether he or she's working that night. If other employees call in sick or you get slammed with traffic you weren't expecting, having this extra person on the schedule can be a lifesaver. If you don't need that person, she gets a bonus night off. Be sure to rotate this duty, especially if you don't need the on-call staff very often. Most employees work because they need the money.

	Monday	Tuesday	Wednesday	Thursday	Friday	Saturday	Sunday
	Average Covers Lunch/Dinner	*Average Covers Lunch/Dinner*	*Average Covers Lunch/Dinner*	*Average Covers Lunch/Dinner*	*Average Covers Lunch/Dinner*	*Average Covers Lunch/Dinner*	*Average Covers Lunch/Dinner*
	60/100	*60/100*	*60/100*	*75/120*	*80/165*	*100/165*	*100/60*
Job Classification	*Employees Required to Fill Position*						
Wait staff	3.0/4.0	3.0/4.0	3.0/4.0	4.0/5.0	5.0/6.0	6.0/6.0	6.0/4.0
On-call wait staff	0.0/0.0	0.0/0.0	0.0/0.0	0.0/0.0	0.0/2.0	0.0/2.0	0.0/0.0
Bartender	1.0/1.0	0.0/1.0	0.0/1.0	0.0/1.0	2.0/2.0	2.0/2.0	2.0/1.0
Bussers	1.0/1.0	1.0/1.0	1.0/1.0	1.0/2.0	2.0/3.0	2.0/3.0	3.0/1.0
Greeters	1.0/1.0	1.0/1.0	1.0/1.0	1.0/2.0	2.0/3.0	2.0/3.0	3.0/1.0
Totals	**6.0/7.0**	**5.0/7.0**	**5.0/7.0**	**6.0/10.0**	**11.0/16.0**	**12.0/16.0**	**14.0/7.0**

Figure 17-2:
Job slot list — front of the house.

Putting names to numbers

After you complete your slot lists and know how many people you need for each position, shift, and day, insert specific employees into those slots. At this stage of the game, you turn your attention to employee schedule requests. Decide how you want to run your system for requesting days off. Many people use a master-calendar system combined with a request book. Employees place their names in the request book by the days they want off. Allot space for them to write a reason for a special request, such as a birthday, so that the person writing the schedule can take it into account.

Be consistent in how you resolve conflicts regarding scheduling. Have a policy in place for priority of requests. Many new restaurants use a "dibs" system, meaning that whoever requests it first gets it. More established places use seniority systems effectively. You can base seniority on either hierarchy or tenure with the company.

Then start filling in the blanks in a table or spreadsheet like the one in Figure 17-3. We use the wait staff for Saturday at Heather's Bistro as an example. We filled in a couple names so that you can see how a *double* shows up on the schedule. A double occurs when an employee essentially works straight through, or works two shifts in a single day with a break between them. In this case Steve and Loretta are working both lunch and dinner without a break. Also, this schedule is based on the first-in, first-out philosophy. Some operations reward openers with longer shifts, which mean more tables and usually more money.

Save yourself some time by setting up Figure 17-3 in a spreadsheet or other computer program. You can keep track of expected hours worked, planned time off, and so on much more easily.

Lunch		
1.	Open	9a.m. - 3p.m.
2.	Open	9a.m. - 3p.m.
3.	Open	9a.m. - 3p.m.
4.	Close	11a.m. - 5p.m.
5. STEVE	Double	12p.m. - 7p.m.
6. LORETTA	Double	12p.m. - 7p.m.
Dinner		
1. STEVE	Double	12p.m. - 7p.m.
2. LORETTA	Double	12p.m. - 7p.m.
3.	Setup	4p.m. - 9p.m.
4.	Setup	4p.m. - 9p.m.
5.	Close	6p.m. - 11p.m.
6.	Close	6p.m. - 11p.m.
On Call		
1.		
2.		

Figure 17-3:
Wait staff schedule worksheet (Saturday).

You have to find a balance between your business levels and staffing levels. Good waiters won't stay where they can't make money. While you're getting a feel for business levels, you'll probably be *overstaffed,* or have too many people for a given shift. Try to make corrections as soon as you can.

Don't get complacent when writing your schedule. You must adjust your schedule to the business on particular weeks or days of the weeks, in particular weather, and so on. Holidays, traditional vacation times, ethnic or religious occasions, sporting events, and the like all affect your business, either positively or negatively. The degree to which it affects your business varies from concept to concept. During Super Bowl Sunday, many restaurants are dead, but if you're a pizza delivery or a sports bar, you should be rocking.

Setting Up Policies to Live (or Die) By

The best way to establish your policies is to write them down and then consistently implement them. Be as specific as possible and try to anticipate most potential problems before they happen. When appropriate, make sure to include the consequence for infractions, up to and including termination. Put all your policies together in one easy-to-use reference called your employee manual. (Check out Chapter 13 for details on creating and maintaining your employee manual and getting it to your employees.)

Scheduling and attendance

If you write a schedule and no one shows up for work, you have a problem. Setting an effective attendance policy goes a long way toward minimizing employee problems. Figure 17-4 shows an example of an effective, comprehensive attendance policy.

Develop a policy for handling schedule changes. Generally speaking, employees are responsible for finding replacements to cover their shifts, but managers should approve replacements. Managers can refuse replacements for a variety of reasons, including performance difference between the two employees (if the replacement is a brand-new server, he probably can't handle the same workload as the ten-year veteran) or the fact that extra hours worked by the replacement will cause her to get overtime pay.

Post schedules at a consistent time each week. You set the standard for punctuality and respect by keeping this commitment to your employees.

Attendance Policy

Being on time and ready for work is part of good attendance. If you are late or plan on being absent, you place an extra burden on fellow employees. If unusual circumstances cause you to be late or absent, you must call your supervisor at least two hours in advance so that someone can be located to cover your shift until you arrive. If your supervisor isn't available, you should leave the following information with another manager:

- Name
- Reason for absence or lateness
- When you expect to be in
- Phone number where you can be reached

Leaving a message does not relieve you of the responsibility of speaking with your supervisor personally. You must continue to call until you make contact with your supervisor. Do not rely on friends, relatives, or fellow employees to report your absence or lateness.

Absences of more than one day must be reported daily, and a doctor's certificate of illness may be requested for any absence due to illness. Consecutive absences will require a doctor's note. Absences of more than four days due to illness or disability will require an approved medical leave of absence.

Failure to follow the proper call-in procedure may result in disciplinary action.

Figure 17-4:
Sample
employee
attendance
policy.

Smoking

"Smoke 'em if you got 'em" is a common refrain among restaurant employees. But you need to create some boundaries for the sake of your business. Decide how you want to handle smoking by employees on company time and on company grounds to maintain your image. You need to tailor your policies to match your business philosophies and to your specific location, but here are some examples that we've seen:

✔ Don't allow any smoking at any time anywhere on your premises.

✔ Establish a nonsmoking restaurant, but allow employees to take smoke breaks outside your restaurant between shifts. Specify a smoking area away from the customers' entrance and require smokers to clean up the area on a regular basis.

✔ Provide a break room where smoking is permitted. This model is used in many old-school hotels. But if you've ever smelled an employee break room where smoking is permitted, you realize what an eyesore (and nose sore) these rooms can be, especially to your nonsmoking employees.

Drinking or using illegal drugs

You should have a strong, clear, enforceable policy that is in line with local laws. Figure 17-5 shows a good example of such a policy.

Figure 17-5:
Sample
drug and
alcohol
policy.

> **Drug and Alcohol Policy**
>
> The illegal use, consumption, possession, distribution, or dispensation of drugs or drug paraphernalia and the unauthorized use, possession, or being under the influence of alcohol, controlled substances, or inhalants on company premises, in company vehicles, or during work hours is prohibited.

Uniforms and grooming standards

A uniform of some kind is mandatory for most restaurants. Many places don't allow you to work in the clothes you came in, even if it is your uniform. You must change on site, leave your uniform for the company laundry, and pick up a clean, sanitary uniform at your next scheduled shift. This system works best for BOH employees who wear chef whites that are maintained by a laundry service. It can also work in large hotels, or very fine dining restaurants, with a large laundry budget. If you're not providing uniforms, and their cleaning, for your staff, managing this system is tough. You're probably better off requiring that they wear the accepted uniform during their shift, and not worry about when they change.

Here are a few ideas to keep in mind as you choose uniforms for your employees:

✔ Uniforms for the wait staff, bussers, and bartenders should complement, enhance, and reinforce your concept. Hip, trendy restaurants demand hip, trendy servers with hip and trendy clothes. Other places can get by with more casual uniforms.

Uniforms must be functional to work in. Employees must be able to move freely and carry plates, trays, and the like. Don't attire your wait staff in high heels, particularly the men. Sure they look good, but stilettos are tough to find in the largest sizes.

✔ In most cases, the restaurant issues and maintains uniforms for dishwashers, cooks, and chefs. You should include a policy for handling the uniform and penalties for misuse or abuse.

Your concept and geographic location have lots to do with your grooming standards. You can limit jewelry to no rings except wedding or commitment rings. Decide on your policy for visible tattoos. Make some boundaries for facial hair. Many operations don't allow earrings for men and limit the number for women. Here are a few grooming standards that are non-negotiable:

✔ Employees must restrain hair extending beyond the shoulders.

✔ Nails should be clean.

✔ Employees must not have noticeable body odor.

✔ Employees must not wear an excessive amount of cologne.

Back-of-the-house (BOH) employees are seen by customers from time to time, so they should be held to the same grooming standards as the front-of-the-house (FOH) employees.

Disciplinary measures

In some cases, despite your best attempts, rules do get broken. Here's the standard sequence of corrective action:

1. Verbal warning

2. Written warning

3. Suspension

4. Termination of employment

The window of time for a progressive discipline system should be very short. Get on down the road if an employee doesn't respond to your progressive discipline system.

Place all written documentation regarding discipline measures in the employee's file. Documentation helps you establish patterns of behavior over an employee's tenure with your company. The more documentation you have to back you up in the case of a terminated employee who brings a suit against you or your company, the better.

Some offenses are cause for immediate termination and don't require progressive discipline. Poor service, violence, coming to work impaired by drugs or alcohol, or theft may demand immediate termination.

If you've built your organization right, no one is indispensable. And to an extent, your employees should know it. They should know that every single day, they should do their job to the standard set for them or risk losing it. You've established goals, standards, policies, and so on. You've done the research and developed your concept, which you want your staff to help maintain. If you run into resistance to your standards and policies, eliminate the obstacles, even if that means firing an employee. Don't be afraid to fire employees who don't meet your standards.

If you terminate an employee, follow your written disciplinary policy to the letter. Your policy should include language stating that the employee must turn in all company property on his last day. Make sure that terminated employees know that if company property isn't returned in good condition, you may deduct the cost of it from their last paycheck.

Offering Benefits

Decide what benefits you can realistically afford to give to your staff. Each benefit has options. Health insurance plans are available at a wide range of costs, with an equally wide range of coverage. Retirement plans and pensions programs vary less, but they still have some flexibility. Consult your insurance agent to determine what benefits you can actually afford.

From an employee's standpoint, taking away or reducing benefits is never a good thing. Make sure that you can afford what you're offering over an extended period of time, at least a year. When your premiums go up the following year (notice that we said *when,* not *if*), decide whether you will pay the difference or pass along some of it to your employees. Breaking the news to employees that they'll have to contribute more out-of-pocket money is always tough, but with the rising costs of health care, it's the reality of every industry.

If you're a new or small business, you may not be able to afford health insurance or a pension plan. Don't forget the nontangible benefits you can give your employees, such as preferred parking spots, preferred scheduling, birthdays off, long-term career planning, on-the-job training, and so on. They may not cost you much, but they should matter to your employees. Even the prestige of working in a certain restaurant can be a benefit.

Free or reduced-cost shift meals are a fairly standard restaurant employee perk. Your meal program may actually be fairly complicated. Maybe employees get free meals when they're working but only a 50 percent discount when they're not. Often, the free shift meal is served at a specific time and is available to all employees. In other places, employees order off the menu at a discount before or after their shift.

Chapter 18

Running a Safe Restaurant

In This Chapter
▶ Taking food safety seriously
▶ Making cleanliness a priority
▶ Providing protection to everyone in your restaurant

Safety first! You hear that from the time you can walk (or run with scissors). The rule about safety is no different in the restaurant business. You just have to consider safety on a broader scale. As a restaurant owner or manager, you're responsible for the safety of everyone on your premises, including your diners, employees, and vendors. No small task! You can implement countless safety measures, but this chapter focuses on a few biggies: cleanliness, food safety, hand washing, and general safety precautions.

Making Sure Your Food Is Safe

Food safety is one of the most important aspects of running a restaurant. Constant attention to keeping your restaurant clean and organized is the best way to keep food safe. Cleanliness prevents other problems from developing (like vermin or bug infestations) and organization ensures that food is properly stored and your customers' are gastronomically safe.

Some people approach food safety by trying to do the minimum and get away with what they can to avoid the hassle. But our view is simple: *Always follow safety guidelines,* period, because it's the right thing to do — for you, your reputation, and your guests' health. If you have a passion for the business, you want only the best for your customer. Your reputation is reflected in how you treat your food and equipment and in the steps you take to maintain it. Plus, some health departments do use fines for violations as a big source of revenues. Follow their rules and don't give them a reason to fine you.

Each state, county, and municipality has its own specific rules related to the type of establishment you run. Laws and ordinances are different if you're a free-standing restaurant, a café in a bookstore, or a taco truck in a parking lot. Contact your local health department for laws that apply to you. Check out the government section of your phone book and look for headings like "health department," "department of health," and "food safety." Or take a look online at `www.cdc.gov/other.htm#states` and find your state or county.

Blaming bacteria

Bacteria cause foodborne illness. Two of the most common bacteria that cause foodborne illness are salmonella and *Campylobacter.* Their symptoms are similar to most foodborne illnesses and include fever, abdominal cramping, and intestinal distress. If an individual already has a compromised immune system, is elderly, or is very young, the bacteria can cause a life-threatening infection. Both pathogens are almost always present in raw poultry, but you can easily kill them by:

- ✔ Cooking poultry completely
- ✔ Avoiding *cross-contamination,* or spreading bacteria from one type of food to another through improper handling and storage (see the section "Preventing cross-contamination," later in this chapter)

Another common bacteria is *E. coli,* which lives in the intestine of cattle and makes its way to meat through improper handling. Symptoms (which can be life-threatening if the person isn't treated properly and promptly) usually don't include fever, but *E. coli* can cause vomiting, diarrhea, and possibly kidney failure, especially in children. *E. coli* infections are often traced back to beef products, most commonly ground beef. But remember that the bacteria can transfer to anything the raw meat comes into contact with, including foods that will never be cooked, like lettuce.

Health departments are pushing to require restaurants to cook ground beef to well done. If *E.coli* is present on the surface of the steak, the cooking process likely kills it, so cooking it to medium or so is usually safe. But, if you cook a burger to medium-rare, much of the burger is raw. The center of the burger may have been the surface of the meat at one point, but the grinding process has now made it the raw center.

These are by no means the only bacteria you should be on the lookout for. Botulism can be present in canned goods. Vibrio is sometimes present in shellfish. And staphylococcus, commonly called *staph,* can contaminate prepared food in your coolers. Some bacteria, like staph and vibrio, can't be killed in the cooking process. So check with your local health department for a complete list of bacteria you should be aware of and how to avoid them.

Battling illness — time and temperature

Your two biggest opponents in the war on foodborne illness are time and temperature. Watch out for the danger zone (the ideal temperature zone for bacterial growth): between 40 degrees and 140 degrees Fahrenheit. Rapidly cool or heat foods so that you can avoid this zone for prolonged periods — don't let foods stay in this zone for more than two to four hours. Hold your food, or keep it, at a temperature above or below this zone, at all other times.

Some foods, like raw chicken, arrive at your door contaminated. Count on it. How you handle the food after it enters your restaurant makes the biggest difference. A chicken breast mildly contaminated by salmonella left out at room temperature for 12 hours becomes highly contaminated and can cause illness. But even when contaminated food makes it into your restaurant, you can implement procedures to ensure that it doesn't make it to your customers. Here's a quick list of tips to keep your food safe:

- Always store perishable foods at the proper temperature, below 40 degrees or above 140 degrees, depending on the food.

- Cool cooked foods that won't be served immediately as quickly as possible. Current laws require you to cool food to 70 degrees Fahrenheit within two hours and 40 degrees Fahrenheit within four hours. Pay particular attention when cooling large quantities of food. Use ice wands and ice baths, and separate large quantities into smaller containers to cool foods quickly.

- Always hold foods at the proper temperature, above 145 degrees Fahrenheit or below 40 degrees Fahrenheit.

- Always cook foods to the proper temperature (see your local health department's requirements for details) before *holding,* or keeping at the proper temperature until service.

- Provide access to calibrated, sanitized thermometers to check food temperatures at every point in the production process.

- Practice FIFO (first in first out). Set up a rotation system so that you're using the oldest products in your inventory first. This process cuts down on waste by reducing spoilage and ensures that you and your staff are in the know about what's on your shelf, how long it's been there, and what condition it's in.

- Reheat foods only once. Toss the remainder. Because some bacteria are *heat stable* (meaning heating doesn't kill them), the more often you reheat foods, the more likely they are to be contaminated. If you're tossing a lot of food, heat smaller portions until you establish your *par levels,* or the amount of a supply (in this case prepared food) you should have on hand for a given period of time (in this case between prep periods). See Chapter 14 for details on establishing your pars.

✓ Always thaw food in a cooler or with a rapid thaw process (such as under running water in a designated sink, if your local health department allows this method). Never leave food out at room temperature to thaw.

You can also make sure that your staff isn't spreading diseases. Institute mandatory, consistent, and enforced hand-washing policies. See the "Implementing proper hand-washing procedures" section later in the chapter for specifics. Have the kitchen staff use latex gloves whenever working with food. This step protects the food from the people (and their germs) and provides a first line of defense from burns, cuts, and similar boo-boos. Require your staff to change into work clothes at work to avoid bringing in contaminants from the outside.

Preventing cross-contamination

Contamination is the unintended presence of a harmful substance or organism in food. So *cross-contamination* occurs when a bacteria (or other substance or organism) that's present in one food accidentally spreads to another food, usually through improper handling and storage. If you've read the previous section, you're likely on the lookout for the usual contamination suspects, like ground beef and raw chicken. But cross-contamination is probably the single largest food safety problem because the contamination happens accidentally and you may not even be aware of it.

Your best line of defense against cross-contamination is a good offense. Implement proper handling and storage practices, and you're on the road to a restaurant free of foodborne illness. Here are a few tips to get you started:

✓ Provide plenty of work space for staff working on a variety of foods at the same time.

✓ Clean and sanitize knives, utensils, and equipment before and after use.

✓ Provide sanitizer buckets with properly concentrated sanitizer solutions and clean towels. Check with your cleaning product supplier for the details on how to use your particular products.

✓ Use hard plastic or rubber non-absorbing food-grade cutting boards rather than ones made of wood, cleaning and sanitizing them between each and every use.

✓ Use separate cutting boards for raw foods, cooked foods, and foods you serve raw, like fruits. Color code the boards to keep them straight.

Monitoring food safety outside the kitchen

Food safety isn't a concern that stops at the kitchen door. The way you and your front-of-the-house staff handle dishes after you leave the kitchen affects the safety of your food and your diners. In the front of the house, avoid these potential food safety hazards:

- ✓ **Waiters touching food or beverages with hands:** They should touch only the plate or glassware, not the contents.

- ✓ **Waiters or bussers with dirty hands:** Some workers may clear dirty dishes and then not wash their hands before returning to the dining room. Effective hand washing is a must for everyone in your organization. See Figure 18-1, later in the chapter, for the proper hand-washing technique.

- ✓ **Possible cross-contamination situations:** If a food server is slicing lemons, make sure he's not using a slicer that just sliced deli meats and wasn't cleaned and sanitized afterward.

- ✓ **Expired perishables in the wait station reach-in:** On a shift-to-shift basis, waiters should check milk, cream, and butter to confirm that they have current use-by dates and that they don't smell bad. You especially need to do this check during slow business periods or when you've ignored the rotation schedule.

- ✓ **Dropped tongs or utensils on buffets:** Watch out for these germ carriers and replace them immediately with clean ones.

- ✓ **Improper stacking of food:** The bottoms of plates and containers may be contaminated. Create a barrier (a tray, plastic wrap, or the like) to keep bacteria from the bottom of one container from contaminating the top of another.

- ✓ **Dirty utensils at the dessert station:** Change the ice cream scoop, pie servers, and the like at the servers' dessert station once an hour, unless you keep the utensils inside the cooler.

Monitoring food safety outside the restaurant

Despite the efforts of the FDA (Food and Drug Administration) to ensure that the food coming in your doors with the FDA stamp on it is a safe, quality food product, problems can still occur between the time the food leaves the processing plant or farm and the time it gets to your cooler. Inspect your orders when they arrive to ensure proper product quality (greens and produce are fresh and free from rot and pests, for example). Demand the proper handling by your suppliers. Ensuring proper storage before the food gets to you is just as important as storing it properly in your possession.

If you serve organic or vegan dishes, confirm that your purveyors meet the standards that you've promised to your diners. If the producer is using pesticides, your clientele probably considers that use a food safety issue. Likewise, if you're buying vegan veggie soup that has cream solids listed as an ingredient, your vegan patrons may be pretty upset.

Some shellfish, such as oysters, can contain illness-causing pathogens, like vibrio, that can make you sick when you eat them raw. If you're purchasing shellfish to serve in your restaurant, you must buy from a registered, authorized dealer and save all documentation related to the purchase, including invoices and tags from the individual shellfish bags. This information is critical in protecting you and your customers if someone traces an illness to your restaurant.

Picking up other food safety tools

HACCP (Hazard Analysis Critical Control Point) is a system of tools designed to help restaurants develop cost-effective food safety programs. The HACCP program focuses on the flow of food from receiving to serving, identifying, monitoring, and removing potential hazards along the way.

Your local health department can become your best partner in implementing food safety programs. Ask your inspector about programs that your staff can attend at the department's facility, like SafeServe classes, or consider having a guest speaker at your next staff meeting. Health department staff can educate your staff on proper hand washing practices by using cool visual tools like Glo Germ and UV lighting to spot — and stop — sloppy technique. Don't be afraid to ask the health department about its training services and facilities.

Implementing proper hand-washing procedures

From staph infections to hepatitis C to the common cold, employees bring a variety of bacteria and potential pathogens to work with them every day. To reduce the risk of transferring any of these pesky organisms to your guests, facilities, and products, employees must wash their hands with hot water and soap, before and after their shifts, at designated hand sinks (following proper hand-washing technique, as pictured in Figure 18-1). Employees must also wash their hands at designated hand sinks during their shifts after doing any of the following:

- Using the restroom
- Touching their hair, mouths, noses, or other body parts
- Sneezing or coughing
- Handling dirty dishes
- Handling raw food
- Handling trash
- Eating or drinking
- Smoking or using tobacco
- Handling animals
- Cleaning restrooms
- Tending to a wound
- Coming into contact with bodily fluids
- Becoming contaminated in any way

1. Use water hot enough for the hands to stand.

2. Wet hands, soap thoroughly, and lather to the elbow.

3. Use a brush for nails and scrub thoroughly.

Figure 18-1: Proper hand-washing technique.

4. Using friction, rub hands together for about 20 seconds.

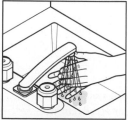

5. Rinse thoroughly under running water.

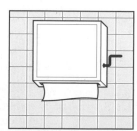

6. Dry hands, using a hot air dryer or single service towels.

Keeping Things Clean

Keeping your restaurant clean is the first step in maintaining food safety. It keeps pests and vermin from sniffing around. Organizing your coolers helps keep foods from spilling, dripping, or falling into other foods. Regularly moving items to clean behind and under them helps keep your products rotated so that none expire and then get used in your menu items. And using fresh containers and pans ensures that you always know when the food was made and that it's safe to serve to your guests.

Cleaning is only as good as your managers. They're ultimately responsible for the cleanliness, health inspection scores, and the processes that make it all work. Hold them to the highest possible standards.

Getting cleaning supplies

Get the right tools for the job. Buy cleaning products designed for cleaning commercial kitchens. These specialized products cut the kind of grease load a restaurant kitchen puts out, polish stainless steel as only a professional can, and truly sanitize the kind of bacteria and toxins that you find in a kitchen. The typical restaurant kitchen needs these cleaning supplies on hand:

Soap for the hand sinks	Dish machine detergent
Hand sanitizer for the hand sinks	Dish machine rinsing aid
Floor cleaner	General sanitizer
All-purpose cleaner	Silver, copper, or stainless steel polisher
Degreaser	Oven cleaner
Glass cleaner	Coffee pot and machine cleaner
Pot and pan soak	

These chemicals can be very dangerous! Keep the following safety tips in mind as you educate your staff about cleaning supplies:

✔ Keep the MSDS (Material Safety Data Sheet) paperwork for all these chemicals on file at all times. That paperwork contains detailed information on safe handling procedures and instructions for dealing with accidental ingestion, exposure, and contact.

✔ We wish it went without saying, but we'll say it anyway: Never store chemicals near food, including the food in dry storage. The fumes can permeate things like lettuce. And you run a tremendous contamination risk if something spills, sloshes, or sprays on any food products.

✔ Observe your staff closely until you're comfortable with their use of chemicals. You must use these chemicals in their proper ratios to maintain the safety of your staff and patrons (not to mention your wallet).

In addition to cleaners, you need the tools to use those cleaning products, including mops and mop buckets, a fresh supply of towels, small buckets for sanitizer solution, brooms, squeegees, scrubbing pads, and cleaning brushes.

And just to make sure that we cover everything, here are a few more tips:

✔ **Consider locking cleaning supplies:** Set up a requisition system, which can benefit you in a couple ways:

- You can control the amount of chemicals in use at a given time.

- You create accountability for proper procedures. If someone has to ask a supervisor for the degreaser, you know who's accountable, and you can be reasonably sure they're using it (or not).

- You limit the opportunity for employees to supplement their home cleaning supplies by borrowing them from your restaurant.

✔ **Assign different towels different jobs:** You can use one stripe color for cleaning and dealing with any chemicals, another color for general kitchen use (like wiping down surfaces), and a third type of towel — of the lint-free variety — solely for wiping down plates and stemware.

✔ **Never use steel wool or stainless steel scrubbing pads:** As they disintegrate with use, they leave behind bits that get into food.

✔ **Schedule cleaning for times other than at closing time:** Things can get overlooked when people are trying to get out after work.

Scheduling your cleaning

The longer you let your kitchen go, the harder it is to clean and the more likely that lack of cleanliness can develop into a bigger problem. Grease erodes paint. Uncovered food invites pests. Old food contaminates new food. Set the standard with exhaustive daily and shift-to-shift cleaning schedules.

Go through your kitchen and note everything that you need to clean and then assign each item a schedule. Don't forget that many items need the occasional heavy-duty cleanup, in addition to daily cleaning. Divide the duties by the employee or job title in a given area to begin to map out your schedule. Base your cleaning schedule on your type of operation. For example, a restaurant featuring fried foods has different cleaning needs than a sushi bar.

Your master cleaning schedule should be part of your operational manual (see Chapter 13). The *master cleaning schedule* should explicitly state what to clean, who should clean it, when to clean it, and how to clean it. Take a look at Table 18-1 for an example schedule based on just one piece of equipment. Create an elaborate cleaning schedule that covers every piece of equipment, every fixture, and every surface in your restaurant.

Table 18-1			Sample Master Cleaning Schedule
Who	*What*	*When*	*How*
Fry cook	Fryer	Between every shift and at close	Turn off fryer; allow grease to cool. While grease is cooling, wipe down exterior surfaces, using spray degreaser. Rinse and finish with stainless steel polish. Filter grease. Wipe down inside of the fryer with a dry towel, remove any food bits. Replace clean, filtered grease. Cover fryer with half sheet pan to prevent light exposure to grease. Run fryer basket through the dish machine. Make sure they're thoroughly dry before use.
Fry cook	Fryer	Every Friday	Same as above, but replace old grease with new rather than strain it.

After you put together your list of things that you need to clean, you decide when to have someone clean them. In the following subsections, we've put together suggested timelines for some of the common kitchen tasks.

Use this section to create your own schedule, but check your equipment for the manufacturer's cleaning recommendations. Some equipment (like combination ovens) have a self-cleaning cycle and recommended cleaning schedule. Always follow the manufacturer's directions.

Must-do's several times each shift

Here are some things that need to be done several times each shift, as needed:

- ✔ Change water in the dish machine.
- ✔ Brush grill between cooking fish and steak.
- ✔ Sweep the line and prep areas.
- ✔ Switch cutting boards.
- ✔ Change sanitizer water.
- ✔ Empty trash.
- ✔ Break down boxes.
- ✔ Change out ice wells.

Cleaning, shift after shift

You can have workers do these tasks on a shift-by-shift basis:

- Sweep the walk-in and dish area.
- Mop the entire kitchen.
- Clean the fryer.
- Filter the fryer oil.
- Send range grates to the dish machine.
- Change sanitizer solution in sanitizing buckets.
- Clean and sanitize all surfaces (reach-ins, prep tables, and so on).
- Hose down mats.
- Wipe down walls, surfaces, and hood vents behind hot line.
- Empty steam table. Clean, sanitize, and refill with fresh water.
- Clean the employee bathroom and locker room.

A cleaning a day . . .

Assign tasks like these on a daily basis:

- Empty equipment and hood grease traps.
- Change foil linings on catch pans of grill, range, and flattops.
- Clean the can opener.
- Remove all the hood filters and run them through the dish machine.
- Put in a rotating deep-cleaning and maintenance schedule; for example:
  - Monday: Sharpen knives.
  - Tuesday: Oil the omelet pans and cast iron cookware.
  - Wednesday: Fill flour, sugar, and other bins in dry storage.
  - Thursday: Apply commercial drain cleaner to floor drains.

 Restrict deep cleaning tasks to Monday through Thursday (or Sunday through Wednesday, depending on your restaurant) because typically the remaining days of the week are too busy, and your staff won't have time for extra cleaning tasks. Just keep up with your daily and shift cleaning on busy days and leave the heavy-duty chores for slower days.

- Create a list of requests for your maintenance staff. Try to assign at least one of these each day during your slower times.

Week in, week out

Make quick work of these more intense weekly jobs with preventive maintenance throughout the week. Figure out your *down days* — days when you have the least amount of inventory in the coolers — and detail the coolers inside and out. Sunday or Monday is usually a great day for this process, because your stock is down from the busy weekend.

- ✔ Empty reach-ins and thoroughly clean and sanitize them. Judge the contents and keep or toss. Reorganize and replace items as needed.

- ✔ Pull the hot line out, if possible, and clean the walls and floor behind and below the line. This task helps you maintain cleanliness, sanitation, and safety. Grease can build up here and catch on fire.

- ✔ Delime the sinks, drains, and faucet heads.

- ✔ Clean the coffee machine.

- ✔ Deep-clean the ovens. Always follow your manufacturer's instructions for cleaning your particular kind of oven. Appropriate cleaning regimens vary greatly, so make sure you know how to clean yours safely.

That fun monthly cleaning

Break these jobs up between employees and spread them out over the month, doing yourself a favor in the labor category and staving off a mutiny.

- ✔ Turn the cooler fans off. Remove the covers. Wipe the fans. Clean the covers.

- ✔ Deep-clean the freezers.

- ✔ Empty and sanitize the ice machine.

- ✔ Check all filters on the reverse osmosis machine, water softeners, and the like.

- ✔ Calibrate ovens. Place an oven-safe thermometer in your oven; set your oven to 350 degrees. After the oven indicates it's reached the appropriate temperature, wait a few minutes for the thermometer to register the actual oven temperature. Make sure that both the oven and thermometer register 350 degrees. If not, repeat the test with a different thermometer. If you get similar results, your oven may not be calibrated properly. Call a technician to test the oven and adjust the temperature if necessary.

- ✔ Calibrate thermometers. Place stick thermometers in a full glass of ice filled with water for one minute to register the correct temperature, which will be 32 degrees. If the thermometer doesn't register 32 degrees, adjust the small dial under the head of the thermometer until the thermometer reaches 32 degrees. Some stick thermometers can't be calibrated. If you find that your thermometer isn't registering the correct temperature and you can't adjust it, toss it in the trash. We recommend that you only buy stick thermometers that can be calibrated.

✔ Prepare for "bug night" in conjunction with your exterminator. Bug night is the night that the exterminator comes to spray for pests. Your exterminator can provide you exact requirements based on what he's treating and the process he uses to treat it. The process you'll follow is specific to the process he uses. Basically, you need to protect your work areas and surfaces from the chemicals.

✔ Sharpen the slicer. (You may have to do this sharpening weekly, depending on the volume of slicing.)

✔ Deep clean walls and ceilings.

✔ Pull everything from dry storage and wipe down the shelves. This cleaning usually coincides with inventory count. See Chapter 14 for more on inventory management.

✔ Change out any pest traps.

✔ Restock your first aid kit.

✔ Deep-clean kitchen floors with a motorized floor scrubber.

✔ Update MSDS (Material Safety Data Sheets, which spell out instructions for safely using any chemicals in your business) you're missing.

Yearly safety stuff

You get to take care of the administration of safety stuff once a year. In most cases, you need to hire a professional to come in and do these jobs for you:

✔ Check fire suppression systems.

✔ Check fire extinguishers. (*Note:* This requirement can vary depending on where you live. Some states or cities may require that this job be done twice a year.)

✔ Clean hoods twice a year or more, if you're putting out a lot of grease.

✔ Clean the pilot lights on all your gas equipment, like your ovens, grills, and ranges. Refer to the cleaning instructions for your particular equipment.

✔ Call for service and maintenance on all your equipment.

✔ Update permits and licenses, as necessary. These documents validate your safety compliance.

Opening and closing procedures

Opening and closing procedures are an important part of cleanliness for several reasons. During opening you confirm that everything is in tip-top shape and that the restaurant is ready to safely prepare meals for the day to come. During closing, you preserve any products for the next shift, get rid of vermin-attracting material from the previous shift, and make sure that all surfaces are free from grease to avoid slips and spills for the next shift.

The opening kitchen manager or chef makes sure that everything was cleaned the night before. He's also responsible for ensuring that all the food has made it through the night. And he must make sure that the opening staff is onboard and knows how to start the restaurant day right.

Opening procedures

Here's the short version of the way a manager may start his day:

- Confirm that coolers and freezers are working properly and have been working properly overnight by checking temperatures.
- Ensure that clean rags and aprons are available for staff.
- Read log entries from the previous shift to check that equipment is working properly.
- Verify that equipment is working properly.
- Conduct a sweep of all vermin traps.
- Do a sweep of all food storage areas to make sure that all food is wholesome and no stinkers are hiding anywhere.

Use this list as a starting point for creating your opening crew's duty list. Add your own food production requirements to round it out:

- Pre-clean any surfaces before food prep begins. This step ensures the surface is clean in case it didn't get sanitized the night before.
- Put out clean sanitizers, buckets, and rags.
- Verify that you have sufficient dish chemicals to get through the shift.
- Confirm all ice bins and water wells are clean. Fill them with fresh ice.
- Make sure that all pans and holding containers are clean. Always use fresh pans, not the ones the food was stored in overnight. If you don't change the pans every day, they eventually become carriers of foodborne bacteria over a period of days.
- Clean and stock the bathrooms.
- Line all trash cans.

Closing procedures

A closing manager has the benefit of the cleaning schedule to keep everyone on track. But she should look for shortcuts that past shifts may have taken. Is the slicer clean underneath the guard? Does the top of the mixer have a dough farm on it? Is the can opener growing fungus? She should note any equipment problems or deep cleaning required in the log book. Before she leaves, she makes sure that

- ✔ Doors are closed and locked.
- ✔ Coolers are sealed.
- ✔ All food is labeled and contained properly.
- ✔ Things that should be covered are covered.
- ✔ Nothing is improperly stored or dripping cross-contamination.
- ✔ The dish machine is empty and cleaned.
- ✔ All trash is appropriately disposed of.
- ✔ No one leaves without checking out with the manager or chef on duty.

Taking Precautions to Protect Your Customers and Staff

The following sections provide tips on a few of the big safety issues in the restaurant world, including first aid and emergency procedures. Check out Chapter 12 for info on responsible alcohol service.

First aid

With the number of sharp implements (from knives to slicers to can openers) and heating elements (including deep fryers, tilt skillets, and even coffee pots) found in restaurants, accidents are bound to happen. Your restaurant needs a basic first aid kit with the following supplies:

Assortment of adhesive bandages	Antiseptic wipes
Gauze	Eyewash
Assortment of nonstick pads	Sterile eye patches
Waterproof first aid tape	Burn gel
Antibiotic ointment	Finger cots (latex gloves for one finger)

Some restaurants also include some OTC (over-the-counter) medications, like pain reliever, cold medicine, antihistamines, and antacids, in their kits or cabinets. These meds are helpful. You must weigh the cost of these supplies against the benefit you receive from them and make your own decision.

Never give any medication out of the first aid kit to a guest. Giving guests aspirin or an antacid may seem like good customer service, but if they have an allergic reaction to the medication, you could get into serious legal trouble.

Consider training your staff in CPR (cardiopulmonary resuscitation) in case a guest has a heart attack or stops breathing. The Heimlich maneuver (designed to help choking victims) is a must-know for restaurant employees. You can find people to provide training at your facility, or you can encourage your employees to get training on their own. Give them a complimentary meal if they get certified. Go to the National Safety Council's Web site at `www.nsc.org/training/selectagency.cfm` to find training in your area.

In the event of an emergency

Your local fire marshal decides how many emergency exits you must have and where you have to put them. Your local codes tell you specifically what kind of doors you have to have, what kind of hardware you should put on the door, which way the door has to swing, and on, and on. Very important stuff, but it varies from county to county and state to state. Check with your local office for the specific ordinances you may be subject to. Here's a general list of good tips to keep in mind regarding emergency exits:

- ✔ They should always be unlocked from the inside.

- ✔ You must clearly mark them. Make sure that you have lighted emergency exit signs.

- ✔ They must be accessible at all times. Never block an emergency exit, even with a movable barrier, like a trash can.

- ✔ If you install *panic hardware* (hardware that sounds an alarm when tripped), make sure that it's properly marked. Nothing is more embarrassing than a diner accidentally tripping an emergency siren.

Make sure that all employees know the escape routes. Instruct your staff to help diners exit your restaurant in the event of an emergency.

Program your telephones with emergency numbers and post instructions for dialing them. If all else fails, post the emergency numbers so anyone who sees the list knows who to call, even if he can't figure out the memory dial.

Chapter 19

Building a Clientele

Advertising draws guests to your door. In Chapter 16, we help you design and implement public relations and advertising strategies to get the word out and bring the customers in. But customers are free agents. Just because they give your establishment a shot doesn't mean they'll return. How you deliver on your implicit or explicit promises to the customer after they're in their seats makes the difference between one-time customers and a regular *clientele* — patrons you want to have in your restaurant and who put money in your pocket by returning again and again with their friends, family, and colleagues. The best ad campaign in the world won't help you for long if you don't build a strong base of loyal customers by meeting and exceeding expectations.

Establishing a clientele transcends being popular. It's about being permanent. Just like doctors, lawyers, mechanics, and beauticians, you develop a loyal clientele based on how you deliver on their wants, needs, and expectations. You won't survive for long by serving one-time-only customers.

A lot of clientele building is common sense, not rocket science. Most people know the right things to do to make people feel special, important, and valuable. But few people actually do it. That's where we come in. In this chapter, we remind you of the importance of exemplary customer service and outline practical strategies that you can use every day to begin building or expand on your loyal customer base. We shed light on an often-overlooked opportunity to gain a loyal customer — customer complaints. And we outline some long-term clientele-building techniques to keep them coming back.

Any successful restaurant has to innovate and bring new people in the door. The trick is to continue to do it, while you keep your regulars.

Understanding Who Your Customer Is

After you've researched your target audience (see Chapter 4) and designed the appropriate marketing strategies (see Chapter 16), you get to turn your attention to the actual human beings. In the same way that you have a few dates before you decide to marry someone, you have to get to know your customers and court them before they become your clientele. Understanding your customer begins with listening to what your customer has to say. Talk and *listen* to your guests. Ask the right questions, and they'll give you the keys to their repeat business.

Know the people who eat regularly in your business, and don't underestimate the value of learning and using their names. For some customers, simply saying hello and calling them by name is enough to gain their repeat business.

Observing and listening

You must get to know your customers in order to figure out what motivates them to pick your restaurant over another one and how to encourage them to come back again and again (with friends). Discover what they want (or think they want) by watching their behaviors, asking questions, and listening to what they have to say. Here are a few ideas to get you started:

✔ **What are they eating?** Your menu mix analysis and other sales reports can give you the snapshot of what's happening (see Chapter 20). But to understand the complexities of the choices they're making, talk to them. And more importantly, listen to them.

✔ **What are they doing besides eating in your restaurant?** Get to know your customers, not just their food and drink preferences. Find out what other activities they're involved in. Use that info to find ways to get them to visit you more often. For example, ask yourself the following questions about your customers:

  • Do they play or watch sports?

  • Do they have kids, and if so, do they want to bring them in, too, or get away from them for a few hours?

  • Are they health or weight conscious?

  • Do they dine in your restaurant before (or after) another activity like shopping, attending the theater, or attending religious services?

✔ **How does value play a role in their decision-making?** Are they looking for the largest portions for the lowest price or high quality at a reasonable price? Or is value not a primary concern as long as the quality is top notch?

✔ How do local preferences and tastes affect their choices? You may have seen the coolest new martinis at the food and beverage show in New York. But if you're located in small town where bar orders overwhelmingly consist of domestic beer, you may sell very few martinis — regardless of how cool you think they are.

Playing on their tendencies

Consider your customers' wants and desires and incorporate them into your concept to help build a loyal customer base. Take a look at the following list for an idea of how this approach works. If your customers

✔ **Buy mixed drinks:** You can offer a specialty cocktail menu.

✔ **Like live entertainment:** You can offer live music one night a week.

✔ **Order salads and lighter items:** You can offer more choices in this category, at higher margins.

✔ **Come in after a softball game:** You can give them a team discount.

✔ **Read the paper while drinking their morning coffee:** You can have newspapers available.

✔ **Ask for a particular kind of wine:** You can order their favorite wine if they come in often enough.

✔ **Often special-order their breakfast:** You can add a special build-it-yourself menu option.

✔ **Don't eat seafood, ever:** You can educate them about your offerings, or dump them. The seafood, not the customers.

✔ **Don't like the far walk to the parking lot:** You can offer valet service.

✔ **Like to watch sports:** You can buy extra TVs and offer drink promotions during sporting events

✔ **Drink lots of draft beer:** You can expand your draft beer selection.

If you want more of a certain kind of diner, figure out what these types of diners want and give it to them. But you can't please everyone, so make changes to your business and your concept only as a concerted effort to gain the increased patronage of a certain type of diner. If you don't want more kids in your restaurant, don't make it especially kid friendly.

Meeting and Exceeding Expectations

People come to restaurants ready to spend money. They're not simply browsing or window shopping. They're coming to your restaurant with an expectation of good, wholesome food; efficient service; and courteous treatment. Fewer places deliver those things than you might expect. Because restaurants regularly fall short of their customers' expectations, a pleasant dining experience often is heralded as revolutionary when it does occur.

Diners have expectations, regardless of whether you're the hot dog wagon outside the plant or the nameplate restaurant of a famous visionary chef. Coauthor Andrew recalls a conversation with a world-class chef, whose commitment to superlative guest service is legendary. The chef said that guests come to his restaurant already expecting and demanding the finest foods, wines, and service in the world. Just delivering on that isn't enough. You have to look at each individual guest and figure out how to exceed his or her expectations, no matter how lofty. And every employee in the restaurant should be committed to delivering this level of customer service, to every diner, every day.

No matter how successful you are, never make customers feel like they're lucky to be in your restaurant.

The minute customers walk in your door, they should experience the best you have to offer. Your host staff is your first exposure to the guest. If you frustrate a diner here, it's tough to turn them around. You have to quote the right wait times and work the reservation system with enough padding in case you have guests who are lingering over coffee. In fact, you never know what might happen in a restaurant, so giving yourself a little extra time is a good idea. If you quote customers 15 minutes and you seat them in 5 minutes, they love it. But don't exaggerate the wait time just to exceed their expectations. If you tell them the wait will be an hour, and then seat them in 5 minutes, you don't impress anyone. But remember, there's no reason to tell customers that the wait will be shorter than it is.

Chicago chef and restaurateur Gabriel Viti is a master of building a clientele at his nameplate restaurant, Gabriel's, in Highwood, Illinois. Not a single night goes by that he's not the first person you see when you walk in the door and the last hand you shake on the way out. He greets you by name, and welcomes you into his restaurant as if he were inviting you into his home. He conveys a level of comfort and assurance that everything will be magnificent because he knows you and is personally committed to your individual dining enjoyment. He never gives off the vibe that you're lucky to be in his restaurant. Rather, he appears to be overjoyed that you have joined him this evening, and he'll see to your needs.

Good customer service is *not* a revolutionary concept — that's the way it should be everywhere, all the time. Here are some ways to exceed your customers' expectations:

- ✓ **Do the extras for people in your restaurant.** Don't just tell them where the restroom is; escort them discreetly. Entertain their kids. Slip a couple two forks when only the husband orders dessert.

- ✓ **Give them a story to tell.** Give them something positive to talk about the next day at work. Table visits are important to get to know your customers, but move beyond, "How is everything?" Join them in tasting the new port you just brought in. Talk to them about an upcoming wine dinner they may be interested in. Let them know about a cool food festival that's coming to town and give them tickets.

- ✓ **Find things that matter to them and capitalize.** Don't just serve them dinner. Find out what they enjoy and leverage that to form a relationship outside of the restaurant. If they like hockey and you have season tickets, consider giving them tickets to a game. If a regular diner is into wine and you're going to tour a local vineyard, invite him to come along.

- ✓ **Send cards to your regular clients.** Send them real, handwritten holiday cards. Reference specific conversations that you've had with them. Then build on the relationship over the next year.

- ✓ **Show your customers that they're important to your success.** Invite them to participate in focus groups, sit on the advisory board for your restaurant, or be part of a VIP club. Make them feel like they have an ownership stake in your restaurant, and they'll share the experience with others, which hopefully means more business for you.

Turning Unsatisfied Guests into Repeat Customers

Successful restaurateurs attempt to exceed guest expectations 100 percent of the time. *Attempt* is the keyword here because, as hard as you may try, you won't walk away at the end of the day with an unblemished track record.

Every customer service situation is an opportunity to make a customer for life. People remember the bad. If you do it right nine times but mess it up the tenth time, that's what they remember. You need to make the problems go away. You want customers to remember that the tenth time, you fixed it. And they usually do.

Of course, avoiding problems in the first place is the best possible scenario. Prevention is worth ten pounds of cure in the restaurant business. With fickle customers, shrinking margins, and limitless dining choices, you need to make it a priority to avoid doing things that result in unsatisfied customers. Here are a few basic things you can do to help ensure happy diners:

- ✔ Make sure that the temperature is right — not too hot and not too cold.

- ✔ Seat guests in the best possible place.

- ✔ Place clean menus, silverware, glassware, and tableware at every table, every time.

- ✔ Keep your restrooms in tiptop shape.

- ✔ Quote accurate wait times, and even err on the side of caution. Customers don't get mad if you seat them early.

But, despite your best efforts, problems will occur. So in this section, we provide tips for staying alert and recognizing problems and show you how to turn an unsatisfied guest into a repeat customer.

Some guests walk into your restaurant unhappy. Other guests like to show off — they're in the business and want everyone to know it. And some people always complain, like to complain, or just can't help themselves. Whether the gripe is legitimate or not, you have to filter through *all* the complaints, dealing with the bogus ones, to get the opportunity to correct a real problem. One of the worst situations is failing to recognize a genuine problem that a customer is having. You never have the opportunity to correct it. You don't get a second chance. The customer just doesn't come back.

Recognizing unsatisfied guests

If every guest that had a problem said, "Hey you, I have a problem," *we'd* have no problem recognizing that clear-cut message. But, in the real world, many guests don't let you know. So, you need to perform some detective work to make sure that all's well that seems well. If you see any of the following "clues" from your guests or on tabletops, investigate the problem. Check in with their server to get the whole story before you visit the table.

- ✔ **Human periscopes:** Look for people looking up and around and then back down. Typically, these folks don't have something they need. It could be a missing menu page, a refill on a soft drink, or extra napkins for a spilled drink. You want to get guests what they need as soon as possible so they can go back to enjoying their time in your restaurant.

- ✔ **Half-eaten food or food left on a plate:** Maybe the customer plans to box it up to go home, but confirm it. You want empty plates going back to the dish area.

✓ **Empty glasses:** People like full glasses of their beverage, especially non-alcoholic drinks, so replenish the water, soda, and iced tea regularly.

When asking guests about a refill on their alcoholic beverages, make it easy for them to say yes. Ask, "How about another glass of wine?" instead of "Do you have enough wine?" You can even take the next step and recommend a wine for their next course.

✓ **Watch gazing:** Customers who keep looking at their watches may not be wondering where their food is, but investigate the situation anyway.

✓ **Waving, snapping, and other hand motions:** If you see customers making these gestures, it's not good. Hopefully, you can get to them quickly and fix the problem before they leave. Even if you feel "attacked" by someone in this agitated state, do your best to maintain your composure and resolve the situation. Also remember that even if you can't win back this customer, other customers are watching to see how you handle the situation. Don't risk losing them as well.

✓ **Aloofness:** If you see people who are laid back in their chair and not looking happy and engaged, this behavior isn't an automatic problem. Some couples go out and never say a word to each other. Just because they don't appear to be enjoying each other doesn't mean there's anything you can do about it. As you gain experience, you'll be better able to judge the nuances of a diner's body language, but until then, consider stopping by the table to check in with these types of diners.

✓ **"Safe" orders:** If customers order chicken in your seafood restaurant, they may be afraid of the menu and simply need some educating. Don't let them miss what you do best.

Giving special treatment to big spenders

The diamond-crusted, jet-setting, super high rollers of the Las Vegas casinos — moguls, tycoons, robber barons, sheiks, and stars — are lavished with attention at every turn. They have their own attendants, concierge, shoppers, and chefs. They get the best tables at the restaurants, the finest seats at the shows, and unlimited access to the high-stakes tables. Why? Because they wager (and generally lose) more cash in one weekend than many restaurants gross all year.

You may not have guests in your restaurant tipping $600 for an espresso or $100 for prompt and courteous cocktail service, but the message is clear: Take care of those who take care of you. You need to treat your key regular clients with kid gloves, or they'll pack up their large wallets and go find someone who will. Remember our golden rule: Never make it hard for someone to give you money!

Making things right

As corny as it sounds, the customer is always right. Resist the urge to reverse the blame on the customers because they were grumpy or petty. Accept the responsibility for their complaint. And remember, do your best from the start to not give them a reason to complain.

1. **Listen to the guest.** Let your customer tell you what's wrong and even how he thinks you should fix it. Sometimes just having an outlet to vent for a moment can start the process of resolution and calming down.

2. **Apologize or thank the guest, depending on the situation.** A sincere apology can go along way toward resolving your long-term relationship with them. Sometimes guests may just have a recommendation or an idea that can really improve your business, not an actual problem. Thank them for their interest in your business and their patronage.

3. **Fix the current situation.** Figure out how you can correct the current problem. If a customer is completely dissatisfied with her entrée or it isn't up to the usual standards, you may consider removing the item from her check. But giving a free dinner or dessert isn't always the answer. Do what you can to serve customers a quality meal before they leave. If the steak is overdone, get them one that's cooked the way they like it. If their pasta is cold, get them a fresh portion. Or ask them if you can bring them something else.

Providing a quality meal and service in the face of a problem gives you a huge opportunity: Some of your best, most loyal clients come from what started as a bad situation. The way you handle the situation is what can make the difference in where the relationship goes from here.

4. **Rectify the long-term situation.** Don't patronize or placate your customers. They want to know that someone has heard their problem, fixed it, and will take steps to make sure that it doesn't happen again. If theirs is the fourteenth overcooked steak on the same shift, you probably have a problem with the grill (either the person manning the station or the equipment itself.) Take the steps necessary to investigate what the true problem is and fix it. Customers hate for someone to listen but at the same time seem to blow them off. Give them your name and your card. Tell them to see you the next time they come in. Your sincerity and follow-through are essential in ensuring that they come back again.

Utilizing Long-Term Loyalty Strategies

Building a clientele requires you to bring in repeat customers, again and again. Sure you can get them in the door. You can even keep them coming for a few months. But how do you keep them interested after you're no longer the hottest new thing? You do it by keeping a balance between maintaining what made you popular in the first place and new, exciting events and menu offerings. Give customers an incentive for dining with you more often. Invite them to events at your restaurant. Contact businesses in your area to make sure they know what you offer. The following sections show you how.

Hosting a diners club

Belonging to a restaurant's diners club is kind of like getting frequent flier miles for dining. Usually, it's a variation on a common theme: You come enough, and you get a free meal. Fast food places have punch cards. Pizza places give free pizza when a customer collects ten box tops. Some restaurants charge a small fee to join their frequent diner club and offer some very high-end perks. After earning a certain amount of points, a customer gets gift certificates, wine, or even spa treatments or trips to wine country.

The prizes or perks don't have to be extravagant. You could partner up with a gourmet shop in town and give discounts on cooking lessons. The more appealing the perks are to *your* customers, the better your response will be.

Orchestrating theme dinners

A *theme dinner* is an event that you host at your restaurant that's separate from the regular menu and oriented around a theme. The theme is limited only by your imagination. You can plan a theme around the food, beverages, or a combination of the two. Or you may want a dinner that features a celebrity personality, soap opera star, guest chef, or author. Another option is to host a dinner that doubles as a charity event, perhaps including a silent auction.

You can still make money on a charitable function. But you must donate a portion of the money to charity.

Wine dinners are a common event for upscale restaurants. Maybe your local chamber of commerce wants to showcase local wines, and the ostrich council is in town and wants to promote flightless birds on restaurant menus. Your chef is interested because he's from the Serengeti. You can get everyone together and host an ostrich and local wine-pairing combo. You can contact people from your mailing list for advance sale tickets. Here are some other ideas for theme dinners:

- Scotch and cigars
- Holiday themes, like St. Patrick's Day or Mardi Gras
- Colors, featuring foods and drinks of a certain color (for example, red could include tomatoes, cabernets, red onions, red meat, and strawberries)

✔ Ethnic cuisine

✔ Period dinners, featuring historic, throwback, or retro themes

✔ Ingredient-focused, such as mushrooms, heirloom tomatoes, caviar, or Spam

✔ Collaborative dinners, in which, for example, several chefs or winemakers work together to put on an event

Courting local businesses

Every guest isn't created equal. We're not saying that you shouldn't treat each guest with the same amount of courtesy and respect. Just recognize that some customers have the potential to bring in more additional business than others. You can beef up your word-of-mouth advertising exponentially if you treat someone in a dining decision-making position with extra courtesy and an occasional free meal.

For example, maybe the office manager who orders all the catered client lunches at the building next to you comes in a couple times a month. Another guy in accounting from the same company comes in at least once a week for lunch and then occasionally gets carryout for dinner, too. The office manager may be a good candidate for an occasional free lunch. She may not come in as often as the guy from accounting, but she has the potential to mean more money for your business. If she's making the buying decisions for an office, consider giving her a reason to choose you.

Here are a few other specific ideas that may work for your business:

✔ If you're part of a business association, partner with other people in your group to offer each other discounts on products and services.

✔ Make the rounds to introduce your business to the concierges of the local hotels. Make sure that they know you're out there with a quality product. Send them an occasional lunch, a nice bottle of wine, or other perk that helps them remember your restaurant first when hotel guests ask for dining suggestions.

✔ Make friends with a few cab drivers, rental car agents, and retail shops. Be known in the places that your customers frequent.

Don't forget the ancillary businesses related to your business. Court your vendors and colleagues. People know they're in the restaurant business and ask them for recommendations. Give them a reason to suggest your place. Don't forget other chefs and restaurateurs in your community who aren't in your direct market segment. If someone asks them where they go for Mexican, you want to be that place, assuming you're a Mexican restaurant.

Laying the foundation for a mailing list

A *mailing list* is a list of your customers that you maintain for the purpose of marketing to them. You can include the following types of content in the material you send to those on your mailing list:

- ✔ Special events at your restaurant
- ✔ Periodic discounts to encourage customers to come in
- ✔ Menu changes
- ✔ Opinion surveys
- ✔ Regularly updated newsletters that contain all of the above, along with appealing content such as recipes or wine reviews

The info you request from your clientele for the mailing list can be very detailed or very brief. At a minimum, your mailing list should include the customer's name and address. You can use the addresses to determine where your guests are coming from. But having a list of customers' addresses also lets you know the areas where you're not attracting customers from so you can target those areas with future promotions. To make your mailing list even more useful, consider asking for this information as well:

- ✔ **E-mail address:** E-mail is a great way to do a fairly inexpensive, quick promotion to your clientele. But remember that not everyone has e-mail and therefore may not be able to receive your newsletter or promotion.

- ✔ **Birthday or other special dates, such as an anniversary:** Acknowledging special events can make lifelong customers.

- ✔ **Business address:** This information can be helpful if customers are interested in hearing about business-focused events, like a discount on catering, delivered lunches, and so on.

- ✔ **Preferences:** Do they like scheduled events? Do they see you only in conjunction with specific holidays? Do they come only for a celebration?

Eventually, you build a picture of your mailing list customers. You can track how long they've been on your list. If they were on your original list, you may like to know that fact eight years down the road. You can also get a sense of how often they visit you.

Ask your customers how they want you to contact them. Typical choices include the following:

- ✔ Via mail
- ✔ Via e-mail

   ✔ Via phone

   ✔ Don't call me, I'll call you

Although people may be surprised and delighted by a house call from their doctor, they'll be freaked out if their local restaurateur makes a surprise visit. Usually e-mail or snail mail is the way to go.

You can sign people up for your mailing list in many different ways. Here are some ideas:

   ✔ **Web site:** Be sure that your Web site has a place for visitors to sign up for the mailing list.

   ✔ **Comment cards:** Leave a space for customers to include their name and address. Check out Chapter 20 for more info on comment cards.

   ✔ **Mailing list sign-up card:** Customers can fill out this card at the register. It's like a comment card, only without the comments.

   ✔ **Business card drop for a free lunch:** When patrons drop their cards for a drawing for a free lunch, you can add these names to your mailing list.

   ✔ **Customer request by phone or letter:** Some patrons may call or write to ask to be added to the mailing list.

Check your mailing list for duplicate entries to save you some money in mailing costs. You don't want the same person on the list three times.

The people on your mailing list are inviting you to contact them. Don't screw it up. Be courteous and efficient with your communication. And don't forget about them. Use the names you collect to market your business.

Your point-of-sale (POS) company may offer to install some kind of credit card capture and spyware on your system. The basic premise of the software is that by running someone's credit card through your system, you automatically build a database entry for that person, with name, address, and so on, that adds the person to your mailing list. Put yourself in your customer's shoes. If it would violate your privacy to have this information captured about you without your knowledge, you probably don't want to add this functionality to your system. Although this kind of thing happens all the time, as a small business owner, you may not want to feel the wrath of that guest who doesn't appreciate it. Weigh your options carefully.

You can also buy mailing lists from companies that allow you to target a certain demographic group in your area. You can specify income range, geographic location, and so on, and the company provides the information to you for a fee.

Chapter 20

Maintaining What You've Created

• •

• •

*W*hether you're considering opening a restaurant or you're already up and running, you have to understand how to read the financial numbers to figure out how your restaurant's actually doing. If you only watch the money coming in, you may have a very wrong perspective on how successful you truly are (or aren't). Many restaurants bring in lots of money in sales, only to watch it disappear in the trashcans (waste) or out the back door (theft) before it turns into a profit, while others don't earn sales they could have had by implementing suggestions from their customers and staff.

In this chapter, we help you take a look at your current numbers and figure out what they mean. We show you how to listen to suggestions and complaints from all the well-meaning (or bitter) employees, diners, and professionals, in and around your restaurant. And we help you figure out how to respond to keep your restaurant running smoothly and profitably.

Evaluating your company's financial performance doesn't just mean reading the numbers and looking for changes. Take the next step and figure out why numbers are changing, why they match (or don't match) your predictions, and how to get them all going in the right direction.

Evaluating Financial Performance

Running your business by the numbers is critical. We don't mean for you to throw your common sense out the window. You have to have controls in place, do regular reviews of your numbers, and rely on your brain (and experience if you have some) to dig deeper when the numbers aren't right.

Keep up with your business on a shift-by-shift, daily, weekly, and monthly basis. Don't let the details sneak up and surprise you after it's too late. Don't miss the opportunity to make the corrections. Use the sample worksheets and the figures in this section and throughout the book to keep up with your numbers and the costs they represent.

Daily business review

Your *daily business review* is a report that you create by recording your sales figures, labor costs, and customer counts (and any other pertinent financial info or business conditions) every day. By recording this info in one place, every day, you build a history of your business that allows you to compare figures across previous days, months, and years to establish patterns and determine whether you've gained or lost ground in individual categories. Graphing this data and cataloging it over time are essential. You can find a sample in Figure 20-1, but develop your own review that tracks data in the categories important to your particular business.

Daily Business Review Week of								
	Monday	Tuesday	Wednesday	Thursday	Friday	Saturday	Sunday	Totals
Sales								
Sales (L/Y)								
Food Sales								
Food Sales (L/Y)								
Beverage Sales								
Beverage Sales (L/Y)								
Labor Cost								
Labor Cost (L/Y)								
Labor %								
Labor % (L/Y)								
Food Cost % (Est.)								
Food Cost % (L/Y)								
Cover Count								
Cover Count (L/Y)								
Check Average								
Check Average (L/Y)								
Food Ck Avg								
Food Ck Avg (L/Y)								
Bev Ck Avg								
Bev Ck Avg (L/Y)								
Food/Bev Mix								
Food/Bev Mix (L/Y)								

Figure 20-1:
Sample daily business review.

Your POS (point of sale) system (see Chapter 15) may already have a version of this review built into it. Check your system or check with your salesperson to take advantage of features you may not be using.

Build a history of your business, and you'll benefit in big ways. Here are a few things a daily business review can do for you:

✔ Determine whether a current promotional event is affecting your sales compared to last year.

✔ Confirm whether your overall volume is increasing over time. Remember, if you want to grow 10 percent a year, you have to grow 10 percent a day. (Not literally of course, but you get the picture.)

✔ Alert you to the beginning of a problem, but not necessarily what the problem is. For example, you may see that your liquor sales are down compared to the previous week, but it may not tell you why. You almost always need further investigation to get to the heart of the problem. If you dig deeper into other places, like your logbook, your reservation book, and any other appropriate resources, you discover that you had a large rehearsal dinner the previous week that accounts for a jump in your sales last week and now you're actually back to "normal."

✔ Establish patterns. Over time, you should start to see trends and patterns emerge in your sales figures. For example:

• Maybe your beverage-to-food mix is dropping on certain nights. Match it up with the staff schedules to see who's working and figure out if someone's not selling, or worse.

• If your labor costs climb because a highly paid sauté cook is picking up shifts as a prep cook, talk to the chef about what's up.

• If your cover count (number of guests in the restaurant for a particular shift) is constant but your check average plummets, did your chef put a bologna sandwich for $2.99 as the special?

• If cover counts remain the same at the bar but your beverage average takes a dip, look for drink giveaways.

Income statement

The *income statement* can also be called a profit and loss (P & L) statement. It summarizes your expenses and sales and gives you your bottom line profit for the month. Many restaurants run monthly, quarterly, and annual statements. Some places use abbreviated, concise documents, while others create detailed documents with page after page showing every budget line in a category. For an example, check out the income-statement figure in Chapter 5 for a sample income statement. Use one column of this 6-month statement to get a feel for what your income statement may look like. Again, this statement doesn't diagnose your problems, but it identifies symptoms that can help you discover what's ailing you.

Our favorite income statement format provides comparative data in addition to the month's actual data. So, this type of income statement has three columns — the actual numbers, the numbers you projected you'd do, and the historical numbers from the same period last year.

Cash flow analysis

Keep a constant eye on your *cash flow,* the flow of money coming into (sales) and going out (expenses) of your business. Prepare a report like the one in Chapter 5. Use as many real figures as you can (such as the invoices you know you need to pay next week) and forecast the rest (like what your sales will likely be next weekend) as accurately as possible. A restaurateur must know not only how much money he has at any given time, but also how much he owes (or will owe very soon) in order to stay ahead.

Don't expect to get credit extended to you — especially if you're new to the business. If obtaining credit is tough, keeping control of your cash, receivables, and payables is even more important. Here are some tips:

✔ **Weigh the benefits of discounts from suppliers for quick payment versus other uses for the cash.** If you're looking for the money to go out slower than it's coming in, for whatever reason, you may not be able to take advantage of some savings offered by suppliers. Many times you'll get, say, a 5 percent discount if you pay within 10 days rather than the standard 30 days. But some months require you to hold on to the cash for those extra 20 days instead of taking the discount. Maybe you need to pay your equipment service guy for 25 extra hours of labor to fix the range. Or maybe you need to upgrade the bathroom fixtures.

✔ **If your cash flow numbers aren't where you'd like them to be, reducing your inventory is a great place to start.** If your money is tied up in extra inventory you don't need, it's not working for you. Keep enough inventory to run your business efficiently. Keep the cash flowing your way and pay out as slowly as you can without incurring penalties.

✔ **Large parties or banquets can be a boon for your cash flow situation.** If you have to make large, expensive purchases for the party (like cases of champagne or expensive cuts of meat), get at least part of your money in advance. But be careful, if you take money in, say a $5,000 deposit, and count it as a sale two months before the event make sure you spend it on things for the party. Get the money in advance, but use it wisely.

✔ **Beware the danger of house accounts.** A *house account* allows individuals or businesses to run a tab and pay it at regular intervals, such as monthly, instead of paying each time they dine with you. House accounts can go sour quickly, especially as the charges add up. The fact is, in this day of easy plastic money, no one needs a house account. Why wait until the end of the month to get paid (if you get paid at all)?

In Figure 20-2, we map out how your cash flow might look on each day of the month. We use several assumptions (we had to start somewhere), including:

✔ Your sales are constant at $5,000 each day.

✔ Half your diners pay in cash and the other half pay with credit cards.

✔ Your credit card company charges you 3 percent of the total transaction as a fee. And credit card funds (less the transaction fees) are deposited into your account with a 3-day lag time.

✔ Your operating expenses (includes food costs, labor, and so on) are 88 percent of sales.

✔ Your rent is $5,000 per month and paid on the 15th of the month.

✔ You're working on a 30-day month.

✔ You pay half of your bills weekly and the other half on the last day of the month.

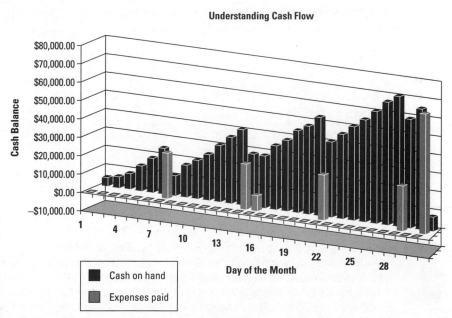

Figure 20-2: Understanding cash flow on a daily basis.

Your cash flow may look very different depending on things like your sales (which usually fluctuate depending on the day of the week) and your bill payment schedule. But this figure shows you how quickly the money goes even in an efficiently run restaurant.

Evaluating Operations

Operational reports show you other factors that have an impact on your profitability. These reports aren't standard business reports, like the financial reports in the preceding section; instead, they're specific to the restaurant business.

Menu mix analysis

A *menu mix analysis* (like the one in Figure 20-3) is a report used to evaluate the profitability of your menu on an item-by-item basis. It provides data on what's selling (and what's not) and, more importantly, how much money you're making off each item.

Menu Item Name Dinner Items	Number Sold	Popularity %	Item Food Cost	Item Sell Price	Item Food Cost %	Item Profit *Price-Cost*	Total Cost *Cost x # Sold*	Total Revenue *Price x # Sold*	Total Profit *Revenue -Cost*	Profit Category	Popularity Category	Menu Label
Ribeye	47	15.1%	$4.82	$18.95	25.4%	$14.13	$226.54	$890.65	$664.11	Low	High	**Workhorse**
Pasta and Marinara	32	10.3%	$1.18	$9.95	11.9%	$8.77	$37.76	$318.40	$280.64	Low	High	**Workhorse**
Chicken Caesar Salad	14	4.5%	$2.13	$12.95	16.4%	$10.82	$29.82	$181.30	$151.48	Low	Low	**Dog**
Roasted Pork Loin	15	4.8%	$3.84	$18.95	20.3%	$15.11	$57.60	$284.25	$226.65	High	Low	**Challenge**
Cioppino	15	4.8%	$5.84	$24.95	23.4%	$19.11	$87.60	$374.25	$286.65	High	Low	**Challenge**
Mixed Grill	14	4.5%	$7.00	$29.95	23.4%	$22.95	$98.00	$419.30	$321.30	High	Low	**Challenge**
Grilled Salmon	23	7.4%	$3.25	$18.95	17.2%	$15.70	$74.75	$435.85	$361.10	High	High	**Star**
Shrimp Scampi	18	5.8%	$6.42	$24.95	25.7%	$18.53	$115.56	$449.10	$333.54	High	Low	**Challenge**
Filet Mignon	46	14.8%	$6.58	$21.95	30.0%	$15.37	$302.68	$1,009.70	$707.02	High	High	**Star**
Arrozo con Pollo	23	7.4%	$3.33	$17.95	18.6%	$14.62	$76.59	$412.85	$336.26	Low	High	**Workhorse**
Shrimp Diablo	26	8.4%	$6.42	$24.95	25.7%	$18.53	$166.92	$648.70	$481.78	High	High	**Star**
Sausage Pizza	38	12.2%	$2.32	$8.95	25.9%	$6.63	$88.16	$340.10	$251.94	Low	High	**Workhorse**
Total or Overall	311	100%					$1,361.98	$5,764.45	$4,402.47			
Average		8.3%	$4.43	$19.45	20.0%	$15.02						

Figure 20-3: Example of menu mix analysis.

You're looking for your menu to reflect a target overall food cost percentage. (You figure *food cost percentage* for individual dishes by taking the cost of all the ingredients used to make a dish and dividing it by the menu price.) To come up with the overall percentage, you have to take the overall cost of the food sold and divide it by the overall revenue you received from that food. (Take a look at Chapter 9 if you need more of an explanation on food cost and food cost percentage.)

Use a computer to create your menu mix. Many POS systems come with this functionality. If your system doesn't, create your own by using Excel or another spreadsheet program. Automating this process saves you a ton of time in calculating the figures, leaving you more time to actually analyze them and make changes as appropriate. (Take a look at Chapter 22 for information on where to buy spreadsheets already created for this purpose.)

Tracking your menu

Use your own menu mix analysis (we use the example of Figure 20-3 in our discussion) to answer these questions:

✔ **Which items are the most popular?** Our most popular items are our steaks. Both the ribeye and the filet are hot sellers, with 47 and 46, respectively, sold on the night we're looking at.

✔ **Which items are bringing in the most revenue dollars?** Notice that it's not usually those that have a low food cost percentage. Pasta with marinara sauce has a low food cost percentage but also a comparatively low *profit margin,* or the difference in the cost of the item and its price.

✔ **Which items have the highest and lowest profit margins?** Our highest margin item is the mixed grill at $22.95; our lowest is the sausage pizza at $6.63.

✔ **Are you maximizing your sales of your highest profit margin items?** Look at both the cioppino and the mixed grill. They're both high-profit items that are currently low in popularity. Think about ways to improve sales of these items to increase profit. The following are descriptions of the standard menu labels in Figure 20-3:

- **Star:** Profit is high and popularity is high

- **Workhorse:** Profit is low and popularity is high

- **Challenge:** Profit is high and popularity is low

- **Dog:** Profit is low and popularity is low

Ultimately, you need to set your own criteria for evaluating your menu mix. Typically, you decide what dollar amount determines high or low profit for your operation. In Figure 20-3, we use the average profit margin of our menu items as the cutoff, $15.02, so anything above $15.02 is considered a high-profit item, and anything below that is a low-profit item.

Working with the mix

Use only similar items when you're comparing them. For example, Figure 20-3 includes only dinner entrées. We don't include desserts, appetizers, or sandwiches, because not everyone orders one of these items. If you were to evaluate a dinner item compared to a dessert, you'd be comparing apples to oranges (or, more accurately, pasta to cheesecake). Most people who come to your restaurant for dinner will order a dinner entrée. Sure, some people order an appetizer as an entrée, others may split an entrée, and someone else wants a sandwich from your lunch menu, but in most cases, they order a dinner entrée. After dinner, some guests order desserts, and some don't.

Look at your menu mix over time. Figure 20-3 represents a single dinner shift, but the more info you get over a longer period of time, the more accurately you can view your data. Run menu mixes weekly, monthly, and at intervals that correspond to your business levels. If you have lots of traffic in the summer but not much in the winter, you may run them weekly, monthly, and seasonally. You may see that your summer customers eat very differently than your winter customers, so you may change your menu to match their preferences.

If you're changing your menu quarterly, seasonally, weekly, and so on, save a paper or electronic version of the menu so that you can look back on preparation methods and side dishes. Your POS may just tell you that you sold 18 orders of salmon in a day, but it won't necessarily tell you whether the salmon was grilled, sautéed, or roasted on a cedar plank unless you make each of these separate POS items. This system means more data entry but the informational return will be valuable in evaluating your menu mix. These menu details can complete the picture that your POS starts. Also, save special occasion menus, from holidays such as New Year's Eve, Valentine's Day, and Mother's Day. After you've been in business several years, the holidays blend together, so don't rely on your memory to keep track of it all.

If you run across items that aren't selling, consider the reasons before you decide how to adjust your plan. Here are some questions to get you started:

- ✔ **Are you charging too much?** Take a look at Chapter 9 for pricing your menu properly.

- ✔ **Is your menu description appealing?** Look at Chapter 9 for tips on making dishes sound like they're worth every penny and more.

- ✔ **Is the item ideally placed on the menu?** Chapter 9 gives you tips and tricks for placing your high-margin items where diners look most often.

- ✔ **Is the item intimidating to your diners?** Pushing the limits is okay if you have a core group of more-adventurous diners. Just keep in mind that the less well-known items may take longer to catch on. Make sure you have the cash reserves to wait it out until they take off.

- ✔ **Is your staff educated about the item?** Maybe you can do additional training with your staff about these high-margin items, and create an incentive program to sell them.

At times, raising the price of an item can actually improve its sales. You could cross a price barrier in the consumer's mind (some people won't pay more than $19.95), or you may create prestige and a market for the item (while others won't consider choosing something that isn't over the $20 mark). A price increase is also an incentive for wait staff that likes to *upsell* — encourage diners to choose higher quality (or additional) menu items. Check out Chapter 9 for info on pricing your menu right the first time.

Purchasing and inventory analysis

The true test of any purchasing and inventory program is in how well it performs in the real world and brings you closer to your goal of profitability. You may be purchasing right and pricing your menu right, only to be giving food away because it's not prepared right, ends up in the trash can, or walks out the back door. Use a cost of goods sold (COGS) report (see Figure 20-4) to help you figure out how your hard work in this area is really measuring up. In a nutshell, a COGS report measures your true and actual food cost percentage. It won't tell you why the number is too high or too low. You'll definitely need to dig deeper if it doesn't match your expectations.

While you almost always write "COGS," you never say "cogs"; instead you always say, "cost of goods sold."

	Beginning Inventory (A)	Purchases (B)	Ending Inventory (C)	Sales (D)	COGS
Food	$2,800.00	$8,700.00	$2,700.00	$29,678.00	29.65%
Liquor	1,345.00	750.00	1,296.00	4,120.00	19.39%
Beer	895.00	300.00	910.00	2,700.00	10.56%
Wine	3,200.00	350.00	2,100.00	6,800.00	21.32%
Total	$8,240.00	$10,100.00	$7,006.00	$43,298.00	26.18%

Figure 20-4: Sample cost of goods sold (COGS).

To figure your COGS:

1. **Figure out your beginning inventory (A).**

2. **Tally your invoices for the products you purchased during the time period you're reporting on (B).**

Create an *invoice log* to track your invoices and assign the invoices to categories that mirror your COGS categories.

3. **Figure out your ending inventory (C).**

4. **Add your beginning inventory and your purchases (A+B) and subtract your ending inventory from your invoices (A+B-C).**

5. **Divide that total by your sales (D), so [(A+B-C)/D] to get your COGS.**

The more categorized your data is, the more easily you can spot problems, but the tougher it is to get an overall picture. Figure out what's best for your business. You may decide that you want all alcoholic beverages to be included in a single category, rather than in three categories, as in Figure 20-4. Most restaurants count nonalcoholic beverages, like tea, coffee, and soda, in their food costs rather than in their beverage costs. But some restaurants count bottled water, juices, and so on with the beverage or bar costs because these items are often kept in the liquor storage area. There's no right way to count them, but be consistent no matter how you categorize. Mark the invoice for the item in the same category that you mark the sale.

The National Restaurant Association (which you can find out how to contact in Chapter 22) can help you find your local office, which has norms and comparison data specific to concepts like yours in your local market.

Evaluating and Using Feedback

Feedback is a blessing and a curse. Every operation must continue to innovate or die, and some of the greatest opportunities for innovation come from feedback. Your employees and your customers are sources of feedback, both positive and negative. But figuring out what to do with the information you receive isn't always easy. Sometimes, the feedback represents a preference and doesn't actually shine light on an actual problem. You have to figure out how to sort through all the info and react appropriately.

If you're asking for feedback but you don't act upon it, people can resent it. They may feel that you aren't listening or don't care about their point of view. If at all possible, follow up with them and let them know that you considered their point of view and chose a different path. Choosing to make a different decision is way better than appearing to ignore your employees or customers. If you know that a recommendation won't work, let them know, gently, during the same conversation. You may say something like, "I agree. The doorframe would look better if it was black. Unfortunately, our landlord requires all the tenants in this building to keep them sea-foam green."

Paying attention to customer feedback

Customers provide feedback in all kinds of ways; some formal and some not so formal. Seek out every opportunity you can to get their feedback because, ultimately, their collective opinion matters. Your customers make the final decision on the success of your business.

Table talk

Visit guest tables informally as often as you can. Many guests won't stop you to let you know about something, but if you stop by their table, they may spew a fountain of feedback that you never anticipated.

Table chats are also a great way to get positive information. Too often, you're called to a table by a frazzled server or, even worse, an angry guest. Improve your odds by visiting tables of happy, smiling guests as well. Give your business cards to happy people, who then can tell their friends they "know" the manager. (See Chapter 19 for more details on building your clientele.) Here are some tips for reading between the lines when you talk to tables:

- ✔ **Find ways to bring yourself into a conversation.** Pour a wine refill if you're passing by and ask how they like their food.

    Watch for signals that indicate a table doesn't want any attention, and then don't bother those diners. Avoid tables where you notice private conversations (people talking quietly with their heads close together) or obvious signs of emotion — crying qualifies.

- ✔ **Keep the tone of your questions positive or at least neutral.** Ask, "Isn't that calamari delicious?" or "How is your filet mignon?" not "Is everything okay?" The word *okay* isn't positive in this business. It's never a goal and shouldn't be an acceptable standard.

- ✔ **Ask open-ended, rather than yes/no questions.** You're more likely to get helpful feedback rather than a polite, "Yes, thanks."

- ✔ **Be specific.** Know your menu well enough to recognize it half-eaten on a plate. People are impressed when you can ask, "How's your Arctic char tonight?" instead of "How's the fish?" Adding extra touches to the conversation helps: "The red and black caviar sauce is a home run. I had that for lunch. It was great."

    If you don't know what guests are eating, don't guess. Confusing two entrees can be embarrassing to you.

- ✔ **Remember names and faces.** Remembering regular customers can help build a rapport that can lead to some great specific feedback.

Comment cards

We recommend that you use some form of comment card in your operation as a feedback tool. Figure 20-5 shows a sample comment card. Your comment card may be longer or shorter than the sample shown, depending on what you want to know about your guests' experience. You may prefer to have just general categories (food, service, atmosphere, and so on) rather than specific questions related to each category. Some restaurants add a space for the diner to compare them to other similar restaurants.

Strike a balance between asking every possible thing you want to know and not getting specific, helpful info. This approach works for a couple reasons. People won't fill out a comment card if it's too long. If people do fill it out, they may just be going through the motions rather than providing good, relevant feedback. (For help with dealing with customer complaints, take a look at Chapter 19.)

Guest Comment Card

We value your patronage and appreciate your valuable feedback on our service, food quality and your dining experience.

Please circle your rating on a scale of 1-10, 1 being the lowest, and 10 being the highest.

1. Reception

Courtesy & friendliness of door host	1 2 3 4 5 6 7 8 9 10
Accuracy of wait time	1 2 3 4 5 6 7 8 9 10
Service of bar staff	1 2 3 4 5 6 7 8 9 10
Overall Impression	1 2 3 4 5 6 7 8 9 10

2. Server

Courtesy	1 2 3 4 5 6 7 8 9 10
Speed	1 2 3 4 5 6 7 8 9 10
Attentiveness	1 2 3 4 5 6 7 8 9 10
Product Knowledge	1 2 3 4 5 6 7 8 9 10
Overall Impression	1 2 3 4 5 6 7 8 9 10

3. Food

Presentation	1 2 3 4 5 6 7 8 9 10
Temperature	1 2 3 4 5 6 7 8 9 10
Taste	1 2 3 4 5 6 7 8 9 10
Overall Impression	1 2 3 4 5 6 7 8 9 10

4. Overall Dining Experience 1 2 3 4 5 6 7 8 9 10

_____

_____

_____

_____

_____

_____

_____

5. How often do you frequent our restaurant?

First time ☐   1-4 times a year ☐   monthly ☐   more often ☐

6. What did you like best about our restaurant?

_____

_____

_____

7. Was there anything you didn't like?

_____

_____

_____

8. What could we do to make your dining experience better?

_____

_____

_____

Date _____   Number in Party _____

Occasion _____
(business, entertaining, celebration, etc.)

Server's Name _____

Your Name _____

Address _____

City _____ State _____ Zip _____

Telephone _____

Email address _____

Would you like to be on our mailing list? ☐ Yes ☐ No

Figure 20-5:
Sample comment card.

Don't get so desensitized to the feedback that you ignore people who are sincerely alerting you to an existing problem. Most people aren't trying to gouge you, take advantage of you, or get free stuff. Keep your cynicism in check. Look at each complaint independently and weigh its merits before dismissing it or acting on it.

Responding to professional criticism and praise

Professional criticism takes many forms, ranging from the local paper's restaurant critic to the colleague sitting next to you at a trade-show conference. You have to grow a thick skin to weather the constant commentary on your business, your lifeblood, your baby.

Take all reviews and criticism with a grain of salt. If a critic praises you, treat it as reinforcement for doing things the right way. If the review is negative, evaluate it and formulate your reaction. But know that if the criticism is public, like a review, others will read it or hear it and form their own opinions. It can mean an increase or a decrease in sales.

As hard as it may be, don't react emotionally if you receive a negative review. Investigate the details in the review objectively, to see if the critique is valid. Use it as an opportunity to reevaluate your concept, menu, and processes. And you can always use it as a reason to rally the troops.

The best way to get a good review is to run your business the right way, every day. Sure, if you recognize a food writer, you can go out of your way to treat her right. You may be able to pick a reviewer out if her table orders more food than a party of her size might typically eat, but they often bring in guests as a cover. If you can pick out reviewers, you can kiss up and get your good review. But if you don't demand excellence every day in every way, your wave of success will be short lived. If you treat every diner with the same courtesy you show a restaurant critic, you're sure to get a good review.

If you're lucky enough to get a good review, don't put everything on autopilot. Keep doing what got you there. A good review usually means an increase in business. Exceed the new diners' expectations because the bar will be set high.

In politics, they call it the Big Mo — momentum. You gotta take advantage of it. Some restaurateurs try to make the money while they're riding the wave by jacking up the prices. This approach is strictly a matter of personal choice and management style. If your concept is based on a value-oriented promise, you may not want to raise prices. Instead, you may want to find a way to increase the number of diners you can seat. If exclusivity is essential to your concept, however, raising prices may be just the thing to do to capitalize on your newfound fame.

Make the most of any industry awards and distinctions — local or national — that you, your restaurant, or your employees receive. If your restaurant gets the vote for the "Best Taco under $3 in Town," let everyone know about it. If you win a Grand Award from *Wine Spectator* magazine, capitalize on it. Use any public praise or honors as an opportunity to praise yourself and your staff. Include newspaper and magazine clippings in your PR and advertising campaigns (see Chapter 16). Incorporate them into your décor by framing the actual award and displaying them for diners to see. Tastefully using this info somewhere on your menu or at your entrance (to give a potential patron that little extra nudge) is also a good idea.

Listening to employee feedback

Talk to your staff at all levels to get feedback. Find opportunities to regularly go one-on-one with servers, bussers, line help, dishwashers, and the manager on duty. Use formal and informal opportunities to get the word on what's really going on from your employees' standpoint. Keep communication flowing through all the departments in your organization. Solutions sometimes come from unlikely places. Here are some ways to get the scoop:

✓ Use the manager's logbook to communicate problems with service, food, or employees. The more people who know what's going on, the more likely it is that you'll be able to establish patterns and fix the problem. If you notice that server Brian constantly serves cold and overcooked food but no one else does, maybe the problem is really with Brian rather than the kitchen. Maybe he's ordering incorrectly or not running his food in a timely matter.

✓ Schedule regular staff meetings for the entire staff and departmental meetings as well. You may find that you get very different feedback at each meeting.

✓ Get a suggestion box. Some employees won't speak up in meetings or come to you directly with a suggestion. The anonymity of the suggestion box can be just the way to pull that next great idea out of them.

Your employees provide customer feedback that's somewhat filtered. It may not be the same information you'd get straight from the customers themselves. An employee, intentionally or not, puts his own spin on the situation and may offer solutions. It's up to you to decide what problems to respond to. If you're talking to different people and you're hearing the same things repeated, consider employees' input.

Part V
The Part of Tens

The 5th Wave
By Rich Tennant

"SCREAMING OR NON-SCREAMING?"

In this part . . .

It wouldn't be a *For Dummies* book without a Part of Tens. Our take on this part includes ten or more myths about running a restaurant, resources for restaurant managers and owners, and our favorite stories that provide some insight into the strange world of restaurants.

Chapter 21

Ten Myths about Running a Restaurant

. . . .

In This Chapter

▶ Looking behind the scenes

▶ Setting clear expectations for what lies ahead

. . . .

*O*ne of the biggest reasons people don't stay in the restaurant business is that they don't have realistic expectations of what the job is really like. (The other heavy hitters are that it's really exhausting, time consuming, unappreciated . . . but we digress.) In this chapter, we dispel some of the most common myths while keeping our fingers crossed that we don't scare you away.

Running a Restaurant Is Easy

The restaurant business captivates and intrigues people. People think it's glamorous and exciting. Customers see you working where they play and assume that it's one big party after another. What these starry-eyed, would-be restaurateurs don't see is what goes on behind the scenes, *each* and *every* day.

A typical chef's or restaurant manager's morning (we're talking before 11 a.m. here) might include all these activities: Getting in at 5 a.m. to inspect and accept deliveries. Starting soups and sauces at 6 a.m. Calling in last-minute orders for tonight's party of 50 that booked yesterday evening. Calling the equipment service technician about the steamer that went down in the middle of last night's shift. Creating a prep list. Supervising the staff. Finding replacement staff to fill in for late employees, call-offs, and no-shows. Ensuring that the dining room is ready to go before the restaurant opens. Performing a line check to confirm that all food is ready to go before the restaurant opens. Creating specials, such as a soup of the day and salad/sandwich combo. Fending off the persistent salesperson who has to talk to you this minute about the new glow-in-the-dark chicken tenders.

That's quite a to-do list to complete before 11 a.m. But that's not all: Then you push the paper to track sales, forecast revenue, and pay bills. If the liquor authority wants to know where you got a case of vodka, you have to be able to produce the receipt. If the health department is investigating a foodborne illness outbreak related to oysters, you better have the tags for your shellfish on file. If the state unemployment office needs confirmation that an employee quit and wasn't terminated, you need accurate employee files.

If you're building a new business or want to move beyond maintaining an existing one, you spend even more time developing marketing and PR strategies, looking for the best deals from your vendors while preserving the quality of your products, and recruiting a top-notch staff.

If you eat out a lot because you don't like cooking at home, how happy are you going to be creating meals for other people every day, holidays and weekends included, for 14 hours a day? You're at the restaurant before opening *and* after closing. The real world opens, closes, and has a life — all within the hours that make up your workday. Running a restaurant is easy if you do it only one day. Talk to us on day 2, 3, or 1,753.

I'll Have a Place to Hang Out

Lots of people use this myth as one of the top reasons they should start a restaurant. They picture themselves hanging out and chatting with people at the bar or walking through a kitchen a-buzz with cooks. They imagine getting paid while watching the World Series in a bar full of their friends. Whatever the specifics of your vision, if you're looking to own a place where you can hang out, you better be willing to pay other people to do the hard work.

It's essential for anyone running a restaurant, either as the owner, chef, or manager, to be in the restaurant and watch what's actually happening. If you're hanging out, you're not seeing what's going on in the supply room, at table 42, or out in the parking lot. Plus, hanging out socially in the restaurant can be a drain on your bottom line, especially if you're buying the drinks.

Note the big difference between being friendly with your staff and being friends with your staff. If you're hanging out in the bar with your staff, you're in the danger zone. Ultimately, if you're drinking socially, instead of just testing a wine or having an occasional beer with a regular customer, in your place of business, you're taking a risk. Odds are, eventually, you're going to make a fool of yourself. Whether you believe it now or not, your casualness will change the way employees look at you and respect you.

I Can Trust My Brother-in-Law

This dilemma — deciding whether to include relatives in your business — isn't unique to the restaurant business. Our general advice is "Don't get involved in business with your family, because it's hard to get out of business with your family." Many companies implement rules against hiring family members because it creates unnecessary complications.

If, for whatever reason, you absolutely, positively must hire your brother-in-law, sister, cousin, or anyone else who shares your family tree, use these tips to minimize miscommunication:

- ✔ **Be very clear about his responsibilities.** Somehow, by virtue of genetic or marital ties, people get strange ideas about what decision-making powers they have and what rights and privileges they enjoy. If they're not partners in your deal, explicitly tell them so.

- ✔ **Treat a family member as you would any other employee.** Don't be overly critical or ultralenient with them. Watch out for the "coach's kid" mentality, even though everything they do is a reflection on you. Your staff is always watching, and they do compare notes.

- ✔ **Explicitly go over your expectations with him, especially detailing rules about cash-handling and inventory procedures.** When you mix money with family, people justify a lot, including helping themselves to loans, a case of wine, or a bottle of ketchup. Make sure that family members understand what is acceptable and what isn't. Family members often need even more info about the rules. Also, make sure that the details of his compensation are detailed and clearly defined so that he's not tempted to take liberties he's not entitled to.

Never use family labor as an assumed safety net. If you think that your family will always be available to pitch in at a moment's notice, they may have other ideas on the subject. And don't assume that your kids have a burning desire to follow in your footsteps. Make sure that they share your goals. Your family and your business will suffer if you force family members to give up their own dreams just to keep the family business going.

The Neighbors Will Love Me

For reasons that you may never know, your neighbors may have preconceived ideas of what you and your business are like. They may have had a bad experience with your predecessor. Maybe it was a noisy bar, or maybe the previous tenant didn't maintain the exterior well. Still others are nasty as a way of entertaining themselves.

You can't kill yourself in order to make your neighbors like you. You can, however, be a responsible part of the business community and hope that they return the attitude. Be sensitive about the upkeep in your area, including any common areas you share with other tenants. Let them know about special events that may cause extra noise and traffic, and invite them. If the guy who runs the dry cleaning shop next door is a huge baseball fan, and Joe Morgan, author of *Baseball For Dummies,* is going to be in for a wine dinner, let him know and invite him to the dinner.

Cultivate friendly relationships with your local police officers and firefighters. They're part of the larger community, as well as prospective customers. They usually can't take free food, but you can offer specials for members of the public service community.

Get to know your neighborhood. Many restaurants become sort of a concierge service for diners who want info on local bookstores, movie theaters, hot nightspots, and so on. But temper your neighborliness with good old-fashioned self-interest. If neighbors are looking for a great bartender and you have one, don't send them elsewhere.

I've Been to Culinary School, So I'm Ready to Run the Show

Attending culinary school is a great head start, but it's just that — a start. Many schools have dropped the prerequisite of work experience before starting school. Graduating from culinary school is the beginning of your career, not a shortcut. Most kids fresh out of school have never hired or fired employees, negotiated with salespeople, placed orders, dealt with unions, or fixed equipment in the middle of a shift. You don't learn to deal with the controlled chaos of a restaurant in a classroom, not even one that looks like a restaurant.

Attaining the title of chef is akin to becoming a general. You have to live through the battles, suffer losses, and come out on the other side. You have to show fortitude and put in your time. Be patient. When the title comes, you'll appreciate it much more.

I'm Going to Be a Celebrity Chef

The popular media has elevated many restaurant chefs to celebrity status. The work of celebrity chefs has gone a long way to shaping the culinary scene in this country and in the rest of the world. Having talked to many of these chefs, we've found that they think the idea of newfound fame is humorous, in the sense that for years they drove a stove for a living. Their careers haven't been all book signings, TV shows, and speaking engagements. People don't see the grueling hours they've spent cleaning grease traps, being screamed at by pan-wielding European chefs of the previous generation, and mopping out coolers. These celebrities didn't attain their status overnight.

Many of these chefs have built wildly successful restaurants and spent thousands of dollars on public relations, agents, and specialized training just to get their first shot as a media personality. All this media attention takes time away from their restaurants, which sometimes suffer from the celebrity chefs' lack of presence on the scene. On the flip side, many great chefs aren't interested in being media chefs, but that fact doesn't diminish their influence, impact, talent, or passion for their true calling: being a chef first and foremost.

My Chili Rocks, So I Should Open a Place

Just because you're good at making chili (or anything else, for that matter) for two, four, or six people as a hobby, don't assume that you can turn it into a job. Running a restaurant is so much more than cooking well. It involves being a salesperson, host, purchasing agent, human resources manager, accountant, and efficiency expert all rolled into one. And few places succeed based on the power of a single dish, so it's a little risky to put all your beans in a single chili bowl. But with this warning in mind, remember that all is not lost for your dream of opening that little chili joint. Coffee bars, ice cream parlors, and hot dog carts can all do well, especially with a large population to draw from. Variety isn't always the spice of life. You may get lucky.

I Can Cut the Advertising Budget

In any business when sales are down, owners and managers naturally begin looking at places to cut the budget. All too often the advertising and marketing budgets are among the first to be cut. Assuming that your advertising is effective, cutting it *will* matter. When sales are down, you need more people coming in the door, and you need the people who are coming in the door to spend more money. Effective advertising can accomplish this goal and more than pay for itself.

Instead of cutting your marketing budget, evaluate how you're currently spending your money and what you're getting in return. If you're placing ads in local publications, review your ad placement. Maybe you should actually spend a bit more and spring for the back cover so that more people see it. Evaluate how well the actual ad attracts the customers you're seeking.

Wraps Are Here to Stay

Trends, by definition, don't last. They're white-hot ideas, entrees, presentations, or whatever that capture the public's interest and then fad . . . er, we mean fade, into the distance. Think wraps, frozen yogurt, merlot, and the $40 hamburger. All still have their place in the hearts of the dining public (except maybe the $40 burger), but they've settled into their proper places on menus everywhere. Wraps gave way to bowls. Frozen yogurt lost ground to its grandfather, frozen custard. Merlot at best shares the stage with red zinfandel, pinot noir, and shiraz. The list goes on. Don't invest yourself too much in the food equivalent of a "one-hit wonder." It's great to get in at the beginning and ride the wave of a trend, but maintain your flexibility and be ready with Plan B when the bottom falls out — because it will.

I'll Be Home for the Holidays

Home is where the restaurant is. It's a myth that you'll be home for many, if any, of your family's special occasions — not to mention weekends or Tuesday night dinner. You can always find exceptions, like a restaurant located in a business district without much traffic on weekends or holidays. But usually, when people are celebrating special occasions, they often turn to restaurants. So guess where you'll be? You guessed it: working.

Many restaurants, especially those close to retail areas, rely on the weeks between Thanksgiving and New Year's Day to turn in their biggest revenue. So if your wife's birthday falls on December 15, you can pretty much forget about taking the day off. You'll likely be working a banquet, catering an office party, or trying to keep the kitchen from crashing at the expo station.

Not only are you working, but many of your key people likely won't be, so you'll be working even harder. Many of the folks whom you depend on throughout the year request time off during these busy times. You can't expect people to do what you're not willing to do yourself. And if several of your key people are missing, you need to be there to watch for disasters.

Chapter 22

More Than Ten Resources for Restaurateurs

*E*ven though our goal is to present you with a highly readable, very thorough, and (dare we hope) entertaining guide to running a restaurant, we're realists. We can't answer every question in one book, so this chapter provides you with some of the resources we've used at one point or another along the way.

We find inspiration and ideas in just about every cookbook we pick up. The list would get out of control quickly if we listed even just our favorites. Our advice: Read lots and read often. But don't feel like you have to beef up your book budget initially. Check out your local library for cookbooks on virtually every style of cuisine and country. After you find your favorites that you go back to again and again, get your own copy for the restaurant.

In addition to reading the business-specific resources in this chapter, keep in touch with what your diners are reading, seeing, and hearing. Don't forget to check out the dining section of your local paper, consumer foodie magazines such as *Bon Appétit* and *Gourmet,* the ever-popular Food Network, and Web sites such as FoodNetwork.com (www.foodtv.com). See Chapter 4 for more on keeping up with your consumers.

There's no better resource (save one: your customer) than your own personal history and experience with your restaurant. Keep a logbook and update it daily, or even multiple times each day. *The Manager's Redbook,* (DataWorks, www.managersredbook.com) is the industry standard for keeping track of everything — the weather, maintenance and repairs, summaries of guest complaints, ordering notes, and anything else you need to remember for the future. Things change fast, blend together, and are tough to keep track of. The more detailed you can be, the better resource you build for you, your managers, and the future of your business.

Checking Out a Few Books

By purchasing the book you're holding now, you've taken a great first step on the road to restaurant management. Here are a few more references in specific areas of the business that can help you make your goal of running a successful, profitable restaurant a reality.

✔ *The New Food Lover's Companion* by Sharon Tyler Herbst (Barron's Educational Series) is the essential guide to 6,000 culinary and dining terms. This resource is a must-have for any culinary or hospitality professional. It gives you easy-to-understand definitions and descriptions of ingredients, techniques, and other food and dining terms. This reference book can help you add pizzazz to your menu, by exploring ingredients you may not be familiar with and by adding dimension to your descriptions of your already-present menu items, without feeling it in your food cost percentage. See Chapter 9 for more details on writing and developing your menu.

✔ If you're brand-new to the world of wine, *Wine For Dummies,* 3rd Edition, by Ed McCarthy and Mary Ewing-Mulligan (published by Wiley) is a great place to get your passport. It gives you practical information about wine terms, appellations, and vintages. It also gives you essential tips on buying, tasting, ordering, and storing wine. Depending on your experience, your concept, and your goals, this may not be your only wine book, but it should definitely be your first.

✔ Containing nearly 1,000 drink recipes, *Bartending For Dummies,* 2nd Edition, by Ray Foley (published by Wiley) definitely belongs in your restaurant library. Other books that you may want to include are *The Joy of Mixology* by Gary Regan (Clarkson Potter), and *The Bartender's Black Book* by Stephen Kittredge Cunningham (Wine Appreciation Guild). Depending on your clientele, your concept, and so on, you may also want to invest in a specialized book or two. You can find books on scotch, bourbon, and other spirits, as well as titles dedicated to making the best martini or the perfect margarita. Chances are if you specialize in it, someone's written a book that can help.

> ✔ *Service That Sells! The Art of Profitable Hospitality* by Phil Roberts (Pencom) is essential reading for anyone who works in the front of the house. Managers, wait staff, and bartenders can benefit from reading this book. It gives concrete tips for maximizing your sales with every guest that walks through the door, which is essential for every profitable restaurant. Get several copies to loan out, or make it part of your new-hire package. The investment will pay for itself in almost no time.

Flipping through Magazines

The great thing about magazines is that most also have Web sites. Many Web sites have free newsletters. Sign up for several freebies and then decide which ones work best for your business.

You may qualify for actual free subscriptions to the hard copy magazine. Publishers offer free subscriptions to restaurant industry professionals. You fill out a lengthy form about your business, including ranges of sales and expenses, and then you find out whether you qualify. Although publishers have the final say on who gets their freebies, they want as many people to have their magazines as possible. Your odds of qualifying are better if you're involved in purchasing decisions at the restaurant. Check out TradePub.com's list of possible food and beverage freebies to see whether you qualify. Go to www.tradepub.com and click on the food and beverage link.

Like restaurateurs, magazines cater to those who pay the bills — in their case the customer the advertiser. So take the views and information they present with a grain of sea salt.

> ✔ *Restaurants & Institutions* targets both the pizza place down the street (commercial) and the hospital cafeteria (noncommercial). This magazine covers a lot of case studies and helpful information about how different business adapt (or don't) to changes and trends. You can find trend information and up-to-the-minute industry news at the Web site (www.rimag.com). The magazine is free for qualified subscribers.

> ✔ *Nation's Restaurant News* offers good product and equipment information, as well as trend information. Unless you're a subscriber to the print magazine, you face a lengthy required registration process to view anything at the Web site (www.nrn.com). It's free but long. After you're in, check out the segment info, trends, and applying current events to the business, calendar of events, like trade shows, conferences and so on. If you subscribe to the magazine, you get access to exclusive info on the Web site, such as targeted segment studies (studies that report trends within specific segments of the restaurant business), trend reporting, and so on.

Taking Advantage of Additional Online Resources

Technology has finally worked its way into the restaurant business. Web sites are becoming more important everyday as we run our restaurants like the businesses they are. Look to these organizations and Web-based resources for help in getting the most from your business, your staff, and your government.

National Restaurant Association

The industry voice on Capitol Hill, the NRA (Charleton Heston isn't part of *this* NRA) provides excellent support, networking opportunities, and industry research valuable to every restaurant owner. It provides subscription-based trend information compiled state by state. Find helpful info about locating suppliers of everything from food to furniture, and get advice on consultants, technology, and everything in between. Locate your local chapter at its national Web site, www.restaurant.org. The association has lots of business-specific information about laws, taxes, and other financial issues. You can find reports providing its analysis of the industry and its predictions for the future of the business for sale at their Web site.

Small Business Administration

The Small Business Administration (SBA) is *the* source for business laws and regulatory assistance for every small business. The SBA has information on starting, financing, and managing your business, with tons of free forms, sample business plans, balance sheets, income statements, and cash flow statements. Look here for help with getting an SBA loan. Check out Chapter 6 for tips on working with the SBA to get a loan to start your restaurant.

At the SBA Web site (www.sba.gov), don't miss the FAQs, or *frequently asked questions,* on starting your own business. Even if you're well on your way toward opening your doors, this site is worth a visit to double-check your timeline and assumptions.

RestaurantOwner.com

RestaurantOwner.com (www.restaurantowner.com) is a great site, with paid access to excellent spreadsheets, articles, and management tools. If you don't have a fully integrated point of sale (POS) system, consider investing some money in membership for this site. You can find business planning tools and professional report spreadsheets to get you up and analyzing your business in no time. Don't miss the online seminars and downloadable workbooks with info about specific concerns, like lowering your food cost, managing your purchasing program, hiring and keeping the best staff, and so on.

Note that the best content on this site isn't free, but it's well worth the investment.

Hcareers.com

Hcareers.com (www.hcareers.com) is geared for both employers and employees in the hospitality industry. As you may have guessed, the H in its name stands for hospitality. At the time of this writing, 2,500 employers were posting jobs for over 10,000 positions worldwide, including some of the biggest names in the business. This site is a great source for finding quality managers, chefs, and other professionals in the business. Premier recruiters in the business use this site, so this is your shortcut to the cream-of-the-crop applicants.

The Food Channel

The Food Channel (www.foodchannel.com), not to be confused with www.foodnetwork.com, is the premier source for current industry trend information maintained by the industry's leading trend watchers, market insiders, and food futurists. Sign up for its fantastic weekly newsletter, *The Food Channel Trendwire,* for a nominal fee. The folks here do the research, and you benefit from their expert analysis, dedication to the business, and unparalleled experience.

RecipeSource

Need a recipe for tandoori chicken, shrimp with citrus mojo, or killer barbecue? Go to RecipeSource (www.recipesource.com) for a starting point and create variations to make it your own. Recipes are organized by ethnic cuisines by region and type of dish.

Entrepreneur.com

This nameplate site for *Entrepreneur* magazine (www.entrepreneur.com) covers issues from start-up to marketing to management, providing in-depth and pertinent consumer information, sales and growth strategies, and how to streamline your business through proven technology. It's essential reading for every small business owner.

You may need to read it with an eye toward applying it to the restaurant business. But it offers great information for writing business plans, finding capital, handling legal issues, and dealing with other concerns shared by business owners across every industry.

Chapter 23

Ten (Or So) True Restaurant Stories That You Just Couldn't Make Up

The restaurant business has no shortage of colorful characters. Whether it's customers, staff, suppliers, or colleagues, if you look around you can always find something to smile about. Here are a few of our favorites.

Déjà vu All Over Again

A guy called a restaurant and said to the manager, "I'd like to confirm a reservation that was never made." The manager repeated what the caller said, just to make sure he heard it correctly. "That's right," the guy said. "I have a party of ten people coming in tonight at 7:30." The manager said, "We'd love to have you, but we can't guarantee that we can take ten of you at that time tonight." The guy said, "You have to. I'm confirming it." The manager said, "But you never made the reservation." The guy said, "That's what I'm doing now, confirming my reservation that wasn't made." The manager worked him in later that night, fairly close to 7:30.

The Eyes Have It

It was a really cold Sunday night. A gregarious man with Coke-bottle glasses was chatting people up and buying them drinks. The closing manager was in the bar for a while but went to the office to start closing procedures. He was a little wary of the customer, but he wasn't sure why. A short time later, the bartender called the office to ask the manager if he'd allow the customer to pay with a check. The bartender said, "I know it's not right, but his girlfriend's got his wallet and she's out shopping. He's got no ID, just a business card." The manager came out to the bar to discuss the situation with the customer.

The customer informed the manager that he could "buy and sell this place," that he had an American Express Platinum card. The manager, having some experience with credit cards said to the customer, "I know Amex will let you get an authorization over the phone if you give them the right answers to the security questions. Let's call them." The manager and customer ran the gamut of credit-card companies with no luck. The customer ran through the list of things he could leave as collateral, all virtually worthless.

The manager called the police to help mediate. The cops talked with the manager to get his input on how he wanted to handle the situation. The manager said, "I want some kind of insurance that he's coming back to pay this tab. I want his glasses and his coat." One cop said, "It's in the teens! You're gonna send this guy out with no coat?" The other cop said, "Forget that! Take his shoes, socks, and underwear, too!" The manager was satisfied with just the extra-thick glasses, the coat, and a worthless watch. The customer left the check, which turned out to be a forged business check that he stole from his employer. The check bounced.

Free Pie Guy

A guy walked into a restaurant and helped himself to a piece of pie. The manager politely stopped the "customer" to ask what was up. The "customer" said, "I came for my free pie. The waitress told me to come back for a piece of pie whenever I want, because mine was bad last time. You owe me a piece of pie." The manager said, "What was her name? What did she look like?" The "customer" said, "I don't know. She was old." The manager said, "Do you have any more info, a card, something in writing from her? Can you give me a better description?" The customer said, "She had gray hair, I think." That cleared it right up.

Dealing with any customer-service issues on the spot is usually best. If you decide to "make it right" on the diner's next visit, make sure to give him a signed business card (preferably yours) detailing the specifics of your offer.

(Coat) Check, Please!

A guy walked up to a restaurant manager and proclaimed, "My coat's been stolen. My wallet, passport, everything was in it." The manager headed to the coat-check area to confer with the checker. The customer stopped him and said, "No, I hung it over there." The manager looked where the customer was pointing and saw the hooks by the counter-service area under a big sign that read, "Leave it at your own risk. We have a coat room. Check it in."

Priceless

After eating his meal, a customer presented his waiter with what he said was his father's credit card. Despite the waiter's protest, the customer insisted that he could use this card. The manager got involved in the situation and suggested that the customer call his father and have him fax his authorization. "He'll never authorize it," the customer said. "It'll get paid, but I can't ask permission." The manager let the customer leave, but only after taking the customer's driver's license, which he said he would hold until the customer paid for his meal. A month or so passed and the customer didn't return to pay. The manager received a phone call from a business owner in Texas, who begged, "Please, you gotta give the license back. This guy owes me money, and I need him to come back to Texas to work so he can pay me. He can't get on a plane without it." The manager and the business owner had extended conversations about the situation, and ultimately the business owner wired the money to the restaurant to free the license from limbo.

Chefs Behaving Badly

At a book signing at a gourmet shop owned by a world-renowned chef/restaurateur, an elderly woman pointed out that the black truffle butter was a bit cheaper at the gourmet shop down the street. The chef graciously set down his glass of wine, cleared his throat, and then recommended that she go buy it at the other store immediately. The lady, familiar with this chef's reputation as a tyrant was flabbergasted and responded that she would tell all her friends how terribly he had treated her.

He paused, looked here directly in the eyes and calmly sneered "Tell them *both* and get the hell out of my store."

He's Got Marty Feldman Eyes

A visiting restaurant manager elected himself to help an urban restaurant rid itself of a rodent problem, or more correctly, a problem rodent. The chef bragged that he was going to get it with a BB gun, but a couple days later, the problem lingered. Around midnight one night, the visiting manager was coming out of the office and saw the rodent out of the corner of his eye. The huge rat tried to run past him. The manager reached to grab anything to hit it with. As the rat ran past him, it stepped on a glue trap and continued running down the hall with the glue trap stuck to its foot. The manager managed to find a long stick with something heavy on the end. He whacked the rat as it ran past. It turned to him and hissed, going on the offensive. The manager pummeled the rat with his makeshift club, eventually killing it. Still full of adrenaline, the manager decided to create a display worthy of his prize. He rigged up a hanger and some kitchen twine, and then quickly ran to get a witness. He found the night-crew cook who always looked half asleep and usually gave the manager a hard time. The cook came around the corner and, to his now bug-eyed surprise, he saw a dead rat the size of a cat hanging from a rafter in the middle of the office by its tail.

Ladies' Night

The street level of a primarily residential building was occupied by a fairly busy restaurant. On Sunday afternoons, the management showcased a light jazz band as a way to bring in new business. The third-floor neighbor continuously complained about the noise from the music. After extended discussions, the manager asked the neighbor, "Ma'am, can you hear the music when the bus passes? I can't even hear it in the restaurant when the bus passes." She admitted, "No, I can't hear the music then, but I'm used to the bus."

Finally, the management cancelled the Sunday jazz band. The noise-hating neighbor came in about six months later to take advantage of their two-for-one Ladies' Night specials. The bartender knew she was the main reason the restaurant no longer played jazz, so he wasn't thrilled to see her. She also had discouraged some of his regular customers from sitting at the bar that night because she was "saving some seats." When she got the bill at the end of the night, she questioned the bartender. Instead of getting two-for-one drinks, she was charged for all of her drinks. The bartender said, "There's no mistake. That special is for *ladies*."

The Drink's on Me

A waiter was working in a busy restaurant at a resort over Easter weekend. A slew of families were in the restaurant enjoying brunch for the holiday. The waiter was preparing a drink tray full of soft drinks, bar drinks, milk, orange juice. . . . You name it, it was probably on this tray. A waitress working a nearby section asked him, "Hey, could you drop an OJ on Table 92 for me?" The waiter happily obliged. When he got to the table, where about 11 people were sitting at a table for 8, he began to set down the juice. As he was setting it down, the guy across the table yelled, "Look out!" as the entire tray slowly and irretrievably tipped onto a customer. In slow motion, each individual piece of stemware dumped its contents onto the customer before crashing directly on his head. As the waiter tried to help clean up the diner, he knocked over the glass of OJ that started the avalanche and was the only glass left standing at that point. The table was in absolute hysterics before the last glass even fell. They became regulars and requested the waiter every time.

So You Like My Tie?

Diners come from around the world to eat at a world-class restaurant in Chicago. Some wait for months to get a reservation and, as they wait, their anticipation builds. The owner takes these expectations seriously and trains his staff to respect them as well. He insists that his staff not only meet but exceed their expectations. At a standard price of more than $500 per person, exceeding their expectations is tough to do. The restaurant has an unwritten policy that if a guest compliments the waiter on his $100+ Armani tie, the guest will find that tie gift-wrapped for him at the end of his meal to take home as a gift, free of charge.

Gentlemen, Start Your Sterno

The Greatest Spectacle in Racing (the Indianapolis 500) demands the Greatest Spectacle in Catering. It's a 'round-the-clock adventure for about three weeks every May. One morning, the head chef came in to start his day at the customary 3:15 a.m. start time to prepare for serving around 40,000 meals for the day. He saw his *hot camp* (the area set up to make the hot food) totally destroyed by a massive storm the night before, despite the precautions they'd taken. Tents were mangled and sagging to the ground under the weight of water. He called in reinforcements and rallied the troops to get the camp reassembled so that they had a chance to get the 10,000 breakfasts done by 7 a.m. Teamwork saved the day, or so they thought.

Just as they were in the midst of the *fire* (finishing the cooking process), the entire electrical system powering the bank of convection ovens went down. Ovens full of breakfast blintzes, ham and onion frittatas, sausage, and bacon, all dead. One chef shot off a cursing barrage as only a highly caffeinated, kitchen guy working 20 straight 20-hour days can. Another cook ran off to call the electrician. Meanwhile, the clock was ticking and the food had to go out. The two remaining chefs came to it at the same time with a light in their eyes: Sterno. Off-premise caterers have Sterno like Starbucks has stir sticks. They loaded the convection ovens with cans of Sterno to finish the food. Another crisis averted before 7:00 in the morning.

Frosty the Newbie

A new manager was training in each of the various stations in the kitchen before assuming the helm. After her kitchen training was completed, her line guys made her perform one last rite of passage. In their open kitchen concept, it was common to see the line cooks "flaming" the sauté pans to the delight of the diners. The sauté pans, with a bit of oil, are heated in a line of gas burners. When they're hot, a cook walks down the line and quickly pours water in the hot oil, causing large flames that burn out quickly. The new manager had to perform this traditional maneuver before her training was complete. The manager hesitated and let the oil get a little too hot. As the manager poured her water, the flames seemed higher than usual. Suddenly, the fire-suppression system over the range began pouring white puffs of dried chemicals over the range, flooding the dining room with harmless, but very annoying, clouds of chemicals. The entire restaurant had to shut down and wait for a fire inspection and a system reset before opening again.

Radio Fryer

In a very busy luxury restaurant in Denver, a cook considered it his right to blare music in the kitchen. He didn't even turn it down when the chef was in the kitchen trying to talk to the staff. Day after day, for close to a week, he and the chef had the same discussion about the loud radio. The next morning, on the chef's "day off," the cook turned the radio on once again. He thought he was pulling one over on the chef. The chef walked in the door, looked the cook in the eye, but walked past him. He grabbed the radio, placed it into a fry basket and tossed it into the 350 degree fryer. Then he walked back to the cook and said, "When that's done, I need you to clean that fryer," and calmly walked to his office.

Index

• C •

• F •

FOR DUMMIES®

The easy way to get more done and have more fun

PERSONAL FINANCE

0-7645-5231-7

0-7645-2431-3

0-7645-5331-3

Also available:

Estate Planning For Dummies
(0-7645-5501-4)

401(k)s For Dummies
(0-7645-5468-9)

Frugal Living For Dummies
(0-7645-5403-4)

Microsoft Money "X" For Dummies
(0-7645-1689-2)

Mutual Funds For Dummies
(0-7645-5329-1)

Personal Bankruptcy For Dummies
(0-7645-5498-0)

Quicken "X" For Dummies
(0-7645-1666-3)

Stock Investing For Dummies
(0-7645-5411-5)

Taxes For Dummies 2003
(0-7645-5475-1)

BUSINESS & CAREERS

0-7645-5314-3

0-7645-5307-0

0-7645-5471-9

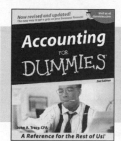

Also available:

Business Plans Kit For Dummies
(0-7645-5365-8)

Consulting For Dummies
(0-7645-5034-9)

Cool Careers For Dummies
(0-7645-5345-3)

Human Resources Kit For Dummies
(0-7645-5131-0)

Managing For Dummies
(1-5688-4858-7)

QuickBooks All-in-One Desk Reference For Dummies
(0-7645-1963-8)

Selling For Dummies
(0-7645-5363-1)

Small Business Kit For Dummies
(0-7645-5093-4)

Starting an eBay Business For Dummies
(0-7645-1547-0)

HEALTH, SPORTS & FITNESS

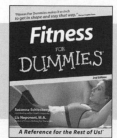

0-7645-5167-1

0-7645-5146-9

0-7645-5154-X

Also available:

Controlling Cholesterol For Dummies
(0-7645-5440-9)

Dieting For Dummies
(0-7645-5126-4)

High Blood Pressure For Dummies
(0-7645-5424-7)

Martial Arts For Dummies
(0-7645-5358-5)

Menopause For Dummies
(0-7645-5458-1)

Nutrition For Dummies
(0-7645-5180-9)

Power Yoga For Dummies
(0-7645-5342-9)

Thyroid For Dummies
(0-7645-5385-2)

Weight Training For Dummies
(0-7645-5168-X)

Yoga For Dummies
(0-7645-5117-5)

Available wherever books are sold.
Go to www.dummies.com or call 1-877-762-2974 to order direct.

FOR DUMMIES®

A world of resources to help you grow

HOME, GARDEN & HOBBIES

0-7645-5295-3

0-7645-5130-2

0-7645-5106-X

Also available:

Auto Repair For Dummies
(0-7645-5089-6)

Chess For Dummies
(0-7645-5003-9)

Home Maintenance For
Dummies
(0-7645-5215-5)

Organizing For Dummies
(0-7645-5300-3)

Piano For Dummies
(0-7645-5105-1)

Poker For Dummies
(0-7645-5232-5)

Quilting For Dummies
(0-7645-5118-3)

Rock Guitar For Dummies
(0-7645-5356-9)

Roses For Dummies
(0-7645-5202-3)

Sewing For Dummies
(0-7645-5137-X)

FOOD & WINE

0-7645-5250-3

0-7645-5390-9

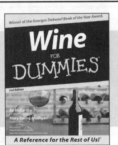

0-7645-5114-0

Also available:

Bartending For Dummies
(0-7645-5051-9)

Chinese Cooking For
Dummies
(0-7645-5247-3)

Christmas Cooking For
Dummies
(0-7645-5407-7)

Diabetes Cookbook For
Dummies
(0-7645-5230-9)

Grilling For Dummies
(0-7645-5076-4)

Low-Fat Cooking For
Dummies
(0-7645-5035-7)

Slow Cookers For Dummies
(0-7645-5240-6)

TRAVEL

0-7645-5453-0

0-7645-5438-7

0-7645-5448-4

Also available:

America's National Parks For
Dummies
(0-7645-6204-5)

Caribbean For Dummies
(0-7645-5445-X)

Cruise Vacations For
Dummies 2003
(0-7645-5459-X)

Europe For Dummies
(0-7645-5456-5)

Ireland For Dummies
(0-7645-6199-5)

France For Dummies
(0-7645-6292-4)

London For Dummies
(0-7645-5416-6)

Mexico's Beach Resorts For
Dummies
(0-7645-6262-2)

Paris For Dummies
(0-7645-5494-8)

RV Vacations For Dummies
(0-7645-5443-3)

Walt Disney World & Orlando
For Dummies
(0-7645-5444-1)

Available wherever books are sold. Go to www.dummies.com or call 1-877-762-2974 to order direct.